AI and Society

AI's impact on human societies is and will be drastic in so many ways. AI is being adopted and implemented around the world, and government and universities are investing in AI studies, research, and development. However, very little research exists about the impact of AI on our lives. This book will address this gap; it will gather reflections from around the world to assess the impact of AI on different aspects of society as well as propose ways in which we can address this impact and the research agendas needed.

Chapman & Hall/CRC Artificial Intelligence and Robotics Series
Series Editor: Roman Yampolskiy

For more information about this series please visit: https://www.routledge.com/Chapman--HallCRC-Artificial-Intelligence-and-Robotics-Series/book-series/ARTILRO

AI and Society
Tensions and Opportunities

Edited by
Christo El Morr

CRC Press
Taylor & Francis Group
Boca Raton London New York

CRC Press is an imprint of the
Taylor & Francis Group, an **informa** business

A CHAPMAN & HALL BOOK

First edition published 2023
by CRC Press
6000 Broken Sound Parkway NW, Suite 300, Boca Raton, FL 33487-2742

and by CRC Press
4 Park Square, Milton Park, Abingdon, Oxon, OX14 4RN

CRC Press is an imprint of Taylor & Francis Group, LLC

ISBN: 978-1-032-19416-5 (hbk)
ISBN: 978-1-032-19870-5 (pbk)
ISBN: 978-1-003-26124-7 (ebk)

DOI: 10.1201/9781003261247

Typeset in Minion
by MPS Limited, Dehradun

Contents

vi ▪ Contents

Contributors

Josephina Antoniou
School of Sciences
University of Central Lancashire (UCLan)
Cyprus
Larnaca, Cyprus

Kristine Bærøe
Medical Ethics and Philosophy of Science
Department of Global Public Health and
Primary Care
University of Bergen
Bergen, Norway

Elizabeth Borycki
School of Health Information Science
University of Victoria
Victoria, Canada

Nicola Luigi Bragazzi
Africa-Canada Artificial Intelligence and
Data Innovation Consortium (ACADIC)
York University
Toronto, Ontario, Canada
and
Department of Mathematics and Statistics
York University
Toronto, Ontario, Canada

Ruben Brave
CEO Entelligence.nl
and
Co-founder Internet Society
NL MMGA Working Group
Amsterdam, The Netherlands

Neal DeRoo
Department of Philosophy
The King's University
Edmonton, Alberta, Canada

Mika Desblancs
School of Computer Science
McGill University
Montreal, Quebec, Canada

Serban Dinca-Panaitescu
School of Health Policy and Management
York University
Toronto, Ontario, Canada

Teodor Dinca-Panaitescu
Department of Communications
York University
Toronto, Ontario, Canada

Ena Dua
School of Gender, Sexuality and Women's
Studies
York University
Toronto, Ontario, Canada

Jake Okechukwu Effoduh
Africa-Canada Artificial Intelligence and
Data Innovation Consortium (ACADIC)
York University
Toronto, Ontario, Canada
and
Osgoode Hall Law School
York University
Toronto, Ontario, Canada

Christo El Morr
School of Health Policy and Management
York University
Toronto, Ontario, Canada

Nadine Y. Fares
School of Law
University of Edinburgh
Edinburgh, UK

Kesha Fevrier
Department of Geography and Planning
Queen's University
Toronto, Canada

Anis Germani
Internal Medicine, MPH
Université Saint Joseph
Beirut, Lebanon

Rachel Gorman
School of Health Policy and Management
York University
Toronto, Ontario, Canada

Torbjørn Gundersen
Centre for the Study of Professions
Oslo Metropolitan University
Oslo, Norway

Minna Horowitz
University of Helsinki
Helsinki, Finland
and
St. John's University
Queens, New York, USA
and
Advocacy and Digital Rights
Central European University
Center for Media, Data and Society
   (Democracy Institute)
Budapest, Hungary

Kalypso Iordanou
School of Sciences
University of Central Lancashire (UCLan)
   Cyprus
Larnaca, Cyprus

Manar Jammal
Information Technology Department
York University
Toronto, Ontario, Canada

Michael Janzen
Department of Computing Science
The King's University
Edmonton, Alberta, Canada

Petri Kettunen
Department of Computer Science
University of Helsinki
Helsinki, Finland

Jude Dzevela Kong
Africa-Canada Artificial Intelligence and
   Data Innovation Consortium (ACADIC)
York University
Toronto, Ontario, Canada
and
Department of Mathematics and Statistics
York University
Toronto, Ontario, Canada

Aleksi Kopponen
Ministry of Finance
Helsinki, Finland

Bushra Kundia
School of Health Policy and Management
York University
Toronto, Ontario, Canada

Andre Kushniruk
School of Health Information Science
University of Victoria
Victoria, Canada

Tommi Mikkonen
Faculty of Information Technology
University of Jyväskylä
Turku, Finland

Marko Milosavljević
Journalism at the Research Centre for
    the Terminology of Social Sciences and
    Journalism
University of Ljubljana
Ljubljana, Slovenia

Fabrice Muhlenbach
Laboratoire Hubert Curien
UMR 5516, Université de Lyon
Saint-Etienne University
Saint-Etienne, France

Michaela Pňaček(ová)
Cinema and Media Studies
York University
Toronto, Ontario, Canada

Matti Rossi
Department of Information and Service
    Management
Aalto University
Espoo, Finland

Anna-Mari Rusanena
Cognitive Science
Department of Digital Humanities
Faculty of Arts
University of Helsinki
Helsinki, Finland

Federica Russo
Faculty of Humanities
University of Amsterdam
Amsterdam, The Netherlands

Amanda Turnbull
Schulich School of Law
Dalhousie University
Halifax, Nova Scotia, Canada

Ondrej Uzovic
Independent Software Engineer
Bratislava, Slovakia

Hildegarde Van den Bulck
Communication Studies and Head of the
    Department of Communication
Drexel University
Philadelphia, Pennsylvania, USA

Teppo Vesikukka
DataLit, Science and Technology Studies
Faculty of Social Sciences
University of Helsinki
Helsinki, Finland
and
Department of Design
University of Aalto
Espoo, Finland

Tero Villman
Finland Futures Research Centre (FFRC)
University of Turku
Turku, Finland

Joseph Vybihal
School of Computer Science
McGill University
Montreal, Quebec, Canada

Jean Wagemans
Faculty of Humanities
University of Amsterdam
Amsterdam, The Netherlands

List of Reviewers

Abdallah Shami, University of Western Ontario
Alexandra Creighton, York University
Alexis Buettgen, Center for Research on Work and Disability
Allen McLean, University of Saskatchewan
Anne Jackson, York University
Colin Pascal Van Noordt, Tallinn University of Technology
Eleni Christodoulou, Duke-NUS Medical School
Emmanuel Salami, University of Lapin
Fabrice Muhlenbach, University of Saint Etienne
Farah Magrabi, Macquarie University
Hossam Ali-Hassan, York University
Jalal Kawash, University of Calgary
Jean-Christophe Bélisle-Pipon, Simon Fraser University
Jude Dzevela Kong, York University
Karine Gentelet, Université du Québec en Outaouais
Kean Birch, York University
Mehdi Adda, Université du Québec à Rimouski
Michaela Pňaček, York University
Mohammad Khalidi, The City University of New York
Nadine Fares, The University of Edinburgh
Nadine Kachmar, Université du Québec à Rimouski
Nicola Luigi Bragazzi, York University
Nicolas Abou Mrad, École Pratique des Hautes Études
Pierre Maret, University of Saint Etienne
Rand Hirmiz, York University
Regina Rini, York University
Reihaneh Moghisi, York University
Sabine Fernandes, York University
Serban Dinca, York University
Susanna Lindroos-Hovinheimo, University of Helsinki

Taina Pihlajarinne, University of Helsinki
Torbjørn Gundersen, Universiy of Oslo
Tripat Gill, Wilfrid Laurier University
Valentina Al Hamouche, VCA Education
Yahya El-Lahib, University of Calgary

I

AI in Health: Contextual Challenges

The Human Factors of Artificial Intelligence – Where Are We Now and Where Are We Headed? Lessons Learned From AI in Healthcare

Andre Kushniruk and Elizabeth Borycki

School of Health Information Science, University of Victoria, Victoria, Canada

CONTENTS

DOI: 10.1201/9781003261247-2

INTRODUCTION

Advances in artificial intelligence (AI) are progressing rapidly and are already touching our lives in many different ways. The technologies involved are many and varied, as are the applications. Advances in areas of AI are constantly in the news, including articles about the application of natural language processing, predictive analytics, decision support, and robotics. Applications of AI are appearing at an ever-increasing and rapid rate. As such, it should be noted that AI is not a singular technology, but rather an array of different technologies that are being applied in a wide range of domains. The application areas of AI are varied – from areas such as business and education to medicine and healthcare. The technologies associated with AI have evolved over the past several decades and are at differing levels of maturity. Overall, AI has had a long history initially dating back to the 1960s and earlier (Buchanan, 2005), and there have been a number of distinct cycles of promise and productivity. To continue to make progress today, it is important to consider what approaches to AI have worked in the past, as well as what issues have been encountered along the way. In this chapter, it will be argued that greater consideration of human factors is needed. It will also be argued that much can be learned from understanding issues that have been encountered historically, in terms of how AI can be integrated into human activities.

The lead author of this chapter (A.K.) has had experience of working in AI going back a number of decades, including research work during the heyday of the 1980s and subsequent iterations of development and application (in areas such as nuclear power, transportation, and healthcare). Despite the excitement about developments in AI, a number of recurrent issues and challenges have appeared that have made the application and widespread adoption of many AI technologies challenging. It will be noted that many of these issues persist. This includes understanding how specific AI technologies can best be applied in our work and daily lives. It will also be shown that since AI has already had a long history in the deployment of the technologies, much can be learned by considering AI in light of human factors. Along these lines, the chapter will begin by exploring the relationship between the two fields of AI and human factors. Examples from a number of domains will be discussed with a focus on human factor–related challenges and lessons learned in applying AI in healthcare. A number of perspectives will be presented for considering AI within the context of human factors broadly, including the impact of the technology at the individual, work group, and organizational levels.

AI AND ITS RELATIONSHIP WITH HUMAN FACTORS

AI applications refer to computer-based systems that can be said to perform tasks that would otherwise be said to require human intelligence. AI refers to not just one type of technology, but rather is an umbrella term that includes a range of technologies, including machine learning, natural language processing, knowledge extraction techniques, text analytics, image processing, and automated speech recognition, as well as growing number of new and emerging applications and methods. Academically, the field of AI spans several decades of research with key activities occurring at major academic centers worldwide. Despite the very wide variation in techniques and methods involved in AI, the commonality from an end user's perspective is that AI applications are typically designed to perform tasks that would normally be performed by humans and be considered to display intelligent behavior (Nilsson, 2014; Russell & Norvig, 2016). In many cases, such systems have been designed to replace humans in doing specific tasks, while others have been explicitly designed to work synergistically with humans to carry out tasks requiring some degree of intelligence.

The field of human factors refers to the discipline devoted to the study of the relationship among humans and the tools they use, including computer systems and advanced applications such as artificial intelligence (Carayon, 2006). These include factors at the cognitive, social, and organizational levels (Kushniruk & Borycki, 2008). The scope of the field is broad, touching on aspects of system usability at the level of the individual user of a technology such as AI, but also relating to understanding the interaction between technology and humans for carrying out work and group tasks synergistically. In addition, human factors at the organizational, policy, ethical/legal, and political levels are also critical and at play in determining how technology such as AI will interface with humans (Kushniruk & Borycki, 2008).

As AI applications are ultimately designed to support humans and their activities, there has been a long and at times tenuous relationship between the two fields of human factors and AI. Indeed, many of the failures of AI to be adopted attributed to a lack of sufficient consideration of how the two fields can work together (Kushniruk & Borycki, 2021). Furthermore, as will be argued in this chapter, the ultimate success or failure of AI innovations has been closely tied to issues related to human factors and the need to integrate AI appropriately into human work and activity.

THE MANY APPROACHES TO AI IN HEALTHCARE

The history of AI in healthcare spans several decades and can be characterized by a number of phases of activity and interest. Some of the earliest work was in the development of computer systems that were designed to mimic physicians in performing and providing advice around diagnosis, treatment, and management of diseases and illnesses. Such applications, termed "expert systems", began to be developed in the 1970s and 1980s (Shortliffe et al., 1975). These systems were considered to be "knowledge-based systems", as they were designed to contain and apply knowledge embedded in rules and other computer-based representational schemes. Many were designed to provide computer-based advice and consultation in areas such as disease diagnosis and treatment planning (Shortliffe & Cimino, 2014). Over the subsequent years, a great many university and commercial laboratories were developed to advance many directions in AI. Work ranged from developing effective methods for representing knowledge with AI systems to machine learning, image processing, and research in natural language processing.

There has been considerable hope (as well as hype) for AI to be able to improve healthcare and transform it to become more effective and efficient. However, the history of AI has also been characterized by a number of "AI winters" – the term describing periods where the promise of AI appears to have led to unrealistic expectations, resulting in a subsequent downturn in funding and interest for a period. Yasnitksy (2020) argues that these cycles of leaps and drops in popularity will continue as new and inexperienced researchers take up work in this area with unrealistically high expectations initially (before realizing the complexity of the AI endeavor). With respect to AI research and development, this has corresponded to periods where the emphasis has switched from emphasis being placed on work in AI (with the objective of developing fully autonomous applications requiring little or no interaction with human users) to a greater focus on human–computer interaction. This followed from the realization that many AI failures may have resulted from leaving the human "out of the loop", thus leading to alternating cycles of renewed work in human factors.

In considering the periodic cycling of activity and interest in AI over the past several decades, Grudin (2009) has noted that the periods of "winter" corresponded to times when issues related to the need for more emphasis on human factors became apparent (in response to the development of AI applications that failed to sufficiently take human factors into account). According to this perspective, failure of many AI systems to be adopted may then have led to increased research and interest in human factors in relation to AI as a response. For example, after considerable activity in AI in the 1980s in medicine, by 1990 it was increasingly recognized that in medicine, AI systems needed to be interfaced more carefully with the work activities of healthcare professionals. This is an issue that persists for many AI applications to this day. Miller and Masarie (1990) in their seminal paper entitled "The Demise of the 'Greek Oracle' Model for Medical Diagnostic Systems" made this point explicitly when they considered AI expert systems developed up that point in time, where the model for the interaction between human and system was deemed to be driven by the AI system. Such systems were developed with insufficient understanding of how the system would fit into the real diagnostic process of the human physician. Since the 1990s, a strong resurgence of interest in AI applications has emerged. This has included continued work in extensions of knowledge-based systems for applications in automated alerting and reminding physicians about patient health issues (Musen et al., 2021) to improvements in areas such as natural language processing systems and automated speech recognition (e.g., used for automated speech recognition for dictation by health professionals).

Some of the most promising areas in AI research and development have been related to advances in neural networks over the past several decades. This work appeared in conjunction with increased computing power to run such applications, leading to advanced approaches known as deep learning (LeCun et al., 2015). This has subsequently led to a wide array of applications of neural network approaches in areas such as image processing in radiology and pathology (Lakhani & Sundaram, 2017). Much of this work has been effectively integrated into a number of uses, including automatically flagging potential tumors, cancers, and areas of interest for health professionals to attend to from automated analysis of images. In some cases, such systems have been shown to have better accuracy than human clinicians in diagnosis in some specific areas such as dermatology. In addition, the integration of automated image processing of X-rays and other diagnostic tests and images into the decision-making process has proven to be successful and is transforming areas such as radiology and pathology (Yu et al., 2018). However, despite the potential of AI to transform healthcare, a number of human factors issues have been described and continue to appear in the literature on AI, which will be discussed in turn.

RECURRENT HUMAN FACTOR–RELATED CHALLENGES WITH AI IN HEALTHCARE

In this section, we will examine how consideration of human factors, including human capabilities and work activities, is essential for the effective application of these technologies in a range of domains including healthcare. A number of issues and challenges for applying AI in healthcare include the following.

Integration of AI Within Existing Healthcare Practice

One of the most persistent and recurring issues in attempting to bring AI technology to healthcare practice has been difficulty in effectively integrating the technology into actual healthcare practice and work activities. Despite the considerable amount of research that has been carried out into developing AI algorithms and testing AI systems in isolation, the understanding of how to optimize the boundaries of the technology and the human is still a work in progress. As an example, designers of early AI systems were critiqued for not considering how they would be used in medical practice (i.e., how and when they would be invoked to help in the process of diagnosis or treatment planning). As noted above, a seminal paper by Miller and Massarie (1990) argued that systems that were designed to essentially replace the decision-making processes of human physicians (rather than helping them solve their natural decision making) often failed to be adopted in practice. Despite many advances since then, the literature is still full of examples of how AI technologies failed to be appropriately integrated into medical and healthcare practice in a practical way. Examples of more recent applications that have encountered this problem include reports of issues in the integration of IBM Watson oncology system (designed to provide treatment planning for cancer cases) into a hospital's electronic information ecosystem in Texas (Schmidt, 2017; Strickland, 2019). As another example, the recent addition of an AI-based telehealth system known as Babylon was found to disrupt the organizational structures within the healthcare system in the United Kingdom. As a consequence, this application has faced serious adoption issues for becoming integrated fully into the National Health System in the United Kingdom (Burgess, 2017; Oliver, 2019).

Assessing Impact of AI on Work and Cognition

In our previous work, we have argued for the application of human factors analysis techniques that go beyond testing of systems in isolation to testing of systems in their "natural environment" of use – e.g., in clinical, office, and home settings, by applying user requirements gathering techniques that consider the user, the task, the technology, and the context of use (Kushniruk & Turner, 2012). Furthermore, the work activities and information needs of human health professionals, patients as well as lay people need to be better understood to create a true technology–human collaboration. It could also be noted that some of the issues around integration have also been encountered with attempting to bring other information technologies, such as electronic health records, into healthcare. In particular, the integration of new AI technologies within the complex workflow of healthcare processes and activities has proven to be challenging. To address this, the approach promoted by Li and colleagues (2012) argues for careful and repeated testing of the impact of AI applications to assess the impact of AI on time-constrained clinical activities that will be critical to improving the likelihood of adoption. Along these lines, Borycki and Kushniruk (2010) argue for a cognitive-socio-technical approach to analyzing the impact of AI not only on decision quality, but also assessing the impact of AI on work activities, human cognition as well as impact on workflow.

Understandability and Explainability

A major area of research that has emerged is that of understandability and explainability of AI systems (Preece, 2018; Gunning & Aha, 2019). Early rule-based AI systems attempted to deal with this by displaying to end users the actual rules used by the system to come up with decisions and actions automatically. Currently, popular and dominant AI techniques based on neural networks and deep learning algorithms are, however, less understandable to the human end user. This is the case as the computational results of these types of AI systems are based on patterns of activation of large number of interconnected nodes (using a range of statistical functions) making the system's explanation of their activation less human understandable and making their decision making something of a "black box" from the typical end user's (e.g., physician or other health professional) perspective. A number of different visualization and other methods have been proposed to help with this problem, but this is still a research area in the human factors of AI (Arya et al., 2019). This issue is also highly related to the issue of trust and liability of end users of AI systems they use in healthcare, where the consequences of decisions and actions made by human health professionals may be critical and potentially life threatening if based on incorrect advice from an AI system. As such this requires the ability to trace the processing that led to any computer-based recommendations or advice (Shin, 2021).

Safety, Accuracy, and Error Modes for AI

The accuracy and safety of AI applications in healthcare, as in many other domains such as transportation, nuclear power, and other critical areas, is of utmost importance. From the human factors literature, a wide range of approaches have been developed for understanding and improving the accuracy and safety of life-critical systems and applications.

For example, the study of error modes (from domains where failure of systems and individual system components is focused on such as aeronautics) has become the basis of ensuring the safety of new technologies and improving their safety record. For example, the classic "Swiss cheese" model from the work of James Reason has been applied to improve the safety of airliners and other life-critical applications (Reason et al., 2006). This approach involves analyzing the layers of defenses within a system that can serve to detect and prevent error, and the model can be used to explain how errors result from "holes" in these defenses. The application of such methods has, however, been slower to be adopted in testing and optimizing AI applications for safety in areas such as healthcare. In recent work, Kushniruk and colleagues have called for the application of a full range of human factors methods for testing and ensuring the safety of AI applications by applying a "layered" and iterative approach (Carvalho et al., 2009). Such approaches involve rigorously testing new information technologies, beginning with a detailed study of the system or application in isolation, followed by simulation testing, and finally by testing systems for safety in "near live" conditions of use. Such testing is needed prior to putting out the new technology in widespread use (Li et al., 2012) as at each stage any potential safety issues or concerns can be rectified.

Usability and Usefulness of AI

The usability of healthcare information systems refers to the ease of use of systems in terms of their effectiveness, efficiency, learnability, and satisfaction with use (Preece et al., 1994). Issues around the usability of many conventional healthcare information systems have been widely reported in the literature (Kushniruk & Patel, 2004). In addition, many problems with the usability of AI applications have also been reported over the past decades (Kushniruk & Borycki, 2021). New forms of information systems must not only integrate well with existing systems in hospitals and clinical settings, but must also be easy to use, not be distracting and must not detract negatively from human cognitive and physical activities. In the busy and complex world of healthcare, this can be a challenge for adding any type of new technology, and AI applications are no exception. In order to work well and fit with the healthcare environment, AI applications must be designed to complement current healthcare practices and activities. This in turn requires a better understanding of healthcare processes, and an understanding of where and how AI technologies can best be inserted in the human–machine joint system in order to maximize efficiency, effectiveness, safety, and usability. This will be needed in order to ultimately improve patient care and health outcomes using the technology (Kushniruk et al., 2013). In addition, for the adoption of any new technology to occur, the technology needs to be considered to be useful to the end users of such systems.

Legal, Ethical, and Trust Human Factors Issues

Some of the most critical human factors related to the adoption of AI in healthcare (as well as in many other domains) are related to issues around legal and ethical concerns. These are related to general issues around end users and organizational trust of new systems such as AI applications (Siau & Wang, 2018). In order to use and apply many AI technologies, both the end users (e.g., physicians) and the organizations they work for (e.g., hospital systems) must be trusting of the systems, both in terms of their accuracy but also regarding legal liability. This is especially important if an error occurs or the result of use of the system that results in adverse medical or health events. In order to mitigate such issues and increase trust for new technologies in healthcare, FDA (Federal Drug Administration) approval is often sought, as it is essentially a "stamp of approval" for new health products and technologies. However, to date, there are many more AI applications being made available than those that have received FDA approval. Indeed, current issues include developing effective methods for testing and approving new algorithms and approaches to healthcare technology and the need for having conducted clinical trials for AI systems (to ensure they are both effective and do not introduce errors). As such, regulatory approval for new AI technologies will provide a level of trust in their use as well as provide some level of legal "comfort" to organizations such as hospitals where they are deployed. New approaches to risk management with AI applications will need to be developed as well to increase trust in systems and mitigate concerns over legal and ethical human factors and issues (Price et al., 2019).

Issues Around Potential Bias in AI Systems

Many of the current AI applications in healthcare include systems that apply neural network technology and specifically statistical methods known as machine learning. Using these approaches, large data sets are typically fed into the system to allow it to be "trained" by creating weighted patterns of interconnections. Such a trained system can then be applied in order to identify new patterns (e.g., from patient or image data), classify them medically, and provide diagnosis as well as recommendations. The accuracy, generalizability, and nature of data used to "train" such systems has been critical. It has been found that if care is not taken in selecting the training sets of data, then biases contained in that data will creep into and become embodied in the resultant system, thereby affecting the output of the AI system (Roselli et al., 2019). This will in turn affect the performance and outcomes of such systems when they are given new data to analyze. Developing approaches to ensuring the validity and generalizability of data used to drive modern AI applications (and to ensure that bias does not enter into the AI system's processing) is currently a research area undergoing considerable interest.

Issues Around Context of Use and Application with AI

Related to the issue of potential bias, it has been found to be critical that AI systems take into account regional, cultural, and a range of other contextual human factors. Historically, early AI systems were often reported to work well within the constrained context of the hospital, location, and medical domain they were initially developed in. However, the same often impressive results were not found when the same system was used in new and different locations and contexts. This has also been the case with a number of current AI systems, where a system developed at one location or in one country did not seem to work as well in the new location. This phenomenon has been reported throughout the history of AI applications in many domains. To mitigate such effects, more effective and thorough testing of AI systems will be needed before they are released on a widespread scale and across different locations and clinical contexts. One approach to explicitly describe the interaction among user types, tasks required by a system, and contextual factors is the User–Task–Context matrix proposed by Kushniruk and Turner (2012). Using this approach, the types of users, what tasks they can use a system for, and the contexts for using a system are all explicitly specified in the requirements in designing information systems, including AI systems.

Issues Around Acquisition and Maintenance of Knowledge Within AI Systems

A recurrent issue with many AI applications has been termed the "knowledge acquisition bottleneck", which refers to the issues and difficulties in obtaining, updating, and maintaining the knowledge required by many systems to run (Wagner, 2006). With rule-based AI systems, this issue was encountered early on and led to the development of knowledge acquisition systems that were designed to support the acquisition of new knowledge from human experts. This new knowledge would then be incorporated in the knowledge bases of AI systems. With many current systems based on machine learning algorithms and neural networks, the issue around knowledge acquisition remains. This includes the need to obtain data sets that will lead to effective AI system performance and accuracy, which can be difficult to obtain and maintain. In applications of AI in automated alerting and remaindering systems (which have been incorporated in many currently used systems such as electronic health records), the maintenance of the knowledge used to drive interactions with end users has also proven to be more complex than had been previously understood. In addition, considerable resources are needed to ensure that knowledge is up-to-date and contextually relevant to decision making at the point of care where it comes into play with end users (Li et al., 2012).

Need for Common Sense Reasoning and Understanding at a Deep Level by AI

The level of understanding embodied within and required by AI systems to be effective has been a debated issue that has been addressed both by technologists and philosophers. For example, chatbots have been used to simulate human-like conversations using text messages in chat or automated text-to-speech. Many such applications have appeared in health (Abd-Alrazaq et al., 2019). However, in areas such as psychiatry, the limitations of such systems for applications such as counseling patients with issues such as depression need to be taken into account. This includes consideration of the depth of understanding of such systems. In many cases is at what could be considered a shallow level, with the systems simply mimicking human conversation with no real or deep understanding, leading to potentially unsafe interactions with users in many healthcare areas (also leading to potential legal liability if recommendations made by the AI application are unsafe). In addition, machine learning applications in healthcare that have proven to be fairly accurate (e.g., systems designed to analyze images of skin lesions in screening for skin cancer) are often limited to being effective in a very specific range of user interactions (e.g., flagging specific skin cancers) rather than demonstrating reasoning or decision making at any broader level. These issues relate to the discussion around the characterization of "strong" versus "weak" AI, where AI is seen as existing on a continuum based on the degree of actual intelligence and cognition embodied in an AI system (Sharkey & Ziemke, 2001; Flowers, 2019).

Deciding on the "Right" Balance Between Human and AI Interaction

The balance between what aspects of decision making and reasoning should be performed by humans and what can be handled by AI has been debated for a number of decades, and ultimately depends on the type of application being considered. For example, a range of AI technologies have been incorporated into robotic surgery, which has proven to be very effective for use in many types of operations, allowing surgeons to do surgeries otherwise difficult or impossible and also being less invasive than traditional surgery (Magnuson et al., 2016; Nichols et al., 2019). Such systems do not work autonomously, but rather there is a balance between the actions of the human surgeon and the system, as the robotic system augments and extends human capabilities. In such applications, achieving the "right" balance between what the system can do and what the human can do is critical. There are parallel advances in aviation, where there has been a trend toward greater computer control of flight. However, if the right balance is not achieved, this may result in an error and a sense of lack of control by the human operator of the technology, where the computer-based system may seem to override or overly constrain the human user. This can also lead to what is known as automation bias (Goddard et al., 2012). Human factors methods of analysis are needed to help define the right boundary and balance between human action and robotic interaction and control. Advances in this direction have been made by Shneiderman (2020) who has proposed a novel approach known as the "Human-Centered Artificial Intelligence (HCAI)" framework, which considers and helps to clarify the issue of control and context for AI systems. The HCAI framework takes into account multiple dimensions, including the level of control by humans as well as the level of automation, emphasizing the need to consider the levels of each required by different types of AI system applications in order to design and provide effective technology.

Defining Effective Modes for Human–AI Interaction

From a human factor and human–computer interaction perspective, the selection of an effective mode for human–machine interaction is a critical design decision. The subsequent effectiveness of the system will be a function of how well the technology fits into actual human activities. From the literature on AI, not only in healthcare but in many domains ranging from business to aerospace, there have been a number of different approaches to the design of human–AI interaction modes. This has ranged from systems that are consulted for advice and critiquing of human decisions, systems that may run completely in the background (including systems that may provide preprocessing of images) to systems that are designed to work synergistically with human operators and users (Kushniruk & Borycki, 2021). Further work is needed to classify and consider the different modes of human–AI interaction that are possible. In addition, the emergence of robotic technology throughout the industry has led to considerable work in the area of delineating possible human–robotic interaction modes, an emerging area of research and development (Goodrich & Schultz, 2008).

LESSONS LEARNED – WHERE HAVE AI SYSTEMS BEEN EFFECTIVE IN HEALTHCARE?

Deciding on how and when to integrate AI into work activities that were previously done by humans is an important goal of current work applying human factors in AI research. From examining the large literature on AI applications in healthcare, a number of generalizations can be made as to what type of applications have been most successfully adopted (Buch et al., 2018). Some of the most successful applications, in the context of actual adoption of the AI technology in healthcare are as follows (Kushniruk & Borycki, 2021):

- Providing automated data analysis and generation of decisions that would otherwise not be possible to obtain within time constraints (e.g., real-time analysis of patient monitoring data for predicting trends).

- Replacing tedious or time-consuming administrative tasks that could be done automatically.

- Providing diagnosis for specific types of conditions where a high degree of accuracy can be achieved (e.g., identification of malignant moles from images).

- Ability to analyze large streams of data that would otherwise be impossible for humans or that would lead to cognitive overload.

- Providing safety checks (e.g., automated alerts, reminders, and guidelines) on human decision making and operations in safety-critical domains.

- Providing decision support for complex tasks where the AI system or application serves as a "catalyst" to help the human with steps in their problem solving and decision making.

- Ability to extend human capability with AI-controlled and AI-supported technologies that go beyond human mental or physician capabilities (e.g., robotic surgery).

CONCLUSION: BRINGING AI AND HUMAN FACTORS TOGETHER

AI technologies promise to lead to advances in many fields including healthcare (He et al., 2019; Buch et al., 2018). However, as described in this chapter a number of complex issues exist and have been encountered along the way. In this chapter, it has been argued that many of the most critical issues are related to human factors. Furthermore, human factors were broadly described as dealing with the interaction of systems with humans at multiple levels. This includes understanding the system–human interaction, from the individual user of a system up to the complexity of the application of AI technology in complex organizational and situational contexts. Along these lines, it was argued that greater emphasis needs to be placed on understanding the human factors involved in integrating AI technologies into complex work domains. Greater emphasis needs to be placed on understanding the users of such systems and applications, the tasks they use the technology for, and the context of use of the technology itself (Kushniruk & Turner, 2012). In previous work, we have argued for the need for more thorough usability and human factors testing of AI systems during their design and before their release. This would likely need to involve "near live" simulation and more extensive testing with AI designs and applications "in-situ" before finalizing and going live with them (Li et al., 2012). In this chapter, it has also been shown that interest in AI has cycled over the past few decades, along with the advancement of improved AI technologies and computing power. However, it has also been demonstrated that a number of key issues related to human factors have remained and appear to be recurrent. This will necessitate the need for more work at the intersection of AI and human factors.

Finally, the adoption of AI technology in healthcare or any other domain can be considered in the context of Roger's theory of diffusion of innovations (Rogers, 2010). This theory provides a set of generalizations that can be applied when considering the spread of innovations. Application of this theory has indicated that many technologies may go through a period of adoption, whereby different types of users (ranging from technology enthusiasts in the beginning to the majority users and finally "laggards") adopt new technology at different points in time and represent a different and distinct type of user groups. How humans understand, navigate and communicate knowledge will be essential to know in order to implement technology that will be effective and become adopted. This is still the case when considering new and emerging technologies such as AI innovations (Patel & Kushniruk, 1998). Understanding the impact of system on healthcare will become increasingly important as AI technology becomes incorporated within patient-facing applications. Such applications have allowed patients and lay people to directly interact with health information systems such as health portals and patient information systems to access and their own patient data (Cimino et al., 1998). In addition, AI-based chatbots are now being used directly by patient populations and are becoming more accessible to the wider population (Abd-Alrazaq et al., 2019). In our current work, we are examining the use of human factors engineering to better understand the use and the users of new technologies such as AI. This work is aimed at lessening the barriers to adoption of technologies that have been proven to be useful, usable, and needed in order to optimize human activity (Kushniruk & Borycki, 2021).

REFERENCES

Abd-Alrazaq, A. A., Alajlani, M., Alalwan, A. A., Bewick, B. M., Gardner, P., & Househ, M. (2019). An overview of the features of chatbots in mental health: A scoping review. *International Journal of Medical Informatics, 132,* 103978.

Arya, V., Bellamy, R. K., Chen, P. Y., Dhurandhar, A., Hind, M., Hoffman, S. C., … Zhang, Y. (2019). One explanation does not fit all: A toolkit and taxonomy of AI explainability techniques. *arXiv Preprint,* arXiv:1909.03012.

Borycki, E. M., & Kushniruk, A. W. (2010). Towards an integrative cognitive-socio-technical approach in health informatics: Analyzing technology-induced error involving health information systems to improve patient safety. *The Open Medical Informatics Journal, 4,* 181.

Buch, V. H., Ahmed, I., & Maruthappu, M. (2018). Artificial intelligence in medicine: Current trends and future possibilities. *The British Journal of General Practice, 68*(668), 143–144. 10.3399/bjgp18X695213

Buchanan, B. G. (2005). A (very) brief history of artificial intelligence. *AI Magazine, 26*(4), 53.

Burgess, M. (2017). The NHS is trialling an AI chatbot to answer your medical questions. *Wired UK (2017, January 5).* https://www.wired.co.uk/article/babylon-nhs-chatbot-app

Carayon, P. (2006). *Handbook of human factors and ergonomics in health care and patient safety.* 2nd Edition. CRC Press.

Carvalho, C. J., Borycki, E. M., & Kushniruk, A. (2009). Ensuring the safety of health information systems: Using heuristics for patient safety. *Healthcare Quarterly, 12,* 49–54.

Cimino, J. J., Sengupta, S., Clayton, P. D., Patel, V. L., Kushniruk, A., & Huang, X. (1998). Architecture for a web-based clinical information system that keeps the design open and the access closed. In *Proceedings of the AMIA Symposium* (p. 121). American Medical Informatics Association.

Flowers, J. C. (2019). Strong and weak AI: Deweyan considerations. In *AAAI Spring Symposium: Towards Conscious AI Systems* (Vol. 22877). http://ceur-ws.org/Vol-2287/paper34.pdf

Goddard, K., Roudsari, A., & Wyatt, J. C. (2012). Automation bias: A systematic review of frequency, effect mediators, and mitigators. *Journal of the American Medical Informatics Association, 19*(1), 121–127.

Goodrich, M. A., & Schultz, A. C. (2008). Human–robot interaction: A survey. *Foundations and Trends® in Human–Computer Interaction, 1*(3), 203–275.

Grudin, J. (2009). AI and HCI: Two fields divided by a common focus. *AI Magazine, 30*(4), 48.

Gunning, D., & Aha, D. W. (2019). DARPA's explainable artificial intelligence program. *AI Magazine, 44*(2), 44–58. 10.1609/aimag.v40i2.2850

He, J., Baxter, S. L., Xu, J., Xu, J., Zhou, X., & Zhang, K. (2019). The practical implementation of artificial intelligence technologies in medicine. *Nature Medicine, 25*(1), 30–36.

Kushniruk, A., & Borycki, E. (2021). The human factors of AI in healthcare: Recurrent issues, future challenges and ways forward. In Househ, M., Borycki, B., & Kushniruk, A. *Multiple perspectives on artificial intelligence in healthcare* (pp. 3–12). Springer: Cham.

Kushniruk, A., Nohr, C., Jensen, S., & Borycki, E. M. (2013). From usability testing to clinical simulations: Bringing context into the design and evaluation of usable and safe health information technologies. *Yearbook of Medical Informatics, 22*(01), 78–85.

Kushniruk, A. W., & Borycki, E. M. (Eds.). (2008). *Human, social, and organizational aspects of health information systems.* Hershey, PA, USA: IGI Global.

Kushniruk, A. W., & Patel, V. L. (2004). Cognitive and usability engineering methods for the evaluation of clinical information systems. *Journal of Biomedical Informatics, 37*(1), 56–76.

Kushniruk, A., & Turner, P. (2012). A framework for user involvement and context in the design and development of safe e-Health systems. In *Quality of Life through Quality of Information* (pp. 353–357). IOS Press: Amsterdam, Netherlands.

Lakhani, P., & Sundaram, B. (2017). Deep learning at chest radiography: Automated classification of pulmonary tuberculosis by using convolutional neural networks. *Radiology, 284*(2), 574–582.

LeCun, Y., Bengio, Y., & Hinton, G. (2015). Deep learning. *Nature, 521*(7553), 436–444.

Li, A. C., Kannry, J. L., Kushniruk, A., Chrimes, D., McGinn, T. G., Edonyabo, D., & Mann, D. M. (2012). Integrating usability testing and think-aloud protocol analysis with "near-live" clinical simulations in evaluating clinical decision support. *International Journal of Medical Informatics, 81*(11), 761–772.

Magnuson, J., Genden, E., & Kuppersmith, R. (2016). *Robotic head and neck surgery.* Thieme: Brazil.

Miller, R. A., & Masarie Jr., F. E. (1990). The demise of the "Greek Oracle" model for medical diagnostic systems. *Methods of Information in Medicine, 29*(01), 1–2.

Musen, M. A., Middleton, B., & Greenes, R. A. (2021). Clinical decision-support systems. In Shortliffe, E. H., & Cimino, J. J. *Biomedical informatics* (pp. 795–840). Springer: Cham.

Nichols, A. C., Theurer, J., Prisman, E., Read, N., Berthelet, E., Tran, E., … Palma, D. A.. (2019). Radiotherapy versus transoral robotic surgery and neck dissection for oropharyngeal squamous cell carcinoma (ORATOR): An open-label, phase 2, randomised trial. *The Lancet Oncology, 20*(10), 1349–1359.

Nilsson, N. J. (2014). *Principles of artificial intelligence.* Elsevier Science: United States.

Oliver, D. (2019). Lessons from the Babylon Health saga. *BMJ, 365,* l2387.

Patel, V. L., & Kushniruk, A. W. (1998). Understanding, navigating and communicating knowledge: Issues and challenges. *Methods of Information in Medicine, 37*(04/05), 460–470.

Preece, A. (2018). Asking 'why' in AI: Explainability of intelligent systems – Perspectives and challenges. *Intelligent Systems in Accounting, Finance and Management, 25*(2), 63–72.

Preece, J., Rogers, Y., Sharp, H., Benyon, D., Holland, S., & Carey, T. (1994). *Human–computer interaction.* Addison-Wesley: Spain.

Price, W. N., Gerke, S., & Cohen, I. G. (2019). Potential liability for physicians using artificial intelligence. *JAMA, 322*(18), 1765–1766.

Reason, J., Hollnagel, E., & Paries, J. (2006). Revisiting the Swiss cheese model of accidents. *Journal of Clinical Engineering, 27*(4), 110–115.

Rogers, E. M. (2010). *Diffusion of innovations,* 4th Edition. Free Press: United Kingdom.

Roselli, D., Matthews, J., & Talagala, N. (2019, May). Managing bias in AI. In *Companion Proceedings of the 2019 World Wide Web Conference* (pp. 539–544).

Russell, S. J., & Norvig, P. (2016). *Artificial intelligence: A modern approach.* Pearson Education Limited: Malaysia.

Schmidt, C. (2017). MD Anderson breaks with IBM Watson, raising questions about artificial intelligence in oncology. *JNCI: Journal of the National Cancer Institute, 109*(5). 10.1093/jnci/djx113

Sharkey, N. E., & Ziemke, T. (2001). Mechanistic versus phenomenal embodiment: Can robot embodiment lead to strong AI? *Cognitive Systems Research, 2*(4), 251–262.

Shin, D. (2021). The effects of explainability and causability on perception, trust, and acceptance: Implications for explainable AI. *International Journal of Human-Computer Studies, 146,* 102551.

Shneiderman, B. (2020). Human-centered artificial intelligence: Trusted, reliable & safe, University of Maryland Human-Computer Interaction Lab Technical Report 2020-1 (January 6, 2020). http://www.cs.umd.edu/hcil/trs/2020-01/2020-01.pd

Shortliffe, E. H., & Cimino, J. J. (2014). *Biomedical informatics: Computer applications in health care and biomedicine.* Springer: Spain.

Shortliffe, E. H., Davis, R., Axline, S. G., Buchanan, B. G., Green, C. C., & Cohen, S. N. (1975). Computer-based consultations in clinical therapeutics: Explanation and rule acquisition capabilities of the MYCIN system. *Computers and Biomedical Research, 8*(4), 303–320.

Siau, K., & Wang, W. (2018). Building trust in artificial intelligence, machine learning, and robotics. *Cutter business technology journal, 31*(2), 47–53.

Strickland, E. (2019). IBM Watson, heal thyself: How IBM overpromised and underdelivered on AI health care. *IEEE Spectrum, 56*(4), 24–31.

Wagner, C. (2006). Breaking the knowledge acquisition bottleneck through conversational knowledge management. *Information Resources Management Journal (IRMJ), 19*(1), 70–83.

Yasnitksy, L. (2020). Whether be new "Winter" of artificial intelligence? In Antipova, T. (Ed.), *Integrated science in digital age, ICIS 2019. Lecture notes in networks and systems,* Vol. 78 (pp. 13–17). Springer Nature: Cham, Switzerland.

Yu, K. H., Beam, A. L., & Kohane, I. S. (2018). Artificial intelligence in healthcare. *Nature Biomedical Engineering, 2*(10), 719–731.

CHAPTER 2

Artificial Intelligence and Safety in Healthcare

Elizabeth Borycki and Andre Kushniruk

School of Health Information Science, University of Victoria, Victoria, Canada

CONTENTS

INTRODUCTION

Artificial intelligence (AI) has been integrated into many technologies. AI's integration has been used to support user decision-making as well as organizational and societal processes (Matheny et al., 2019; Househ et al., 2021). Yet, there are concerns in many communities about the safety of AI and this has been an important area of discussion,

DOI: 10.1201/9781003261247-3

debate, and research globally. This is especially the case in healthcare (Borycki & Kushniruk, 2021). The healthcare community, which includes health professionals, healthcare administrators, health informatics/technology professionals, and individuals, who receive healthcare, has concerns about AI-driven technologies in terms of their ability to support safe, efficient, and effective patient care and health-related processes. This is the case in hospitals, clinics, and the homes of patients (Borycki et al., 2021; Richardson et al., 2021). According to the literature, physicians are concerned about the impact of AI in influencing their decision-making (e.g., providing incorrect information or diminishing the quality of their decisions by introducing bias). Physicians and legal societies are concerned about how AI could lead to patient harm (Jiang et al., 2017; Price & Gerke, 2019). Nurses identify the need for compassion to be integrated into care provided by AI and advocate for identifying evidence-based strategies and approaches to safely implement the technology into the healthcare digital ecosystem (Borycki et al., 2013; Robert, 2019; Borycki & Kushniruk, 2021). Patients are concerned that AI technologies may lead to decreased patient choice regarding treatments, misleading conclusions by health professionals due to bias in the algorithms, and inappropriate or ineffective healthcare (Richardson et al., 2021).

In this chapter, the authors define safety and the issues around safety that arise when considering the application and use of AI. The authors will use healthcare as an example of how AI is shaping our expectations surrounding the safety of the technology.

OBJECTIVES OF THE RESEARCH CHAPTER

The objectives of this chapter are as follows:

1. Define AI safety.

2. Describe the benefits of AI.

3. Describe AI safety issues and challenges.

4. Review the current norms around the safety of AI and an example of how AI is shaping our perceptions and expectations regarding safe use in healthcare.

5. Solutions going forward.

6. Future research directions.

The chapter begins by defining health technology safety as it applies to AI technologies.

DEFINING TECHNOLOGY SAFETY

In the field of health informatics, assessing the safety of AI has emerged as an important aspect of professional practice (Price & Gerke, 2019; Borycki & Kushniruk, 2021). In healthcare, health professionals (e.g., physicians, nurses, pharmacists) and patients are interested in learning about the safety of AI when it is used to support health-related decision-making (Price & Gerke, 2019; Robert, 2019; Richardson et al., 2021). Similar concerns have emerged in the health informatics professional community (Borycki & Kushniruk, 2021). Health informatics professionals often lead health technology procurements for regional health authorities, or they may be involved in the design, development, implementation, and maintenance of these new technologies. Therefore, ensuring the safety of AI technology functioning and long-term use is a critical aspect of health informatics professional work (Kushniruk et al., 2010). A major category of AI is known as machine learning, which focuses on the development of algorithms that can improve their performance on tasks (e.g., medical diagnosis) through the automated analysis of data (Challen et al., 2019). Today, the application and use of machine learning and other forms of AI present a number of challenges, particularly with regard to safety.

Many AI researchers and authors have attempted to define AI safety. Broadly speaking, AI safety can be defined as the tools, testing approaches, and methods that are used to ensure that AI, when deployed, does not harm humanity (Feige, 2019). Many AI technologies are used in our society; for example, in healthcare AI can aid in the diagnosis of disease and identify deterioration in a patient's condition. AI has also been used to improve the safety of healthcare, supporting health professionals as they prescribe medications and monitor a patient's health status using AI-enhanced alerts, reminders, and alarms (Matheny et al., 2019; Househ et al., 2021). Alternatively, AI technologies can cause technology-induced errors (TIE). TIE are one type of error that arises from the design, development, implementation, and/or interactions between the AI technology and the new work processes that it generates, when it is used in daily life or within the context of an organization (Borycki & Kushniruk, 2008, 2021). To illustrate, given the advances and new applications of AI in healthcare, several researchers are studying and attempting to understand how AI improves safety as well as how it may introduce new opportunities for medical error (He et al., 2019; Price & Gerke, 2019).

THE BENEFITS OF AI: HEALTHCARE AS AN EXAMPLE

Much of the AI healthcare research has focused on the design, development, and use of AI as a diagnostic and prognostic tool in hospitals (Choudhury & Asan, 2020; Jiang et al., 2017); for example, AI is being applied to electronic health record (EHR) data to support physician decision-making. EHRs are the main technology used in healthcare. EHRs collect substantial amounts of patient data. They are used in hospitals to support health professional communication, decision-making, and patient care activities in medical units, surgical units, obstetrical units, intensive care units, etc. AI techniques such as machine learning and natural language processing techniques are being studied for their application and use in healthcare as a way of improving patient safety outcomes. Most of this research has been on topics such as the design and application of machine learning and natural language processing approaches to the analysis of large volumes of different types of patient health data (found in EHRs, monitoring devices, and other health data collection devices).

According to a recent systematic review by Choudhury and Asan (2020), AI safety research in healthcare focuses on the application and use of AI technologies in five main areas with an aim to improve the safety of healthcare provided to patients for:

- Drug safety
- Prevention of adverse drug events
- Clinical reporting
- Clinical alerting
- Clinical alarms

In the drug safety and adverse drug event literature, AI technologies have been applied to activities such as identifying the presence of drug–drug interactions that might harm patients (e.g., cause an allergic reaction). Patients are prescribed medications in a hospital, clinic, or office by a physician, nurse practitioner, or pharmacist. Other applications of AI in the area of drug safety include the use of AI tools to monitor for and prevent safety events such as administering the wrong medication to the wrong patient, providing a patient with the wrong dose of a medication (leading to a drug overdose) and the reconciliation of medications, when a patient transitions from one healthcare setting to another (to make sure the patient is prescribed the appropriate medications no matter where he or she is in their health journey from hospital to home) (Choudhury & Asan, 2020). To illustrate, if a citizen (who is taking several medications for a chronic illness) is hospitalized for an acute exacerbation of a disease then a physician, nurse practitioner, pharmacist, and/or nurse would be provided with detailed information about the medications the patient is taking at home. Such information would be provided to the physician or nurse practitioner to support the appropriate selection and prescribing of medications, while the patient is hospitalized for treatment of the illness (Monkman et al., 2013; The Electronic Medication Reconciliation Group, 2017). AI technologies could process and enhance health professionals' decision-making regarding treatment approaches while at the same time letting the health professionals know if there is a drug–drug interaction (Choudhury & Asan, 2020).

Developers of AI technologies have focused their efforts on improving the quality of clinical reports in healthcare; for example, AI has been used to identify and analyze safety incidents and patient feedback reports submitted by health professionals who work in hospitals or clinics and by patients who have received care in either of these settings (Choudhury & Asan, 2020; Davy & Borycki, 2021; Li et al., 2021). Such information could inform the development of interventions that can improve the quality and safety of patient care (Palojoki et al., 2017). In this case, AI helps to identify and analyze safety events or patient feedback reports, where the information could help to improve patient care processes (Choudry & Asan, 2020).

AI has also been applied to the analysis of patient laboratory test results and vital sign report data. AI-related enhancements have included supporting the review and use of patient laboratory test results and vital sign information in clinician diagnostic and treatment-related decision-making in hospitals and clinics. Research at the intersection of EHRs and AI has largely focused on extracting information about patients. AI can also improve the identification, review, and analysis of vulnerable patient populations such as those individuals, who are at an increased risk of bleeding, postoperative surgical complications, mortality, and future health events. Here, researchers have analyzed EHR data found in hospitals to identify the characteristics of individuals, who experienced a health event such as increased bleeding. The data from the EHR and the algorithm that was developed based on that data are applied to future patients, helping to identify those patients that have the same characteristics (and are therefore at risk for a health event such as increased bleeding). The algorithm then alerts the health professionals to the individual's vulnerability so that extra precautions such as additional monitoring can be undertaken to prevent any such health issues, should they arise (Choudry & Asan, 2020).

AI techniques have been used to improve alarms and alerts for medical and monitoring devices in intensive care units (such as ventilators, intravenous pumps, and cardiac monitors). The algorithm triggers an alarm for the health professional to hear when a patient's condition warrants immediate intervention. This research has included applying AI in improving the performance of alarms and reducing the number of false alarms (such as false alarms on patients receiving cardiac care in intensive care units) in hospitals. Some AI research has focused on improving clinical alarms by developing algorithms that more effectively classify patient vital sign data in hospital intensive care units, predict the occurrence of adverse events when a patient is receiving care in a hospital, identify medication-related adverse events when a doctor is prescribing medications in a hospital or at a clinic and signaling health professionals about a deterioration of the patient's health condition, when the patient is receiving treatment and care in a hospital (Jiang et al., 2017; Challen et al., 2019; Choudhury & Asan, 2020).

In summary, the benefits of AI are significant. AI can be used to improve human safety especially when it has been developed for use in healthcare settings. The examples mentioned in the previous paragraphs are only a few descriptions of how AI has been used to support the diagnosis of disease and improve patient safety. As described above, AI has also been used to improve the prescribing process by alerting health professionals about drug–drug interactions, and vulnerable patients so that they receive additional medical attention whether in a hospital or clinic. Even so, safety issues remain a concern when considering AI applications in healthcare.

SAFETY ISSUES AND CHALLENGES OF AI: HEALTHCARE AS AN EXAMPLE

In the next decade, research will need to focus on several key safety issues and challenges in AI, including (1) improving the quality, credibility, accuracy, completeness, and the breadth of data collection so that AI algorithms work well in healthcare, (2) improving the design and development of AI algorithms to improve their ability to identify and predict current and future health issues, (3) testing these algorithms so as to ensure that they are effective over and above currently used approaches to detecting and predicting disease, and (4) explaining what algorithms do so that the humans, who use these technologies know their limits in supporting health professional, patient, and family decision-making (see Table 2.1 for examples of research in this area).

TABLE 2.1 Key Safety Issues, Challenges, and Examples

Key Safety Issue/Challenge	Example
1. Improving the quality, accuracy, credibility, completeness, and breadth of data collection	In one study, researchers identified that up to 28% of patient diagnoses were missing from an electronic health record (Madden et al., 2016). Given this amount of missing data, health professionals, patients, and family members will need to ask questions about the EHR data used to develop algorithms and whether any of that data was missing (and understand how missing data may have affected the algorithm's ability to detect a health issue).
2. Improving the design and development of AI algorithms to identify and predict current and future health issues effectively	Researchers have identified that AI may be biased; for example, an algorithm that has been designed and developed using data from one population may not be effective in detecting health issues in another population (Reddy et al., 2020). To illustrate, an AI algorithm that detects skin cancer in a light-skinned population may not be effective in detecting skin cancers in a darker skinned patient population and thereby place the darker skinned population at risk for a skin cancer diagnosis being missed. Patients and health professionals need to understand what data was used to develop the algorithm to understand its limitations and to use this information when considering the recommendations made by the algorithm (Lashbrook, 2018).
3. AI algorithms need to be tested to ensure that they are effective over and above currently used approaches to detecting and predicting disease.	Healthcare researchers are now able to compare AI algorithms in terms of their effectiveness to help identify those algorithms that represent an improvement over currently used AI. For example, a group of German researchers is examining how well different algorithms are working to identify skin cancers for the purpose of seeking out the most effective algorithm for use in a physician's office (Brinker et al., 2019).
4. Explaining what algorithms do so that the humans who use this technology know its limits in supporting decision-making.	With AI being applied to our health and when there are decisions that influence life and death, patients, families, and health professionals need to understand the application of AI to the diagnosis of disease and to treatment. There has emerged a pressure on being able to explain what the AI does and whether it is appropriate to apply. Here, a patient or family member may wish to understand how the AI improves a health professional's decision-making in their case (or if the technology has limits in terms of diagnosing disease or supporting treatment of an illness) (Adadi & Berrada, 2020).

As outlined above, many issues still exist when considering AI technologies, their readiness, application, and safe use to support healthcare. The hope is that advances in this research will improve the quality and speed with which health professionals and/or patients (and their families) can identify potential health issues, support their treatment of disease, and have their health-related decision-making supported (Choudhury & Asan, 2020).

AI SAFETY: CULTURAL NORMS

AI technologies have improved aspects of healthcare. Yet, concerns about AI safety persist among health professionals and patients. We also know that each year new technologies are being designed, developed, and approved for use. This is particularly the case in the health sector. We know that as each technology is inserted into the process of care, there are opportunities to improve safety and/or inadvertently introduce new types of medical errors (Borycki & Kushniruk, 2021; Borycki et al., 2013). As has been pointed out earlier in this chapter, AI like other health technologies has this potential too (Borycki & Kushniruk, 2021). To illustrate, there have been published reports that have documented health professional and public concerns surrounding AI. Specifically, there have been calls for greater transparency surrounding AI technologies. Both groups wish to know (1) what the technology does, (2) when the technology is being used, (3) what research supports the technology's use, and (4) how it affects the quality of their reasoning and decision-making. These are common questions for patients and health professionals (i.e., those whose lives may be affected by AI) (He et al., 2019; Price & Gerke, 2019).

Health professionals and patients are increasingly demanding more transparency when AI is introduced to healthcare as there is an expectation that the technology supports the identification of common to rare health events. Consumers and health professionals expect AI technologies to identify important health issues, and in cases where this is not possible, to provide information about the boundaries and drawbacks of using the technology (He et al., 2019; Borycki & Kushniruk, 2021; Richardson et al., 2021).

Robust AI solutions that are being developed for healthcare use, require large amounts of data for training and validation such as the patient data found in EHRs. Once implemented, these technologies need an ongoing supply of data to continue to train (i.e., teach the AI to interpret and learn from the data), validate (i.e., determine how well the AI performs on a new data set), and test (and improve) the AI over time by applying it to new data sets or a data set that has been updated with new data (Jiang et al., 2017; He et al., 2019; Matheny et al., 2019; Tao et al., 2019; Kim et al., 2020). To illustrate, half of the patient data from an EHR could be used to develop an AI algorithm. Once the algorithm is developed, the other half of the patient data (that has not been used in algorithm development) is used to determine how well the AI performs on the data set. To ensure the algorithm works well on other EHR data sets, it is applied to patient data from a different EHR from another healthcare organization or from another country. To improve these algorithms, some researchers have suggested that there is a need to access large data repositories across countries for there to be enough data to effectively test and validate some AI solutions. Many available data sets are limited in size and therefore data sets may be of insufficient size to train and validate AI technologies adequately (in some cases even data captured at a country level may be of insufficient size to ensure the safety of the AI) (Kim et al., 2020; Borycki & Kushniruk, 2021).

Researchers and policymakers have suggested that countries and healthcare organizations pool their data to create data sets large enough to test and validate AI algorithms and to prevent biases introduced by these data sets. To illustrate, Kim and colleagues (2020), developed, tested, and validated an AI solution for breast cancer detection by using data from three different countries (i.e., Korea, the United States, and the United Kingdom). Kim's research highlights the importance of large, ethnically broad, and racially diverse data sets being used to test AI technologies for their effectiveness and to prevent bias from being present in the algorithm.

Such needs for large data sets have led to a demand for technology products and digital infrastructures that enable safe and secure use of large data sets (i.e., so that the data set can be anonymized and patient privacy can be protected in a secure environment) (He et al., 2019; Kim et al., 2020). Here, technology products that support de-identification of patient data, patient privacy, and security data are necessary before large data sets can be made available to create full and robust AI technologies to preserve the safety and privacy of those individuals who have contributed their data to those data sets. Furthermore, until large data sets can be accessed in the context of development, testing, and validation of some AI technologies, administrators, clinicians and consumers may question the quality and safety of the AI in detecting health-related issues to sufficiently support diagnostic reasoning and decision-making by healthcare providers and consumers. Here, there is a need to provide transparency regarding the potential biases introduced by using small, homogeneous data sets for training and optimizing AI applications (He et al., 2019; Price & Gerke, 2019; Kim et al., 2020; Househ et al., 2021).

Beyond traditional AI technology validation, there have emerged calls from the medical and health informatics communities to add additional layers of testing and validation before a system is deployed for real-world use (Borycki & Kushniruk, 2021). To illustrate, Apple® watches are being tested in clinical trials by physicians to determine the effectiveness of AI in detecting atrial fibrillation (a heart condition that causes the heart to beat quickly) as compared to conventional electrocardiograms of the heart currently used in cardiac settings (Raja et al., 2019). In addition to this, physician groups have suggested there is a need to verify AI technology product claims on local data sets, as the AI may have been developed and validated on a patient data set that differs from the local patient(s) health data to which it is being applied. Patient characteristics may vary by region and these regional differences, whether they are based on sex, gender, race, ethnicity, or environmental context, affect the AI technology's predictive reliability and safety (Price & Gerke, 2019).

Physical evidence of the presence or absence of disease holds considerable promise for creating powerful AI algorithms. Cancer researchers are developing algorithms that attempt to predict the presence or absence of cancer. Research has demonstrated that it is possible to confirm the quality of a predictive algorithm in identifying individuals at risk for disease with physical observations and test result data. To illustrate, researchers from

Korea, the United States, and the United Kingdom were able to confirm the predictive quality of their algorithm for a breast cancer diagnosis with biopsy data. In their study, biopsy data provided additional confirmation of the presence or absence of cancer and provided insights into the quality of the AI as well as opportunities for additional refinement of the technology (Kim et al., 2020).

Some physicians have suggested that AI technologies (much like other technologies such as decision support systems, mobile technologies, and other types of devices used in healthcare) need to be studied using a randomized clinical control trial approach in real-world settings as compared to usual care. These researchers have suggested this would help to determine whether the technology (1) could improve health outcomes and (2) provide a superior intervention as compared to other types of medical/technology interventions currently being used by healthcare practitioners to diagnose disease and identify risk. Such knowledge of the impact of AI provides insights into whether introducing the new technology provides any additional benefit over and above existing approaches and technologies that we use in healthcare. This type of research could be reviewed by organizational and government decision-makers before there is an investment in AI technologies that do not help patients or may be costlier to use than those currently in use in healthcare (Jiang et al., 2017; Price & Gerke, 2019).

To ensure that clinicians feel comfortable with using AI, physician organizations are calling for transparency regarding what technology does, when the technology is being used in the process of care, how the AI application may affect decision-making and reasoning, the limits of its effectiveness, and how it compares to other technologies currently in use. Such transparency would allow clinicians to develop an understanding of the technology and how it works as well as to identify the technology's limits. This research extends to the area of AI explainability so that its human users (e.g., physicians) will be able to understand (and accept) the AI's decisions and trust what the AI is doing (Jiang et al., 2017; Price & Gerke, 2019; Sujan et al., 2022). This is a critical area of research as some forms of AI have been criticized as acting as "black boxes" in the sense that we know the inputs to their processing (e.g., sets of data) as well as the outputs (e.g., decisions generated by the AI) but the intervening processing (between the inputs and outputs) that generated decisions may be less understandable or explainable in human terms.

Finally, the context of AI use is emerging as an important area of research that will need to be considered as part of the future of healthcare. Healthcare systems are highly digitized. Yet, much work is still needed to fully digitize healthcare. To illustrate, although Canada has been digitizing its patient health records for over 20 years, this digitization remains uneven where EHRs are concerned. In Canada, 100% of diagnostic images and patient demographics are available digitally, yet only 63% of information about a patient's dispensed medications and lab test results are available (Gheorghiu & Hagens, 2016). In a recent (2021) Organization for Economic Co-operation and Development (OECD) country report, 85% of healthcare data sets were available nationally in Canada with some gaps (e.g., in areas such as diabetes and cardiovascular care data). Canada ranked 10th among the 23 countries that were compared for health data set availability, maturity, and use (OECD, 2021).

EHRs are supposed to provide a lifetime of digital records of patients' health history, but gaps in the data remain. EHRs are important data collection tools and repositories of patient information. Globally, there has been a move toward implementing EHRs across countries and healthcare settings are uneven (El Morr, 2018). A considerable amount of patient data remains paper-based (see the Canadian example above). The data, as a result, are incomplete and therefore AI algorithms developed using these data would be impacted in terms of their accuracy and safety (i.e., given that patient data would be missing from the data set). We are seeing new health data collection tools and interventions that take the form of mobile health apps (Martínez-Pérez et al., 2013), remote monitoring devices (Chaudhury et al., 2017), and public health information systems (Yasnoff et al., 2000) increasing and creating data sets that are not fully integrated with EHRs, again influencing the development of algorithms using these data sets negatively in terms of their accuracy and safety.

It is important to recognize that healthcare has its own vast and complex digital health ecosystem and introducing new AI applications should be considered within that context. There is a need to understand where and when the technology could be used most effectively and to insert the technology at that point in the patient's care process. Furthermore, healthcare providers need training and support to use AI to understand the quality of the AI being used and the boundaries of its effective application (Price & Gerke, 2019). Lastly, healthcare administrators need to consider AI technologies within a global healthcare context. Adding costly technologies that have little to no benefit over and above existing approaches to patient treatment and management may lead to negative impacts on patient care – diverting monies away from proven treatment approaches to one that needs further research can lead to system-wide costs.

NEED TO REVIEW THE CURRENT NORMS AROUND THE SAFETY OF AI: HEALTHCARE AS AN EXAMPLE

AI is quickly being integrated into society and healthcare is part of this process. Health professionals such as physicians and nurses are increasingly becoming aware of the issues and considerations associated with developing, testing, and validating AI technologies so that their outputs and suggestions are reproducible. This is especially the case when considering the impact of the data upon introducing bias into the AI algorithm's performance (e.g., based on sex, race, ethnicity). Going forward, for AI technologies to be fully accepted and adopted for use by health professionals and consumers, an understanding needs to be built. Health professionals and consumers need to be able to evaluate the quality and safety (including the boundaries) of the AI tools' application and use. There is also a need to understand the processes associated with its development and validation, including an understanding of the type of data that was used to develop the AI tool and the limitations of the data set. This is especially the case for clinicians who may be using the technology to make decisions and where there is a mismatch between the nature of the data used to develop the AI tool and the patient they are trying to diagnose; for example, a physician who is using an AI tool to support his or her decision-making regarding the presence or absence of a melanoma should be aware of the type of data set that was used to train the algorithm. If the data set used to train the algorithm did not include darker skinned individuals then the physician should not rely solely on the algorithm to decide whether a skin lesion may be cancerous. Here, the physician may still biopsy the lesion and send it for additional review even if the algorithm suggests that there is no cancer cell present. Understanding how AI applications affect healthcare practices and decision-making is critical in developing trust in the technology as trust influences subsequent use (He et al., 2019; Matheny et al., 2019; Yampolskiy, 2019; Richardson et al., 2021).

SOLUTIONS GOING FORWARD

There are a number of solutions for addressing AI safety issues from a regulatory, organizational, and health professional/patient perspective. The ultimate adoption of AI will depend on how a number of complex regulatory, economic, and political issues are addressed, as there are many stakeholders who would be affected by the successful application and use of AI technologies in healthcare. It will be critical to address issues, which range from the technical to the social, for moving AI into the mainstream. In addition to the safety of AI technology, policymakers, clinicians, and administrators will need to consider the cost-effectiveness of AI and its health impacts before the technology is fully integrated and adopted into healthcare. Given the high costs and current constraints on healthcare spending, AI will need to be shown to reduce health costs while at the same time increasing the positive health impacts associated with its use.

Regulatory Organizations

The first of these issues will be the development of a responsive regulatory environment that allows for in-depth review and understanding of how the technology was designed, developed, and tested. One of the leading regulatory organizations in healthcare internationally is the Food and Drug Administration (FDA) in the United States. The FDA is developing and improving the regulation of AI and ML technologies. The FDA's work includes developing policies and an action plan for approving AI- and ML-based software for use in healthcare. Policy and guidance documents are being worked on with an aim to focus on AI governance, use, and reporting (i.e., on safety events leading to patient harm or death). In this policymaking, the FDA plans to provide oversight of AI from its development (before it is brought to market) to after it has been implemented and any changes in the algorithm that takes place after it is implemented in healthcare settings (i.e., this is called postmarket surveillance of technologies). Such oversight would allow for real-time monitoring of the impacts of AI and a better understanding of the effects of changes to the technology on health over time (Food and Drug Administration, n.d.).

Government and Healthcare Organizations

Healthcare procurement organizations in government, regional health authorities, and health maintenance organizations (HMOs) have an important role in this process. Rigorous and informed procurement practices that are transparent will also need to be developed to include health informatics professionals, health professionals, and healthcare consumers. Physicians and nursing and legal societies are calling for increased scrutiny of AI and the contexts of the technology's use in hospital and clinic settings. There is a recognition that given the potential impacts of AI on the quality of the diagnosis of disease, predictions regarding the presence or absence of disease, and the quality of patient care, organizational procurements must be intensive and provide additional scrutiny of the technology for successful local implementations to take place (e.g., a local hospital) (Price & Gerke, 2019). Organizations will need to identify, where in the healthcare process the technology would best support clinicians and healthcare consumers. This may involve testing the technology using varying different strategies and approaches in the local (HMO) or regional health authority (Kushniruk et al., 2010). As part of implementing AI, training approaches (that include a critical review of the potential safety issues and boundaries of the technology's effectiveness) would need to be included in this work going forward.

Health Professional and Patient Perspective

Health professionals and patients will need to learn about how algorithms are designed, developed, and tested. In addition, health professionals need to understand, when such technologies fail and what types of questions to ask about the AI technology being deployed in their organizations especially when AI is applied to the diagnosis and treatment of patients. To date, several medical schools have announced the integration of AI into the medical curriculum to develop physician competencies in these areas (Wartman & Combs, 2019). As a society, potential and actual patients would need to develop data science and AI literacies to be able to understand how the technology is being used and to consent to its use (in order to understand its implications for healthcare). This involves learning about how to discern between a "good" algorithm and one that may not apply to their individual health situation much as there is a need to understand how health information on the internet may or may not apply to their current situation.

Economics of AI

Lastly, the economics of AI will add a layer to understanding AI safety and its health and economic impacts. Currently, the evidence surrounding the health and economic impacts of AI is limited. There is a need for the economic evaluation of these technologies, including the development of economic models to evaluate the effect of different types of AI on cost and health. To date, research suggests that evaluations of AI have focused on the impact of the technology on cost rather that health impacts or benefits of using AI. Researchers have suggested new models and methods of health economic evaluation will need to be developed to assess the true cost-effectiveness of AI in healthcare. To date, this has been difficult, due to the speed of the evolution of AI (Voets et al., 2022).

In contrast, the industry has focused on how AI can transform healthcare from a workforce and organizational perspective by improving diagnostics, care delivery, chronic disease management, patient self-care, and triage of patients (based on their health conditions). Industry and policymakers are actively examining and developing possible use cases for AI in healthcare. To date, the scale of AI solution adoption has been small, but it is expected that the pace of adoption will accelerate. Policymakers are considering what will be needed to accelerate the adoption of AI such as skills training for health professionals, who will use the technology, through to data science literacies for patients. As well, there has emerged a growing focus on the need to develop the health informatics/technology workforce that will design, develop, implement, and update AI in the future. This new type of health professional will need to consider the data quality, accuracy as well as safety (in addition to cost and health impacts) of AI (Spatharou et al., 2020).

FUTURE RESEARCH DIRECTIONS

Although considerable research in the area of AI in healthcare has emerged, more is needed. Researchers will need to continue to focus their efforts on data set quality, algorithm validity, ensuring data privacy and security, examining the effects of the context of use, and how the technology may fit into the current digital ecosystem in our society. Researchers will need to develop the use of cases for AI to better understand where and when the technology can be safely and effectively used to maximize its health impacts and also to ensure that it is cost-effective (relative to currently used approaches to the diagnosis, treatment, and management of health and disease). Benchmarks will need to be developed for varying aspects of AI. The health, safety, and economic impacts of AI will need to be assessed and benchmarks (and measures) to be set to ensure that the technologies meet or exceed the expectations of the public, health professionals, administrators, policymakers, and regulators. Over time, as society's norms and expectations change regarding AI, these activities will need to be revisited. There will be a need to determine the AI competencies that will be needed by society and by health professionals who use these technologies and to identify effective strategies for educating these groups. New roles will emerge in health informatics/information technology as AI is designed, developed, tested, implemented, and maintained over time. In the future, AI technologies and their safety will form a foundational component of research in the area.

CONCLUSIONS

AI has made significant contributions to society, especially in the application of these technology tools to patient health monitoring and healthcare processes. AI has improved the quality and safety of some societal processes. AI's design, development, and implementation continue to grow. However, in the upcoming years, several safety issues will need to be addressed surrounding the safe deployment of AI. Researchers, health informatics and technology professionals, administrators, and users of the technology will need to develop strategies and approaches to support continued research and safe application of AI in many settings. There is a need to develop the science behind implementing AI technologies so that health professionals and administrators know that the technology provides improvements in care over and above those technologies that are currently being used. Lastly, informatics/technology professionals, health professionals, and patients will need to become trained and be part of the process of providing additional scrutiny of AI applications to ensure both their effectiveness and safety.

ACKNOWLEDGMENTS

This chapter was, in part, supported by a research grant from the Michael Smith Foundation for Health Research, British Columbia, Canada.

REFERENCES

Adadi, A., & Berrada, M. (2020). Explainable AI for healthcare: from black box to interpretable models. In *Embedded systems and artificial intelligence* (pp. 327–337). Springer: Singapore.

Borycki, E. M., & Kushniruk, A. W. (2008). Where do technology-induced errors come from? Towards a model for conceptualizing and diagnosing errors caused by technology In Kushniruk, A. W., & Borycki, E. M. (Eds.), *Human, social and organizational aspects of health information systems* (pp. 148–166). IGI Global: Hershey, Pennsylvania.

Borycki, E. M., & Kushniruk, A. W. (2021). The safety of AI in healthcare: Emerging issues and considerations for healthcare. In Househ, M., Borycki, E., & Kushniruk, A. (Eds.), *Multiple perspectives on artificial intelligence in healthcare*. Springer Verlag: New York.

Borycki, E., Kushniruk, A., Nohr, C., Takeda, H., Kuwata, S., Carvalho, C., … Kannry, J. (2013). Usability methods for ensuring health information technology safety: Evidence-based approaches. Contribution of the IMIA working group health informatics for patient safety. *Yearbook of Medical Informatics, 8*, 20–27.

Brinker, T. J., Hekler, A., Hauschild, A., Berking, C., Schilling, B., Enk, A. H., … Utikal, J. S. (2019). Comparing artificial intelligence algorithms to 157 German dermatologists: The melanoma classification benchmark. *European Journal of Cancer, 111*, 30–37. 10.1016/j.ejca.2018.12.016

Challen, R., Denny, J., Pitt, M., Gompels, L., Edwards, T., & Tsaneva-Atanasova, K. (2019). Artificial intelligence, bias and clinical safety. *BMJ Quality & Safety, 28*, 231–237.

Choudhury, A., & Asan, O. (2020). Role of artificial intelligence in patient safety outcomes: Systematic literature review. *JMIR Medical Informatics, 8*(7), e18599.

Chaudhury, S., Paul, D., Mukherjee, R., & Haldar, S. (2017, August). Internet of thing based healthcare monitoring system. In 2017 8th annual industrial automation and electro-mechanical engineering conference (IEMECON) (pp. 346–349). IEEE.

Davy, A., & Borycki, E. M. (2021). Copy and paste in the electronic medical record: A scoping review. *Knowledge Management & E-Learning: An International Journal, 13*(4), 522–535. 10.34105/j.kmel.2021.13.028

El Morr, C. (2018). *Introduction to health informatics: A Canadian perspective*. Canadian Scholars: Toronto.

Feige, I. (2019). Artificial intelligence (AI) safety can be broadly defined as the endeavour to ensure that AI is deployed in ways that do not harm humanity. https://faculty.ai/blog/what-is-ai-safety/#:~:text=Artificial%20Intelligence%20(AI)%20Safety%20can,do%20not%20harm%20humanity.

Food and Drug Administration (n.d.). Artificial intelligence and machine learning in software as a medical device. https://www.fda.gov/medical-devices/software-medical-device-samd/artificial-intelligence-and-machine-learning-software-medical-device

Gheorghiu, B., & Hagens, S. (2016). Measuring interoperable EHR adoption and maturity: A Canadian example. *BMC Medical Informatics and Decision Making, 16*(8). 10.1186/s12911-016-0247-x

He, J., Baxter, S. L., Xu, J., Xu, J., Zhou, X., & Zhang, K. (2019). The practical implementation of artificial intelligence technologies in medicine. *Nature Medicine, 25*, 30–36. 10.1038/s41591-018-0307-0

Househ, M., Borycki, E., & Kushniruk, A. (2021). *Multiple perspective on artificial intelligence.* Springer: New York.

Jiang, F., Jiang, Y., Zhi, Y., Li, H., Ma, S., Wang, Yl., … Wang, Y. (2017). Artificial intelligence in healthcare: Past, present and future. *Stroke and Vasular Neurology, 2.* 10.1136/svn-2017-000101

Kim, H. E., Kim, H. H., Han, B. K., Kim, K. H., Han, K., Nam, H., … Kim E. K. (2020). Changes in cancer detection and false-positive recall in mammography using artificial intelligence: A retrospective, multireader study. *The Lancet Digital Health, 2*(3), e138–e148.

Kushniruk, A., Beuscart-Zéphir, M. C., Grzes, A., Borycki, E., Watbled, L., & Kannry, J. (2010). Increasing the safety of healthcare information systems through improved procurement: Toward a framework for selection of safe healthcare systems. *Healthcare Quarterly, 13*(Sp), 53–58. 10.12927/hcq.2010.21967

Lashbrook, A. (2018). AI-driven dermatology could leave dark-skinned patients behind. *The Atlantic.* https://www.theatlantic.com/health/archive/2018/08/machine-learning-dermatology-skin-color/567619/

Li, Y., Shyr, C., Borycki, E. M., & Kushniruk, A. W. (2021). Automated thematic analysis of health information technology (HIT) related incident reports. *Knowledge Management & E-Learning, 13*(4), 408–420. 10.34105/j.kmel.2021.13.022

Madden, J. M., Lakoma, M. D., Rusinak, D., Lu, C. Y., & Soumerai, S. B. (2016). Missing clinical and behavioral health data in a large electronic health record (EHR) system. *Journal of the American Medical Informatics Association, 23*, 1143–1149. 10.1093/jamia/ocw021

Martínez-Pérez, B., De La Torre-Díez, I., & López-Coronado, M. (2013). Mobile health applications for the most prevalent conditions by the World Health Organization: Review and analysis. *Journal of Medical Internet Research, 15*(6), e2600.

Matheny, M. E., Whicher, D., & Israni, S. T. (2019). Artificial intelligence in health care: A report from the national academy of medicine. *JAMA, 323*(6), 509–510.

Monkman, H., Borycki, E. M., Kushniruk, A. W., & Kuo, M. H. (2013). Exploring the contextual and human factors of electronic medication reconciliation research: a scoping review. *Studies in Health Technology and Informatics, 194*, 166–172.

OECD (2021). OECD Working paper number 127. https://www.oecd.org/officialdocuments/publicdisplaydocumentpdf/?cote=DELSA/HEA/WD/HWP(2021)4&docLanguage=En

Palojoki, S., Mäkelä, M., Lehtonen, L., & Saranto, K. (2017). An analysis of electronic health record-related patient safety incidents. *Health Informatics Journal, 23*(2), 134–145. 10.1177/1460458216631072. Epub March 7, 2016.

Price, W. N., & Gerke, S. (2019). Potential liability for physicians using artificial intelligence. *JAMA, 322*(18), 1765–1766.

Raja, J. M., Elsakr, C., Roman, S., Cave, B., Pour-Ghaz, I., Nanda, A., … Khouzam, R. N. (2019). Apple watch, wearables, and heart rhythm: Where do we stand? *Annals of Translational Medicine, 7*(17), 417. 10.21037/atm.2019.06.79

Reddy, S., Allan, S., Coghlan, S., & Cooper, P. (2020). A governance model for the application of AI in health care. *Journal of the American Medical Informatics Association: JAMIA, 27*(3), 491–497. 10.1093/jamia/ocz192

Richardson, J. P., Smith, C., Curtis, S., Watson, S., Zhu, X., Barry, B., … Sharp, R. R. (2021). Patient apprehensions about the use of artificial intelligence in healthcare. *NPJ Digital Medicine, 4*(1), 1–6.

Robert, N. (2019). How artificial intelligence is changing nursing. *Nursing Management, 50*(9), 30.

Spatharou, A., Hieronimus, S., & Jenkins, J. (2020). Transforming healthcare with AI: The impact on the workforce and organizations. McKinsey & Company, 10.

Sujan, M., Pool, R., & Salmon, P. (2022). Eight human factors and ergonomics principles for healthcare artificial intelligence *BMJ Health & Care Informatics, 29*, e100516. 10.1136/bmjhci-2021-100516

Tao, C., Gao, J., & Wang, T. (2019). Testing and quality validation for AI software: Perspectives, issues, and practices. *IEEE Access, 7,* 120164–120175. 10.1109/ACCESS.2019.2937107

The Electronic Medication Reconciliation Group (2017). *Paper to electronic medrec implementation toolkit,* 2nd edition. ISMP Canada and Canadian Patient Safety Institute.

Voets, M. M., Veltman, J., Slump, C. H., Siesling, S., & Koffijberg, H. (2022). Systematic review of health economic evaluations focused on artificial intelligence in healthcare: The tortoise and the cheetah. *Value Health, 25*(3), 340–349.

Wartman, S. A., & Combs, C. D. (2019). Reimagining medical education in the age of AI. *AMA Journal of Ethics, 21*(2), 146–152.

Yampolskiy, R. V. (2019). *Artificial intelligence safety and security.* Taylor and Francis Group: CRC Press.

Yasnoff, W. A., O'Carroll, P. W., Koo, D., Linkins, R. W., & Kilbourne, E. M. (2000). Public health informatics: Improving and transforming public health in the information age. *Journal of Public Health Management and Practice, 6*(6), 67–75.

CHAPTER 3

The Politics of Artificial Intelligence in Healthcare: Diagnosis and Treatment

Anis Germani

Internal Medicine, MPH, Université Saint Joseph, Beirut, Lebanon

CONTENTS

DOI: 10.1201/9781003261247-4

INTRODUCTION

No other mammal in the animal kingdom projects itself into the future as much as humans do. We recall the past and act in the present only to plan, organize, or predict the future. The future is the only temporality in which humans, as individuals and species, exist. Reflecting on that future does not go without reflecting on the future of technology. After all, the ability to develop tools was the main evolutionary advantage of our ancestors. Tools compensated for our weak biology. Our skin is thinner than fur hides, our nails not as sharp as claws, our teeth not as piercing as tusks, and our bodies not as nimble or as sizeable as other animals. Humans sharpened silex to skin hides, tamed fire to soften food, built shelters to survive harsh environments and evade predators, and created animal traps and agricultural tools … not just to survive, but to thrive. Many thousands of years later, we find ourselves at a new technological juncture, that of artificial intelligence (AI). This tool is just as vital for our survival as all the ones that came before it. However, unlike pre-20th-century tools, its potential for salvation and destruction is of equal measure.

The average layperson's first perception of AI may be quite polarized. And rightly so, when movies, books, video games, articles, conferences, and legislations seem to adopt a dichotomous perception of AI as a tool for humanity's salvation or its demise. This dichotomous prism via which the public sphere perceives AI is not universal, however, it is understandable when the very name of the tool in question indicates that for the first time in the history of humankind, our evolutionary advantage (intelligence) can be replicated. The fact that this advantage is unconstrained by the laws of nature (artificial), only supplements the hopes and fears of the beholder. Among the numerous applications of AI, nowhere other than in healthcare do its implications reach the extreme heights of polarization. After all, nothing is as intricately related to the self as the health of the body inhabited by that self. And where else do all individuals find themselves universally in a position of vulnerability, as they do when confronting their own mortality by seeking care. The artificial cannot encompass the full complexities of the human experience, while intelligence (especially one that is alien) cannot be trusted with vulnerability. The fearsome debate around AI in healthcare was expected, from the tool's nomenclature, and is also justified, by our reasoning's future temporality. However, it is problematic on two fronts. Firstly, it undermines, by exaggerating, the nature of this tool. After all, AI technology can be boiled down to be described as a statistical model. And secondly, by taking the creators of these models (us humans) out of the equation. Individuals and societies become mere spectators to a technology that is created, honed, and perfected of its own accord. Much to the detriment, and maybe relief, of engineers at Amazon, Google, IBM, and Microsoft.

DEFINING "INTELLIGENCE"

Although AI is a very real and concrete branch of computer science, defining it is closer to pinning down an abstraction. Asking an engineer, a neurologist, and an avid fan of science-fiction to define exactly what "is" an AI would yield different opinions that converge on certain points as much as they diverge on others. The first would go about explaining all the intricate mechanisms that go into coding and training an AI, the second would explain the complexities of the human brain and how unlikely it is for a machine to surpass it, and the third would describe AI as a benevolent or maleficent god-like entity. However, all three would agree that present-day AI technology has a long way to go before reaching its full potential. This divergence comes as no surprise when the very words used by experts to decorticate and define AI may seem either misleading or overly ambitious, and certainly alienating, to the average layperson. Machine learning (unsupervised, supervised, semi-supervised), Black Box, Nature Language Processing, Deep Learning, Neural Network … these words evoke different understandings, and even feelings, to different beholders. The average reader would freak out at the very sight of the words "unsupervised machine learning operating as a black box", whereas an engineer would probably chuckle at this last sentence, knowing it simply means that data is being clustered when the coder did not input enough instructions to define a clear methodology for the AI to follow (James et al., 2013). From a medical perspective, this would be an algorithm that clusters patients into groups based on similarities in their medical records, without providing any prediction on their risks of developing certain diseases. But the lack of widespread technical knowledge and the use of an alienating vocabulary are not the only reasons behind the abstraction of AI. The abstract concept of "intelligence", is another such reason. One of the earliest and most widely adopted definitions of machine intelligence was derived from Alan Turing's test which can be briefly summarized as "if a machine talks like a human, it is intelligent" (Turing, 1950). The acceptability of this definition was further encouraged by the technology industry massively investing in human speech synthesizing programs such as Google's Assistant, Amazon's Alexa, and Apple's Siri (Pataranutaporn et al., 2021). Another textbook definition of AI is a machine capable of mimicking human-like behavior. Far from attempting to delve into the philosophical debate of defining human intelligence, one thing is clear, we have yet to understand the biological mechanisms behind intelligence to even begin replicating it in machines. So what really is AI? It is a broad category of statistical algorithms used for "modeling and understanding complex datasets" (James et al., 2013). In simpler terms, AI processes large amounts of data by sorting it, in order to find similarities, differences, correlations, or better visualize the data, to accomplish predefined goals, set by the programmer, who feeds the AI all the necessary data, criteria, and conditions to accomplish its goal. An AI is therefore not completely autonomous, it requires human intervention to build it, give it purpose, train it to correctly process data, and more importantly equip it with the tools to perceive the data in a way that is useful to us humans. The senior principal researcher at Microsoft Research, Kate Crawford, goes as far as to argue that "AI is neither artificial nor intelligent. Rather, AI is both embodied and material, made from natural resources, fuel, human labor, infrastructures, logistics, histories, and classifications. AI systems are not autonomous, rational, or able to discern anything without extensive, computationally intensive training with large datasets or predefined rules and rewards. In fact, AI as we know it depends entirely on a much wider set of political and social structures" (Crawford, 2021). This definition is critical to steer away from abstracting the very real and technical nature of AI, as well as to understand its impact and challenges, and to elaborate strategies to overcome them.

IS THERE AN AI IN THE HOUSE?

Evidence-based medicine relies on two pillars: knowledge and experience. Over time, medical studies have grown in complexity and scope in the hopes of capturing the most objective observations that might be universally applicable. Ironically enough, the culmination of medical knowledge has resulted in the elaboration of processes for establishing diagnoses and dispensing treatments in the form of algorithms. Currently, these algorithms are regularly executed by medical professionals in their day-to-day practice. The very foundations (accumulation of theoretical and clinical data) and organization (diagnosis and treatment algorithms) of healthcare are, in a way, perfectly adapted for automation. Traditional programs are technically unable to take into account the many interlinking factors involved in the decision-making process of dispensing care: past medical and surgical history, familial history, epidemiological statistics, current chief complaint, and associated symptoms, known food and drug allergies, current medications, past and current electrophysiological test results, up-to-date evidence-based recommendations. AI, however, is fully capable of simultaneously processing data for all these variables in order to aid in the best possible course of action (Gennatas & Chen, 2021). The two most useful types of AI in healthcare are support vector machines (SVM) and artificial neural networks (ANN), which respectively account for 42% and 31% of medical studies involving the use of AI between 2013 and 2016 (Jiang et al., 2017). SVM aid in classifying patients based on their outcomes. For example, an SVM can look over COVID-19 patients' medical records to stratify them into low- and high-risk groups, or it might look over radiological imaging and classify patients as sick or healthy. An SVM trained to diagnose COVID-19 using images of chest X-rays scored an accuracy of 97.48% (Hassanien et al., 2020). On the other hand, ANN are complex webs of mathematical functions that treat input information to come up with predictive outcomes. For example, they may aid in establishing likely diagnoses based on an input list of symptoms, or predict the most effective treatment plan for certain conditions. ANN were able to predict the presence of prostate cancer in men more accurately than the standard PSA test (Djavan et al., 2016). The rising number of published medical research involving the use of ANN has increased nine folds between 2013 and 2016, while nearly doubling between 2015 and 2016 alone, this speaks to their promising potential applications in healthcare (Jiang et al., 2017). To paraphrase a Syrian saying, "knowledge that is not useful is like ignorance that is not harmful". In that vein, how will AI be useful to patients?

Electronic Health Records

AI would not have existed were it not for "big data". Despite being first theorized in the fifties of the past century at the Dartmouth Summer Research Project on Artificial Intelligence, AI would have never taken form were it not for the large amounts of data amassed since the advent of the internet (Anyoha, 2017). Luckily for the health sector, electronic health records (EHRs) have already been adopted across the world – albeit in varying amounts between high- and low-income countries. EHRs contain all medically relevant data pertaining to a patient: vital signs, medical history, laboratory and radiological reports, immunization, dates of admission to healthcare facilities, names of physicians, and even their DNA sequencing data when applicable (Centers for Medicare & Medicaid Services, 2021). The entire Chinese health sector relies on EHRs, in the United States (US) 96% of hospitals and 86% of office-based physicians used EHRs in 2017, and in Italy, 85% of health services use EHRs (Tikkanen et al., 2020). While accurate statistics are lacking in lower income countries, studies have shown that the deployment and use of EHRs remain limited and below the World Health Organization's (WHO) Sustainable Development Goals (Kumar & Mostafa, 2020). As patients' access to medical services increases, their life expectancy increases, and chronic diseases (that have long histories and require detailed follow-up and tailored interventions) become the main cause of death, EHRs become larger and more complex for any single practitioner to fully grasp and extract relevant information. The star readers of medical records in the world of AI are Natural Language Processing algorithms (NLP) that transform physical records into EHRs, then unsupervised learning algorithms can reduce the volume of those (now readable) records to be used at will in supervised algorithms such as the aforementioned SVR and ANN. The deployment of an NLP at the Humanitas Research Hospital allowed the Emergency Department staff to reduce the time required to accurately identify patients suffering from syncope by 96% when compared to manually reading through their records (Dipaola et al., 2019). Another NLP combined with an ANN was able to accurately identify 90% of children suffering from child abuse based only on their medical records prior to them being taken in by child protection services (Annapragada et al., 2021).

AI may even participate in the writing of medical records. Physicians were found to spend 50% of their time manually entering data into EHRs (Sinsky et al., 2016). Companies are already working on AI programs that, with time and training, can write into a patient's EHR without requiring any human intervention (Coiera et al., 2018). On the nursing front, a proprietary algorithm embedded into EHRs was developed to calculate the Rothman Index, which can predict the deterioration of a hospitalized patient within 24 hours, using 26 variables (vital signs, clinical assessment, electrophysiological results). Compared to traditional monitoring mechanisms, this algorithm captured 54% more deteriorating patients and reduced false alarms by 53% (Finlay et al., 2013).

AI does not only streamline the delivery of care with high accuracy but also the conduction of research, by accessing large data samples without having to resort to the long and tedious process of data collection. Cohort studies are already being conducted using AI and EHRs (Cimino, 2017). More importantly, AI has bolstered efforts to unravel complex genetic mysteries encoded in the 3 billion base pairs that constitute the human genome. Previously costly and time-consuming studies aiming to identify genetic risk factors for diseases can now be conducted much more efficiently using patients' genetic data and phenotypes already documented on their EHRs (Li et al., 2020). On a global scale, fully automated AI has been developed to track data streams, news feeds, and social media content such as Twitter posts in order to identify early warning signs of threats to public health, monitor epidemics, and predict disease levels. Among these systems are MedISys (2004), HealthMap (2006), and SENTINEL (2019) (Zeng et al., 2021). The use of AI in healthcare has already shown promise in improving the delivery and quality of care, predicting diseases and conditions in advance, monitoring and predicting outbreaks of diseases, and streamlining research that is ever-growing in scope and complexity.

EVIL MEANS OR EVIL ENDS?

The process, which capacitates AI to automate certain aspects of healthcare, is not itself automated and requires constant human intervention.

Is AI a Substitute for Knowledge?

First, scientific knowledge must be acquired. For AI to perceive the world in a way that is useful to its users, it must be taught the rules under which this world operates. A classic example is that of an AI tasked with identifying causes and risk factors for death by drowning. A naive AI (being a statistical tool) would find that when temperatures rise, so do drownings, i.e., that hot weather causes drowning. How would it be expected to know that humans tend to swim more in hot weather, thereby increasing deaths by drowning? Human behavior, which an average person might label as "commonsense", is a confounding factor for AI. Commonsensical assumptions do not exist for AI unless a programmer specifically accounts for them. Until reality in all its complexity is fully modelized, complete reliance on AI cannot be achieved, particularly in healthcare, where human behavior and environmental factors are at the center of preoccupation. An AI tasked with establishing diagnoses would assume that a middle-aged shopkeeper in a rural area presenting with lower back pain is suffering from a rheumatoid disease, before probably considering a lumbar disk hernia; as shopkeepers in rural areas are more likely to aid their customers with carrying their shopping than in urban areas.

Programming commonsense is not the only limit of AI capabilities, but also medical knowledge itself. AI finds correlations, not causations. It does not explain the pathophysiology, describe cellular pathways, or establish treatment modalities. Quite the opposite, the aforementioned information is inputted within AI to achieve useful results. The misconception that AI is an autonomous intelligent machine that can singlehandedly advance science and medicine is actually driving investment away from clinical research towards AI research and development. According to a survey of healthcare and life sciences executives conducted by KPMG, one of the four largest accounting firms in the world, investments in clinical trials finished last in the top five areas of investments for the next two years, while telemedicine and automation landed in first and second place (Krishna et al., 2021). This does not bode well, neither for the improvement of medicine nor AI as these models will be deprived of better knowledge to process data. The hype around AI has even led to squandering funds over wishful thinking. In 2015, it was found that Theranos – a nine billion dollar startup claiming to use AI technology to perform a full range of blood tests from a small finger-prick sample – was defrauding its investors. People were eager to believe that AI created a solution for an unsolved scientific problem, when the company was, in fact, diluting blood samples and delivering false results, sometimes indicative of HIV and cancer to patients (Carreyrou, 2015). It is important to remember that AI has not automated the attainment of knowledge, and is only as useful and accurate as our present-day scientific knowledge allows it to be.

AI and Data Monopolies, Foes, or Natural Allies?

Second, a lot of data has to be gathered. AI and big data are two sides of the same coin. However, many problems arise in the constitution of datasets, matters of privacy, consent, bias, and access. Our highly digitized world has created massive amounts of data, from credit card information to social media activity, location tracking, and medical records … The very nature and sheer volume of this information entail that only a few corporations and institutions have the capabilities and resources to gather and store such data, notably the so-called GAFA (Google, Amazon, Facebook, Apple) and the US National Security Agency (NSA). This creates *de facto* monopolies of data. Data-opolies (Stucke, 2018) are problematic, not just because they keep free marketeers awake at night, but specifically because they pose monumental risks to the data itself. This becomes all the more dangerous when that data is health related.

Privacy and Agency

The first and most obvious risk is that of privacy. Concentrating data in the hands of a few facilitates hacking or leaking large datasets from one single firm, as opposed to smaller ones from multiple firms. In parallel, a monopolized market reduces the need for data firms to improve their privacy protection, as market competition is absent (Stucke, 2018). The Office for Civil Rights at the US Department of Health and Human Rights reported 599 health data breaches in 2020, affecting 26 million individuals. In 2021, the number of breaches decreased to 578 but the people affected were over 40 million, of which 3.5 million were the victim of one single breach at the Florida Healthy Kids Corporation; this testifies to the dangers of data-opolies (Office for Civil Rights, 2021). Another privacy-related issue is a patient's ability (or lack thereof) to opt out altogether from having their health data collected since AI learns by processing the largest and most diverse datasets. Will access to the latest AI-powered medical treatments be conditioned on the relinquishing of ownership over one's medical records?

A Mosaic of Segregation

The second point of concern is based on the "mosaic theory", suggesting that seemingly worthless disparate information, once aggregated and combined, can take on significant importance (Ma, 2021). Combining health-related data with personal information, credit card purchases, location data, and social media activity can have unimaginable consequences. In 2016, an AI that filters job applications, developed by Kronos, consistently rejected applicants suffering from mental diseases by diagnosing them in a questionnaire (O'Neil, 2016). Health data aggregation could lead to the systematic banishment of members of the workforce from jobs by simply looking over their medical records. Anyone suffering from HIV, cancer, heart disease, or is currently pregnant would simply and secretly, be rejected without their knowledge. This can be extrapolated into a dystopian scenario of "health segregation", where people with certain health issues would live, work, and have access to services depending on their health status.

Coded Bias

Thirdly, data-opolies are a breeding ground for biases and exclusion. A well-understood fact among researchers is that data is only as good as the process in which it was collected. Secondary data analysis is fraught with inconveniences, from heterogeneous labeling and grouping of data to the poor quality of the collection. Data-opolies are obsessed with homogenizing data. This can either be achieved by imposing a uniform mechanism of data collection, using electronic health record software that is unaffordable to most low-income countries and institutions (Kumar & Mostafa, 2020); or by developing costly AI that would homogenize data. In both cases, data in low-income situations are systematically disqualified from the collection, and the biases prevalent in the institution or algorithm collecting and homogenizing data are systematically applied. This only reinforces the prevalent biases resulting from exclusion, in our current medical knowledge, as the proportion of white participants in clinical trials from 1997 to 2014 reaches 86%, and systematically excludes minorities (Knepper & McLeod, 2018). Bias does not only arise from skewed collection mechanisms, but also from the very act of labeling data used to train any AI. Kate Crawford explains that "to create a training set is to take an almost infinitely complex and varied world and fix it into taxonomies composed of discrete classifications of individual data points, a process that requires inherently political, cultural, and social choices"(Crawford, 2021). The underlying political challenges of data collection – mainly achieving North/South economic equity – and the political nature of data labeling and aggregation, should steer us away from seeking a simple one-size-fits-all recipe to create fair and representative datasets. Having universally accessible, scientifically diligent, and transparent data collection and aggregation mechanisms would however have to be at the heart of any technical outline of these processes.

Doctor or Engineer?

It is no secret that as it stands today, AI is still far from being intelligent, according to any and all definitions of intelligence. The arduous task of finessing these programs rests on the shoulders of an army of workers and end-users (in this case, healthcare workers). If there is one thing Jeff Bezos excels at, it is finding solutions to complex problems by exploiting human labor. As Amazon's AI programs failed to execute certain tasks, Bezos devised "Mechanical Turk", a scheme employing approximately 250,000 human workers (Robinson et al., 2019), earning on average two dollars an hour (Hara et al., 2018), to execute simple tasks that are too complex for an AI. He not-so-ironically called it "artificial artificial intelligence" (Pontin, 2007). Astra Taylor more accurately describes it as "fauxtomation", or the act of completely obscuring labor behind an imagined halo of automation (Taylor, 2018). Fauxtomation relies on the alienation of labor by fragmenting and dispersing it through space and time, and disconnecting it from the value it's producing.

On the other end of the AI assembly line, lies the users. Tech giants' workers cannot infuse AI with the real-life experience required to optimize its algorithms. This is where healthcare workers don the invisible hat of tech workers. Indeed, healthcare workers are expected to spend more time interacting with machines, not just as users, but as trainers. It is already estimated that 70% of a healthcare practitioner's time is spent on administrative work (EIT Health; McKinsey & Company, 2020). The share of time spent away from a patient will have to decrease even further during the transition to automated healthcare, as practitioners would have to train AI on top of completing administrative tasks. Adapting AI to the healthcare setting and tailoring it to practitioner needs is an essential part of automating delicate and time-consuming healthcare tasks. Once achieved, automation would radically change the very nature and day-to-day practice of healthcare providers, who would devote most, if not all, their time to interacting with patients on a humanistic level and prioritizing their experience of disease over clerical work and standard care. However, the long and arduous task of training must neither be sidelined as a part of "user experience" and therefore, healthcare workers must be remunerated for the additional service they are rendering; nor should it compromise the quality of patient care by reinforcing the temporal wedge between practitioners and their patients.

I HAVE READ AND AGREE TO THE TERMS AND CONDITIONS

Our current experience with giving consent for a machine to execute certain tasks or to use information is restricted to the End User License Agreement or Terms of Service agreement box we hastily check to create an online account or install a software. A study found that among its 80,000 participants less than 8% spent enough time reading the license agreement before giving their consent (Böhme & Köpsell, 2010). These results might seem surprising only in how optimistic they are, as it is hard to imagine anyone sifting through pages and pages of highly specialized legal and technical jargon when in the end there is no real choice being offered. Refusing to consent simply bars the user from accessing the technology. Checking that box, however, is equivalent to signing a legally binding document.

This frank abuse of the very notion of consent in the technology sector is the root of many fears people hold when imagining AI-driven healthcare. Informed consent in healthcare is as far as can be from a Terms of Service agreement, despite both holding the same legal standing. Skipping the conversation with a healthcare provider explaining the significance of a diagnosis, the risks and benefits of a treatment option, and alternative options, is not possible. Drowning a patient with medical publications and complicated jargon instead of providing a clear and well-adapted explanation voids any consent form that might be signed later on. Being denied all care for refusing one treatment option is also plainly unethical.

This divergence between the notions of consent in technology and healthcare raises many questions as these two sectors intricately merge with AI. There is no consensus around the answers to these questions, as ethical standards vary between countries, communities, and individuals, and are set over time and with experience. These ethical challenges abound, however, for the sake of clarity, a few will be listed below. First, should a patient be made aware that AI is being used at the hospital, in case they would want to refuse the AI access to their medical file? Can the patient benefit from all that the AI has to offer while still opting out of sharing their personal information? Second, if that patient divulges their medical information, should they be made aware that the tech company that developed the AI is aggregating their personal information in a dataset that may or may not be sold or used by another AI that might impact their credit score or chance of employment? Third, when informing a patient of their diagnosis, is the treating physician expected to not only understand but also explain the intricacies of the many AI algorithms involved in reading imaging and blood test results, analyzing pathology samples and medical records, that were involved in reaching that diagnosis and ela-borating treatment plans? If not, is consent still truly informed? If a patient was part of a minority group, would they be made aware of the biases under which the AI operates? Would the AI offer a treatment plan tailored to the patient's beliefs and expectations, such as respecting their request not to be resuscitated, or transfused with blood, despite both having detrimental outcomes? If the AI misdiagnosed a patient and subjected them to dangerous procedures and emotional strain, who would be held responsible for the malpractice, the physician acting as a human supervisor, the AI's developing company, or the AI itself? Would the patient be allowed access to the AI's algorithms on which their life depends, or do they fall under company secrets? These questions are but a sample of the many unanswered ethical dilemmas emanating from the employment of AI in healthcare. Any attempt to answer them today in absolute and certain terms is futile. However, keeping them at the forefront of preoccupations while coding AI and writing AI-related legislation will be imperative to ensure their appropriate employment in the future.

HEALTHCARE POLITICS OF AI

While reflecting on the politics of AI, MIT professor Joseph Weizenbaum – recognized as a father of modern AI – describes the machine as "a fundamentally conservative force. It has made possible the saving of institutions pretty much as they were, which otherwise might have had to be changed" (Ben-Aaron, 1985). This depiction of AI might not have been concerning to the average individual who traditionally favors stability prior to 2019 (with the exception of us few self-declared revolutionaries). However, the COVID-19 pandemic has shown that the most adaptable healthcare systems were the most efficient at tackling the emergency. Early travel bans, countrywide lockdowns, social welfare, redistribution of human and material resources, redirection of research and production … All of these decisions were as radical as they were unprecedented. How would a hypothetically-in-charge AI have fared, during the first days of the pandemic, when all the data it had at its disposal were experiences of previous pandemics and a long track record of favoring profit over health? Probably no better than the average conservative politician (think a Donald Trump or Jair Bolsonaro-like AI saying COVID-19 is no worse than the flu (Tollefson, 2020)). That is not to say that this hypothetical AI would not have changed course and defied all basic mathematical logic shortly after enough data had been gathered on the rates of infection, mortality, and even detrimental economic repercussions. We would certainly not be finding ourselves in the absurd position we find ourselves today where, at the time of writing, only 8% of people living in poor countries have received one dose of the vaccine, while the highly vaccinated Global North hoards millions of doses instead of distributing them to end the pandemic (Guarascio, 2022).

Contrary to Wizenbaum's stipulation, however, AI as a tool for automation, will inevitably and radically change the political economy of our societies; whether for the better or the worse, that remains to be seen. It is difficult to estimate when exactly that change will happen and what sector will be hit first. The steam engine ushered in the industrial revolution of the 18th century. It was dubbed a revolution because of its abrupt onset, as well as its widespread repercussions across all aspects of society. To claim that it was a well-expected and preunderstood event would turn the very name of this epoch into a misnomer. It is not naive to expect that the advent of AI (or any other technological advancement for that matter) will improve the quality of life of all humans, that better care will be systematically delivered, that labor in the health sector will be relieved of the constraints of meager and time-consuming tasks. The pertinent question is *how much* will each socioeconomic class benefit?

Class Longevity

It is fair to expect that AI-driven healthcare will bring about a general improvement in longevity and mortality rates, however, should access to this technology be restricted to a wealthy minority, we are sure to expect a further widening of the life-expectancy gap between rich and poor. In 2019, people born in high-income countries already lived 18.1 years more than those in low-income countries (World Health Organization, 2019). Certain causes of death (particularly non-communicable diseases) might be eliminated or reduced for those who can afford to employ AI to monitor, diagnose, and treat them; whereas those who cannot, would simply die just as they do today. From this perspective, AI has the potential to reinforce class segregation by supplementing it with biological segregation. The rich would lead healthier longer lives, while the health of the poor would only slightly improve. But it has also the potential to flatten out class-related health disparities. Access to medical consultations for early diagnoses and better health choices would be universally available on any gadget. Automation would allow laborers more leisure time, meaning less exposure to physical and psychological stressors. Pricey "best doctors" or "best hospitals" would cease to exist, as the same AI-driven healthcare, using the same data, would be uniformly present across health systems.

Capitalism Without Labor

Another expected change will be at the macrolevel of the political economy, intricately related to health as to any other sector. According to Marxist theory, profit under capitalism is generated by expropriating labor of the value it creates (Marx, 1996). At the zenith of automation, AI will trigger a conundrum: how can profit be generated when there is no labor to create value? In other words, AI will bring about the end of "classic" capitalism, one way or the other. One does not have to subscribe to Marxist ideology to see it. Google's CEO recognized that AI technology will have an impact on humanity that is "more profound than electricity or fire" (Petroff, 2018). In fact, this paradox of capitalism is being addressed as of today, even when we are still probably decades away from AI-driven automation. Some, particularly tech billionaires, have already started resolving this conundrum to their advantage: profit will be made via the ownership (and therefore patenting) of AI technology.

The California Patent Rush

Between 2008 and 2018 the number of AI patents registered yearly rose from 22,913 to 78,085. A report examining the ownership of these patents found that IBM, Microsoft, Google, and Siemens held the top five biggest portfolios; with Microsoft owning the most useful or "technically relevant" patents. In terms of yearly patent applications, it is worth noting that the US comes in first place with 279,145 applications, whereas China, in second place, recorded four times less than that amount with 66,508 applications (IPlytics, 2019). A study on healthcare-related AI patents found the US to be first in both technology development and as a target of non-resident registration of patents (Xin et al., 2021). The entire medical technology industry is booming, a boom accelerated by the COVID-19 pandemic. Global revenues from the medical technology industry rose 37% between 2011 and 2020, reaching 384 billion US dollars, and are expected to reach 600 billion in 2024 (Stewart, 2020).

Patenting in healthcare is problematic on many levels. It makes medical treatments inaccessible to those who cannot afford them, such as the lifesaving diagnostic tests and treatments for HIV, drug-resistant Tuberculosis, Hepatitis C (Frontline AIDS; International Treatment Preparedness Coalition, 2019), and COVID vaccines (Rocca & Maurer, 2021). In other words, patents are a public health hazard. On an ethical level, the commodification of healthcare through patents reduces the quality of care provided to patients, threatens the public good, and implies that some human lives are more valuable than others (Pellegrino, 1999). On a legal level, it is a violation of the Universal Declaration of Human Rights which states *"all human beings are born free and equal in dignity and rights"*, and guarantees the right to adequate health (as opposed to a luxury to be afforded). The most troubling (and likely) prospect, is the corruption of AI-driven healthcare with patenting. As it stands today, medical drugs, tests, and equipment can be patented, whereas "products of nature" such as genes cannot as per the 2013 US Supreme Court ruling (Kesselheim et al., 2013). Scientific knowledge is, to some extent, shared regarding new diagnostic procedures, treatment modalities, disease pathophysiology, etc. But, as AI technology flourishes, what is to be the fate of these new diagnoses and treatments? Will the patent protection of AI extend to the new diagnostic modalities and treatments, discoveries of new scientific and medical knowledge, and patient medical histories and symptoms? This would mean the compartmentalization and absorption of what we call today the "scientific community" into tech companies. Scientific and medical knowledge would fall under "trade secrets", thereby even circumventing the "products of nature" categorization. Healthcare would be fully commodified, when the way a healthcare provider takes the medical history of a patient, reads their medical file, examines them, and analyses their lab results, when the thought process behind establishing a diagnosis, and when the recommendation of treatment modalities, are all patented under the umbrella of an AI algorithm.

CONCLUSION

This grim future is what Yanis Varoufakis calls "Techno-Feudalism", a post-capitalist system where large tech monopolies expand to own almost every part of the economy, even humans themselves by harvesting and weaponizing their personal data (Varoufakis, 2021). This future is, however, far from fated. The AI revolution holds great promise. Like any revolution, it promises to free the masses from poverty, segregation, need, and alienating jobs; but it is also at risk of being coopted by those who seek to monopolize and monetize the technology. That is why the real challenge posed by AI to healthcare is not the technology itself, it is the same people that today seek to privatize care, impose austerity, and defund research. Political mobilization and action will prove essential, as the future of AI and its users is being decided today. While it is no easy task to pre-emptively change an uncertain future, there are certain political levers of change that can be activated today in order to increase the likelihood, if not guarantee, the path which AI will take. One of these levers is the fight for data privacy laws, another is the call to break up corporate monopolies or the regulation of AI development and use. The most important lever and goal, however, remains taking healthcare off the market altogether. As long as there is profit to be made from care, abuse will surely follow. Once "healthcare as a right" is fully entrenched within our legislations, communities, within our deepest personal convictions, then, and only then, will it be immune to any perceived threat, whether it is artificial technology or human greed.

REFERENCES

Annapragada, A., Donaruma-Kwoh, M., Annapragada, A., & Starosolski, Z. (2021, February 26). A natural language processing and deep learning approach to identify child abuse from pediatric electronic medical records. *PLoS One, 16*(2). 10.1371/journal.pone.0247404

Anyoha, R. (2017, August 27). The history of artificial intelligence. *Science in the News (Harvard University)*. https://sitn.hms.harvard.edu/flash/2017/history-artificial-intelligence/ (accessed 28 December 2021).

Ben-Aaron, D. (1985, April 9). Weizenbaum examines computers and society. *The Tech, 105*(16). http://tech.mit.edu/V105/N16/weisen.16n.html

Böhme, R., & Köpsell, S. (2010). Trained to accept? A field experiment on consent dialogs. *SIGCHI Conference on Human Factors in Computing Systems (CHI '10)* (pp. 2403–2406). Association for Computing Machinery: New York, USA. 10.1145/1753326.1753689

Carreyrou, J. (2015, October 16). Hot startup Theranos has struggled with its blood-test technology. *The Wall Street Journal*. https://www.wsj.com/articles/theranos-has-struggled-with-blood-tests-1444881901 (accessed 1 January 2022).

Centers for Medicare & Medicaid Services (2021, January 12). *Electronic Health Records*. CMS.gov: https://www.cms.gov/Medicare/E-Health/EHealthRecords (accessed 27 December 2021).

Cimino, J. J. (2017). Classification of clinical research study eligibility criteria to support multi-stage cohort identification using clinical data repositories. *Studies in Health Technology and Informatics*, 341–345. 10.3233/978-1-61499-830-3-341

Coiera, E., Kocaballi, B., Halamka, J., & Laranjo, L. (2018, October 16). The digital scribe. *NPJ Digital Medicine, 1*. 10.1038/s41746-018-0066-9

Crawford, K. (2021). *Atlas of AI*. Yale University Press. 978-0-300-20957-0

Dipaola, F., Gatti, M., Pacetti, V., Bottaccioli, A., Shiffer, D., Minonzio, M., … Furlan, R. (2019, October 14). Artificial intelligence algorithms and natural language processing for the recognition of syncope patients on emergency department medical records. *Journal of Clinical Medicine, 8*(10), 1677. 10.3390/jcm8101677

Djavan, B., Remzi, M., Zlotta, A., Seitz, C., Snow, P., & Marberger, M. (2016, September 21). Novel artificial neural network for early detection of prostate cancer. *Journal of Clinical Oncology, 20*(4). 10.1200/JCO.2002.20.4.921

EIT Health; McKinsey & Company (2020, March). Transforming healthcare with AI: The impact on the workforce and organisation. https://eithealth.eu/wp-content/uploads/2020/03/EIT-Health-and-McKinsey_Transforming-Healthcare-with-AI.pdf

Finlay, G., Rothman, M., & Smith, R. (2013, December 19). System, measuring the modified early warning score and the Rothman index: Advantages of utilizing the electronic medical record in an early warning. *Journal of Hospital Medicine, 9*(2), 116–119. 10.1002/jhm.2132

Frontline AIDS; International Treatment Preparedness Coalition (2019). *The problem with patents: Access to affordable HIV treatment in middle-income countries*. Make medicines affordable. https://makemedicinesaffordable.org/wp-content/uploads/2020/02/The-problem-with-patents_pages_web.pdf

Gennatas, E., & Chen, J. (2021). Artificial intelligence in medicine: Past, present, and future. In Xing, L., Giger, M., & Min, J.(Eds.), *Artificial intelligence in medicine* (pp. 3–18). United Kingdom: Elsevier Academic Press.

Guarascio, F. (2022, January 14). Poorer nations forced to dump close-to-expiry COVID vaccines. *Reuters*. https://www.reuters.com/business/healthcare-pharmaceuticals/more-than-100-million-covid-19-vaccines-rejected-by-poorer-nations-dec-unicef-2022-01-13/

Hara, K., Adams, A., Milland, K., Savage, S., Callison-Burch, C., & Bigham, J. P. (2018). A data-driven analysis of workers' earnings on amazon mechanical Turk. *Proceedings of the 2018 CHI Conference on Human Factors in Computing Systems* (pp. 1–14). Association for Computing Machinery: New York, USA. 10.1145/3173574.3174023

Hassanien, A. E., Mahdy, L. N., Ezzat, K. A., Elmousalami, H. H., & Aboul Ella, H. (2020). Automatic X-ray COVID-19 Lung Image Classification System based on Multi-Level Thresholding and Support Vector Machine. 10.1101/2020.03.30.20047787

IPlytics. (2019). *Who is patenting AI technology?* Iplytics: Berlin. https://www.iplytics.com/wp-content/uploads/2019/03/IPlytics-AI-report.pdf

James, G., Daniela, W., Hastie, T., & Tibshirani, R. (2013). *An introduction to statistical learning with applications in R*. Springer: New York. 10.1007/978-1-4614-7138-7

Jiang, F., Yong, J., Zhi, H., Dong, Y., Li, H., Ma, S., …Wang, Y. (2017, June 22). Artificial intelligence in healthcare: Past, present and future. *Stroke and Vascular Neurology, 2*. 10.1136/svn-2017-000101

Kesselheim, A. S., Cook-Deegan, R. M., Winickoff, D. E., & Mello, M. M. (2013, July 10). Gene patenting—the supreme court finally speaks. *New England Journal of Medicine*. 10.1056/NEJMhle1308199

Knepper, T., & McLeod, H. (2018, May 9). When will clinical trials finally reflect diversity? *Nature*, 157–159. 10.1038/d41586-018-05049-5

Krishna, S., Campana, E., & Chandrasekaran, S. (2021). *Thriving in an AI world: Unclocking the value of AI across seven key industries*. KPMG. Retrieved from https://advisory.kpmg.us/content/dam/advisory/en/pdfs/2021/thrivingai2021.pdf

Kumar, M., & Mostafa, J. (2020, January 23). Electronic health records for better health in the lower- and middle-income countries: A landscape study. *Library Hi Tech, 38*(4), 751–767. 10.1108/lht-09-2019-0179

Li, R., Chen, Y., Ritchie, M., & Moore, J. (2020, March 31). Electronic health records and polygenic risk scores for predicting disease risk. *Nature Reviews Genetics*, 493–502. 10.1038/s415 76-020-0224-1

Ma, W. (2021). Breaking the big tech monopoly. *Horizons*, (18), 166–179. https://www.cirsd.org/en/horizons/horizons-winter-2021-issue-no-18/breaking-the-big-tech-monopoly

Marx, K. (1996). *Capital: A critique of political economy*, Volume I. Engels, F. (Ed.), Regnery Publishing: Washington, D.C.

O'Neil, C. (2016, September 1). How algorithms rule our working lives. *The Guardian*. https://www.theguardian.com/science/2016/sep/01/how-algorithms-rule-our-working-lives

Office for Civil Rights (2021). *Breach portal: notice to the secretary of HHS breach of unsecured protected health information*. U.S. Department of Health and Human Services. https://ocrportal.hhs.gov/ocr/breach/breach_report.jsf (accessed 1 January 2022).

Pataranutaporn, P., Danry, V., Leong, J., Punpongsanon, P., Novy, D., & Sra, M. (2021). AI-generated characters for supporting personalized learning and well-being. *Nature Machine Intelligence*, 1013–1022. 10.1038/s42256-021-00417-9

Pellegrino, E. D. (1999). The commodification of medical and health care: The moral consequences of a paradigm shift from a professional to a market ethic. *Journal of Medical Philosophy*, 243–266. 10.1076/jmep.24.3.243.2523

Petroff, A. (2018, January 24). Google CEO: AI is 'more profound than electricity or fire'. *CNNMoney*. https://money.cnn.com/2018/01/24/technology/sundar-pichai-google-ai-artificial-intelligence/index.html

Pontin, J. (2007, March 25). Artificial intelligence, with help from the humans. *The New York Times*. https://www.nytimes.com/2007/03/25/business/yourmoney/25Stream.html

Robinson, J., Rosenzweig, C., Moss, A., & Litman, L. (2019, December 16). Tapped out or barely tapped? Recommendations for how to harness the vast and largely unused potential of the mechanical Turk participant pool. *PLoS ONE*. 10.1371/journal.pone.0226394

Rocca, F., & Maurer, P. (2021). Red cross red crescent: We need new extraordinary steps to increase access to COVID-19 vaccines and we need them now. *International Committee of the Red Cross*. https://www.icrc.org/en/document/red-cross-crescent-access-covid-vaccines

Sinsky, C., Colligan, L., Li, L., Prgomet, M., Reynolds, S., Goeders, L., … Blike, G. (2016, December 6). Allocation of physician time in ambulatory practice: A time and motion study in 4 specialties. *Annals of Internal Medicine*, 753–760. 10.7326/M16-0961

Stewart, C. (2020, September 22). *Total global medical technology revenue from 2011 to 2024*. Statista: https://www.statista.com/statistics/325809/worldwide-medical-technology-revenue/

Stucke, M. (2018, March 27). Here are all the reasons it's a bad idea to let a few tech companies monopolize our data. *Harvard Business Review*. https://hbr.org/2018/03/here-are-all-the-reasons-its-a-bad-idea-to-let-a-few-tech-companies-monopolize-our-data (accessed 1 January 2022).

Stucke, M. E. (2018, March 19). Should we be concerned about data-opolies? *Georgetown Law Technology Review*. 10.2139/ssrn.3144045

Taylor, A. (2018, August 1). The automation charade. *Logic Magazine*. https://logicmag.io/failure/the-automation-charade/

Tikkanen, R., Osbron, R., Massialos, E., Djordjevic, A., & Wharton, G. (2020). *International profiles of health care systems*. The Commonwealth Fund. https://www.commonwealthfund.org/sites/default/files/2020-12/International_Profiles_of_Health_Care_Systems_Dec2020.pdf

Tollefson, J. (2020, October 5). How Trump damaged science — And why it could take decades to recover. *Nature*, (586), 190–194. 10.1038/d41586-020-02800-9

Turing, A. (1950, October). Computing machinery and intelligence. *Mind, 49*(236), 433–460. 10.1 007/978-1-4020-6710-5_3

Varoufakis, Y. (2021, June 28). Techno-feudalism is taking over. *Project Syndicate*. https://www. project-syndicate.org/commentary/techno-feudalism-replacing-market-capitalism-by-yanis-varoufakis-2021-06

World Health Organization (2019). *World health statistics 2019: Monitoring health for the SDGs, sustainable development goals*. Geneva. https://www.who.int/publications/i/item/ 9789241565707

Xin, Y., Man, W., & Yi, Z. (2021, December). The development trend of artificial intelligence in medical: A patentometric analysis. *Artificial Intelligence in the Life Sciences*. 10.1016/j.ailsci.2 021.100006

Zeng, D., Cao, Z., & Neill, D. (2021). Artificial intelligence-enabled public health surveillance—From local detection to global epidemic monitoring and control. In Xing, L., Giger, M., & Min, J. (Eds.), *Artificial intelligence in medicine technical basis and clinical applications* (pp. 436–453). Academic Press.

II

AI Impact: Social and Legal Aspects

CHAPTER 4

Analysis of the Impact of Algorithms on Siloing Users: Special Focus on YouTube

Joseph Vybihal and Mika Desblancs

School of Computer Science, McGill University, Montreal, Quebec, Canada

CONTENTS

DOI: 10.1201/9781003261247-6

INTRODUCTION

The impact of artificial intelligence (AI) and technology on society is undeniable. In *Weapons of Math Destruction*, Cathy O'Neil (2017) states that "If we had been clear-headed, we all would have taken a step back at this point to figure out how math had been misused … But instead … new mathematical techniques were hotter than ever … A computer program could speed through thousands of resumes or loan applications in a second or two and sort them into neat lists, with the most promising candidates on top" (Crawford, 2021). Kate Crawford in her recent book *Atlas of AI* mentions that "I've argued that there is much at stake in how we define AI, what its boundaries are, and who determines them: it shapes what can be seen and contested" (Crawford, 2021). Recently, the Senate Commerce subcommittee (2021) hearings with whistleblower, Frances Haugen, calling for transparency claiming that Facebook entices users to keep scrolling to increase the opportunity for advertisers to reach these users resulting in side effects harmful to children and women (Senate Commerce Subcommittee, 2021). The misuse of algorithms, unintentional or intentional, is a great concern given that society is very trusting in computers.

The Internet has changed the speed at which information can be shared as anyone with an Internet connection is able to disseminate their ideas to a wide audience. While this phenomenon is not new, YouTube has recently received a lot of attention. The low barrier of entry to publishing videos on the platform has caused a spike in the amount of independent political pundits; a little less than half of the most popular news channels are independent of any news organization and over a third center around a single personality. Furthermore, given that over 73% of adults and 94% of 18–24-year-olds turn to YouTube for news (Stocking et al., 2020), understanding what kind of content is being watched and information disseminated is crucial to measuring the platform's impact on today's democracies. In recent years, YouTube has been accused of being a vector for online radicalization and in 2020 had to ban open white supremacists such as Stefan Molyneux and Richard Spencer (Stocking et al., 2020). Along with its hosting of in-cendiary content, the YouTube recommendation system has also been accused of gra-dually pulling users towards more extreme content by recommending and promoting videos that become more "hard-core". A *New York Times* article claimed in 2018 that the recommendation system had a bias toward inflammatory content and users who watched mainstream news sources were quickly presented with far-right videos (Tufekci, 2018). The article argued that this tendency was not a bug but a feature; the algorithm was simply exploiting our natural attraction towards watching more inflammatory content. In June 2020, Google announced that it changed its guidelines to better manage racist content, terminated over 25,000 channels, and took steps to limit recommending in-flammatory content (BBC News, 2020). YouTube's impact on political news dis-semination remains important yet Google's changes have received little scrutiny.

The impact that recommendation systems have on individuals is a function of the form of interaction the individual engages with the recommendation system. This form of interaction is higher order, in that it is not controlled by the recommendation system but is centered on the user's behavior. For example, the recommendation system may show the user a set of recommendations some of which the user has already viewed. The user might not view the repeated recommendations again. It is this higher order search space the user explores: the things they want to see. That search space is constrained by what the recommendation system offers to the user, but the user further constrains the space. To study user siloes, we need to traverse this higher order search space and see how it impacts the recommendation system. In this chapter, we suggest ways to access this higher order search space (or Meta Space).

Our study focuses on the impact of YouTube's recommendation system in placing individuals into silos, unintentionally encouraging people to focus on a point-of-view while ignoring other views that may balance or critique their bias. The chapter will focus on experiments our group conducted with the YouTube platform. Our experiments explore different perusing techniques. We discuss these results in relation to the YouTube algorithm's current ability to silo users.

RECOMMENDATION SYSTEM MECHANICS

In contrast to a recommendation system, a traditional database stores information in records that are relatively independent from one another. For example, when depositing $5.00 at an ATM machine, the bank's database will record this transaction as a database record. The record will contain, as a minimum, the date, user ID, account number, and amount. If we wanted to retrieve information from the database, we would need key information to search on, like the date of the transaction. We could ask, "Display all the transaction at a particular date" or "list all the dates Alice deposited $5.00". To perform a more advanced search the record would need to have *metadata*, information (a field in the record) not directly related to the transaction that created the record. If metadata is present, then we could also perform more in-depth queries like *cross-linking* (e.g., all account holders that are teenagers) and the ability to *group information* (e.g., list all of Alice's bank accounts). These deeper searches are defined by an organization's purpose for doing such reporting. Google, for example, claims they record only statistical metadata and do not record specific statistics about individuals. They then profit from that information through targeted advertisement or the sharing of those statistics with interested third parties. Population statistics instead of tracking an individual's statistics (Jannach et al., 2021).

A recommendation system's database is more like a graph. Each database record is a node of the graph, and every arc is metadata. At least two types of metadata are stored: categorization information, which is supplied by content creators and may also be auto-generated by the host system (e.g., Genre, publisher, tags), and population statistics ("type" of people who frequently visit a node, "click" interaction tracking, group "join" tracking, search "query" writing). In addition to the content database (the YouTube videos), the system also keeps a traditional database of statistics about users (individual's personal interactions with the system) that may or may not be private information (e.g., Google claims they share population statistics but not personal statistics). The rationale is that the way an individual interacts with the system statistically is proportional to what the individual wants.

The goal of the recommendation system is to *document* and *exploit* interaction statistics for an individual. Business goals are related to *profit* and product *loyalty*, which may conflict with social concerns.

The process of documenting interaction statistics requires methods to associate a user with their interaction statistics, the common way is a password-protected user account. This restricts the number of individuals who can access the account, resulting in higher confidence that the statistics belong to the individual. An indirect way of creating an account is through the IP address of the device used to access the system. The likelihood that the IP-based account refers to a single individual is less likely, but not zero given the use of cell phones and personal laptops. At worst, the IP-based account provides statistics about a closed community (like a family or friend group). Recommendation systems can use the IP metadata to realize that two accounts, one an IP-based account and the other a username/password account, when on the same IP address are related in some way. Recommendation systems can also use the IP metadata to associate accounts resulting in cross-recommendations between presumed "family" and "friend group" members. For example, your spouse searches for diapers and it also shows up in your YouTube feed.

A user of a recommendation system interacts with the system in two modes: passive click (click a video to play) and active interaction (input search key or join a group). Each mode results in the gathering of statistics. Passive click is the default mode. In default mode the system watches the user recording specific statistics: video selected, length of video watched, pause length in front of a video, time of day user interacts with the system, view habits by time of day, associations by IP address with other users, genres frequency, etc. In active mode, the user typically enters a query into the search box for specific information. The intentional search is a strong indicator of interest in the topic. The user can also "join" a "channel" or "group" to indicate a strong preference for the material published by the provider of that channel. Commonly in a modern recommendation system, the user begins in default mode after logging in. The user is presented with a list of recommendations even before interacting with the system based on their past behavior. The way the individual interacts with this initial offering reinforces (or modifies) the statistical decisions made by the system.

A user session is measured as the period between when a user logs into the system (this could be automated by simply starting the app) and when the user logs out of the system (or automated by closing the app). During that session, the user performs a series of actions over time. These actions are related to a traversal of a graph. The root node of the graph contains the initial recommendations presented to the user when they first login. How they respond to the initial recommendations determines the path they follow through the graph. Each node of the graph is a set of recommendations presented to the user. After selecting a recommendation, the system presents additional recommendations (the next node in the graph). We define depth as being the number of nodes traversed from the root node to some stopping point. For example, the user can choose to "stop" by returning to the root node at any time by selecting a "home" button. The root node may or may not display the same information. If it displays the same information, then this is a cyclic graph. If the algorithm displays different nodes, then this is a tree (a graph without cycles). Note, it is not required that the algorithm that displays the root node recommendation is the same algorithm that presents the follow-up node recommendations.

Recommendations are based on a *policy*. A policy is a set of rules or a strategy for selecting videos from the system's catalog. These policies are *black boxes* to an outside investigator. These policies are proprietary. However, the actual policy can be teased out based on how it responds to specific inputs. These policies will manifest themselves based on observations of the form: videos grouped together, videos shown (hid) to (from) the user, node population, and the evolution of the root node over subsequent sessions.

RECOMMENDATION SYSTEM WEAKNESSES

The weaknesses in a recommendation system are directly related to the policies or technologies in question. The algorithm may not be intentionally constructed as biased. The recommendation is a function of the limits in the policy or technology. These limits can be expressed in many ways: algorithmic artifacts, fairness, business interests, etc. Let us look at two examples that highlight algorithmic artifacts.

Example 1: Artificial neural network job placement and implicit bias.

An artificial neural network (ANN) is a statistical pattern matcher. Given a set of example data, it can on its own determine the most common features belonging to the example set of data. The larger the number of examples, the greater its ability to extract even finer features that are in common to all the parameters in the example set. Assume we use an ANN to help an organization select its next employee. Assume we have decided to create an example set of all the greatest employees of this organization. Without prejudice, we give the ANN the curriculum vitae (CV) of all the greatest employees. This would contain information like their name, place of birth, school, degree, where they lived, age, gender, etc. It is hard to know what features an ANN identifies as significant since that knowledge is kept as fractional numbers (scores and weights) stored within the cells of a matrix the ANN uses to identify significant features. These fractional number patterns are determined via the interaction of the algorithm with the examples presented to the ANN. What if it so happens to be that the greatest employees for this organization happen to come from affluent neighborhoods and that past managers favored hiring men? The ANN would select strongly for men from affluent neighborhoods. This is called *implicit bias*. The organization did not intentionally want the algorithm to select affluent men. Notice that the bias arises from both the dataset used for learning (the selected CVs – we can call this the *policy*) and the way ANNs detect important features (the algorithm – we can call this the *technology*).

Example 2: Sorting genre preferences and silos.

Simple tracking algorithms use counting and thresholding when making recommendations. Let us look at this simple algorithm: count the number of times a user visits a genre and sort that tracking list from highest to lowest. Display recommendations in sorted order for all values greater than a threshold value. Values below the threshold would not be displayed. The threshold is used to reduce the volume of recommended objects and to remove uninteresting objects. The threshold could be an absolute number, or it could be a percentage. An absolute number would have the effect that recommendations would not be made for a given metadata until the user visits that metadata n times, where n is the absolute threshold value. A percentage value would display recommended objects regardless of the number of times the user visited a genre. For example, if the user is new to the system and only visited a single provider, then that visit constitutes 100% of the statistics, and assuming the threshold is 50%, it would display the object. A side-effect of this type of algorithm is observed when a user, for some reason on a particular day, becomes interested in a topic and visits that topic frequently resulting in the visit count (for that metadata) to increase causing it to be sorted to the top of the list and recommended more frequently to the user. This is useful to the user for a time, but when the user is no longer interested in this topic the system will continue to recommend the topic (since it remains sorted above the threshold). The user must actively interact with objects tagged with different metadata to force these new meta statistics to sort above their previous interest. This is an example of a silo effect. When the algorithm begins to favor recommending one topic above others based on the sorted metadata count. The unintended effect is to show only one kind of information to the user over a long period of time. This is manageable for users with diverse interaction habits since they purposefully influence the statistics, but for passive users who rely on the default behavior of the system, the objects presented to them could hover around specific content for longer periods of time, while at the same time hiding from sight other content. In the above example, the technology of counting, sorting, and thresholding has a siloing effect.

In analysis, it is important to identify not only the policy but the technology. In some cases, the policy and technology are highly integrated and can be viewed as the same thing. In the literature, policy is often viewed as integrated (Steck et al., 2021). But we argue that policy and technology should be kept separate when possible. We define *policy* as human choices in terms of input data used for learning. *Technology* is defined as the side effects of algorithms.

HOW TO ANALYZE A RECOMMENDATION SYSTEM?

This section is an introduction to software probing, where probing will be discussed in general terms. The next section, Analysis of YouTube, will describe the way we implemented these general principles.

Recommendation systems are proprietary software and are therefore black boxes. The only way to determine the nature of a black box (to determine the policy it uses) is to probe and see how it behaves with input stimuli (datasets). The output of the black box given the input stimuli form statistics that is proportional to the underlying policy and technology.

To probe a black box, we need to be aware of three important algorithmic qualities: (a) upper and lower bounds, (c) high-probability cycles, and (c) edge cases. Upper and lower bound analysis determines the behavior of the algorithm during extreme probing. This helps determine the algorithm's boundaries. In other words, beyond this point, the algorithm cannot go. High-probability cycles identify the most common way users interact with the system and how the system behaves in those conditions. Edge cases are low-probability cycles, conditions in which the algorithm is rarely in, but must still be considered for a small population of use cases.

These three important algorithmic qualities express themselves differently based on the underlying policy and technology that make up the recommendation system. These policies and technologies produce a recommendation search space the user interacts with, but there is a meta-search space that is an expression of the combined interaction of the policies, technologies, and the user. For example, the recommendation system's recommendations will express differently when using a list, a tree, or a graph (as seen in the examples discussed previously). Assuming a graph, the number of connections and the quality of the metadata on the connections determine the type of queries that can be invoked on the graph. This impacts the quality of the recommendations displayed to the user. If the recommendation has an object the user has previously seen, the user may remove that object from consideration. We referred to this previously as the user's Meta-Space, it is the search space in the user's mind. That is the real search space.

What boundaries, common cycles, and edge cases does the user's meta-search space have?

A search space is often viewed as a graph since cycles are observed in recommendation systems. In other words, the same recommendation is encountered later. However, users interact with a recommendation system on a session basis. This means the user interacts with the recommendation system over a period, and then they exit the recommendation system and visit it again at another time. This period represents an entry point into the graph (called that root) and the interactions with the system during the session (click, then new recommended objects) is the *search path*. It is acceptable to think that during a session a user will rarely interact with a recommended object more than once (meaning, if they watch a movie, they probably will not watch the movie again during the same session). If this is the case, then during the session the graph reduces to a tree. In other words, the user will ignore objects they have seen before and only search through pathways they have not previously followed in that session. It is possible that the policy would take note of cyclic interactions by the user (user watches a movie twice in the same session) to strengthen certain types of recommended objects, however, since this can be assumed to rarely happen, this behavior could be analyzed during an edge case probe, not for boundary or common-cycle analysis.

A recommendation system logs user interactions during each session. These interactions form statistics that modify the set of objects recommended during a subsequent session (or during the same session as they travel down a search path). These recommended objects can be classified and reflect the underlying policy. Studying how the root or search path changes during a session and between sessions reveal the underlying policies employed by the recommendation system. With enough data points, a distribution can be graphed giving confidence that a particular policy exists within the recommendation system.

Assuming the meta-search-space reduces to a tree, then (1) the upper and lower bound analyses of a tree are depth-first and breadth-first search, (2) the common cycles can be estimated from surveys of large populations of users, and (3) the edge cases must be handled case-by-case (one example was given previously).

Depth-first and breadth-first searches are extreme behavior interactions with a tree. In both cases, the tree is searched exhaustively. Depth-first search interacts with the tree by selecting the first recommendation presented, regardless of what it is, until it exhausts that path. Then, it goes up the branch and selects the second recommendation, and so on. In breadth-first, every recommendation is watched in the ply before going down to the next ply. Breadth-first search focuses on the set of recommended objects presented to the user, and how watching all the objects impacts subsequent recommendations. In some recommendation systems, depth-first and breadth-first interactions are unrealistic. However, this type of probing reveals features of the underlying policy. In other words, general conclusions about features of the policy of the form "at most it can do this" or "in the worst case, it can do that" are revealed.

Surveying a large population of users will tease out common practices. A common practice is defined by a set of interactions users commonly perform during a session. For example, login, see initial offering, pick the best object, watch it, pick from the next set of recommendations, watch that, go back to root, see the offerings, watch another one, then logout. Writing probing software that follows these common practices, together with the boundary cases, helps to reduce the range of divergent paths. In other words, the change in recommendations observed from the common practices probing is compared to the boundary probing. If a common practice sequence of interactions has a depth or breadth element (truncated to a finite length), then extreme behavior can be extrapolated using the boundary analysis. It can be said "most users experience this x but some users will experience that y", where x is the common cycle and y is the boundary cycle. In other words, if a user does x for a while and then happens to do y, a statistical prediction can be made.

ANALYSIS OF YOUTUBE

Previous Work

A *New York Times* article cited by Tufekci (2018) claimed that the YouTube recommendation system had a bias toward inflammatory content and users who watched mainstream news sources were quickly presented with far-right videos. In 2019, Ledwich and Zaitsev (2020) published a paper that contradicted these claims. They found that

YouTube's recommendation algorithm actively discourages viewers from visiting radicalizing or extremist content, instead favoring mainstream media and cable news. The authors built a dataset of over 816 political and influential YouTube channels. Each of these channels was manually annotated using a list of 18 tags. Using individual videos from tagged content creators, the authors collected information about the recommended videos with a scraping script. The authors' algorithm viewed and collected information about these videos using an anonymous account that had not "watched" any previous videos. The YouTube recommendation system had no "user history" on which to base its recommendations. The authors investigated the recommendations of an individual video without traveling down the recommendation space. Thus, their study focuses on the recommendation system's political behavior for isolated videos without history. Given that recommendation systems base their recommendations on historical user interaction statistics, we do not believe their study accurately portrays the YouTube recommendation system.

Ledwich and Zaitsev (2020) list of 816 political channels was later extended to include annotations for over 6,500 content creators (Clark & Zaitsev, 2020). The authors used a channel discovery and classification method which generates political affiliation tags using user channel subscriptions. The model can predict political affiliation tags with higher degree of agreement with human annotators, agreeing between 84% and 97% of the time. The model achieved precision and recall values of 89.1% and 77.9% for left-leaning channels, and 86.3% and 92.3% for right-wing channels. We have chosen to re-use an updated list of annotated political channels from January 1, 2022, generated by Clark and Zaitsev's method with 11,645 content creators (Clark & Zaitsev, 2020).

Our Work

We classify videos using tags associated with YouTube channels from the 11,645 content-creators annotated dataset described previously. For our scraping, we created different authorized YouTube accounts to take into account user history. We have chosen to assume that the user will not view a video multiple times during a YouTube session. However, they may repeat view a video at another session. By session, we mean logging back into a YouTube account after having deleted its entire account-linked user history and data. We delete an account's entire account-linked user history and data before starting another session so that a user's history built over the course of an expansion does not influence the recommended videos of another session. To properly mimic user engagement in a video, the algorithm "watches" videos for three minutes or until the maximum length of the video is reached, whichever is shorter. By "watching" the video, we hope to better mimic the human user interaction on YouTube.

Given the above, the upper and lower bound analysis is equivalent to a depth-first and breadth-first search of the recommendation tree. The high-probability cycle for the most common user behavior was determined using a survey of 187 YouTube users. We leave edge cases for future work.

We present only the upper bound, lower bound, and common-cycle experiments. Figure 4.1 is the expansion algorithm.

```
Begin:

    if depth or breadth:
        root_rec = YouTube_Search(random(Curated_list));
    else:
        root_rec = YouTube_Search(common_use_behavior());

    recs = Top(root, n); // top n recommended videos

    count = 0;
    Expansion(recs, count);

End.

Expansion(recs, count):

    if count == m: stop // m is based on probing depth

    if depth:
        Expansion(Top(YouTube_Search(depth_select_first(recs))), n), count+1);
    if breadth:
        Expansion(Top(YouTube_Search(breath_select_next(recs))), n), count+1);
    if common-cycle:
        Expansion(Top(YouTube_Search(random_or_politicalBias_select_one(recs))), n), count+1);

End.
```

FIGURE 4.1   Expansion algorithm.

Next we detail the different expansion types. Each expansion description follows algorithm 1. Figure 4.2 depicts breadth-first boundary experiment. Figure 4.3 depicts depth-first boundary experiment. Figure 4.4 depicts important results from our survey. Table 4.1 depicts the curated left-/right-leaning seed videos.

BREADTH-FIRST EXPANSION

In breadth-first expansion (see Figure 4.2), the algorithm begins with the user selecting a YouTube video of interest using active search. This search places the user at what we call the *root recommendations* of the tree. It is the only part of the algorithm that uses a directed search. It is an automated search using a predetermined (curated) set of providers of interest (see Table 4.1) divided into left- or right-wing content-creator sets. Depending on the search bias, a video is randomly selected from that list of videos. The resultant root node is a set of video recommendations dependent on this search. In breadth-first search, we will visit every child video in that resultant list of recommended videos (the ply) before continuing to the next ply. To reduce complexity of our analysis, the algorithm visits only the first three recommended videos irrespective of what the videos contain. Each of those three videos becomes the root of another recursive expansion. In this way, the tree expands ply by ply. The algorithm continues until a ply depth of 4. For each ply, we compute the number of videos whose metadata corresponds to the initial search metadata, in this case, its left- or right-wing rating over the total number of recommendations in that ply. We call this the *silo percentage,* and how it changes over time, we call this the *silo percentage evolution.*

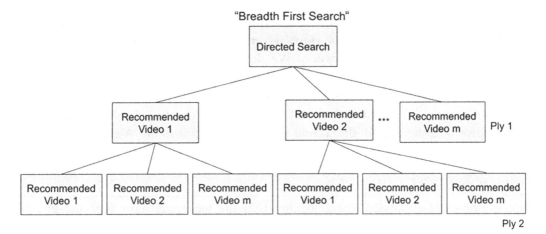

FIGURE 4.2   Breadth-First expansion of YouTube recommendations.

DEPTH-FIRST EXPANSION

In depth-first expansion (see Figure 4.3), the algorithm begins by performing the same initial active mode search as in breadth-first search from the curated list. Then, the algorithm takes the first video recommended, regardless of its content, and watches it. The algorithm is then presented with a new list of recommended videos and watches the very first one, regardless of its content. It repeats this watching of the first recommended video repeatedly up to a ply depth of 6. Then, it returns to the root and watches the next

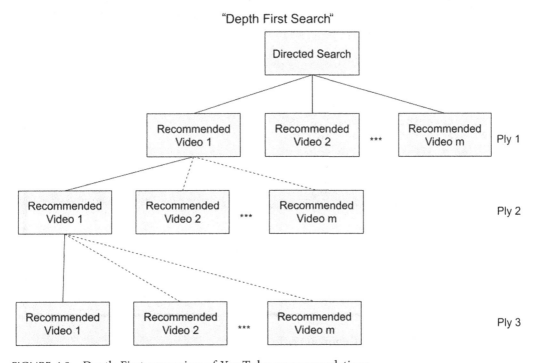

FIGURE 4.3   Depth-First expansion of YouTube recommendations.

recommendation presented, starting a new depth-first traversal of the recommendation tree. Importantly, the original root video recommendations are saved and remain unchanged throughout the entire session. We do this five times. We calculate the silo percentage by following each depth-first search path. We call this a *dive*. We compare the number of silo videos by the number of videos watched from root to leaf for each "dive". We then compute the growth/decrease of the silo bias between each "dive", comparing the first dive with the second, the second with the third, and so on. We call this the *silo evolution value*.

COMMON-CYCLE EXPANSION

In common-cycle expansion, the algorithm uses the technique most reported in our survey. We surveyed 187 YouTube users. The summary of the survey results and some important conclusions can be found in Figure 4.4.

Given the results from the survey, the most common procedure YouTube users follow is directed search by interest (A and D with E) with randomness (F) that sometimes challenges their beliefs (G). They do a depth-directed search up to a ply of 2 or 3 before returning to the homepage (H). They repeat this process a few times. We will call this *the common-cycle procedure*.

The common-cycle experiment will use the following variation of the common-cycle procedure. The algorithm will start by determining the user's intent by using the following rule:

- 80% of the time it will choose to start with an initial left-/right-wing seed from the curated list of videos (Table 4.1) to generate the root recommendations of interest, based on its initial bias.

```
(A) 82% Looks for things they like. (W 77%)
(B) 50% Go back to home page. (W 38%)
(C) 92% Logged into YouTube. (W 88%)
(D) 50% Search for a video. (W 62%)
(E) 56% Same topic scan. (W 54%)
(F) 65% Random - catch attention. (W 63%)
(G) 85% Watch videos challenging beliefs (W 22%)
(H) 81% Depth of 2 or 3 (W 80%)
(I) 95%: in their 20s, student, 90% North American.

Conclusions:
- Three data points greatest difference between men/women (B), (D), (G)
- Most are logged into YouTube (C)
- Look for things they like (A) (some randomly (F))
- search depth 2 or 3.
- W = women
```

FIGURE 4.4 Survey Results for Common Cycle.

TABLE 4.1   Example of Curated Left- and Right-Wing Videos

Title	Content creator	Political classification
A Short History of Slavery	PragerU	Right
Yes, Censorship is Bad	Sargon of Akkad	Right
Leftists MELT DOWN After Elon Musk Condemns Vaccine Mandates	Ben Shapiro	Right
Ben Shapiro Gets SCHOOLED by Neil Degrasse Tyson on Trans Issues	Vaush	Left
The Easy Answer of YouTube Conservatism	Three Arrows	Left

- 10% of the time it will choose a video from the first 25 videos automatically presented to it when it first logged in (called the *homepage videos*).

- 10% of the time it will scan the homepage videos for an opposing point of view, choosing a random homepage video if no partisan video is found.

The algorithm then performs a depth-first search of the recommendation space guided by the user's intent for a ply depth of 2. This will be repeated six times.

For each expansion type, we also compute a *silo evolution value of the user's homepage*. The homepage is the initial set of recommended videos presented to the user when they log into YouTube (at the start of a session). To track the silo evolution of the homepage, the algorithm scrapes a session's YouTube homepage's top 10 videos. Scrapes will occur before the start of each new *ply* in the breadth-first expansion and before each *dive* in the depth and common-cycle expansion. As more probes are performed, the homepage will change over time. We are interested in whether siloing occurs right from the start of their YouTube session.

The analysis of YouTube will be based on three experiments using the three previous expansion types. Experiment 1 uses bread-first search, experiment 2 uses depth-first search, and experiment 3 uses the implementation of the common-cycle procedure described above. For experiments 1 and 2, our analysis will compare *dive statistics* with *dive evolution statistics* between each dive. We will also compute *homepage state statistics* and *homepage state evolution statistics*. We will then generate a table and make observations. For more detailed explanations of the algorithms please refer to the GitHub page (Desblancs, 2022).

RESULTS AND ANALYSIS

Breadth-First Expansion

The results from the depth-first search experiment are summarized in Table 4.2, Figures 4.5 and 4.6. The experiment visited 7,426 videos, which represent trees of width 3 and depth of 4, where each "dive" started at the root, using the root's 5 videos as the beginning.

TABLE 4.2 Tentative Breadth-First Search Experiment Results

Ply	TTL L	TTL R	TTL O
0	1	0	2
1	2	0	7
2	4	0	20
3	5	0	64
Ply	**TTL L**	**TTL R**	**TTL O**
0	2	0	1
1	3	0	6
2	4	1	22
3	8	3	64

Table 4.2 shows the number of videos seen per ply, categorized by left-leaning (TTL L), right-leaning (TTL R), and other videos (TTL O). These initial results show that videos of type Other are favored. Two breath dives are shown for a left-leaning initial directed search. As the dive progresses, the TTL O columns increase faster than the TTL R and TTL L columns.

Silo Percentage and Evolution

In Figure 4.5, we see how breadth-first evolves over depth. In the picture on the left, we have a left-leaning initial directed search. We see that the recommended videos at ply zero show more left-leaning videos, as expected. But as the algorithm progresses breadthwise down the tree, the "Other" videos dominate. A similar story exists for the right-leaning videos. An interesting artifact of our data is that the right-leaning videos are always not the most prevalent, even at ply zero. Also notice that at ply 4 the curve changes direction. We believe this is an artifact of our algorithm. In future experiments, we will dive deeper to see if this pattern persists.

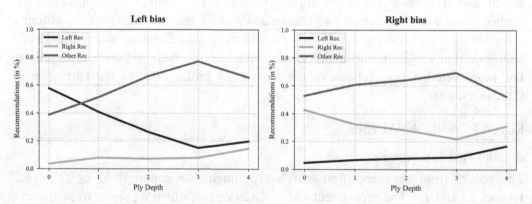

FIGURE 4.5 Average video recommendation types per ply in a Breadth-First Left- and Right-wing tree (in %).

Homepage Ply Percentages

The evolution of the homepage is an important property. It is the initial offering to the user when they login and can influence their outlook. Figure 4.6 shows our experimental results. You can see in breadth-first the homepage is always dominated by "Other" videos. If the user is left or right leaning, the remaining videos reflect their leaning, and the opponent videos (to a much lesser degree) still appear in the feed.

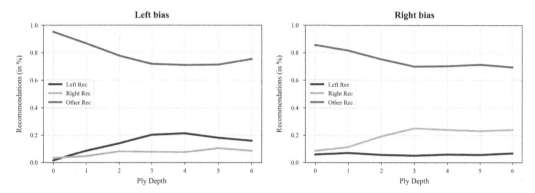

FIGURE 4.6   Average homepage recommendation types per ply after each dive in a Breadth-First Left- and Right-wing tree (in %).

Depth-First Expansion

The results from the Depth-First Search Experiment are summarized in Figures 4.7 and 4.8. The experiment visited 2,448 videos, which represents trees of width 5 and depth of 6, where each "dive" started at the root, using the root's 5 videos as the beginning. This was not an exhaustive depth-first search of every ply, but only the root.

Dive Statistics and Evolution

Figure 4.7 shows the dive statistics and evolution with the percentage of right-, left-wing, and neutral (Other) videos in the top 5 suggested videos at the different video positions, where the position is the order in which videos were visited. The algorithm goes to a ply depth of 6, which is indicated by the vertical dashed lines. After each dashed line the algorithm returns to the root and starts its next dive. Interesting artifacts of the data to notice: (a) at the end of the first dive the bias is nullified by YouTube resulting in a steep rise in neutral videos and a sharp decline in the left/right videos. (b) We see again that right-leaning videos perform more poorly than left-leaning videos. Further study is needed; for example, are left-leaning videos more entertainment based, while right-leaning are more news-based?

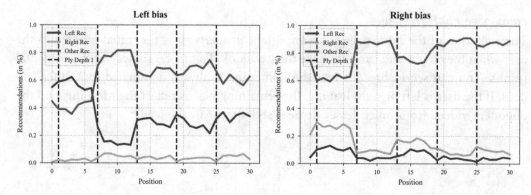

FIGURE 4.7 Average video recommendation types per position in a Depth-First Right- and Left-Wing Tree (in %).

Homepage State and Evolution

Figure 4.8 graphs out the homepage right-, left-wing, and other recommendation percentages on the homepage after dive *n* along with its evolution after the different dives, where 0 is a snapshot when we first login and 6 is a snapshot after the sixth (last) dive. The homepage evolution compared to the breadth-first graphs.

In summary for depth and breadth search, we see that the bias affected greatly the outcome. If the user selected "other" they were presented with left and other videos, but mostly other. If they selected "left" they were presented with left and other videos, but mostly left.

The dive recommendation bias frequency evolution graphs also show this siloing effect is especially strong for trees with left-wing biases. The frequency with which left-wing videos are recommended is greater than the reverse situation. Furthermore, regardless of the tree bias, videos presenting opposite political points of view are rarely recommended.

The homepage evolution shows slight levels of siloing for both biases. However, it is not as strong as the siloing which occurs in the recommendation space. Interestingly, for both political biases, political bias video frequency stabilizes to its highest values directly after the first dive, indicating that while siloing is slight, it happens during the first dive.

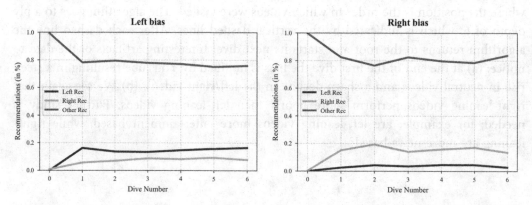

FIGURE 4.8 Average homepage recommendation types after each dive in a Depth-First Left- and Right-wing tree (in %).

Common-Cycle Expansion

The results from the Directed Search Experiment are summarized in Figures 4.9 and 4.10. The experiment visited 1,895 videos. Which represented directed dives of depth 3, returning to the root, and then performing another directed dive, following the *variation of the common-cycle procedure.*

Dive Statistics and Evolution

Read Figure 4.9 in the same way as Figure 4.8 with the notable exception that black dotted vertical lines now indicate points in the algorithm where it has gone back to the homepage instead of to the directed search root recommendations. Notice the artifacts of this figure: (a) siloing occurs to a greater extent for both biases in the common expansion. (b) The neutral (Other) videos compete for dominance. (c) In the right bias, the neutral (Other) videos dominate. An interesting question to explore is whether the competing neutral (Other) video is an attempt to counter siloing through distraction by YouTube.

Homepage State and Evolution

Figure 4.10 is read like Figure 4.8. The artifacts to note in this figure are (a) the neutral (Other) videos dominate the graph but lose ground as bias persistence continues. (b) The homepage reflects the user's bias to a strong degree.

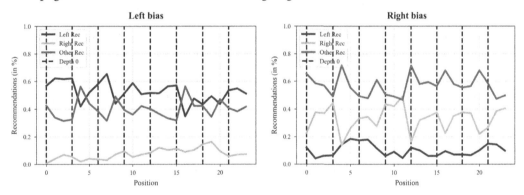

FIGURE 4.9   Average video recommendation types per position in a common-cycle expansion Left- and Right-wing tree (in %).

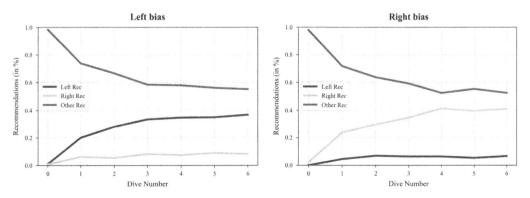

FIGURE 4.10   Average homepage recommendation types per dive in a survey-inspired Right-wing tree (in %).

In summary, following the common-cycle procedure, siloing is present for both political biases with the opposite bias rarely being recommended. However, the recommendation system seems more sensitive to recommending left-wing content than right-wing content. On scrapes with a left bias, the recommendation system suggested an average of around 50% of left-wing recommendations while only suggesting around 30% of right-wing content. Unlike the depth- and breadth-first expansions, however, the frequency of biased recommended videos does not follow periods of constant growth, decreases nor stabilization. The YouTube algorithm also seemed to be sensitive to neutral (Other) choices resulting in a rapid rise in neutral recommendations. However, this rise would decrease when not exploited.

CONCLUSION

The purpose of a good recommendation system is to give the user what they want to see. Based on our experiments, YouTube does this. If the user is left or right leaning and selects 80% of the time their bias of choice, the YouTube platform will present the user with the left- or right-leaning videos, rarely presenting opposing videos. The silo effect is present in our experiments. The user must intentionally select opposing videos to see those videos in their feed. However, the recommender is sensitive to selection changes and displays opposing videos quickly.

The evolution of the user's homepage over time will reflect their bias to a greater degree with little to oppose. Even though the homepage is dominated by neutral videos, these videos do not help expose the user to opposing views. In many cases, this effect is not important, as when purchasing diapers. But it is important when viewing videos on the "benefits" of not eating, or in politics, or conspiracy videos. This homepage bias dominance can lead to confirmation bias and siloed thought.

Interesting questions to study further: What is the reason for the dominance of neutral (Other) videos, is this an artifact of the data, or is this an intentional distraction strategy by YouTube? Is the effect that left-leaning videos are presented more often than right-leaning videos real? To what extent does homepage bias dominance lead to confirmation bias and siloed thought?

REFERENCES

BBC News (2020). YouTube bans prominent white supremacist channels. BBC Business. *BBC News*, https://www.bbc.com/news/business-53230986

Clark, S., & Zaitsev, A. (2020). Understanding YouTube communities via subscription-based channel embeddings. *arXiv* [Preprint] (2020). arXiv:2010.09892.

Crawford, K. (2021). *The atlas of AI.* Yale University Press, p. 217.

Desblancs, M. (2022). Analysis of the impact of algorithms in siloing users: Special focus on YouTube (Version 1.0.0) https://github.com/mika-jpd/YouTube_Radicalization_Recommendations [Computer software]

Jannach, D., Pu, P., Ricci, F., & Zanker, M. (2021). Recommender systems: Past, present, future. *AI Magazine*, 42, 3–6. 10.1609/aaai.12012

Ledwich, M., & Zaitsev, A. (2020). Algorithmic extremism: Examining YouTube's rabbit hole of radicalization. *First Monday, 25*(3), 10.5210/fm.v25i3.10419

O'Neil, C. (2017). *Weapons of math destruction*. New York: Broadway Book, p. 13.

Senate Commerce Subcommittee (2021). Facebook whistleblower Frances Haugen testifies before senate commerce committee. C-SPAN. https://www.youtube.com/watch?v=GOnpVQnv5Cw

Steck, H., Baltrunas, L., Elahi, E., Liang, D., Raimond, Y., & Basilico, J. (2021). Deep learning for recommender systems: A netfil case study. *AI Magazine, 42*, 7–18. 10.1609/aaai.12013

Stocking, G., Van Kessel, P., Barthel, M., Eva Matsa, K., & Khuzam, M. (2020). *A closer look at the channels producing news on YouTube – And the videos themselves*. Pew Research Center. https://www.pewresearch.org/journalism/2020/09/28/a-closer-look-at-the-channels-producing-news-on-youtube-and-the-videos-themselves/

Tufekci, Z. (2018). Youtube, the great radicalizer. *The New York Times*, www.nytimes.com/2018/03/10/opinion/sunday/youtube-politics-radical.html

CHAPTER 5

Affective Change Through Affective Artificial Intelligence

Michaela Pňaček(ová)

Cinema and Media Studies, York University, Toronto, Ontario, Canada

CONTENTS

INTRODUCTION

Emotion and affect received an indirect focus since the Enlightenment philosophy, and only in the mid-1990s did affect theory take a larger sociocultural and philosophical course beyond the realms of post-Freudian psychology. In this chapter, I outline approaches to affect which are crucial for creative practice in artificial intelligence (AI) and

DOI: 10.1201/9781003261247-7

emerging media. I introduce the connection between affect theory, new materialism, and AI. My premise is that AI is an untrustworthy and unethical partner in our everyday lives because it is untransparent, based on abstraction and patterning. Affective AI (known also as emotional AI) – such as facial expression analysis (FEA) and emotion recognition (ER) – as it exists today is based on a rationalist tradition resulting in biases of its trained models which lead to errors. However, if we interact with these technologies with a critical stance and agency, we might gain more control of how we are perceived and interpreted by the machines.

My proposal to make affective AI more trustworthy, lies in implementing new materialist methods when interacting and creating with it. The term is inspired by Rosalind Picard's "affective computing" (Picard, 1997) and it implements emotion theories in practice – it "also includes many other things, such as giving a computer the ability to recognize and express emotions, developing its ability to respond intelligently to human emotion, and enabling it to regulate and utilize its emotions" (Picard, 1997, p. 3). If human decision-making relies on the combination of affect and cognition, could we make AI more ethical and trustworthy by making it "affective" through a controlled human–AI interaction[1] in emerging media, such as expanded reality (XR)[2]? I suggest a form of human–AI co-creation grounded in the framework of affect theory, critical data and technology studies, and surveillance capitalism. It is a way to challenge these systems, democratize them, and diversify them. The aim of this experiment is to test whether it is possible to surpass the boundaries of the brain and the biological body, and whether it is possible to achieve a controlled agency when subjected to affective AI. I develop a methodology based on Karen Barad's "agential realism" (2007) when using affective AI as a creation apparatus.

I differentiate between affect and emotion by connecting the psychological theories of primary emotions used in affective AI (i.e., proto-affect theory) (Tomkins, 2008; Scherer & Ekman, 2014), with social theories of "face work" (Goffman, 1956), post-structuralist approaches to affect (Massumi, 2002; Sedgwick, 2003; Gibbs, 2010; Ahmed, 2014) and new materialism (Haraway, 2016; Barad, 2007). Specifically, I apply Karen Barad's concept of "agential realism", and I look at sociality of affect through the lens of "affective economies" (Ahmed, 2014), and "mimetic communication" (Gibbs, 2010). Moreover, I analyze neuroscientific research on emotion (Ratey, 2002; Damasio, 2005) as it has a major influence on the development of affective AI processes and the design of emerging media. In the conclusion of this chapter, I propose a range of idealistic and radical interventions when designing with AI as an attempt of critical, agentive, and controlled human–AI interaction, co-creation, or a symbiosis if you will.

Last but not least, this chapter represents an attempt to de-rationalize the patriarchal, heteronormative, and colonial structures in technology via delving into sentience and affect. I am not going to dive into medicine, biotechnology, or suggest creating the new Kismet[3] but I focus on barrier-free and accessible technologies through emerging media. I won't tackle the issue of natural language processing, and sentiment analysis due to the large amount of data in these areas.

ERROR AND BIAS IN AFFECTIVE AI

With researchers still wrangling over whether people can produce or perceive emotional expressions with fidelity, many in the field think efforts to get computers to do it automatically are premature — especially when FEA and ER technology could have damaging repercussions. The underlying processes in these technologies are machine learning (ML) and computer vision (CV),[4] which I view as AI apparatuses through which we are being objectified: perceived, interpreted, and constructed. CV is based on human vision, which is not universal: "Sight and vision should not be understood as essential qualities or strictly physiological processes with universal, transhistorical meanings or functions" (Gates, 2011, pp. 9–10). I view ML and CV as tools of human ideologies, which are the magnifying glasses of human perception (and which produce dangerous algorithmic truths).

It is often through an accidental error that innovation and learning happens,[5] but it is also through error of abstraction that bias occurs. At the heart of abstraction in AI, processes lie datafication and patterning. As Lisa Gitelman and Stephen J. Jackson put it, data are always already "cooked" (Gitelman, 2013). Data are never raw. In other words, "how data are conceived, measured and employed actively frames their nature" (Kitchin & Lauriault, 2014, p. 4). I view data and AI through the lens of intersectional feminism, queer software studies (D'Ignazio & Klein, 2020), and sociophilosophical notions of abstraction and error. Data "are the products of unequal social relations, and this context is essential for conducting accurate, ethical analysis" (D'Ignazio & Klein, 2020, p. 10).

Matteo Pasquinelli and Vladan Joler (2020) use the metaphor of "nooscope" to depict the error in datafication and algorithms. They draw a diagram that starts on the bottom with human labor during data processing, its interventions and errors on the left, and machine and statistical bias on the right. Human error on one side, machine error on the other. This error created during the datafication process amalgamates through ML into bias where ML serves as "an instrument of knowledge magnification that helps to perceive features, patterns, and correlations through vast spaces of data beyond human reach" (Pasquinelli & Joler, 2020). They further claim: "Nooscope is described as a machine that operates on three modalities: training, classification, and prediction. In more intuitive terms, these modalities can be called: pattern extraction, pattern recognition, and pattern generation" (Pasquinelli & Joler, 2020).

I position human–AI interaction, emerging media, and emotional/affective AI within the context of surveillance capitalism (Zuboff, 2019), neoliberalism, and psychopolitics (Han, 2017). Shoshana Zuboff addresses the ways ER has become one of the major data supplies that large tech companies capitalize on – "These supply operations are aimed at your personality, moods, and emotions, your lies and vulnerabilities" (2019, p. 199). The collection of biometric data (i.e., gaze tracking, face tracking, pupillometry, heart rate, step count, EEG) serves these companies to predict, and thus influence (and coerce) users' behaviors, needs, wishes, and emotions hidden behind the neoliberal concept of freedom. According to Byung-Chun Han (2017), neoliberal psychopolitics interrogates the notion of freedom as capitalization. Humans become their own projects to perfect themselves and capitalize themselves, which is possible through self-tracking and self-publishing; "Today, we do not deem ourselves subjugated subjects, but rather projects: always refashioning and reinventing ourselves" (Han, 2017, p. 1). These endless possibilities make us into self-producing objects, and they are crucial when we talk about production of the "self" through digitization where our data becomes "biocapital" (Schull, 2018).

Just recently, Meta published an emotion recognition effect on Instagram called *Emoji Picture Effect* (2021), which takes the form of a gamified camera effect. The user's mission is to imitate emojis turning in a wheel around their face on their phone screen and then publish the recorded video. Unless they agree to publish it, they cannot play the game self-serving as a marketing tool. Inadvertently, and through a seemingly innocent game, we are all working for Meta to train their ER.[6] Thus, *Emoji Picture Effect* serves as an example of biocapital (Schull, 2018), which comes from the post-Marxist thought of capital as labor in the neoliberal context of data capitalism. Biocapital includes digital labor that we as subjects produce and give out for free in exchange to increase our "social capital".[7] Within the biometric tracking processes (i.e., step counting, heart rate, face tracking), which take a material form in "the assemblages of sensors, analytical algorithms, and data visualizations that constitute contemporary self-tracking practices" (Schull, 2018, p. 26), human and non-human agents become data workers. Our digital and physical practices, tracked through biometric sensors, develop into digital labor. This is a new regime of labor called "self-quantification" according to Natasha Schull (2018, p. 28). Our collected data train algorithms developed by the Silicon Valley corporations, who capitalize by selling the data and the technologies to third parties. But, within these practices, opacity and error are frequent.

Systems of Facial Expression Analysis and Emotion Recognition in Affective AI

So how do these systems work? Different face expression databases serve as training tools for FEA and ER, and among them one of the first FEA databases was Paul Ekman's Facial Action Coding System (FACS) created in the 1970s.[8] Even though the issues of interpreting emotions from facial gestures are known to be problematic (i.e., due to lack of social context, lack of knowledge of the individual subjects), computer scientists aim to solve these issues by applying different AI processes to the same databases and the same FEA systems, such as FACS, without considering performative, social and cultural aspects of emotions. Kelly A. Gates (2011) deems the constantly changing social contexts and interpretations of emotions hugely impactful. Some of these social approaches are solidified in FEA, which deems the software inflexible as it cannot embrace the fluctuation of contexts and meanings. "There are a wide variety of 'scopic regimes' of the face, a wide range of ways in which people use their faces and interpret the faces of others. Computation is itself a culturally and historically specific way of analyzing faces and modeling visual perception" (Gates, 2011, pp. 11–12). Gates derives her approach from Donna Haraway's (1990) concept of situated knowledge; but here, CV represents the apparatus of human perception and interpretation of face. Through these apparatuses, we empower the systems created by humans (in the tech companies) without even knowing it.

Donna Haraway's work on situated knowledge serves to interrogate the fallibility of human action in data processing (Haraway, 1990). When training CV and ML with data, it is human perception that structures it. Human perception and interpretation of data is culturally and socially situated, and because data labeling is part of this process, CV and ML are "culturally and historically specific, modified, involved" (Haraway, 1990, p. 12). Haraway moreover states, "Vision is always a question of the power to see", and "struggles over what will count as rational accounts of the world are struggles over how to see" (Gates, 2011, pp. 9–10).

I use ML and CV as an illustrative example of systemic differentiation between boundaries of object and subject. Our data generate other data and it is through this process when we, as our quantified selves, become objects in the AI apparatuses – such as ML and CV. These are fed with data produced by the agents (including humans, animals, etc.) themselves by tracking and collecting, which then humans label according to their (fallible) perception – self-quantification – which turns into biocapital. Based on data collection, labeling, inclusion, and exclusion in ML, deep neural networks[9] learn to artificially generate large datasets for their own training to learn to differentiate between the "signal" and the "noise". This is how datafication bias transforms within the apparatus of ML and CV. Concretely, ML feeds its classifications and predictions into CV and that is how computers learn to "see" (i.e., recognize objects, faces, and emotions), and the difference between what is recognized and what isn't recognized becomes larger.

Through databases such as FACS, CV and ML learn to recognize and assign emotions to facial expressions on humans, who learn to perform the emotions for machines (i.e., *Emoji Picture Effect* on Instagram) to reinforce the training of its algorithms and neural networks.[10] Biometric datafication and algorithmization captures "the processes of fragmentation, amalgamation, and aggregation through which selves are made objects and subjects of power in a digitally networked world" (Schull, 2018, p. 35). I call this a cyclical performative dimension of human–AI interaction, and in order to change this cycle, we need to apply critical interventions through agential realism.

AFFECT VS EMOTION – THE FOUR ROUTES

The Primary Emotions Route

Are emotions culturally constructed, or is there really a certain number of primary emotions common to all of mankind? In 1962, Silvan Tomkins developed "psychobiology of differential affects" (Sedgwick & Frank, 1995), which set out the Darwinian psychological direction of certain primary emotions we share with mammals. Tomkins claimed that there were six primary affects, which occurred in pairs: interest–excitement, enjoyment–joy, surprise–startle, distress–anguish, anger–rage, and fear–terror, later he added shame–humiliation, dissmell and disgust (Tomkins, 2008). Tomkins argued that these nine affects manifest a shared biological heritage with what is called emotion in animals, and that they differ from Freudian drives in lacking an object. This theory was further developed by Paul Ekman in the 1970s.

Paul Ekman popularized the notions that humans are thought to have an innate set of basic emotions that are cross-culturally recognizable such as fear, joy, surprise, anger, sadness, and disgust (Scherer & Ekman, 2014). Ekman and his colleague Wallace Friesen undertook a several years long study of facial expressions, "creating a scheme of forty-four discrete facial 'action units' — individual muscle movements combinable to form many different facial displays" (Gates, 2011, p. 22) called Facial Action Coding System – FACS (Ekman et al., 1997). As a result of this study, Ekman claims that humans can reliably infer emotional states from expressions on faces all around the world – implying that emotional expressions are universal.

The primary emotion theory stood unchallenged for a long time but a new cohort of psychologists and cognitive scientists has been revisiting those data and questioning the conclusions. Many researchers now think that the picture is a lot more complicated, and that facial expressions vary widely between contexts and cultures. In 2012, Jack et al. refuted the primary emotions universalism originating from Darwinist essentialism, conducting anthropological research based on simulating Ekman's six primary emotions from gathered data of 30 Western and Eastern culture individuals on their facial avatars. They learned that:

> cross-cultural comparisons of the mental representations challenge universality on two separate counts. First, whereas Westerners represent each of the six basic emotions with a distinct set of facial movements common to the group, Easterners do not. Second, Easterners represent emotional intensity with distinctive dynamic eye activity.
>
> *(Jack et al., 2012, p. 7241)*

Facial expressions can change throughout different cultures, and even in a personal context, our expression might confuse our audience (i.e., our laughter might express anxiety rather than joy). If the interpreter on the other end has enough information about the situation and our character, then they might interpret it correctly. However, more often than not, even humans misinterpret emotions. Why do we expect that a machine could if it's based on fallible human perception anyway?

The Spinozist–Deleuzian Route

In his groundbreaking work *Ethics* written in 1677, Benedict Spinoza develops metaphysics that present emotion and sensation, body and mind, nature and God, as being two sides of one coin. There is only one substance in the universe – God. "Everything else that is, is in God" (Spinoza's Ethics, 2020, pp. 160). He defines emotions analogically, pleasure and pain, the companions of love and hate, are modifications of the body which increase or decrease our active powers. I'd like to make a parallel to neuroscience here: the pain releases dopamine in our brains, which motivates us to action (e.g., to put our hand on the hot stove). However, Spinoza assigns positive and negative qualities to emotions. Beings attain a state of greater perfection and power through an active state of mind, heightened by active emotions such as pleasure, whereas passive emotions such as hate decrease the activity of the mind.[11] The more the mind controls emotions, corresponding to active and positive feelings, the greater its perfection. Power in the sense of potency and actualization of potential is an important aspect of Spinozist philosophy. Happiness is the experience we have when we are actively increasing our power and actualizing our potential. Spinoza's account of emotions collapses the distinction between mind and body: emotions are what physical beings experience through their interactions with each other. Spinoza attributes meaning to emotions, and he considers them "human vices and follies" (Spinoza's Ethics, 2020, p. 162). Nonetheless, humans and their emotions are part of nature, and so rules of nature apply to them in the same way.[12]

The Spinozist–Deleuzian philosopher Brian Massumi defines affect as the third state between different levels of Spinoza's concepts of activity and passivity,

> Spinoza's *Ethics* is the philosophy of the becoming-active, in parallel, of mind and body, from an origin in passion, in impingement, in so pure and productive a receptivity that it can only be conceived as a third state, an excluded middle, prior to the distinction between activity and passivity: affect. This "origin" is never left behind, but doubles one like a shadow that is always almost perceived, and cannot but be perceived, in effect.
>
> *(Massumi, 1995, p. 93)*

Massumi positions affect as something that exists pre-emotionally. He does not situate affect outside of emotion but sees them as different levels of the same entity that transform and echo each other. He defines emotion as subjective quality in a sociolinguistic and personal context, and positions affect outside of these terms, which results in his argument that "affect is unqualified", and "as such, it is not ownable or recognizable, and is thus resistant to critique" (Massumi, 1995, p. 88). On the other hand, "emotion is qualified intensity, the conventional, consensual point of insertion of intensity into semantically and semiotically formed progressions, into narrativizable action-reaction circuits, into function and meaning" (Massumi, 1995, p. 88). Emotion is a cognitively processed affect (which we assign a certain quality, such as "active" or "passive", "positive" or "negative", etc.). Massumi does not suggest that emotion cannot be subject to critical theory, it is the affect that cannot be subject to it because it's not qualifiable. Although affect is "asocial", it is not "presocial", "it includes social elements, but mixes them with elements belonging to other levels of functioning, and combines them according to different logic" (Massumi, 1995, p. 91).

The Performative Route

When affect is processed through cognition – once the signal from the amygdala reaches the prefrontal cortex in our brains – it becomes an emotion. It occurs through cognitive action and relations between agents (human and non-human). These cognitive actions are inherently performative, such as language, bodily and facial gestures, or tone of voice, and Sara Ahmed (2014) calls these relations "contact". She focuses only on human relations – her view residing in social constructivism and performativity – and argues that already when we feel that something is good or bad, it involves "reading the contact we have with objects in a certain way" (Ahmed, 2014, p. 6). Contact involves a process of reading, attribution of significance, it "involves also the histories that come before the subject" (Ahmed, 2014, p. 6). Ahmed stresses the interrelationality of matter, during which "all our actions are reactions, in the sense that what we do is shaped by the contact we have with others" (2014, p. 8). In her terminology, interrelationality becomes "contact". Hence, emotions are relational.

I view emotions as culturally and linguistically constructed performative actualizations of affect. Ahmed posits emotion as cultural construct through language (2014).[13] Whereas Massumi does not identify the biological or the cultural as separate spheres, he still sees emotions as performative, "emotions are embedded in the arbitrariness of language and gestural code (including face) involving cognition, and through which we assign these intensities qualities and which carry meanings in order to be communicated" (1995, p. 89). Ahmed takes this terminology of emotion, and echoes Judith Butler: "Through repetition of norms worlds materialize, and the norms appear as ordinary life through the concealment of this repetition" (Ahmed, 2014, p. 7). She further claims, "Emotions shape the very surfaces of bodies, which take shape through the repetition of actions of time, as well as through orientations towards and away from others" (Ahmed, 2014, p. 7). This cyclical dimension of performativity of emotion and its social distribution is "affective economy" according to Ahmed (2014). Feelings "don't reside in subjects or objects, but are produced as effects of circulation" (Ahmed, 2014, p. 8).

The Neuroscientific Route

I now turn to affect and emotion from the neuroscientific perspective. I simplify this complex physio-chemical process and ask the readers from the field of neuroscience to excuse this simplicity. Ahmed mentions that "emotions are both about objects (our apprehension of them), which they hence shape, and they are also shaped by contact with objects" (Ahmed, 2014, p. 7). These "objects" aren't necessarily material, they can be imagined such as memories. According to neuroscientific research, these judgments are products of interactions between the limbic system and the cortex (Picard, 1997, p. 12). Emotions are directly attached to the attention system, which consists of four parts - one of them is the reward system producing "sensations of pleasure, assigning an emotional value to stimulus, which also marks it for memory" (Ratey, 2002, p. 117). If a similar stimulus is later encountered, the memory recalls emotional responses (joy, disgust, etc.) and then generates a plan of action. Hence, it is the body that remembers these traces of emotions and memories associated with them (we might still feel the burning pain in our hands). Ahmed explains these traces as impressions, the physicality of them being crucial to the interrelationality between different bodies.

Emotions arise through the workings between the limbic system and the cortex in the brain. The amygdala, the central part of the limbic system, is the first one to assign the intensity of the perception before any other information is assigned to it when it reaches the frontal lobes (such as the cortex). It "provides a preconscious bias of intensity to every stimulus you come into contact with, even before you actually pay attention to it. It can, and it does, operate outside consciousness" (Ratey, 2002, p. 121). These intensity assignments to stimuli are called "limbic tagging", and the neurotransmitter dopamine is the reason. Ratey calls it the "learning transmitter" as it is released in response to "pleasurable reward or painful punishments" (2002, pp. 121–122) – we remember that the stove can burn us and so we are more careful next time. Dopamine controls our expectations and thus our decision-making. For instance, when we are in a situation whether we shall study to pass the exam or whether we will pass it even without studying, the brain calculates on the one hand, the probability of failing the test or passing it (pessimistic vs. optimistic expectation based on previous memory and emotional response), as well as the consequence of failing it. Dopamine is important to keep our long-term motivation and the ability to predict the future, such as saving food for the winter instead of eating it right away. If the dopamine concentration changes, it causes either the desire for an immediate reward (ADHD patients, drug addicts, alcoholics) or a complete state of demotivation (which then influences depression).

Brain is social according to Ratey, "the neurons are either making connections with their neighbours or dying for lack of contact" (2002, p. 23). The amygdala assigns intensity to a stimulus (this can be a memory, a bodily sensation, any kind of object, i.e., obstruction in quantum physics) and the released amount of the neurotransmitter dopamine directs the intensity until it is processed in prefrontal cortex as an emotion (fear, joy, etc.). Is affect a neurotransmitter? Is it the hidden capacity in the amygdala waiting to be released? Can we understand affect as the process of making a trace of a feeling that the body remembers?

If we take into consideration the sociality of affect, its transmittive forces, its "stickiness" and the ability to transmit itself between bodies and things, this process of traces of memories in a body is possible. Can we thus consider these "somatic markers" (Damasio, 2005), or gut feelings and intuition as affect? Can affect carry "the trace of past actions including a trace of their contexts" which are " conserved in the brain and in the flesh, but out of mind and out of body understood as qualifiable interiorities, active and passive respectively" (Massumi, 1995, p. 91)? Can this "half a second"[14] of "something" be affect? Is it a trace of a memory, or trace of our emotion or someone else's, which we cannot identify as an emotion yet because we have not processed it cognitively?[15]

Until now, I have introduced four approaches to affect and emotion and how they might be implemented in human–AI interaction: the primary emotions theory, Deleuze-Spinozist affect route, the performative route, and the neuroscientific route. It is my intention to find the resonances amid these different directions through the lens of agential realism in order to critically intervene during interacting with affective AI.

NEW MATERIALISM AND AFFECTIVE AI

Karen Barad, the author of "agential realism" (2007) goes beyond the anthropocentricity of social constructivism and performativity. Her theory posits that "the forces at work in the materialization of bodies are not only social, and the bodies produced are not all human" (Barad, 2007, p. 33). These bodies are "agents" (Barad, 2007). Barad proposes a new understanding of how discursive practices are related to the material world through the lens of quantum physics, where the discursive and the material are intertwined, and not exclusive. It is via this posthumanist lens that I view affective AI; where agential realism is "an epistemological-ontological–ethical framework that provides an understanding of the role of human and nonhuman, material and discursive, and natural and cultural factors in scientific and other social-material practices" (Barad, 2007, p. 26). Inspired by the two premises discussed above, I claim that emotion is the relational materialization of affect, which encompasses the capacity (i.e., potential) of becoming and "mattering" (Barad, 2007).

Another term important for this discussion is Barad's neologism "intra-action" (2007), which can be understood as affect. In her words, intra-action

> signifies the mutual constitution of entangled agencies. That is … the notion of intra-action recognizes that distinct agencies do not precede, but rather emerge through, their intra-action. It is important to note that the "distinct" agencies are only distinct in a relational, not an absolute, sense, that is, agencies are only distinct in relation to their mutual entanglement; they don't exist as individual elements.
>
> *(Barad, 2007, p. 33)*

The interrelationality of emotions is crucial to distinguish from affect's intra-actionality. Emotion arises only as distinct agency (i.e., motivation to action) through the intra-action (i.e., affect) and through its interaction with the environment, it materializes into action (we feel pain, we put away the hand from the hot stove, we remember the fear, we learn not to put hands on hot stoves). This interaction with the environment can be seen as "diffraction" (Barad, 2007). Barad applies diffraction as a process of "mattering" – becoming from the virtual to the actual and vice versa (2007). She claims, "diffraction has to do with the way waves combine when they overlap and the apparent bending and spreading out of waves when they encounter an obstruction" (Barad, 2007, p. 28). Upon encountering an obstruction, waves can diffract into particles (the hot stove is the "obstruction", and when the signal reaches the prefrontal cortex, it "diffracts" into emotion – which includes the motivation to action – which materializes into action: we pull our hand from the stove). A memory associated with an emotion is formed (pain – fear), and we learn not to touch hot stoves. All these processes form "materring", the core of agential materialism as well as quantum physics. Barad defines "mattering" as:

Matter is neither fixed and given nor the mere end result of different processes. Matter is produced and productive, generated and generative. Matter is agentive, not a fixed essence or property of things. Mattering is differentiating, and which differences come to matter, matter in the iterative production of different differences.

(2007, p. 137)[16]

Mattering leads us to the question of virtuality and materiality. An emotion becomes an activation or expression of affect from "a virtual co-presence of potentials on the basis of memory, experience, thought, and habit, surfaces onto a body, and which transmits to, and interacts with other bodies (human and non-human, and other matter)" (Gregg & Seigworth, 2010, p. 187). The agents (human and non-human, subjects and objects) are dynamic – they can change through mattering when encountering an obstruction (i.e., interaction with their environment). Through mattering, they materialize and in this case, affect materializes into emotion, which changes into a performative action such as facial or bodily gestures, tone of voice, language. Thus, "mattering, is a posthumanist performative account of material-discursive practices" (Barad, 2007, p. 148).

As mentioned above, I view affective AI as an apparatus through which human emotions are co-produced. Barad defines apparatus as "a discursive practice", "specific material re-configurations through which 'objects' and 'subjects' are produced" (Barad, 2007, p. 148). These apparatuses are material conditions, which "enact what matters and what is excluded from mattering" (Barad, 2007, p. 148). Apparatuses produce matter, they decide what matters, what is important, what is the signal and the noise. In agential realism, there is no subject or object, however, there are agents which are produced as subjects or objects through these apparatuses. People, faces, emotions are among these agents, and their codification and re-distribution results in a new concept of truth – algorithmic truth – that decides what matters. Pasquinnelli and Joler (2020) and Louise Amoore (2020) dispute the way how we see the world through AI and algorithms en-grained in algorithmic truth. "AI is a new regime of truth, scientific proof, social nor-mativity and rationality, which often does take the shape of a statistical hallucination" (Pasquinelli & Joler, 2020). Anna Munster says, "such techniques significantly transcend and undercut traditional statistical notions of what matters, what is interesting, and what is optimal" (2006, p. 41). She also explains the formative logic of algorithms "to be an arrangement of propositions that significantly generates what matters in the world" (Munster, 2006, p. 41). ML and CV become the powerful apparatuses producing what matters and what doesn't, and thus formulating its own algorithmic truth (residing within error and bias). However, John Cheney-Lippold argues that biases resulting from algorithmic processing are not errors, rather they are reconfigurations with material consequences – "freshly minted algorithmic truth that cares little about being authentic but cares a lot about being an effective metric for classification" (Cheney-Lippold, 2017, p. 16). I would say that bias is an amalgamated error of datafication through the process of algorithmic patterning.

MATERIAL PRODUCTION OF EMOTION

In regards to the relation between agential realism and affective AI, it is the contribution of Erving Goffman on "face work" (1956) which sets the origin of discursive practices of facial expression and emotion. Goffman introduces the concept "front" (1956) as an assemblage of masks and social practices performed in a certain setting that comprise one's self. One has only partial agency on constructing the front as they can only choose from those fronts that are available.[17] Goffman explains the front as a culturally constructed practice, which is institutionalized in terms of the stereotyped expectations to which it gives rise, and tends to take on a meaning. The front becomes a "collective representation and a fact in its own right" (Goffman, 1956, p. 17). He claims that what constitutes social realities is a repetition of acts that become real through social imaginaries. Therefore, only when we perform the fronts in line with the idealized expectation of our audience, and only when this performance is coherent with other performances, only then do we give "true", "genuine", and "valid" performances (Goffman, 1956). For instance, only when we express fear in a way understandable for our audience, only then will they interpret our emotion as fear. This is the legitimization aspect of what constitutes social reality in Goffman's theory. It explains why context (social, physical, and personal) matters when interpreting emotions, but it also explains facial expressions as an arbitrary social construct, or rather "communication". Through re-playing these idealized fronts, we sustain and support the systems in power, and construct ourselves within these systems with little agency. This is in fact the core of Butler's performativity – through performing and repeating acts, we are products (subjects) of discourses.

So how does Goffman's theory help to explain material construction and distribution of emotion through affective AI? FACS represents Goffman's system of fronts – an arbitrary FEA system implemented within ER. Gates describes the attempts of coders to find agreement in facial expression analysis in order to standardize it. This attempt results in the same accountability fallacy:

> The more people and computers can be made to agree about facial actions and intensities (as determined by FACS), the more accurate the classification system is said to be. This means that the "accuracy" of the system is defined not in terms of a correspondence between the system and a person whose face is being analyzed (or the full range of ways a facial expression might be interpreted), but in terms of the system's internal agreement—that is, whether the classification system consistently agrees with itself.
>
> (Gates, 2011, p. 171)[18]

The system chooses from a certain number of FACS fronts, silencing anything that does not fit, and thus eliminating unidentified emotions, facial gestures, etc., for example, the Instagram emoji effect. In order for agents to interact with these technologies, they have to speak "their language" so to say, and have to perform emotions according to this arbitrary system. Moreover, this system is only accountable to itself, and it forms the material expression of emotion, which might mold our own understanding and "feeling" of emotions. Gates says

> The real power of FACS comes into play when this form of 'accuracy' — deriving from the process of standardization—in turn gets pushed back out onto faces, as the standardized coding system comes to define what facial expressions mean and how they work. Facial expressions are made to fit the technology and the decontextualized, mathematical theory of information that informs its design.
>
> *(Gates, 2011, p. 171)*

Our facial expressions and emotions are thus misidentified, misrecognized, and then distributed through tools of "mimetic communication" (Gibbs, 2010), such as emojis, facial recognition applications and many more. The apparatuses of affective AI produce a topography of face and emotion. Our faces and our emotions are analyzed, recognized, predicted, and produced by the apparatuses of ML and CV as dynamic agents, and then performed and transmitted by (sometimes the same but not the same) agents.[19]

MATERIAL DISTRIBUTION OF EMOTION

Through the lens of quantum physics – specifically intra-action, diffraction, and mattering – affect transmission happens all the time and everywhere. But how can we apply it to "social mattering"? As in quantum mechanics, the possibility of transmission of the smallest particles and waves causes changes in larger levels of the universe, in affect theory, it is the transmission between the biological and the social that becomes crucial (i.e., the transmission of affect through media). Gibbs takes the Aristotelian concept of mimesis and turns it into "mimetic communication" as a way to view affect transmission. Nonetheless, she views communication not as transmission of information, but as "action on bodies (or, more accurately, on aspects of bodies)" (Gibbs, 2010, p. 93). Similar to Ahmed, Gibbs echoes the performative force of discourses shaping the body, but she applies it to visuality as a way of seeing things:

> Visuality appears not only as a biophysical phenomenon but also as a social process, a way of relating to what is seen. Mimesis can then be understood as the primary mode of apprehension utilized by the body, by social technologies such as cinema, television, and even the Internet, and by the cultural processes involving crowd behavior, fads, celebrity, and pandemics of anorexia or depression, as well as the processes by which rapid shifts of social and political attitudes may occur.
>
> *(Gibbs, 2010, p. 202)*

Thus, mimetic communication can be viewed as a form of performative affective economy of affective AI and its other forms (including immersive media such as XR). Gates says, "computers 'see' only in a metaphorical sense, only in highly constrained ways, and only with a significant investment of human effort. Computer vision systems are very much constrained by the purposes of their design, and suggesting that a computational model of vision represents an objective, detached form of vision elides the intentions and labor behind the design, deployment, and uses of these technologies" (Gates, 2011, p. 11).[20]

CONCLUSION – A FEW PROPOSITIONS TO CREATIVE INTERVENTIONS TO AFFECTIVE AI

Until now we have established that FEA and ER as forms of affective AI include implicit bias. First, they are based on human vision, which is a combination of actual perception and prediction of reality that deafens the noise, and tends to focus on certain aspects of reality and predict the rest. Then human cognition fills in the gaps. Second, the bias is transmitted during interpretation and labeling of data (i.e., FACS). And third, algorithms solidify these biases. The performative and social aspect of emotion and its distribution through mimetic communication leads to its cyclicality, enforcing these biases on our bodies. My suggestion is to apply agential realism when interacting with AI, even more so when co-creating with it.

Through the new materialist lens, I view FEA and ER as apparatuses of affective AI, which produce and distribute dynamic agents. In this interrogation, it is crucial to remember here that emotion is relational, but affect is intra-actional – it is through its intra-actionality that different agencies emerge. Affect is the capacity (i.e., potential) of becoming and mattering. Applying quantum theory and Barad's agential realism (2007) to affect, it is upon encountering an obstruction (object – virtual or actual) that diffraction (change of matter) occurs. This obstruction can be anything - an emotional trigger, an object, a memory, humans, non-humans, and it can also be an error. Affect then materializes through diffraction into emotion, then into motivation, which morphs into action, an experience, a memory, as well as a physical change.

In conclusion, on a positive note, I decided to list a few propositions and examples on how to interact critically with affective AI.

1. Embrace and code error! Break things! Induce as much diffraction effect as possible according to this scheme: (virtuality) affect – obstruction (error) – diffraction (change of matter) – emotion – motivation – (actuality) action – transmission (impact).

Here, I would like to mention an example that uses the simplification and abstraction of FEA and ER in a positive and impactful way. *Project Convey* (Cox Communications Inc., 2022) is a video chat software for people with autism. One of the symptoms of autism is the inability to recognize the emotions of others. Through the simplification of emojis, it is easier for autistic people to cognitively understand what emotion the person on the other end expresses. Through the use of FEA and ER, emojis are produced on the screen as a translation tool. However, the video chat also includes other forms of communication including the physical and social contexts of the participants. Thus, the emojis are not the sole form of communication, and the agents also implement tone of voice, body gestures, environment, and language. The simplified and abstracted emojis are contextualized and completed through other performative features of communication, making it possible for the participants to recognize errors and correct them, not rely solely on the software, and learn at the same time.

2. Embrace affect and emotion in computation, but with a critical lens!

Could we understand neurotransmitters – especially dopamine – in philosophical terms as affect? If so, how can we implement them in new technologies? In early 2020, the researchers Will Dabney, Zeb Kurth-Nelson, and Matthew Botvinick published the article "A Distributional Code for Value in Dopamine-Based Reinforcement Learning". This article has had a groundbreaking impact on neuroscience as it explains the way dopamine works in the brain based on reinforcement learning algorithms. In order to solve a problem in the human brain, it's crucial to understand future consequences. This is the role of dopamine, which works similarly to the temporal difference learning algorithm (TD). Concretely, "instead of trying to calculate total future reward, TD simply tries to predict the combination of immediate reward and its own reward prediction at the next moment in time" (Dabney et al., 2020, p. 673). When the next moment comes, the predicted expectation is compared, and if it differs, the algorithm calculates this difference and adjusts its old prediction to the new prediction. The aim is to bring these numbers as close as possible. This long discussion of the workings of dopamine in the brain and the temporal difference learning algorithm in AI shows the importance of emotions within decision-making. However, it does not prove that by using this algorithm, we will solve all questions posed here. It is however the first step forward in implementation of affect in AI.

3. Use a multitude of senses and different materials! Machines should incorporate a diversity of receptors inspired by all forms of life (human and non-human), so that they can be in constant exchange with their surroundings!

In expanded reality, other senses and receptors can be included such as smell, touch, and taste, which have more direct contact with our brains than vision and sound (Ratey, 2002). Regarding smell, Ratey explains that "odors can alter heartbeat and blood pressure directly, without mediation" (2002, p. 66). Olfactory fibers are directly connected to amygdala in the brain, which is the center of our limbic system, and the limbic system processes our fear and nurturing behavior for instance. Smell, taste, and touch are non-arbitrary and direct, and they can result in immediate fight or flight emotions such as disgust and fear. Thus, if all our sensoria can be included, we might be able to go through a "super-real"/"surreal" affective AI experience. We need to include different kinds of receptors onto XR gadgets such as HMDs (head-mounted displays), and bodysuits which track not only the bodies of its users, but also constantly perceive and adjust to their outside environment.

4. And finally, it is us who may become the extension of AI and become part of a new form of existence!

I see the future of affective AI as "New AI", an approach which contends that sensory, perceptual, and corporeal data form the frame within which cognitive faculties emerge. The skills and competencies that develop in an artificial entity as it engages directly with the world generate an intelligence that is responsive and develops constantly. This is not AI's singularity, it is rather an agentive interaction between AI and the world (including humans) seen as a symbiotic affective relationship.

NOTES

1 I view co-creation with AI as a controlled method to intervene in these technologies, and as an artistic practice of interactive and immersive user-centric design in emerging media.
2 XR is used as an umbrella term for expanded reality such as virtual, augmented, and mixed reality.
3 Elizabeth Wilson mentions the robot Kismet as a realization of Alan Turing's dream of making a child-like computer, which would develop through interaction with humans, "e.g., from the mid-1990s, a group in the MIT Media Lab began to integrate emotional character into a humanoid robot. 'Kismet' is a child-like robotic head that can express a variety of primary emotions" (Wilson, 2010, p. 53).
4 CV and ML can be explained as:

> AI is the umbrella of these fields, machine learning is a subset of AI, wherein computer vision is also the subset of machine learning. However, CV can be considered as a direct subset of AI. ML and CV are two fields that have become closely related to one another. ML has improved CV about recognition and tracking. It offers effective methods for acquisition, image processing, and object focus which are used in CV. In turn, CV has broadened the scope of ML. It involves a digital image or video, a sensing device, an interpreting device, and the interpretation stage. ML is used in CV in the interpreting device and interpretation stage.
>
> ("Machine Learning in Computer Vision", 2019)

5 Silvan Tomkins says, "The achievement of cognitive power and precision require a motivational system no less plastic and bold. Cognitive strides are limited by the motives which urge them. Cognitive error, which is essential to cognitive learning, can be made only by one capable of committing motivational error, i.e., being wrong about his own wishes, their causes and outcomes" (Tomkins, 1962, as cited in Sedgwick & Frank, 1995, p. 511).
6 See Figure 5.1 in the appendix.
7 Social capital according to Pierre Bourdieu is "the aggregate of the actual or potential resources which are linked to possession of a durable network of more or less institutionalized relationships of mutual and recognition" (Bourdieu, 1986).
8 See section on "Primary Emotions".
9 Deep neural networks are a subset of AI, and their creation originated from the brain and its functions. The neural network "starts working when a developer enters data and builds a machine learning algorithm, mostly using the 'if… else … ' principle of building a program. The deep neural network does not only work according to the algorithm but also can predict a

solution for a task and make conclusions using its previous experience. In this case, you do not need to use programming or coding to get an answer" (Kyrykovych, 2020).

10 Here, I think Haraway's quote on the way science constructs our knowledge of other beings is appropriate:

> Biology is the fiction appropriated to objects called organisms; biology fashions the facts "discovered" from organic beings. Organisms perform for the biologist, who transforms that performance into a truth attested by disciplined experience; i.e., into a fact, the jointly accomplished deed or feat of the scientist and the organism. Romanticism passes into realism, and realism into naturalism, genius into progress, insight into fact. Both the scientist and the organism are actors in a story-telling practice.
>
> *(Haraway, 1990, p. 5)*

11 Further on, he explains this concept in detail, "We see therefore that the mind can undergo great changes, and pass at one time to a higher and at another to a lower degree of perfection; and these vicissitudes or passions explain to us the emotions of pleasure and pain [Laetitiae et Tristitiae]. By pleasure I shall understand in the following pages a passion whereby the mind passes to a higher degree of perfection; by pain a passion whereby the mind passes to a lower degree of perfection" (Spinoza's Ethics, 2020, p. 172).

12 Spinoza says,

> There is nothing in existence which can be attributed to a vice in nature; for nature is always the same and is everywhere one; her virtue and power are everywhere the same; that is, the laws of nature according to which all things come into existence and pass from one form to another, are everywhere and always the same, and therefore the means of understanding the nature of all things must be one and the same, namely, by the universal laws and rules of nature. Hence passions such as hatred, anger, envy and the like, considered in themselves, follow from the same necessity and power of nature as other phenomena ...
>
> *(Spinoza's Ethics, 2020, p. 162)*

13 In her book *The Cultural Politics of Emotion* (2014), Sara Ahmed presents discourse analysis of different texts as examples of affective economies. For instance, she analyzes Darwin's statement *"uncovering the teeth under that furious age"* (2014, p. 3). According to Ahmed, emotions get narrated as a sign of our pre-history, deconstructing the essentialist tendencies of proto-affect theories (primary emotions shared with mammals according to Darwin) (2014).

14 Massumi describes the half-second when affect turns into emotion as "Formed, qualified, situated perceptions and cognitions fulfilling functions of actual connection or blockage are the capture and closure of affect. Emotion is the intensest (most contracted) expression of that capture and of the fact that something has always and again escaped" (1995, p. 96).

15 And for instance, can generational trauma be investigated through this lens?

16 Massumi claims that "The place of non-mediation between the virtual and the actual is explored in quantum mechanics. Just as 'higher' functions are fed the way to the subatomic (i.e. position and momentum) indeterminacy is fed forward. It rises through the furcations leading to and between each of the superposed reality. On each level, it appears in a unique mode adequate to that level ... The use of the concept of the quantum outside quantum mechanics, even as applied to human psychology, is not a metaphor" (1995, p. 98).

17 Goffman claims that "When an actor takes on an established social role, usually he finds that a particular front has already been established for it" (Goffman, 1956, p. 17).

18 For instance, Afdhal et al. recently published an article about their approach which allows their emotion recognition system to classify 18 emotions (primary emotions and their intensities). They describe their research process as follows, "First, we proposed textual definitions of the intensity emotions. Then, we created our emotion recognition system, which is composed of three stages: pre-treatment, feature extraction and classification. We used the deep learning for the feature extraction and the fuzzy logic for the classification. The experimental test demonstrates the efficiency of our system for primary emotions and their intensities' classification compared to other methods" (Afdhal et al., 2021, p. 1848).

19 I use Anna Gibbs' notion of "mimetic communication" (2010), as it is the most suitable concept for my discussion. There are other concepts related to affect transmission, i.e., affect contagion and sociality of affect. However, mimetic communication expresses the performative aspect of agential realism in FEA and ER in the best way.

20 Another aspect of mimetic communication is that it can be seen as an example of synchrony, "a pervasive sharing of form that seems to be the fundamental communicational principle running through all levels of behavior, through both human and animal bodies, and connected to other rhythmic processes in the natural world" (Gibbs, 2010, p. 187). The simplest example of this synchrony is the heartbeat which at some point actualizes into rhythm, which then induces an emotion. Therefore, affect can be transmitted through rhythm, for instance.

REFERENCES

Afdhal, R., Ejbali, R., & Zaied, M. (2021). Primary emotions and recognition of their intensities. *The Computer Journal, 64*(12), 1848–1860. 10.1093/comjnl/bxz162

Ahmed, S. (2014). *The cultural politics of emotion.* Edinburgh University Press.

Amoore, L. (2020). *Cloud ethics, algorithms and the attributes of ourselves and others.* Duke University Press.

Barad, K. (2007). *Meeting the universe halfway.* Duke University Press.

Bourdieu, P. (1986). The forms of capital. In Richardson, J. (Ed.), *Handbook of theory and research for the sociology of education* (pp. 241–258). Westport, CT: Greenwood. https://www.socialcapitalgateway.org/content/paper/bourdieu-p-1986-forms-capital-richardson-j-handbook-theory-and-research-sociology-educ

Cheney-Lippold, J. (2017). *We are data: Algorithms and the making of our digital selves.* NYU Press.

Cox Communications Inc. (2022). *Can emojis speak louder than words?* https://www.cox.com/residential/articles/project-convey.html

Dabney, W., Kurth-Nelson, Z., Uchida, N., Starkweather, C. K., Hassabis, D., Munos, R., … Botvinick, M. (2020). A distributional code for value in dopamine-based reinforcement learning. *Nature, 577*(7792), 671–675. 10.1038/s41586-019-1924-6

Damasio, A. (2005). *Descartes' error: Emotion, reason, and the human brain.* Penguin.

D'Ignazio, C., & Klein, L. F. (2020). *Data feminism.* The MIT Press.

Ekman, P., & Rosenberg, E. L. (1997). *What the face reveals: Basic and applied studies of spontaneous expression using the facial action coding system (FACS).* Oxford University Press.

Gates, K. A. (2011). *Our biometric future.* NYU Press.

Gibbs, A. (2010). After affect, sympathy, synchrony, and mimetic communication. In *The affect theory reader.* Duke University Press.

Gitelman, L. (Ed.). (2013). *"Raw data" is an oxymoron.* The MIT Press.

Goffman, E. (1956). *The presentation of self in everyday life.* University of Edinburgh.

Gregg, M., & Seigworth, G. (Eds.). (2010). *The affect theory reader.* Duke University Press.

Han, B.-C. (2017). *Psychopolitics: Neoliberalism and new technologies of power.* Verso Books.

Haraway, D. J. (1990). *Primate visions: Gender, race, and nature in the world of modern science.* Routledge.

Haraway, D. J. (2016). *Manifestly Haraway.* University of Minnesota Press.

Jack, R. E., Garrod, O. G. B., Yu, H., Caldara, R., & Schyns, P. G. (2012). Facial expressions of emotion are not culturally universal. *Proceedings of the National Academy of Sciences USA, 109*(19), 7241–7244. 10.1073/pnas.1200155109

Kitchin, R., & Lauriault, T. (2014). *Towards critical data studies: Charting and unpacking data assemblages and their work* (SSRN Scholarly Paper ID 2474112). Social Science Research Network. https://papers.ssrn.com/abstract=2474112

Kyrykovych, A. (2020). Deep neural networks [Blog]. *KDnuggets.* https://www.kdnuggets.com/deep-neural-networks.html/

Machine Learning in Computer Vision (2019, May 8). *Full scale.* https://fullscale.io/blog/machine-learning-computer-vision/

Massumi, B. (1995). The autonomy of affect. *Cultural Critique, 31,* 83–109. 10.2307/1354446

Massumi, B. (2002). *Parables for the virtual: Movement, affect, sensation.* Duke University Press.

Munster, A. (2006). *Materializing new media: Embodiment in information aesthetics.* UPNE.

Pasquinelli, M., & Joler, V. (2020). *The nooscope manifested: Artificial intelligence as instrument of knowledge extractivism.* KIM research group (Karlsruhe University of Arts and Design) and Share Lab (Novi Sad). https://nooscope.ai/

Picard, R. W. (1997). *Affective computing.* Cambridge: MIT Press.

Ratey, J. J. (2002). *A user's guide to the brain: Perception, attention, and the four theaters of the brain.* Penguin Random House.

Scherer, K. R., & Ekman, P. (Eds.). (2014). *Approaches to emotion.* Psychology Press. 10.4324/9781315798806

Schull, N. (2018). *Self in the loop: Bits, patterns, and pathways in the quantified self.* 10.4324/9781315202082-3

Sedgwick, E. K. (2003). *Touching feeling: Affect, pedagogy, performativity.* Duke University Press. 10.2307/j.ctv11smq37

Sedgwick, E. K., & Frank, A. (1995). Shame in the cybernetic fold: Reading Silvan Tomkins. *Critical Inquiry, 21*(2), 496–522.

Spinoza's Ethics (2020). In G. Eliot (Trans.), *Spinoza's ethics.* Princeton University Press. 10.1515/9780691197043

Tomkins, S. S. (1962). Freedom of the will and the structure of the affect system. In *Affect, imagery, consciousness, Vol. 1: The positive affects.* (pp. 108-149). Springer Publishing Co. https://doi.org/10.1037/14351-004

Tomkins, S. S. (2008). *Affect imagery consciousness (*The complete edition: Two volumes). Springer Publishing Company.

Wilson, E. A. (2010). *Affect and artificial intelligence.* University of Washington Press.

Zuboff, S. (2019). *The age of surveillance capitalism: The fight for a human future at the new frontier of power.* PublicAffairs.

APPENDIX

FIGURE 5.1 Emoji Picture effect on Instagram, 2022.

CHAPTER 6

Artificial Intelligence Lenses: Citizens' Guide to the Futures with Citizen Digital Twins

Aleksi Kopponen[a], Tero Villman[b], Petri Kettunen[c], Tommi Mikkonen[d], and Matti Rossi[e]

[a]*Ministry of Finance, Helsinki, Finland*
[b]*Finland Futures Research Centre (FFRC), University of Turku, Turku, Finland*
[c]*Department of Computer Science, University of Helsinki, Helsinki, Finland*
[d]*Faculty of Information Technology, University of Jyväskylä, Turku, Finland*
[e]*Department of Information and Service Management, Aalto University, Espoo, Finland*

CONTENTS

DOI: 10.1201/9781003261247-8

INTRODUCTION

In a typical democratic society, such as Finland, which gives a context to this chapter, societal operations are based on resource efficiency and organizational orientation, in the public sector mandated by law and in the private sector driven by business initiatives. This results in task-oriented services and organizations, where it is up to individuals to discover and navigate through the different services they want to use, with little or no connection between related services and markets that do not promote asset sharing, such as customer information.

However, Finland offers a particularly interesting context for studying the effects of digitalization on human well-being. Numerous international indicators show that Finland is one of the most developed, competent (The Digital Economy and Society Index (DESI), 2022), reliable, and even happiest (World Happiness Report, 2022) countries in the world. One of the factors that can be considered a success is that Finland has always invested in its most important capital, the people. The relatively small population (5.5 million) in chilly Northern Europe has had no choice but to work together to succeed. This has pushed the nation to innovate in national and local cooperation across organizational boundaries. As digitalization of the society progresses, people's everyday life in Finland has received increasing attention to people's own ability to utilize digital services for their own benefit and that of their related. Empowering people to take care of their own situation can also significantly improve public health (WHO, 2006) and the national economy (Women's Empowerment and Economic Development, 2012).

Correspondingly, the Finnish society can be considered a small reference state of a democratically functioning nation, whose values, legislation, and activities are at least to some extent comparable to other democratically functioning states around the world (i.e., in North America). For example, the Finnish primary school system can be considered one of the best in the world, and other countries also want to benchmark it.

Because the focus is on organizations that produce services, both digitalization and the use of artificial intelligence (AI) are driven primarily by the needs of organizations and administrations, in particular, due to the tasks based on legislation. Similarly, data interoperability is challenged by legislation and conflicts of interest between actors responsible for data repositories. People are seen as "customers" of particular services rather than individuals living their lives needing different services in different situations and events in life.

In contrast to this task-centricity, a Human-Centric AI Transformation (HCAIT, Figure 6.1) model aims to promote holistic well-being and a smooth everyday life in a society that utilizes AI for the benefit of the people. The planning of activities and service paths is guided by different situations and events in people's lives. The well-being of people is supported through extensive cross-sectoral cooperation. Digitalization and the use of AI aims at improving the flow of life. Data interoperability enables a well-being-enhancing data economy and people's ability to manage information about themselves.

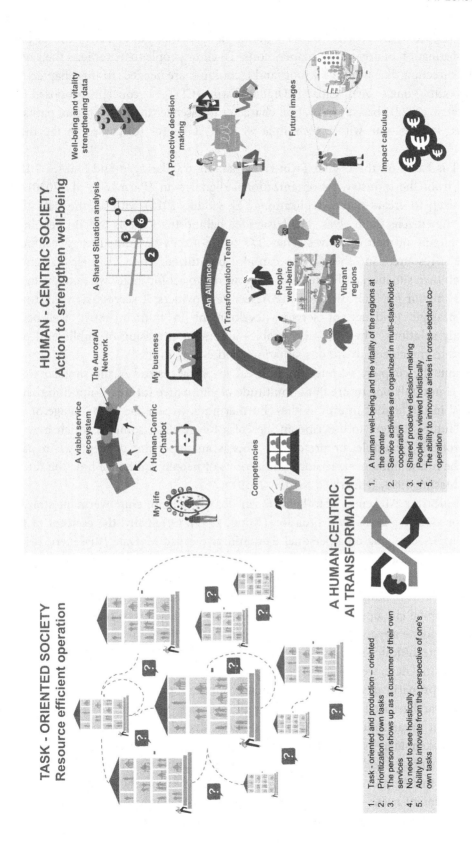

FIGURE 6.1 A Human-Centric AI Transformation (HCAIT) of a Finnish Society, model model version 1.1. Derived from The Finnish National Artificial Intelligence Program AuroraAI, Ministry of Finance, Finland (The Finnish National Artificial Intelligence Program AuroraAI, 2022).

One key feature of the HCAIT model is that it views a citizen as an active role as part of the transformation of organization operations. To allow people to better lead their own lives in the direction they want, new tools and techniques are needed. In this chapter, we propose creating one's own Citizen Digital Twin (CDT, a concept proposed by Kopponen et al. (2022))-based exploration character to discover their own future paths to their desired futures state with a technique we call AI Lenses (discussed in the third section).

The CDT is based on the Digital Twin (DT) paradigm (Glaessgen and Stargel, 2012) originating from the industry, or organizational digital twin (Parmar et al., 2020). It allows a citizen to create digital replications (El Saddik, 2018) with all the data that pertains to the citizens themselves. The basic idea behind the CDT is to help people to form a big picture of their own lives. The CDT will not only be limited to government data, but data resources in other sectors can also be utilized. The CDT helps a person perceive their own situation and to become empowered to act for their own good, using it like a digital mirror for their own good. For service providers, it serves as an informed basis for strategic guidance of service development in human-centric well-being strengthening solutions. The CDT also enables automatic provision of public and private services to the citizen in various situations and events in life.

Throughout the chapter, we refer to "futures" in plural instead of the singular form since there is not only one future but a multitude of alternative futures – a notion that is fundamental in the field of futures studies. Furthermore, we use the term "image of the future" or "futures image" to describe an idea of a future state, some of which may be possible, probable, plausible, or preferable. This is an important concept, as in part, images of the future influence decisions and actions of people and hence how the future is shaped (Masini, 1993; Bell, 1997; Sardar, 2010).

The goal of using AI Lenses is to help in self-observation, an empowerment strategy proposed for assessing one's own situation (Kopp, 1989). Originally, the concept of the CDT was proposed relying on a personal data initiative called MyData (Rissanen, 2016), but it has grown to also include other data sources, some of which can be provided by the citizen to explore different paths that exist, with different choices. Moreover, people's lives consist of a wide number of events regarding the consequences of actions, such as moving to a capital city opens new opportunities, if such data can be made in a fashion that does not violate anyone's privacy. We believe that such noninvasive use of existing data sets is a technical issue, not a principal one, and by offering better tools for managing personal data, we can improve the present-day situation (Herrera et al., 2021).

AI Lenses is primarily designed for personal use, but the approach can also extend to the organizational and societal levels. In democratic societies, where power is distributed among different organizations throughout society, a shared vision among citizens and institutional stakeholders is needed to legitimize and execute reforms. Such visions are formed by studying and seeking consensus through different future images – both positive and negative – that help in understanding the implications to society. When forming the images, the different needs of citizens should be considered, and various divergent paths through life must be supported to embrace inclusion and prevent exclusion. The ability to form a shared vision becomes particularly important at a time when solutions based on AI are being widely adopted in society. Without the ability to form a shared vision of a society that utilizes modern technology and AI, development can lead to an undesirable future for different actors, which could otherwise be avoided. Tensions arise because, for example, the increase in turnover sought by the tobacco industry by expanding its product portfolio does not necessarily increase people's well-being, but may even weaken it.

The chapter is structured as follows. First, we provide background and motivation for our work. Then, we present the concept of AI Lenses to support people's decision-making to act for their future goals in the long run. The concept is demonstrated with a design case, where futures images are used as a tool for probing the well-being of the Finnish youth. Then, we provide an extended discussion including dialogue between opportunities and tensions, and regarding the lessons learned in the process of creating and applying AI Lenses in practice. Finally, towards the end of the chapter, we draw some conclusions.

BACKGROUND AND MOTIVATION

People have always been fascinated by the course of human life and the decisions that affect it at different stages of life. Stories of Gilgamesh (Gilgamesh, Wikipedia, 2022) and the likes have spurred the imagination for decades, and at the same time, they have also inspired self-observation with respect to one's own actions. In the various twists and turns of life, one must be able to make decisions, but without one's own, more far-reaching sense of purpose and dreams, life may only drift from moment to moment and year to year. Therefore, people who want and are able to dream of something better are also in a better position to achieve them, than people who live in the moment without thinking about the future, their desires or the long-term consequences of their actions.

With such interest in personal development – be it fictional or real historical events – it is somewhat surprising that the only link between the games, fiction, and history is usually just our own perception and context. However, this perception and context comes from humans who play games or read books. In particular, we still have not seen a game where a person could participate in a simulation concerning their own life with their own data and desires. We hypothesize that such a simulation would help a person envision what their own life could look like and how choices made in life have an impact on how it will go. Because gaming is natural for different age groups, a gaming environment can increase the security of exploring different options in your own life: What if I start smoking tobacco? What if I go to a vocational school instead of a high school?

Citizen Digital Twin

Digital and physical worlds are in the process of becoming entangled. Various wearable devices and systems have increased people's interest in collecting information about themselves and using it to promote their own health and well-being. We are increasingly confronted with devices that people are willing to invest in and carry as part of their own daily lives. As a result, the amount of data on people's lives, activities, physiological characteristics, and the like has increased significantly. However, well-being-promoting systems mainly focus on improving individual characteristics, for example, an intelligent wristband helps to understand heart rate or its variability, movement, sleep quality, and so on. Even smart breathing exercise devices have been brought to people. Each of these systems usually include some form of a digital service that helps a person take full advantage of the device for their own benefit. Over the years, the services have developed to be even easier to use, more comprehensible and to be used in everyday life. As the ease of use and affordability of these devices increases, so does their usage, and more ordinary people are able to take advantage of them. Typically, the services and data collected by the devices are managed within that device and its service and only a few integrative services are available. Google Fit, for example, is focused on compiling health data and is one of the world's largest integrators from a human perspective.

However, we have not yet seen services that look at people as a whole, since physical health can be seen as only one part of overall well-being. For example, someone may become a millionaire at a young age by coding, but health metrics show that immobility means that at an older age one cannot enjoy a very comfortable life. The holistic well-being of a human consists of other elements, too. For example, according to Stiglitz et al. (2010), well-being can be viewed through eight complementary dimensions (i) material living standards (income, consumption, and wealth), (ii) health, (iii) education, (iv) personal activities including work, (v) political voice and governance, (vi) social connections and relationships, (vii) environment (present and future conditions), (viii) insecurity, of an economic as well as a physical nature.

Together, these dimensions improve the self-image of our own situation. For example, health data could show well-being even when social connections and relationships have suffered or economic activity is not at the level one would like or require. However, this data already exists in both private and public sector data resources. By forming a more holistic view of one's own situation from this information, the so-called CDT can be built, which seeks to imitate a data-based picture of one's own situation.

Our CDT is a new technique intended to help people better understand and manage their daily lives (Kopponen et al., 2022), building on data access and computational infrastructure. The basic idea behind the CDT is to help people form an informative image of their own lives, based on both government information and data resources in other sectors. The CDT helps a person perceive their own situation and to become empowered to act for their own good. For service providers, CDTs serve as an informed basis for strategic guidance of service development in holistic well-being strengthening solutions. The CDT also enables automatic provision of public and private services to citizens in various situations and events in life.

Digital Service Path Formation Problem

Each of us (as citizens) can form our own situational analysis without CDTs or information systems, but real knowledge management is usually reinforced with objective and integrative data to either validate our own subjective perception or open our eyes to look at consequences of our actions that we have not considered at all. Similarly, the problem of perceiving relevant services purely from one's own point of view just by searching for them on the Internet is much more challenging when the information in one's own head is not automatically communicated to the search engine. Human–machine interaction should allow information systems to see the person as a whole instead of individual data sources and perspectives. For example, if a person wants to outline future paths towards their goals such as desired profession, they have to gather understanding from various sources, such as search engines and other online services, making the whole seem confusing, and they may not be able to make meaningful decisions for themselves. Decisions about the next place to study, for example, may be based purely on discussions in one's own family, with a tutor and friends, and surfing on the Internet. Based on these, the decision to study a certain degree, for example, maybe on a very fragile basis. It is challenging for a person to communicate their own situation and their own dreams to service providers' information systems so that the systems could provide the best possible options to move in the direction they want in their own lives. Correspondingly, service information systems are currently not in a very good position to inform people about changes in the society at large. For example, when making decisions about future career and educational choices, it would be in the interest of the individual and society to anticipate possible changes and future opportunities, for example at the time of the expected graduation, rather than simply acting on one's own current needs or information about the system's present – or worst – past states. For these reasons, AI Lenses' concept is based on futures images on which future paths can be built. Futures images seek to describe the society that the future paths might lead to.

Who Controls the Development of Our Society and Its Services?

One of the characteristics that guides the development of society is the incentive of private service providers to provide services to people based on their own starting points and commercial interests, not so much in terms of people's real needs, goals, or the strengthening of human overall well-being. For example, applications that optimize advertising are primarily based on commercial interests and business-to-business agreements. By changing this perspective, an opportunity can be created for the person herself to influence the development of society's services. By helping people to create an overall picture of themselves based on different sources of information, digital services can also be developed to improve well-being and build alternative service paths toward the desired futures images.

In general, people's (citizens') lives are moving in some direction that is under internal and external pressures. Internal pressures can come from one's own goals, while external pressures can be, for example, social or societal. Depending on the society, people are either pushed, pulled or empowered by the interests of those in power, or people are allowed to make as many voluntary choices as possible. A private actor might want to influence a person's decision-making, for example, to study at a high-end private university that aims to do business through teaching and research. In the midst of these different interests, people's ability to plan for their own dreams and goals may be forgotten or at least won't be prioritized.

All the above developments lead to the convergence of different technologies and eventually between technology and people. It is therefore important to support citizens in making informed decisions where their own needs and dreams are part of planning their futures and putting them into practice. Service providers also have a critical role to play in the human-centric service development, to which the HCAIT framework (Figure 6.1) contributes.

Achieving Goals and Desirable Futures by Developing Futures Consciousness

In a world of instant gratification (Cheng et al., 2012) built into the systems and services people use daily and fighting for their attention, individuals are guided towards short-term actions without thinking about the longer term effects of their actions or inactions, and thus become less prone to making an effort for something that may only be achieved through years of consistent work. If people lack dreams, the foundation of society's future begins to erode. As Polak (1973) says, "[t]he rise and fall of images of the future precedes or accompanies the rise and fall of cultures".

Personal visions provide meaning to life, help make changes to career and life, and coach oneself to realize personal dreams (van der Helm, 2009). However, people don't always act in their best interests. For example, while changing negative habits is clearly beneficial, it is also difficult. Achieving one's own dreams requires the ability to imagine and reflect on their own desired futures, and make decisions that are favorable to themselves in the long term so that the desired futures are a little closer after the decisions. This in turn requires futures consciousness, the capacity of individuals or organizations for considering future consequences, possessing a sense of empowerment to influence their own actions, considering alternatives with openness, having a holistic and systemic perspective on society, and pushing to create a better future for themselves and others (Ahvenharju et al., 2018) or in short "the human capacity to understand, anticipate, prepare for, and embrace the future" (Ahvenharju et al., 2021). Thus, developing services and technologies supporting and especially helping to develop this capacity and personal futures should be the goal for both public and private organizations. Possible future paths generated with AI Lenses and based on one's own CDT offer the individual better conditions to make informed decisions in order to achieve desired future states.

Sample Paths to the Future: Preferred Images of the Future of the Finnish Youth

The concept of a human-centric and proactive society is built through different situations and events in life, one at a time. As an example, we report on a study (Villman, 2021) on young persons' life situations and events, involving young people (13–16-year-olds in basic education) as well as experts and decision-makers from different fields across sectoral boundaries. The study process consisted of (i) assessing the current situation of the 13–16-year-olds in basic education; (ii) identifying forces of change; (iii) creating and evaluating future-oriented statements; (iv) constructing alternative images of the future for the life event; (v) constructing images of preferred futures (see Figure 6.2), and (vi) evaluating the preferred futures images. Through participatory visioning, active

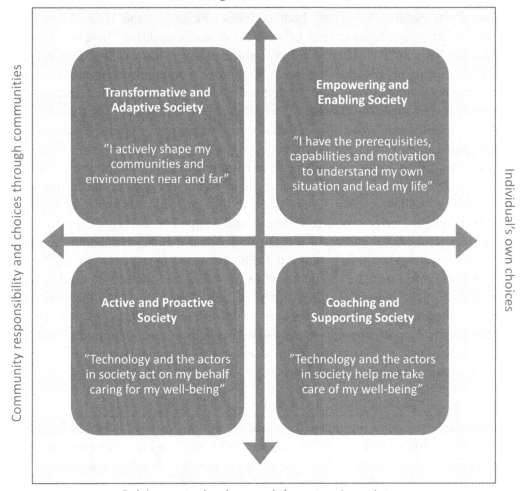

FIGURE 6.2 The preferred futures of a Human-Centric Society in Finland 2040 from the perspective of 13–16-year-olds in basic education (Adapted from Villman, 2021; Villman and Kopponen, 2020).

discussion was made possible and shared desirable images of the future of what a human-centric and proactive society can mean in all its desirability and why it is worth pursuing as a direction were constructed. By taking a bold stand on current problems, such as the COVID pandemic, which seem insurmountable, and looking far enough, it was possible to break free from the acute challenges of everyday life and to create the belief that solutions can be found over time through shared direction, commitment, and action. Visioning seemed to serve as a common platform for encounters, dialogue, learning, and the direction of change so that everyone could realize the vision from their own starting points (Villman, 2021).

The results of the process are portrayed in the form of preferred futures images of a human-centric society in Finland in 2040 from the perspective of 13–16-year-olds in basic education (see Figure 6.2). While constructing alternative futures images during the process, it was possible to identify both desirable and undesirable characteristics regarding the futures and tensions even between the desirable qualities. Then, based on the tensions, the logic for the preferred futures as a matrix was formed. In Figure 6.2, the horizontal axis represents the continuum between "Community responsibility and choices through communities" and "Individual's own choices", and the vertical axis between "Trusting one's own abilities" and "Relying on technology and the actors in society". Jointly, the axes create a set of four distinctive images of preferred futures, which can coexist.

Overall, according to the citizens' preferred future images of their future society, a human-centric society creates opportunities for everyone for holistic well-being while considering and valuing individual differences and the goals of sustainable development (translated from the original source (Villman and Kopponen, 2020)). People have the prerequisites, capabilities, and motivation to understand their own situations and lead their own lives. In addition, technology and different actors in society work together to coach and help people take care of their well-being. When the situation demands it, they act on behalf of the individual, caring for their well-being. Otherwise, they empower people by automating mandatory duties and tasks on their behalf. In this way, people have the ability, support, and opportunity to actively shape their communities and environment, both near and far as part of the communities in which their voices are heard and which adapt according to their needs.

AI LENSES: PATH-BUILDING TO DESIRED FUTURES

Technical support can be introduced to study the options that are available for an individual. The future images make it possible to form desired and undesired images of the future in different situations and events in life. Similarly, a situational analysis of the present moment can be formed utilizing the CDT, which provides an opportunity to understand a person's situation at that very moment.

To examine advancing from the current state towards the desired future, we propose using our AI Lenses (see Figure 6.3 and Table 6.1). With the help of AI Lenses, a Futures Map (Kuusi et al., 2015a, 2015b) connecting personal visions with suggestions of possible paths can be created for the individual to move toward her desired future states. Path creation can be based on data in various information systems, relying on statistics, decision trees, input from personal data sources such as personal health records or measured well-being data, different types of self-assessments made by the individuals, and AI-based techniques such as reinforcement learning about the value of the recommendations made to the user and thereby learns to make more specific recommendations to future users of the service.

Overview

AI Lenses (see Figure 6.3) is a technique that one can use to take the steps toward one's desired futures. Many future images are often also based on role models. Role models can be, for example, athletes, successful persons in business or otherwise only

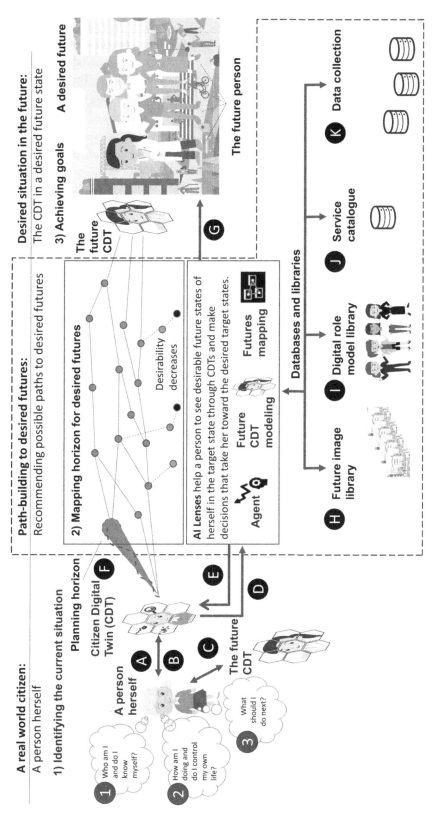

FIGURE 6.3 AI lenses provide a technique for an individual to see possible paths towards desired future states. Labels A–K elaborates opportunities and tensions in discussion section.

TABLE 6.1   Defining Elements for AI Lenses

	Citizen	Path-building to desired futures	Desired situation in the future
Perspective	A person himself/herself	Recommending possible paths to desired futures	The CDT in the desired future state
Phase	1) Identifying the current situation from which to shape future paths to achieve her own goals	2) Mapping the horizon for desired futures gives alternative paths for a person to move toward the desired state and avoid not-desired ones.	3) Achieving goals through the informed decision-making
Elements (in Figure 6.3)	**A person herself** building a situational analysis and acting for her own good by discovering answers to the following questions: 1. Who am I and do I know myself? 2. How am I doing and do I control my own life? 3. What should I do next?	**AI Lenses** help a person to see desirable future states of herself in the target state through CDT and make decisions that take her toward the desired target states.	**The future CDT** in a desired state
	Citizen Digital Twin (CDT) helps to identify their own current situation for building future paths and achieving her own goals	**Agent** suggests possible paths and services to proceed in life based on CDT state and its possible history data. It learns (reinforcement learning) by trial and error from its own actions using feedback from people using their CDTs.	**The future person** in a desired state or other desirable futures states
	The future CDT in a desired state	**Futures map** is generated with the individual to outline possible paths and desirable futures using the role model library that describes example paths to different target states.	**The future image** reflects the context in which the future CDT will be formed.
	Planning horizon for a person to commit to the next steps toward their desired state	**Future CDT modeling** is done using the current state of the CDT, its historical data, a role model library, and selected futures images that create the context for The Future CDT.	

successful in one's own life, which a person sees as if one wants to reach a similar situation in her own life. Similarly, these role models can be taken into a digital form as "a role model CDT" to outline the paths these people have actually taken in their own lives to reach their current CDT state. From the combination of these role models and the images of the future, AI Lenses form a Futures Map and possible paths that a person herself can set out to explore and act on. It should be emphasized, however, that the person herself must make choices about which paths and services she wants to use in each situation.

Simply put, AI Lenses is a technique to provide life scenarios, based on one's own current situation, personal desired goals, and existing data gathered in various services about people in general. It can be regarded as analogous to systems where AI generates a book, based on existing books, other data, and themes provided by humans. Here, the starting point is the CDT, which models the citizen situation at present, based on existing data. The personal goals are then something AI Lenses aims at, based on different choices that take one towards meeting the goals. These choices are supported by national data sets, such as statistics on income, health, profession, and so on. The role of AI is to learn to recommend paths that are most likely to lead toward desired goals.

In addition to the CDT, the AI Lenses apply the conceptual framework Futures Map on the level of individuals to portray the outcomes of their personal futures research processes. While a map consists of symbols and patterns depicting physical scenery, the Futures Map represents a dynamic futures scenery consisting of a vision portraying the preferred futures images, future states as images of alternative futures, and possible paths as scenarios on the Mapping horizon, events and decisions as bifurcation points, and the committed path, a roadmap, on the Planning horizon (Kuusi et al., 2015a). By combining visioning, long-term thinking, short-term planning, action, and reflection it is possible to embrace conscious future-making, learning, emerging opportunities, and uncertainty related to the future. For example, when new information, such as new job opportunities arises, the actor using the Futures Map should reassess the contents of it and change courses of action when necessary to be able to move towards their goals, while being aware of and adapting to both internal and external changes (Villman, 2021; Kuusi et al., 2015a).

The goal of AI Lenses is to support making decisions regarding one's own future, by generating paths to the future, aiming at reaching the desired goals. These paths then allow self-reflection regarding the different options and opportunities. Furthermore, the paths can also be used to identify decisions that may lead to undesirable outcomes. Obviously, scenarios generated by the AI Lenses do not predict the future – there are so many things in life that happen by chance, and things can go wrong, changing paths to the future, even collapsing at worst – but they can act as a tool for considering one's own plans for the future. As Amara (1981) states, the future is not predictable, nor predetermined, but future outcomes may be influenced by choices. Furthermore, personal and environmental characteristics that are not included in the CDT used to generate the paths can either foster or hinder progress.

For society and organizations, AI Lenses can help understand the desired and undesired paths to the future at the population level. Then, informed decisions can be taken on how to develop the society and its services in a fashion that takes the view of individuals into account, enabling them to meet their own goals. This in turn can catalyze the transformation towards a more human-centric society, where public and private services are based on the known needs of citizens, instead of today's model where organizational structures and obligations defined by law form the baseline for public services and markets to define the winners and losers in the private sector.

The CDTs, futures images, and the pathways to reach the desired states also provide new opportunities for service providers to provide services that genuinely support people on their way to their target state. At its best, this type of data contributes to the realization of a human-centric society, with the incentive of organizations operating in the market to produce the services that people really need.

It is recognized that the full-scale implementation of AI Lenses in the short term is hard, due to numerous factors, such as technical and semantic interoperability of futures images, role models, and CDTs. However, AI Lenses could be implemented through targeted populations that benefit a lot from the ability to consider one's actions and their long-term consequences. From this perspective, one promising target group is the Finnish youth because there is anxiety about the future (Doygun and Gulec, 2012). This anxiety can be treated by studying the different scenarios that can be generated, starting from one's own life situation. Furthermore, the resulting scenarios also contribute to a better understanding of the desired futures of the youth and for the youth.

Using AI Lenses is a continuous, even lifelong process in nature that learns and evolves from user behavior and user feedback. The usefulness and interest of the paths recommended by AI Lenses to the user will increase as AI Lenses gain access to the paths and decisions made by people in a similar situation.

A Hypothetical Scenario

Helen (a fictional character) is an eighth-grade comprehensive school student who has begun to reflect on the direction of her own life and the time after next year when her basic education is over. The study counselor has helped Helen understand her own situation and opportunities to move on to the next stage in her own studies. However, Helen has been uncertain about the direction of her own life, which she has sought to outline in conversations with her parents, loved ones, and especially her friends. At the confirmation class, Helen has become acquainted with a "How You Are Doing?" application that has given her a better picture of her own situation with the help of her own CDT. This picture has helped Helen reflect on the current situation and understand her own starting point for the next stage of life after the comprehensive school. A better understanding of her own situation and opportunities has allowed Helen to form new kinds of future images of where she might end up in her life and what she could achieve.

After creating her own CDT in the confirmation class, Helen uses a service that allows her to have a new dialogue about her future CDT. The future CDT modeling is similar to the CDT state modeling in the confirmation class, with the difference that it draws the desired state of the future with the help of AI Lenses. The Future CDT of Helen is formed through a dialogue in which AI Lenses engages in a dialogue of goals and desires, but does so that AI Lenses leverages knowledge of the CDT state to make the future CDT more realistic and achievable.

After a dialogue between Helen and AI Lenses, Futures map service makes the decision as to which future image best fits the context for the future CDT described by Helen. The future image is chosen from the future image library, which contains the pre-processed desired futures of society (see the chapter "Sample Paths to the Future: Preferred Images of the Future of the Finnish Youth"), which Helen does not have to form herself. In addition, AI Lenses makes use of the digital role model library and, together with Helen, seeks to outline whether there are people in the library who have already achieved similar goals, who have described their own situation in their goal (role model) and the paths that led to it. Based on this, Helen selects the role models closest to her goals that she glorified and could imagine aiming for. Utilizing selected role models and other dialogue, AI Lenses forms the future CDT, against which Helen reflects on her own goals. When Helen finds that the future CDT meets her own goals, AI Lenses begins to form the mapping horizon toward the desired state. The mapping horizon forms possible paths and services to be utilized along the way, as well as action proposals that lead towards the goal and have typically been utilized by the chosen role models.

The mapping horizon describes to Helen possible paths along which it is possible for Helen to get closer to her target state. People prefer to take the reward immediately rather than commit to longer-term work for a bigger reward (Cheng et al., 2012). Thus, Helen's planning horizon is made so short that Helen wants to commit to it. Once the picture of the possible paths has been formed, Helen herself makes the decision to commit to the first stage of the path she has chosen, which in this case is just a little bit further to improve mathematics studies towards the ninth grade to allow Helen to increase her probability to move to a sports high school in the neighboring city. As Helen makes these small decisions, another goal-oriented life begins that supports Helen's progress toward her goal state.

First-Hand Experiences in Implementing AI Lenses

The concept of AI Lenses is presently at an early stage, and many of its long-term implications and lessons are still to be discovered. However, the context of the concept offers practical evidence of its feasibility. A common denominator to the research is the Finnish Artificial Intelligence Program AuroraAI of Finland, based on a vision of a human-centric and proactive society (The Finnish National Artificial Intelligence Program AuroraAI, 2022).

A core part of the vision is that all actors of society are incentivized to collaborate to enable people to seamlessly manage the different decisions and events they face during all the stages of their lives instead of focusing only on the organizational responsibilities and efficiency. The change is aimed at increasing the improvement of overall individual well-being benefitting the people, organizations, and society, since "[a] human-centric society is based on the holistic welfare of its people, businesses and society as a whole" (The Finnish National Artificial Intelligence Program AuroraAI, 2022). It is on the basis of acknowledging and harnessing this diversity that a vision portraying a shared ambition can be created to bring people together. In addition to people, the vision should look at the role of AI as part of the transformation, since advanced technologies such as AI need to be considered as actors as well.

To make the vision more concrete, an approach based on life events and different stages in life has been introduced, such as a professional immigrating to Finland, a teenager moving to a different city to study, or an elderly person who faces the risk of unemployment. Then, integrated services have been built at a societal scale, to help citizens in these particular life events. Because one goal of the services is to help people to better understand their situation and possible actions, these life events and related services can be regarded as AI Lenses components for mapping horizon, enabling still very limited service provision toward the desired state. These experiments with life events have demonstrated to us that it is feasible to combine data from different sources, covering both public and private sectors, to help in forming paths to the future.

As for constituting CDTs, the "How You Are Doing?" application mentioned in Helen's scenario is the most concrete vehicle to understand one's own everyday situation, based on input and signals from different stakeholders that help to build CDTs in different contexts. From the perspective of AI Lenses, the application provides a view of a person's situation on day zero, that is, how are you doing today. As the next steps to concretize AI Lenses, we plan to build the tools and services to increase the visibility to the different possible futures, based on paths that one wishes to study.

DISCUSSION

At the individual level, people can improve their quality of life holistically through the data-strengthened self-image that a CDT enables, concretizing other shared visions such as OECD Learning Framework 2030 (OECD, 2022). Service providers hoard data about people anyway. New types of incentive models can unleash the potential of data for the human good instead of narrow monetary benefits (Parvinen et al., 2020). Self-images created at the societal-level and population-level analyses compiled from them also provide significant added value to the public sector and market participants, as a holistic understanding allows people to assess their own needs and dreams to evolve. Analyses can be provided with respect of individual protection so that they only describe human characteristics at the population level. An individual-level picture of the situation is owned by the person himself.

Our proposed concept of AI Lenses strengthens people's (citizens') ability to lead their own future toward their desired future images. Otherwise, a person will end up being only a part of the visions of others. Properly utilized, AI Lenses create the conditions for a human-centric society to be built on the real needs, goals, and dreams of its members. In addition, organizations can take advantage of their members' goals to develop their own operations and services. This strengthens people's ability to dream for themselves in a better way while providing the most real-time information possible to support the change in the way organizations operate.

Overall, the envisioned AI Lenses could facilitate the transformation depicted in Figure 6.1 toward more human-centric, preferable digital technology-enabled societies. It supports forming the futures images, shared situation analysis and proactive decision-making (see the right-hand side of Figure 6.1). Considering the preferred images of the futures in Figure 6.2, AI Lenses would give new means to the futures of a Coaching and

Supporting Society and the Active and Proactive Society. In addition, the focus of the AI Lenses can vary. For example, in the Empowering and Enabling Society the focus could be on the Planning horizon helping to optimize everyday life, and in the Transformative and Adaptive Society in finding ways to shape the environment.

Data from different life events vary, and existing data sources are not typically designed to be combined in life events or between other data sources. Lack of data consistency and different interpretations of concepts can also easily lead to erroneous conclusions. Similarly, protecting privacy can be challenging with certain parameters. While, in principle, the future paths could be public, they could lead to private issues. Coincidences, timing, and context also play a big role, so the data can be somewhat misleading; on the other hand, these cannot be distinguished directly from the data, because what seems to be a coincidence, however, may be a trend.

The CDT is principally a technological vehicle of collecting and integrating citizens' dynamic data from various sources over time. As such, it could incorporate life logs of possibly covering the entire life cycles of citizens. For instance, it could include full records of personal health data starting from the genomic data of each individual. AI Lenses could utilize such data for example to assess the plausibility of the desired futures envisioned by each individual citizen.

A core question, Stevenson (2006) asks, is "who has the right and the competence to construct and select a preferred vision on behalf of any social unit and to work backwards towards enacting the journey into the future?" Answering to this challenge with AI Lenses raises opportunities and tensions (see Table 6.2) which themselves provide a way to weigh ethical perspectives to take advantage of AI Lenses. It is also worth considering whether it is ethical not to improve people's ability to plan their own future from their own starting point.

AI Lenses also raise questions about citizens' equality and the ability to take advantage of the solution to their own advantage. The questions are not easy to answer, given the myriad different needs and constraints of people. Digital Equality draws attention to the fact that everyone has both the opportunity and the adequate knowledge and skills to use a variety of digital services. These digital skills contribute to self-development through AI Lenses. The DESI summarizes indicators on Europe's digital performance and tracks the progress of EU countries (The Digital Economy and Society Index (DESI), 2022). According to the DESI, people's digital abilities in Finland are the best in the EU. According to the study, 76% have basic skills and 50% have above-basic skills (against the EU average of 56% and 31%, respectively) (DESI Country Profile, 2022). On the other hand, it means that up to 24% of the population of the best country lacks basic skills. Achieving equality requires, in particular, the identification and consideration of these 24% needs in the development of AI Lenses.

To conclude, the concept of the proposed AI Lenses includes numerous opportunities to harness AI to pursue people's dreams and thereby put a human-centric society into practice. However, the concept is still in its infancy, so it naturally has a significant number of limitations to consider. First, the implementation should focus on carefully selected life events in which futures thinking and guidance is known to play a significant role or could

TABLE 6.2 Potential Opportunities and Tensions When Applying the Proposed AI Lenses Technique

Labels in Figure 6.3	Description	Opportunities	Tensions
	Interaction		
A	Person interaction with the CDT Service: Defining life situation, service selection, user attributes, data consent for service providers.	Strengthens the knowledge management of one's own situation by combining one's own objective well-being data with subjective experience. Improves taking conscious action toward a person's own desired future images.	The visualization of one's own situation as a CDT Service may not correspond to one's own perception of her situation. The utilized data may also be incomplete or even incorrect.
B	Person reflection by herself: The CDT Service visualizes CDT models and service discovery towards desired future states.	The CDT-based reflection enables the improvement of the subjective self-image with objective data, reducing the biases that arise in a person's own imagery.	The ability to deal with one's own future varies. The user may be empowered by the crude real-life situation analysis, while the more unfortunate person in life may need the support of other people much more.
C	Person interaction with the CDT in a desired future state: Gives a picture of the target state she wants to set for herself by AI Lenses.	Improves one's ability to dream her state of purpose subjectively and objectively. Helps to understand the characteristics associated with the target state.	A person herself may not recognize her own goals, so building a future CDT may be based on one's own limitations or unrealistic imaginations of thinking about her future.
D	CDT State provides information on the CDT situation and how it is been evolving.	CDT State is a replica of the person based on a description and data that a person has given to the system. CDT State allows future planning to be based on holistic and realistic starting points.	Because the human real situation is based on subjective experience and objective data, the digitization of the human situation appears exactly as it was done at a given point in time. Moreover, the CDT State is only one possible projection of the current state, which can also be described in other ways. Incomplete and incorrect information directly affects the condition of the CDT State.
E	Suggestions for possible paths to proceed to the future CDT state.	Supports people to outline possible and realistic paths to progress toward their own desired state. It also helps to understand surprising paths that a person would not normally consider due to their own living environment or the people around them.	Possible paths give only a few options to progress towards the target state. Several options may cause a paradox of choice.
F	A person commits to the next steps towards the desired state in the planning horizon.	Supports a person's commitment to choose and take some (even small) action that lead toward the desired state. Helps to concretely understand what a person needs to do next and what services will help.	Decision-making might be based only on the paths presented by the system, in which case one might not think of other alternatives. It may also be that the proposed path requires more than the person is willing or able to commit to working to get the path forward.

G	Desired future context to be used is selected by AI Lenses based on the CDT.	The future images provide the context for one's own future CDT. Future images are carefully prepared perceptions of the point in time at which your own goals are set. They allow the future CDT to be placed in the most probabilistic context possible.	The context of the future image may change as a person's own situation changes. For example, when one's own life situation changes, the context may also need to be re-examined. AI Lenses may also make false assumptions based on incorrectly entered inputs.

Databases and libraries

H	Future image library provides a context for alternative future images in different situations and events in life.	Carefully prepared future images can be provided as a basis for individuals to plan for their own future. Creating future images of a society in different situations and events in life requires a lot of work that a person does not have to do themselves.	Future images offer some possible future prospects. However, they are not limited to them, as the future cannot be predicted. A person may think that futures are predefined, in which case their own thinking is limited to the given future images.
I	Digital role model library describes the CDTs of people in the target state and the paths that led to it.	Enables the description of realistic and desirable role models for the utilization of individuals and to support their own goal setting. It attracts those who have already achieved the goals to describe their own path towards the achieved goals as exemplary performances.	Digital role models, that give just some ideas of possible desired states, can cause anxiety in people planning for their own future. Many goals really require a lot of work, commitment, and prioritization, which may only become clear afterwards. Many goals could not be achieved if you knew in advance the amount of work required.
J	Service catalog with information about the correspondence of services to different target paths.	Forms an understanding of the services that lead to the desired goal. Helps to understand what kind of services have been useful for people who have achieved similar goals. Using the database, AI Lenses generates service recommendations toward the desired state.	The service information offers only some service possibilities, in which case the person must be able to perceive other services and activities as well.
K	Data collection such as open data or MyData from government officials and private companies) and the CDT models built with the service).	Helps refine the objective knowledge base for AI Lenses' operations, the state of the CDT, and the realism of the future CDT. Reduces the risk of forming a false picture of the person himself.	Data protection issues, as well as ethical issues regarding the use of data, may pose challenges to building a holistic and objective CDT model. For some, the brutality of their own snapshot can be difficult to deal with.

result in beneficial impacts. Second, fostering creativity and experiential aspects of the concept require further research since futures are open for previously unseen possibilities. Third, the formation of desirable future images requires extensive and open cooperation with various stakeholders in order to discover the shared boundaries of preferred futures, which enable the development of many different, yet still desirable futures (see, for example, van der Helm, 2009). Fourth, building a meaningful service ecosystem requires a commitment from service providers as well to develop their services to support people's goal setting and achieving a new kind of value creation in collaboration with different organizations. In addition to the limitations presented, potential technical and possibly also privacy constraints will be identified as the implementation of AI Lenses progresses.

CONCLUSIONS

Desirable and shared societal visions act as a common platform for encounters, dialogue, learning together, and the direction of change, so that everyone can implement the vision from their own starting point. Furthermore, by taking a bold stand on current, seemingly insurmountable problems and looking far enough, societies can look beyond the acute challenges of everyday life and create trust that solutions can be found over time through shared intentions, commitment and action. Through and with the help of AI Lenses proposed in this chapter, it is possible to have an active discussion and create a shared image of what a human-centric and proactive society can mean in all its desirability and why it is worth pursuing as a direction for individuals as well as stakeholders of society.

Without a holistic and systemic view of the impacts of technology and AI on human well-being, equality, and, for example, equality issues, we will not be able to steer the direction of development in the desired way. As Meadows et al. (1992). describe, a "[v]ision without action is useless. But action without vision does not know where to go or why to go there. Vision is absolutely necessary to guide and motivate action. More than that, vision, when widely shared and firmly kept in sight, brings into being new systems".

AI Lenses is a technique based on strengthening people's overall well-being through the achievement of people's own dreams. At the same time, it helps different actors in society to renew their operations to increase their value for their own businesses as well as people who are impacted by their services. AI Lenses provide support to tackle systemic challenges through people's own actions. It can also provide a real opportunity to defend people's own ability to make what they want out of their lives and improve their chances of achieving their own life goals while harnessing opportunities over tensions. The more organizations learn about people's needs toward their goals, the more organizations learn to provide proactive services that help people move toward them.

REFERENCES

Ahvenharju, S., Lalot, F., Minkkinen, M., & Quiamzade, A. (2021). Individual futures consciousness: Psychology behind the five-dimensional Futures Consciousness scale. *Futures*, *128*(April), 102708.

Ahvenharju, S., Minkkinen, M., & Lalot, F. (2018). The five dimensions of futures consciousness. *Futures*, *104*(December), 1–13.

Amara, R. (1981). The futures field: Searching for definitions and boundaries. *The Futurist*, 15(1), 25–29.

Bell, W. (1997). Foundations of futures studies: History, purposes and knowledge. *Human science for a new era*. Vol. 1. Transaction Publishers: New Brunswick.

Cheng, Y.-Y., Paichi, S., & Chiou, W.-B. (2012). Escaping the impulse to immediate gratification: The prospect concept promotes a future-oriented mindset, prompting an inclination towards delayed gratification. *British Journal of Psychology*, *103*, 129–141.

DESI Country Profile, Finland. https://ec.europa.eu/newsroom/dae/redirection/document/80484 (accessed March 20, 2022)

Doygun, O., & Gulec, S. (2012). The problems faced by university students and proposals for solution. *Procedia-Social and Behavioral Sciences*, *47*, 1115–1123.

El Saddik, A. (2018). Digital twins: The convergence of multimedia technologies. *IEEE Multimedia*, *25*(2), 87–92.

Gilgamesh, Wikipedia. https://en.wikipedia.org/wiki/Gilgamesh (accessed January 8, 2022)

Glaessgen, E., & Stargel, D. (2012). The digital twin paradigm for future NASA and U.S. Air Force vehicles. In 53rd AIAA/ASME/ASCE/AHS/ASC structures, structural dynamics and materials conference 20th AIAA/ASME/AHS adaptive structures conference 14th AIAA, p. 1818.

Herrera, J. L., Berrocal, J., Garcia-Alonso, J., Murillo, J. M., Chen, H.-Y., Julien, C., … Mikkonen, T. (2021). Personal data gentrification. *ArXiv Preprint,* arXiv:2103.17109

Kopp, J. (1989). Self-observation: An empowerment strategy in assessment. *Social Casework*, *70*(5), 276–284.

Kopponen, A., Hahto, A., Kettunen, P., Mikkonen, T., Mäkitalo, N., Nurmi, J., …Rossi, M. (2022). Empowering citizens with digital twins: A blueprint. *IEEE Internet Computing*, 1. 10.1109/MIC.2022.3159683

Kuusi, O., Cuhls, K., & Steinmüller, K. (2015a). Quality criteria for scientific futures research. *Futura*, *1*, 60–77.

Kuusi, O., Cuhls, K. & Steinmüller, K. (2015b). The futures map and its quality criteria. *European Journal of Futures Research*, *3*(1), 22.

Masini, E. B. (1993). *Why futures studies?* Grey Seal: London.

Meadows, D. H., Meadows, D. L., & Randers, J. (1992). *Beyond the limits.* Chelsea Green Publishing Company: White River Junction, VT.

OECD. The future of education and skills, Education 2030. https://www.oecd.org/education/2030/E2030%20Position%20Paper%20(05.04.2018).pdf (accessed January 8, 2022)

Parmar, R., Leiponen, A., & Thomas, L. D. (2020) Building an organizational digital twin. *Business Horizons*, *63*(6), 725–736. 10.1016/j.bushor.2020.08.001

Parvinen, P., Laitila, M., Pöyry, E., Gustafsson, R., & Rossi, M. (2020). Advancing data monetization and the creation of data-based business models. *Communications of the Association for Information Systems*, *47*(1). doi:10.17705/1CAIS.04702

Polak, F. (1973). *The image of the future.* Translated and abridged by Boulding, E. Elsevier Publishing Company: Amsterdam.

Rissanen, T. (2016). Public online services at the age of mydata: a new approach to personal data management in Finland. In: Hühnlein, D., Roßnagel, H., Schunck, C. H. & Talamo, M. (Hrsg.), Bonn: Gesellschaft für Informatik e.V.. (S. 81-92).

Sardar, Z. (2010). The namesake: Futures; futures studies; futurology; futuristic; foresight—What's in a name? *Futures*, *42*(3), 177–184.

Stevenson, T. (2006). From vision into action. *Futures*, *38*(2006), 667–672.

Stiglitz, J., Sen, A., & Fitoussi, J-P. (2010). Report by the commission on the measurement of economic performance and social progress. https://ec.europa.eu/eurostat/documents/8131721/8131772/Stiglitz-Sen-Fitoussi-Commission-report.pdf (accessed January 8, 2022)

The Digital Economy and Society Index (DESI). https://digital-strategy.ec.europa.eu/en/policies/desi (accessed March 20, 2022)

The Finnish National Artificial Intelligence Program AuroraAI. https://vm.fi/auroraai-toimintamalli (accessed January 8, 2022)

van der Helm, R. (2009). The vision phenomenon: Towards a theoretical underpinning of visions of the future and the process of envisioning. *Futures*, *41*(2), 96–104.

Villman, T. (2021). The preferred futures of a human-centric society: A case of developing a life-event-based visioning approach. Turku School of Economics, University of Turku, Turku. https://www.utupub.fi/handle/10024/151334

Villman, T., & Kopponen, A. (2020). AuroraAI-visiotyön 2020 tulokset. AuroraAI Vision theme group presentation, December 17, 2020.

What is the evidence on effectiveness of empowerment to improve health? WHO, 2006. https://www.euro.who.int/__data/assets/pdf_file/0010/74656/E88086.pdf. (accessed April 3, 2022)

Women's Empowerment and Economic Development, *Journal of Economic Literature*, 2012. https://www.nber.org/system/files/working_papers/w17702/w17702.pdf (accessed April 3, 2022)

World Happiness Report (2022). https://worldhappiness.report/ (accessed March 20, 2022)

CHAPTER 7

Artificial Intelligence in the Sports Industry

Teodor Dinca-Panaitescu[a] and Serban Dinca-Panaitescu[b]

[a]Department of Communications, York University, Toronto, Ontario, Canada
[b]School of Health Policy and Management, York University, Toronto, Ontario, Canada

CONTENTS

INTRODUCTION

Historically, sports have always played an important role in human society. From their beginnings in ancient cultures, sports have been an important form of entertainment, leisure and recreation while simultaneously teaching important lessons regarding human behaviors. In the past 100 years, the world of sports has made remarkable advancements, shifting from popular pastime to a trillion-dollar industry. Our society is evolving at a frantic pace and the sport industry is no different. The newest phenomenon which can have a pivotal impact on the sports sector is artificial intelligence (AI). Being a new tool, the impact of AI in sport is still unclear. The novelty of AI makes it particularly important to

DOI: 10.1201/9781003261247-9

analyze its potential benefits, the drawbacks as well as the lasting mark this new technology can leave on the world of sport.

Before starting the analysis, certain key terms are defined. Artificial intelligence (AI) is the capability of a technological system to analyze external data, develop learning patterns and apply those patterns in problem-solving scenarios (Wei et al., 2021). AI is extremely effective in data prediction scenarios by using algorithmic learning to make human-like decisions. A subcategory of AI is machine learning, which uses algorithms and past data to help programs improve. Machine learning falls into three categories: supervised learning, unsupervised learning, and reinforcement learning (Fialho et al., 2019). Supervised learning takes input and output data with the goal of making future predictions, while unsupervised uses only input data to group and discover regularities (Horvat & Job, 2020). Reinforcement learning, on the other hand, measures the effectiveness of an operational system. Another key term is neural networks, which represent a key part of the machine learning process generally at the heart of deep learning algorithms (Fialho et al., 2019). One more important thing to note is that all advancements in AI related to sports industry have been possible due to the large volume and availability of match and training data. This availability of data was only possible because of technological improvement in data tracking devices such as motion sensors and video image analysis.

The purpose of this chapter is to investigate the presence of AI in the sports industry from various angles. First, we will analyze to what extent AI is currently being implemented in various sectors of the sports industry. The following components will be analyzed: AI in player recruitment, AI in training, AI in maintaining the integrity of the sport, AI in sports medicine, AI in sports betting, and AI in sports journalism (Figure 7.1).

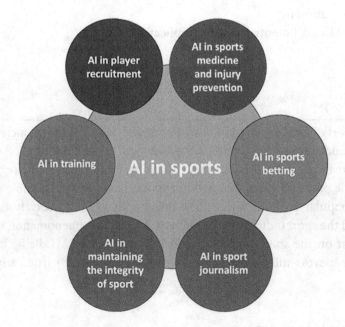

FIGURE 7.1   Applications of AI in sports.

Using a multitude of studies, we look at the positives AI has to offer such as improvements on field performance, as well as the potential ethical drawbacks regarding privacy concerns among others. Additionally, we examine the potential future applications of AI and conclude the chapter by linking our findings with their relevance to society as a whole.

AI IN MAINTAINING THE INTEGRITY OF SPORT

Sports have always been based around the fundamental rules of fair play, respect and integrity. While overcoming adversities, pushing past limits and claiming victory are also key, these elements only have meaning if the game occurred in a fair environment. In sport, the referee is responsible for maintaining parity between players or teams, his role requiring impartiality. Unfortunately, over the course of the last century, there have been many instances where the integrity of sport has been tarnished, with NBA referee Tim Donaghy being a prime example (Mallen, 2019). Donaghy bet on matches he refereed where he controlled the point spread in order to get out of debt (Mallen, 2019). While most referees attend to the integrity of sport, all referees make genuine human errors which can impact the outcome of a game. To limit these human inaccuracies digital electronic technologies have been used for many years, an example being the hawk eye system used in tennis to determine whether a ball is in or out.

While electronic technologies have been a great help in reducing wrong refereeing decisions, they are responsible for slowing down the flow of the game (Mallen, 2019). The implementation of AI on the other hand builds upon these electronic developments providing referees with real-time data in order to optimize decision making. While the implementation of AI in sports refereeing is still in its infancy, early applications are present particularly in association soccer. VAR, short for video assistant referee, is beginning to be equipped with AI elements to help with quicker refereeing decisions. Currently, AI's primary application is to aid referees with offside decisions. For example, in La Liga, Spain's first division, AI uses an automated calibration process which maps out the field of play (LaLiga, 2019). Using the real-time analysis available from broadcasting cameras, the AI computes these images in relation to a 2D model of the field, resulting in accurately drawn virtual offside lines (LaLiga, 2019). Additionally, in gymnastics, the International gymnastics federation has implemented AI technology in its competitions to help with the judging process. Fujitsu's latest Ai laser sensors and 3D modeling technology help detect movements performed by athletes with the scope of offering judges a helping hand in the difficult scoring process (Stefano, 2021). Shaped like a small box, this latest technology tracks athletic movement by analyzing exercise velocities and skeletal positions. This technology does not replace human judges but it does help them confirm difficulty scores if a gymnast contests score or if there is a large discrepancy between the scores of the judges (Keh, 2019).

The usage of AI as an assistant to referees is not exclusive to soccer or gymnastics. Baseball is another popular sport which has implemented AI to maximize decision-making optimization with the help of a system called Trackman (Nasu & Kashino, 2020). This technology determines if a pitch is a ball or a strike. Analyzing multiple details regarding pitches thrown such as velocity, trajectory, and spin rate, Trackman examines the data and creates a strike zone in relation to the pitcher's height rather than the pitcher's stance. Once Trackman determines if a throw is a ball or a strike, the data is transmitted to a tech man who then provides the data to the umpire via an ear piece (Nasu & Kashino, 2020).

AI IN TRAINING

In the 21st century, high-performance sport has become a game of fine margins. Long gone are the days where athletes could rely purely on natural talent and neglect aspects of their training such as physical preparation, diet, and recovery. The implementation of new technology combined with a data-driven approach to training has revolutionized sport. Artificial intelligence is the newest innovation which has already become a popular tool used to maximize various aspects of an athlete's training regiment (Chu et al., 2019). There are two current AI applications in training. The first is centered around the physical aspect, which looks to maximize the effectiveness of strength and conditioning work, while the second application is centered around technical training which uses AI coaching tools in sport-specific training scenarios (Chu et al., 2019).

The majority of AI applications so far in the field of strength and conditioning have been centered around weightlifting. When performed correctly, lifting weights is an excellent training method used universally by athletes to increase attributes such as strength, speed, explosiveness, and power, while simultaneously helping with injury risk minimization (Chu et al., 2019). Improper form in the weight room however can lead to serious injuries, which in some cases can be career ending. The Internet of things (IoT), which represents the interconnection via Internet of devices or sensors that can share data, has the potential to improve training. The sports IoT system uses artificial intelligence to maximize weight training efficiency. By placing IoT motion sensors such as patches or wristbands on an athlete's appendages, as well as on the machine used to perform the exercise, crucial physiological information such as exercise stroke, blood pressure, heartbeat, and breath rate is collected. The data collection process is connected with a real-time Open Pose system which provides a posture analysis of the training participant (Chu et al., 2019). Simulating a 3D model of the trainee movement patterns, a digital coach's ideal movement pattern is then merged with the trainees' in an open Sim system in order to fix discrepancies in exercise form (Chu et al., 2019). This virtual simulation of the body helps athletes understand their innate movement patterns via musculoskeletal geometry and joint kinematics. Any issues regarding form inadequacies will be detected by the virtual coach, which can be merged on a singular body part or the body as a whole depending on an athlete's personal needs. Lastly, data inputs can be used to determine levels of fatigue and reduce potential risk of injury (Chu et al., 2019).

In other instances, AI was used in weight training not only to detect correct movement patterns but also to determine movement time and velocity. By attaching sensors to weight training machines, total force and displacement data was recorded (Novatchkov & Baca, 2013). With the help of AI technology, the data collected was automatically assessed and provided individuals with feedback regarding their movement stability and ability to control the weight when performing a specific exercise (Novatchkov & Baca, 2013).

While AI plays a key role in helping athletes with their strength and conditioning work, it arguably plays an even bigger role in sport-specific training. While maintaining form when performing weight training is critical for injury prevention and maximizing muscle building potential, having the right movement patterns is even more crucial when performing sport-specific actions where the margins for error are incredibly small at the professional level. Golf is one sport which has seen athletes implement AI in their training with opening arms (Li & Cui, 2021). Golf has been a perfect candidate for AI implementations in training given its more static nature and having fewer number of external variables being a non-contact sport (Li & Cui, 2021). Similar to the IoT system used in weight training, there are many technologies which allow golfers to compare their swinging technique in relation to a virtual coach. By using wearable technology sensors placed on the joints, data can be collected, modeled, and compared to the optimized movement trajectories of a trainer (Li & Cui, 2021). One of the most popular technologies used by golfers is MySwing Professional, which is a training tool capable of tracking an athlete's movement and that of their club (Wei et al., 2021). Containing 17 wireless sensors, this full-body motion capture tool comes with a built-in software capable of replay and extensive data storage space (Wei et al., 2021). This is seen as an optimal training tool as it not only precisely records movement, but it also offers an athlete the option to analyze their technique via 3D playback analysis (Wei et al., 2021). Furthermore, athletes can compare their own swing to other golfers that have their data stored within the MySwing software. By storing all sessions, My Swing allows golfers to look back at their old sessions and see how their movement patterns change over time (Wei et al., 2021).

Other sports have also implemented AI training tools capable of performing instant data analysis and processing large amounts of data in real time. For instance, in badminton there is a training tool called pace training system which uses an action-recognition algorithm to determine a player's match pace (Wei et al., 2021). With the feedback provided by the training tool, athletes can adjust and improve their pace on the court in order to perform with greater efficiency. Additionally, taekwondo athletes have also begun using AI algorithms to learn efficient movement pattern techniques directly applicable to their respective martial art. These algorithms are based on a Support Vector Machine and act as a scientific learning tool with correctional properties that look to fix issues with body movement form (Wei et al., 2021).

AI is not only a tool used for athletic training in individual sports, but it is also widely used in team sports. Rather than focusing purely on improving an individual athlete's form or technique, AI in team sport training looks at both the individual athlete's performance level as well as their impact on the team's performance. In futsal for example, studies have been conducted using wearable technologies such as the MBody3 that not only tracks physiological data but also gather positional information regarding a player's spatial awareness on the court (Rodrigues et al., 2020). Collecting player information via electrical firing of major muscle groups located in the legs, the MBody3's data is processed and then differentiated by an algorithm which classified the data in terms of passing, shooting off the ball movement, and jumping. Given the spatial-temporal ability of the MBody3 to collect positional data, players are able to see in what areas of the field they performed certain actions, allowing them to analyze and improve their decision making in the future (Rodrigues et al., 2020).

AI is also a great tool for coaches and scouts to improve their team's performance. Intelligent analysis systems such as the SportVU in basketball provide coaching staff with critical player information and problem-solving solutions (Wei et al., 2021). Present in all NBA arenas, SportVU uses bird's eye view cameras combined with sensors to analyze every single action on the court ranging from passes to court spacing to distance covered (Wei et al., 2021). The data is stored away into a system capable of offering statistical support to analysts but also answering complex questions via data mining and machine learning methods. While it currently is only a complement to scouts and coaches to help with their decision making, it is having an impact on changing traditional coaching methods within the NBA (Wei et al., 2021).

AI IN SPORTS MEDICINE AND INJURY PREVENTION

There is a famous saying in the world of sport that an athlete's best ability is his availability. At the end of the day, it does not matter how talented or technically gifted the athletes are if they are unable to avoid constant injury. When an athlete is injured, everyone loses from the athlete himself to the entire team all the way to the ownership. Every season, the top professional sport leagues fork out millions of dollars on injured player wages. During the 2017–2018 English premier league season, over 217 million pounds were paid to injured players; the NFL paid over half a billion dollars in injured player wages in 2019–2020 (Beal et al., 2019). Despite injuries being unpredictable in nature, new AI applications in sports medicine are having a positive impact on athletes' health all over the world (Beal et al., 2019; Ramkumar et al., 2021). AI's predictive capabilities are revolutionizing sport medicine in two primary ways: by helping facilitate the recovery process once an athlete is injured, and by helping with risk minimization and injury prevention.

One of AI's current applications within an athlete's recovery process is found in the field of radiology (Parker & Forster, 2019). Once an athlete has suffered a serious injury, the first step of his recovery process is undergoing extensive investigations through medical imaging processes such as MRI, CT scans, or ultrasound. Once the results of the respective test are collected, a healthcare professional analyzes them and makes a diagnosis. This is where AI comes into play and helps the doctor with the injury detection process, which is the area where most human errors occur. By implementing a highly accurate algorithm capable of diagnosing injuries, the margin for error significantly decreases, resulting in better treatment options for athletes. Currently, AI algorithms have the capability to determine bone density, detect fracture, and perform differential segmentation for lesions (Parker & Forster, 2019). Given the current trajectory of algorithmic advancement, there may soon be an AI standardized injury diagnosis procedure which will provide key data for specialists to analyze injuries such as fractures and muscular tears (Parker & Forster, 2019).

Another application of AI in the injury recovery process is helping determine how far athletes have progressed in their rehab and if they are ready to return to sport-specific training. Knee injury specifically is an area where the implementation of AI has been well documented (Stetter et al., 2019). In sports requiring sharp changes of direction, knee injuries are by far the most common. In terms of anatomy, the knee's primary function is to bear weight and allow the body to move. Wearable technology (hardware) and artificial neural networks (algorithms) have been utilized in recent years to measure ground reaction force (GRF) in athletes (Stetter et al., 2019). Tracking an athlete's ability to exert force into the ground when at the peak of his conditioning provides a quantifiable baseline which needs to be met before returning to competition. If an athlete's GRF is lower after injury, it means they still need to work on their recovery and gain back their power and explosiveness. Additionally, it is critical not only to look at an athlete's ability to exert force into the ground but also track the knee joint forces (KJF) (Stetter et al., 2019). Using inertial measurement units, data can be collected looking at how effectively an athlete's knee is able to bear forces in situations such as jumps, directional and linear movements. Tracking the knee's loading ability helps predict how certain movements may impact the knee when force is applied to the joint, which is critical data to ensure a safe recovery process. Tracking both GRF and KJF helps trainers create a rehab plan which provides the correct stimulus for the knee depending on the stage of recovery (Stetter et al., 2019).

While injury rehabilitation will always be a large part of sport medicine, modern athletic ideology has shifted its focus toward injury prediction and prevention. Top professional clubs all over the world are collecting more data than ever on their players to ensure they are performing at their peak ability and are not at a risk of injury. Teams in the English premier league (EPL), for instance, use data tracking systems such as STASsport or catapult in both training and match scenarios to track heartbeat, distance covered, number and intensity of sprints (Beal et al., 2019). This aggregation of data gives coaching staff an idea of a player's average workload along with the capability to see when a player has significantly surpassed his workload. Most injuries in the EPL occur due to players overtraining, which is in most cases controllable. Implementing AI as a predictive metric to analyze optimal player workloads drastically reduces the total number of stress-induced injuries (Beal et al., 2019). In a 2016 study, the acute chronic workload ratio (ACWR) was analyzed in rugby players. The acute workload relates to fatigue levels and the chronic workload relates to fitness. It was discovered that an increase in the ACWR leads to more injuries amongst players (Hulin et al., 2016). For cricket players, it was found that injury risk was at its highest when the acute workload was over twice as high as the chronic workload (Kakavas et al., 2020).

When creating an algorithm to predict injuries, there are many factors to consider. In addition to exceeding normal training loads, there are also extrinsic and intrinsic factors which impact injury. Extrinsic factors include the field or the ball while intrinsic factors include a player's age or his past injury history. One of the greatest soccer teams in the world, FC Barcelona has developed a model which predicts player injury by constructing a training data set for each training session (Kakavas et al., 2020). A player's personal data and his workload are collected, the data is being processed and a numerical value of either 1 or 0 is presented. The value assigned indicates if a player will be injured the next game or if they will remain healthy (Kakavas et al., 2020). Similarly, a sports clinic in Cleveland has applied a machine learning algorithm which has successfully predicted injury in the next seasons in the NHL and MBL with an accuracy of nearly 95% (Ramkumar et al., 2021). By looking at personal data, injury history, and performance metrics, they were able to accurately determine future injuries (Ramkumar et al., 2021).

AI not only can predict injuries caused by over training, but it also has the ability to determine when an athlete has suffered a serious concussion, which is critical to offer timely medical help. This application of AI could be tremendously beneficial in a sport like boxing where trauma to the head is constant (Yengo-Khan & Zuckerman, 2020). Using AI-assisted video analysis combined with neural networks, a boxer's movement patterns in the earlier rounds can be analyzed and compared in relation to his movements in the latter rounds of the fight (Yengo-Khan & Zuckerman, 2020). The difference in movement can help determine the extent of the traumatic brain injury a boxer has accumulated and whether is close to being knocked out. The referee would have access to this data in between rounds, and with the help of a medical professional can stop the fight to ensure the athlete's safety (Yengo-Khan & Zuckerman, 2020).

AI IN BETTING

Sports betting has become a major industry player in the 21st century (Hubáček et al., 2019). Sports betting refers to placing a wager on a particular outcome occurring during a sporting event. If an individual bets on a correct outcome they win back their wager and receives additional profit based on the betting odds. If they place an incorrect wager, the bookmaker profits by keeping the bettor's wager (Hubáček et al., 2019). One of the reasons sports betting has become so popular is due to the technological expansion of betting parlors into the online realm. According to a 2019 report, the sports betting market has reached a staggering quarter of a trillion dollars (Beal et al., 2019). With so much money circulating in the industry, the stakes are incredibly high for betters and bookmakers alike. For this reason, Artificial Intelligence is becoming an increasingly popular tool used by betting companies to predict sporting outcomes, reduce uncertainty, and minimize risk (Beal et al., 2019).

What makes sports so beloved around the globe is that they are exciting due to their unpredictable nature. From a betting perspective however, unpredictability can lead to chaotic and undesired outcomes. There is almost an infinite list of factors which influence a sporting result, ranging from the skill level of the participants, the weather, and team tactics. Additionally, the level of uncertainty ranges from sport to sport. Soccer, for example, is the most unpredictable sport due to matches having 3 potential final outcomes: win, loss, or draw. Additionally, the low scoring nature of the sport means that any team has a chance to win the game while higher scoring sports like basketball tend to be more predictable (Beal et al., 2019).

Complexities arise in betting since it is not only possible to bet on match outcomes, but also on other factors such as the exact score line or point spread. Classification models which predict match outcomes are much more accurate in their prediction process than regression-based models which predict factors with greater variance such as scores (Horvat & Job, 2020). Since it is possible to bet on almost any aspect of a sporting event, using an athlete's available performance data can help predict future outcomes and it can be used by bookies. Looking at an athlete's past performances and analyzing their statistics via Deep Learning technology can help determine how well an athlete will perform (Nguyen et al., 2021). This is particularly effective in creating betting odds for individual sports such as MMA or athletics, but can also be useful for team sports, especially if the athlete analyzed is considered a key player (Nguyen et al., 2021). The usage of neural networks analysis, sports analytics, and statistical pattern classification is undoubtedly increasing the accuracy of sports predictions (Nguyen et al., 2021).

AI is not only beneficial to the bookies who make the betting odds but it can also help level the playing field for bettors. The famous saying "the house always wins" remains true because the odds are always in the favor of those who create them. In moneyline bets online where the bettor solely focuses on predicting the winner of a game, it has been discovered that the betting odds payout is less than the actual numerical probability of the event occurring (Hubáček et al., 2019). By predicting potential outcomes with AI and presenting the actual numerical probability associated with an outcome to bettors, betting can be performed in a more ethical manner instead of lining the pockets of big betting companies (Hubáček et al., 2019).

There are also challenges and conflicts that may arise by implementing AI in betting such as jeopardizing the fairness of betting resulted by imparity of information dissemination.

AI IN JOURNALISM

AI is not only a tool used to assist the on-field performance elements of sports, but it also plays a role in sports media, particularly journalism. The primary function of AI in journalism is to create automated content at rapid speeds and in high volume. This methodology is often referred to as computational journalism where algorithms and big data are used to create news. Sports in general play a key role in modern commercialized society where the demand for their coverage is extremely high. Being the largest journalistic market makes sports journalism the optimal segment for AI implementations. AI is extremely expensive to train to produce realistic text writing, and an environment with high volume news stories is necessary (Galily, 2018). The combination of these two elements makes sports journalism the ideal candidate for AI. In addition to the large profit generated by sports journalism, its dependency on scores, statistics, and definite data makes AI implementations easier than in journalistic domains centered around more opinion-based investigations. In many cases, sports journalism writing is formulaic in nature, following certain templates which can be completed by AI (Galily, 2018).

There are many examples of applications of AI in sports journalism. For instance, the Associated Press tested the process of automated reporting for minor league baseball matches with the scope of generating real-time match reports. This made it possible to cover a far greater number of games than in the past without sending teams of hundreds of reporters to attend matches all America in person (Galily, 2018). Another example of

AI application in sports is found in the development of sporting news and results applications. One such app is BeSoccer, one of the largest online soccer communities in the world which provides live scores, news, and statistics (Segarra-Saavedra et al., 2019). Covering over 35,000 sporting leagues worldwide and over half a million teams, BeSoccer relies on AI and algorithmic methodology to provide match coverage. With the implementation of software robots, BeSoccer can analyze millions of matches every year which would not be feasible relying purely on manpower (Segarra-Saavedra et al., 2019).

This transition from traditional journalism toward an AI data-driven approach in sports is not without implications. On one hand, AI in sports journalism has many positives. AI's ability to produce thousands of news stories with remarkable speed, accuracy, and efficiency is an asset. AI not only makes far less errors than humans, but it also learns from a mistake made and does not repeat it twice (Galily, 2018). On the other hand, AI will undoubtedly have an impact on the progression of traditional journalism. The automation process of AI will lead to many journalists being laid off as their work has become obsolete (Galily, 2018). At the same time, however, AI has the potential to create new job opportunities, allowing journalists to perform less mundane tasks and explore more pertinent sports-related questions (Galily, 2018).

AI IN PLAYER RECRUITMENT

Player recruitment is an integral element of the sports world, playing a particularly important role in team sports. This process of recruiting varies from sport to sport, depending on various rules and regulations. For instance, in American sports leagues, players are either drafted or traded while in Europe, players are generally sold between clubs. Despite the differences between leagues and sports, at a fundamental level, the player recruitment process remains the same regardless of cultural and geographical difference. The scope of player recruitment is simply to find players which will have a positive impact on a team's performance. Clubs need to analyze various players and attempt to predict a player's potential impact. In the past, this process of recruiting was purely done by in-person scouting. However, in the 21st century, player recruitment decision making is a much more data-driven approach. AI has also become a key player in the recruiting process. AI algorithms and statistical modeling offer support to scouts to reduce the risk of poor player recruitment decisions. AI uses the large volume of data collected by sports teams to help with all steps of the recruitment process. AI helps determine areas of weakness within the team and analyzes data on potential players which can bolster the roster and helps scouts make informed decisions on which players to sign. Essentially, AI offers support to highly knowledgeable scouts to rate players. This not only reduces scouting budget costs but also increases scouting efficiency (Beal et al., 2019).

Many of the AI developments in player recruitment have occurred in association soccer. Since soccer is the most played sport in the world, by default it also has the largest talent pool of available players. Additionally, the open nature of the soccer market means clubs have a near infinite number of players available to sign. The volume of players on the market makes AI a very important tool to help determine which players are the best suited to improve a respective team. Linear models exist in soccer which take current members of the team and potential recruits and determine how the combinations of players would perform together (Pappalardo et al., 2019). This in many cases can help clubs find players which perhaps have been overlooked and would be budget buys. Furthermore, these data-driven tools help coaches determine which players within their team are underperforming in key areas. Once the weak links within the team are identified, potential replacements can be scouted and ranked with AI in relation to certain specific performance metrics. PlayeRank is an example of one of the new data-driven frameworks in soccer (Pappalardo et al., 2019). Using the information collected by soccer data companies via soccer logs, PlayeRank looks to learn, rate, and rank the data available. By analyzing a player's field statistics, a final rating is presented to each player depending on their on-field input. This final match rating helps simplify a player's performance into one numerical figure which can then be compared to that of other players. What PlayeRank discovered was that the top players do not always perform well but their percentage of excellent performances is far greater than other players. While these new technologies such as PlayeRank provide tremendous insight information for scouts and coaches alike, they are limited since they track data relating to ball touches. This fails to show the bigger picture, since in a soccer match most time is spent with a player, not possessing the ball (Pappalardo et al., 2019). Nevertheless, PlayeRank still provides valuable input to those responsible with a team's player recruitment process.

LIMITATIONS OF AI AND POTENTIAL FUTURE APPLICATIONS

Although its potential has been demonstrated, AI has several limitations. First, the machine learning tools are mostly seen as "black boxes", where both their internal model and decision-making process remain unknown to users (Ramkumar et al., 2021). The work done in explainable AI field, which tries to elucidate the decision of an ML algorithm while simultaneously explaining these decisions after they happen, is often problematic.

Second, there are ethical concerns with respect to data sharing and privacy. AI may be able to identify users even if the algorithm is based on deidentified data. Another situation of concern arises when the user's decision is different from what the expert system recommends. AI should not replace users but rather offer decision support. Moreover, AI systems could be biased, and current design procedures may not be able to identify them.

AI will continue to impact all aspects of professional sports, from the way the game is played and refereed to how the fans are involved. The future of sports includes AI assistant coaches, automated video highlights, and more meaningful automated interactions for fans.

CONCLUSION

It is evident that AI is becoming a much more popular tool that is being utilized in various aspects of sports such as training, recruiting, medicine, refereeing, betting, and journalism to name a few. Although Artificial Intelligence development is still in its infancy, the benefits of its implementation in sport are evident. Maximizing task efficiency through AI in the sport industry will undoubtedly revolutionize sport in a multitude of ways, ranging from more efficiency training regiments to better recovery methods. Athletes, coaches, and fans alike will all benefit from AI advancements. However, certain drawbacks of AI, such as the black box nature of the technology or its potential to replace human workforce, can also make it dangerous. During the next few years, AI will undoubtedly transform sport tremendously, becoming a standardized feature in high performance. With any new technology taking up a key role in society, there are advantages and disadvantages. However, what really matters is how we use AI and ensure that all applications are done in an ethical manner.

REFERENCES

Beal, R., Norman, T. J., & Ramchurn, S. D. (2019). Artificial intelligence for team sports: A survey. *The Knowledge Engineering Review, 34*, e28. doi:10.1017/s0269888919000225

Chu, W. C.-C., Shih, C., Chou, W.-Y., Ahamed, S. I., & Hsiung, P.-A. (2019). Artificial intelligence of things in sports science: Weight training as an example. *Computer, 52*(11), 52–61. doi:10.1109/mc.2019.2933772

Fialho, G., Manhães, A., & Teixeira, J. P. (2019). Predicting sports results with artificial intelligence – a proposal framework for soccer games. *Procedia Computer Science, 164*, 131–136. doi:10.1016/j.procs.2019.12.164

Galily, Y. (2018). Artificial intelligence and sports journalism: Is it a sweeping change? *Technology in Society, 54*, 47–51. doi:10.1016/j.techsoc.2018.03.001

Horvat, T., & Job, J. (2020). The use of machine learning in sport outcome prediction: A review. *Wiley Interdisciplinary Reviews: Data Mining and Knowledge Discovery, 10*(5). doi:10.1002/widm.1380

Hubáček, O., Šourek, G., & Železný, F. (2019). Exploiting sports-betting market using machine learning. *International Journal of Forecasting, 35*(2), 783–796. doi:10.1016/j.ijforecast.2019.01.001

Hulin, B. T., Gabbett, T. J., Lawson, D. W., Caputi, P., & Sampson, J. A. (2016). The acute:chronic workload ratio predicts injury: High chronic workload may decrease injury risk in elite rugby league players. *British Journal of Sports Medicine, 50*(4), 231. doi:10.1136/bjsports-2015-094817

Kakavas, G., Malliaropoulos, N., Pruna, R., & Maffulli, N. (2020). Artificial intelligence: A tool for sports trauma prediction. *Injury, 51*, S63–S65. doi:10.1016/j.injury.2019.08.033

Keh, A. (2019). *Gymnastics' latest twist? Robot judges that see everything.* The New York Times. https://www.nytimes.com/2019/10/10/sports/olympics/gymnastics-robot-judges.html

LaLiga. (2019, February 27). *Artificial Intelligence and VAR take centre stage during LaLiga Innovation Showcase at the Mobile World Congress.* https://www.laliga.com/en-GB/news/artificial-intelligence-and-var-take-centre-stage-during-laliga-innovation-showcase-at-the-mobile-world-congress

Li, C., & Cui, J. (2021). Intelligent sports training system based on artificial intelligence and big data. *Mobile Information Systems, 2021*, 1–11. doi:10.1155/2021/9929650

Mallen, C. (2019). *Emerging Technologies in Sport.* 87–104. doi:10.4324/9781351117906-6

Nasu, D., & Kashino, M. (2020). Impact of each release parameter on pitch location in baseball pitching. *Journal of Sports Sciences, 39*(10), 1–6. doi:10.1080/02640414.2020.1868679

Nguyen, N. H., Nguyen, D. T. A., Ma, B., & Hu, J. (2021). The application of machine learning and deep learning in sport: Predicting NBA players' performance and popularity. *Journal of Information and Telecommunication*, 1–19. doi:10.1080/24751839.2021.1977066

Novatchkov, H., & Baca, A. (2013). Artificial intelligence in sports on the example of weight training. *Journal of Sports Science and Medicine, 2*, 27–37.

Pappalardo, L., Cintia, P., Ferragina, P., Massucco, E., Pedreschi, D., & Giannotti, F. (2019). PlayeRank: Data-driven performance evaluation and player ranking in soccer via a machine learning approach. *ACM Transactions on Intelligent Systems and Technology (TIST), 10*(5), 1–27. doi:10.1145/3343172

Parker, W., & Forster, B. B. (2019). Artificial intelligence in sports medicine radiology: What's coming? *British Journal of Sports Medicine, 53*(19), 1201. doi:10.1136/bjsports-2018-099999

Ramkumar, P. N., Luu, B. C., Haeberle, H. S., Karnuta, J. M., Nwachukwu, B. U., & Williams, R. J. (2021). Sports medicine and artificial intelligence: A primer. *The American Journal of Sports Medicine.* doi:10.1177/03635465211008648

Rodrigues, A. C. N., Pereira, A. S., Mendes, R. M. S., Araújo, A. G., Couceiro, M. S., & Figueiredo, A. J. (2020). Using artificial intelligence for pattern recognition in a sports context. *Sensors, 20*(11), 3040. doi:10.3390/s20113040

Segarra-Saavedra, J., Cristófol, F. J., & Martínez-Sala, A.-M. (2019). Inteligencia artificial (IA) aplicada a la documentación informativa y redacción periodística deportiva. El caso de BeSoccer. *Doxa Comunicación. Revista Interdisciplinar de Estudios de Comunicación y Ciencias Sociales, 29,* 275–286. doi:10.31921/doxacom.n29a14

Stefano, A. D. (2021, March 23). *AI in sports: Current trends and future challenges.* https://www.itransition.com/blog/ai-in-sports

Stetter, B. J., Ringhof, S., Krafft, F. C., Sell, S., & Stein, T. (2019). Estimation of knee joint forces in sport movements using wearable sensors and machine learning. *Sensors, 19*(17), 3690. doi:10.3390/s19173690

Wei, S., Huang, P., Li, R., Liu, Z., & Zou, Y. (2021). Exploring the application of artificial intelligence in sports training: A case study approach. *Complexity, 2021,* 1–8. doi:10.1155/2021/4658937

Yengo-Khan, A., & Zuckerman, S. L. (2020). Preventable deaths, video analysis, artificial intelligence, and the future of sport. *Neurosurgery, 86,* E349–E350. doi:10.1093/neuros/nyz452

The Use of Artificial Intelligence by Public Service Media: Between Advantages and Threats

Minna Horowitz[a], Marko Milosavljević[b], and Hildegarde Van den Bulck[c]

[a]*University of Helsinki, Helsinki, Finland; St. John's University, Queens, New York, USA; and Advocacy and Digital Rights, Central European University, Center for Media, Data and Society (Democracy Institute), Budapest, Hungary*
[b]*Journalism at the Research Centre for the Terminology of Social Sciences and Journalism, University of Ljubljana, Ljubljana, Slovenia*
[c]*Communication Studies and Head of the Department of Communication at Drexel University in Philadelphia, Philadelphia, Pennsylvania, USA*

CONTENTS

DOI: 10.1201/9781003261247-10

INTRODUCTION: PUBLIC SERVICE MEDIA AND DIGITALIZATION

Machine learning, algorithms, automation, and other forms of "artificial intelligence" (AI) permeate all sectors of contemporary societies, including various media. While the implementation of AI in other sectors raises considerable (re)considerations of the role of specific sectors, segments of societies, or professions, the issues raised by AI in the media create specific concerns. As the so-called "fourth estate", "fourth branch of power", and "watchdogs" of democracies, media and journalism perform a crucial role in democratic societies, protecting the interests of citizens and controlling the political, economic, and societal sources of power. If their tasks are increasingly automated and left to AI tools, this specific role of the media comes under pressure and can potentially be compromised or threatened.

The use of AI and big data is recognized in the academic and public fora as re-configuring some of media's most fundamental, even epistemic, principles, from those governing journalism to questions regarding human–machine interplay. Similar to previous technological innovations, the implementation of AI in media has been a gra-dual, incremental, and diverse process, leading to the "cumulative transformation" (Boczkowski, 2004) we are currently witnessing. This takes place in a globally digitized media landscape and affects the media regardless of type, funding, distribution platform, or societal position.

These issues are most pronounced in public service media (PSM), which, historically and politically, represent central segments of the media sector in many parts of the world and which remain the cornerstones of most contemporary media ecosystems from an economic, journalistic, ethical, political, and technological perspective. Explicitly set up to serve the entire nation and to enhance the educational and cultural capital of its citizens-audience through universal access and content provision, AI implementations go to the heart of PSM's mission, principles and responsibilities, as we will show in this chapter. Some studies have even suggested that the way PSM choose to utilize AI's power is decisive to the future of democracy (Tambini, 2021).

In this context, PSM organizations are not just relevant as particularly significant stakeholders in different national media systems, but they also bear a heavy burden as they attempt to exist in global–national and hyper-competitive contexts. These contexts call for drastic changes in the ways these organizations operate and require content and services that serve society at large and its many communities, groups, and individuals. Unlike its commercial competitors, PSM need to be vigilant and transparent in their use of data and technological innovations. This chapter discusses the potentials, reality, and problems that implementing AI, specifically algorithmic systems, brings to PSM and their contribution to society. Here, "algorithmic systems" are understood as de-fined by the Council of Europe: applications that perform one or more tasks, such as gathering, combining, cleaning, sorting, classifying, and inferring data, as well as se-lecting, prioritizing, recommending, and making decisions (CoE, 2020). For example, in the case of news, media use algorithmic systems in production (to gather structured and machine-readable data, assemble information in different formats, and produce and modify content) and distribution (to enable efficient search and utilization of content by users, specific prioritization, and recommendation) (Milosavljević & Vobič, 2021).

Since their inception, public service broadcasting (PSB) institutions, which are increasingly being identified as PSM, have played a cornerstone role in innovations of all kinds while maintaining crucial roles in society. Their multiplatform reiterations have been at the heart of mass communication systems in the 20th century in most Northern and Western European societies (Bardoel & Lowe, 2007; Scannell & Cardiff, 1991; Van den Bulck, 2001) and in former Commonwealth countries. Around the globe, they are considered important in guaranteeing healthy communication ecosystems in existing and emerging democracies (Horowitz & Marko, 2019).

As a result, they have various normative characteristics or core principles assigned to them. The key association of European PSM, the European Broadcasting Union (EBU, 2019), a global advocacy organization for public media, the Public Media Alliance (PMA, n.d.), the Council of Europe (CoE, n.d.), posit the following about PSB/PSM:

1. Refer to broadcasting and related services made, financed, and controlled by the public, for the public. Mostly established by law, they are nonpartisan and independent and are run for the benefit of society as a whole.

2. Are neither commercial nor state-owned, free from political interference and pressure from commercial forces.

3. Provide output designed to inform, educate, and entertain all audiences.

4. Ensure universality – that is, equal service to all audiences – in terms of content and access.

5. Maintain accuracy in and high standards of journalism and excellence in broadcasting.

6. Enhance social, political, and cultural citizenship; promote diversity and social cohesion; and support an informed democracy.

In addition, the EBU lists innovation, including creativity in terms of formats, technologies, and connectivity with audiences, as one of the core PSM principles.

Altogether, these normative characteristics aim to provide alternatives to both state-run and purely market-based profit-driven media. They are also significant in the context of the abundance of user-generated content in today's media landscape, which is often based on unverified information in the era of data-driven global platform power. At the same time, despite normative uniformity, PSM organizations vary in institutional arrangement, budget, offering, reach, and ability to innovate.

PSM organizations have been very much caught up in digitization trends, exploring the opportunities provided by algorithmic systems to improve their performance, fulfill their (often legally) expected and defined role, and thus remain relevant in a digitized media landscape. However, this digitized context creates both opportunities for and threats to the role and key values of PSM.

In this contribution, we argue that these opportunities and threats must be understood at three levels: the wider media context in which PSM operate; their organizational structure and principles, including views on innovation; and the level of specific types of content and audiences. A better grasp of these three layers will allow PSM to interact with AI and big data in a way that respects their core values and principles while remaining relevant in a digitized media world. Therefore, we posit that PSM organizations have a responsibility to fight the establishment of the so-called "algocracies", which are a form of societal governance based on algorithms (Danaher, 2018). These forms are based on the opacity of algorithmic decision-making, which hampers human agency and is the opposite of the citizen-centric principles of PSM.

PSM AND AI: AN UNEASY RELATIONSHIP

Ventures into algorithmic systems and the specific points of attention they raise for PSM have received considerable scholarly attention. A key focus is the question of whether PSM can abide by the same rules and apply the same tools as commercial media when embracing these new digital tools in material gathering, content creation and distribution, and audience relations.

First, several studies have analyzed PSM organizations' increasing involvement with algorithmic systems as part of customized content production and recommender systems, which allow for better provision of relevant content, answer audience expectations, and, in case of mixed financing, create additional revenue. This happens to various extents. PSM organizations usually develop their own systems to compete against platform power (Martin, 2021) for more exposure and personalized services (Sørensen & Hutchinson, 2018; Van den Bulck & Moe, 2018; Vaz-Álvarez et al., 2021).

However, these innovations can undermine some of PSM's core principles, such as universality and inclusiveness. Computational diversity does not necessarily align with public media diversity in the context of algorithm-based recommender systems (Sørensen, 2021). Recommender systems automatically generate lists of products or services – in this case TV shows, video content, podcasts, news articles, and other media content and services – that might be interesting and/or relevant to the user based on previous purchases, interests, searches, and other data. Whereas recommendation systems in commercial media tend to offer users similar (types, genres, or sources of) content, to remain loyal to their core principles, recommender systems of PSM should offer relevant diversity, variety, and plurality of content to enhance the democratic aspect and purpose of PSM. Other studies have focused on the opportunities and threats that AI brings to investigative journalism (Thurman et al., 2019) and on the issues of diversity and inclusion in automation in news production and public service newsbots (Diakopoulos, 2019), finding that quality is not the same as audience preference.

Second, a different set of studies has investigated how the implementation of algorithmic systems involves intermediaries and third parties that provide editorial, technical, marketing, and advertising tools for personalization and recommendation (Hutchinson, 2018; Sørensen & Van den Bulck, 2020; Sørensen et al., 2020). These intermediaries and third parties greatly assist in improving the user experience and can help generate additional revenue. The latter can result from the direct sales of audiences' digital data to third parties or from more personalized and targeted content and advertising. This is what Anderson defines as "the long tail" and "the longer tail", which are opportunities to finetune products and services to small niche audiences not possible in "mortar-and-brick" economies of mass production and economies of scale (Anderson, 2009).

In the area of news, algorithmic systems are part of a larger and longer transformation of journalistic and editorial practices toward quantification and computation (Milosavljević & Vobič, 2021). These systems "might correct our prejudices, our emotional incontinence, and our wild inconsistencies" (Harford, 2021, para. 2). However, these innovations also come with considerable concerns, as suggested by the role of bots in the distribution of disinformation. Some of these opportunities and challenges are generic to legacy media, but many are specific to PSM, as they affect their core values, thus threatening PSM's continued (if contested) mandate, public financing, and, most of all, audiences' trust in these institutions. Trust is always an intrinsic but implicit value for PSM, and it has become an explicit topic in discussions regarding the continued legitimacy and relevance of PSM. The EBU emphasizes the role of PSM as a unique, trusted information source in an increasingly commercial and self-serving ecosystem plagued by the viral spread of "fake news" (EBU, 2019).

Finally, and most importantly, existing studies have confirmed that PSM institutions, while actively utilizing and experimenting with algorithmic systems and wider AI, do not seem to have a specific "PSM strategy for AI". This results in institution-specific approaches that prevent the simple identification or establishment of universal AI-related strategies for PSM. For example, a study of 16 European PSM (Vaz-Álvarez et al., 2021) mapped key AI innovation areas, the use of various AI applications, the use of video-on-demand recommender systems, and future visions for AI and found a wide variety of AI-related intentions and uses across PSM organizations. While they observed a greater presence of third-party services on private/commercial than on public media platforms, Sørensen and Van den Bulck (2020) also found significant differences in the number and types of these services among PSM.

THREE LAYERS OF OPPORTUNITIES AND THREATS

Despite the existing body of work on how PSM organizations may use AI, little is known about the effects of PSM decisions on the use of AI and algorithmic systems and the accompanying tools and third-party services. Are these decisions affected by the national media landscape, the economic, political, and cultural contexts of PSM, the organizational cultures of innovation, the audience, and the genre-specific demands and opportunities – or all of the above? What, if any, are the considerations about societal impact? To understand the advantages and threats of algorithmic systems in PSM organizations, they must be examined from three distinct perspectives: as contextual characteristics of specific national media systems, as organizational configurations, and as audience-specific demands and opportunities for the use of AI and algorithmic systems.

PSM and AI in National Contexts

As PSM organizations are national institutions, economic, political, and even cultural contexts are important in envisioning the potential and analyzing the existing use of algorithmic systems by PSM institutions. In terms of media markets, it seems intuitive that the position of PSM in their particular domestic market affects their embrace of AI and algorithmic systems. A correlation between market position and the resources to invest in innovations, such as AI, is expected, but this is not always the case. Dominant and "wealthy" PSM in small and large markets may have the means to fund digital innovations, but they may also be more affected by commercial competitors wanting to curb PSM efforts. For example, the Finnish Broadcasting Company, a PSM forerunner in digitalization, was challenged for its use of AI for personalization (Hilden, 2017).

In comparative terms, research has found similar uses of AI by PSM in countries with similar media systems within Europe and unexpected differences between similar countries (Van den Bulck & Moe, 2018). Research has suggested a distinction between Nordic, Central (including Germany and Switzerland), and Western European countries in the extent to which PSM institutions involve algorithmic systems and services in the running of their platforms (Sørensen & Van den Bulck, 2020). Other studies (Jääskeläinen & Olij, 2019; Van den Bulck & Moe, 2018) have pointed to significant differences in this regard between PSM within Nordic countries. This suggests that the use of AI by PSM does not fit neatly into typologies that group countries and media systems based on the relationships between media and political systems. Research on former Communist Europe has suggested that the previous history and development of a country's broader digitization, of the wider media market (including the information environment), and of the role of PSM are important variables in understanding the development of AI and algorithmic systems (Milosavljević & Poler Kovačič, 2021). Although AI seems to be necessary for PSM to have a meaningful position in any country, and although the nation-specific features of media markets, political systems, and media cultures may provide various opportunities, no contextual factor can guarantee that a PSM organization can become a harbinger of a distinct, ethical, and citizen-centric use of AI.

PSM and AI in the Organizational Context

The second layer in understanding the PSM use of AI and algorithmic systems is the organizational level. Even if resources are available for PSM to use, the innovation cultures and corporate cultures at large within organizations may differ drastically (Glowacki & Jackson, 2013).

Throughout their history, states with longer PSM traditions, particularly in Europe, have given PSM institutions a mandate to innovate for reasons of technological nationalism. This means innovation in terms of new technological solutions rather than new kinds of content (Van den Bulck, 2008). As these media markets became competitive from the late 1970s onward, they became a source of criticism from commercial players, which considered PSM's innovation opportunities to disturb national markets. The latter was increasingly competitive anyway due to international and global players entering domestic markets in many parts of the world. Academically, it raises questions about control over the processes through which knowledge is legitimated (Hardt, 1998).

Nevertheless, for many PSM institutions, that special place in the national framework of innovation remains part of their organizational thinking and being, continuing to affect their perceptions of innovation and the need for change. For example, it seems that the implementation of digital personalization tools by European PSM has been based more on views regarding technology and innovation than on cultural or market similarities between countries (Van den Bulck & Moe, 2018). These innovation cultures within different organizations could vary from technological optimism and skepticism to stark pessimism. For example, PSM with innovation-driven organizational structures tend to take the lead and show great confidence in the development of AI-based applications, setting up "sandbox" innovation departments, whereas PSM with fewer innovation-oriented organizational principles show more restraint in developing these applications and will have less innovation-oriented structures.

This organizational position in innovation also affects the core purpose of PSM: content production and the accompanying production culture. For example, the implementation of algorithmic processes to gather and assemble data; create news narratives, figures, and graphics; and/or publish and distribute news items changes journalism's internal and external processes (Carlson, 2016). Specifically, AI helps to speed up news production, and keeping in mind journalists' personal style and credibility can increase its weight in creating trust in the news (Túñez-López et al., 2021).

The implementation of AI and algorithmic systems is also affected by the broader corporate culture. Traditionally, PSM institutions across the globe were organized as public administration with public service and a cultural–education logic that permeated the organizational culture. What PSM had to account for was their success in contributing to the collective good, and they had to give reckoning to governments and "licensed participants … broadcasters, politicians, intellectual and cultural elite" (Jakubowicz, 2003, pp. 148–149). In practice, these organizations were often overly bureaucratic and averse to change, slowing down innovation processes (Dhoest, 2004). To adjust to the changing media landscape and in search of legitimacy in a crowded media landscape, PSM across the globe reformed beginning in the 1990s. They embraced new public management ideas and exchanged a cultural–educational logic for competition, audience maximization, and channel branding (d'Haenens & Saeys, 2007; Van den Bulck, 2015). In many cases, civil servants were replaced by managers and lifelong employment by short-term contracts, and remits and goals were translated into short-term program standards, quotas, audience reach, and satisfaction benchmarks. Therefore, PSM responses to the opportunities and threats of AI and algorithmic systems must be understood within the context of such evolving corporate cultures. For example, whereas the organizational restructuring of PSM institutions, such as the Flemish VRT and Norwegian NRK, has created agile institutions quick to respond to digital opportunities and challenges, a lack of reform of US public broadcasting has resulted in PBS remaining at the tail end of digital evolutions (Ali & Van den Bulck, 2021).

In sum, PSM's general, long-standing position and organizational culture of innovation will affect the adoption and adaptation of AI within their working processes. The belief that PSM hold a special place within national cultural and socio-economic frameworks can put them at the forefront of innovation but can also result in a resistance to change so as not to lose that position. Some PSM show "two tracks" within the institution: one prioritizes traditional broadcasting and its practices, and the other believes in cutting-edge innovation as a strategy for survival and societal value creation (Głowacki & Jackson, 2019; Leino, 2021). These internal organizational rifts can play out not only in the overall strategy but also in the practical and operational challenges brought on by digital changes. In general, AI and data-based strategies challenge many PSM practices, ranging from the ethical use of audience data for strategic purposes to storing data in a secure manner and analyzing and managing them effectively and meaningfully (Murschetz, 2021).

PSM, AI, and Different Audiences

The third layer refers to the understanding of the core PSM value of universality in relation to AI and algorithmic services with regard to specific kinds of content and reaching specific audiences. This poses a fundamental challenge to PSM, especially in terms of their societal role and impact. Intrinsic in the principle of universality is that organizations must engage in the production and distribution of a variety of content genres and services, as well as ensure that they reach all audiences. In the mass media era, this two-fold remit of equal reach and diversity of genres was relatively straightforward, catering to a national mass audience. Currently, universality is a major conundrum in the relationship between PSM and audiences. On the one hand, it requires taking into account the shared needs of society, which are more than a composite of individual tastes and preferences. Universality is meant to serve cohesion and a common understanding. On the other hand, in more fragmented media markets (and societies), it also means investing in new content, services, and platforms to reach different audience groups (Savage et al., 2020).

Tailoring news is one of the most frequently discussed uses of AI as a tool to reach audiences. For news to be of interest and relevance to the public, AI provides the opportunity to create "customized news feeds for an audience of just one person" (Haim & Graefe, 2017, pp. 1045–1046), which is sometimes defined as personalized "Daily Me" (Negroponte, 1995). By "doing it for the public" (Deuze, 2005, p. 447), journalists aim for a heterogeneous citizenry with a shared public culture and serve as an "integrative force" for public debate (Dahlgren, 2009, p. 147). However, the use of AI in journalism may not always be the result of a desire to serve audiences. The so-called automated (or robot) journalism seems enticing as a means to create unlimited numbers of news stories on a specific topic at minimal cost, produced faster and more precisely in multiple languages or with automated translations and subtitles (Haim & Graefe, 2017), while stimulating people's engagement through thoughtful customization and personalization, thus fulfilling relevant public service expectations.

However, AI can also harm the ideal of universality (Thurman & Schifferes, 2012), fragmenting the common knowledge base of a society and weakening the understanding of the shared issues of its citizens. The potential role of PSM in countering fragmentation and individualization makes the personalization of news and other content and re-commendations particularly problematic.

Thus far, there have been fewer analyses and a lesser understanding of how AI and algorithmic systems can work in relation to other genres, such as drama and non-fictional entertainment. Traditionally, PSM had particular functions aimed at uniting the citizenry around shared values and cultural identifiers. This, too, can be undermined by fragmentation through algorithmic personalization. Moreover, these genres have parti-cular functions in relation to others, such as news. This is epitomized in scheduling techniques that provide audiences with a balanced diet and often use popular programs to lure audiences to more serious content, with an eye toward society and democracy building (Van den Bulck, 2009).

In a context in which people's trust in the media, particularly news media, is de-creasing (Toff et al., 2020), and the majority of citizens are still doubtful about AI (Vandendriessche et al., 2020), digital innovation efforts need to be audience-centered. Although this may apply to all media, PSM strategies and applications regarding AI and algorithmic systems are expected to start from public interest. Attention to audiences is relevant in terms of audience segmentation (children vs. adults, general interest vs. niche audiences), as programming aimed at youth and children may need to follow different principles from that aimed at the general adult audience. PSM organizations constantly struggle to reach young audiences not only because their media habits are so different from those of older audiences but also because of the many youth subcultures and diverse digital practices that they have adopted (Grönvall et al., 2021). The wide-scale application of AI and algorithmic systems also creates new responsibilities for PSM, as the use of big data that accompanies AI applications comes with questions about and attention to audiences' privacy in ways that do not occur in a traditional broadcast context (cf. Sørensen et al., 2020).

GLOBAL GUIDELINES AND PSM

PSM are not alone in their uneasy relationship with AI. The opportunities and concerns related to the uses and impact of AI on society have been debated in many fora. Optimistic expectations from technological euphoria perspectives on AI and algorithmic systems as tools for a better and more personalized provision of information and services are met by techno-skeptical criticism that views these systems as "opaque, unquestioned, and unaccountable" (O'Neil, 2018, p. 33), raising "questions of power and politics in who gets to design the algorithms and who feels the results" (Crawford, 2021, pp. 40–41).

Recently, these debates have led to the creation of several guidelines. The UNESCO Recommendation on the Ethics of AI (2021), which was signed by all member states, sets the first global normative framework for states to apply. It points to the challenges that AI poses to cultures, social cohesion, inclusivity, and the availability of mediated informa-tion. Similarly, the European Union's 2021 Coordinated Plan on Artificial Intelligence (EU, n.d.) provides guidelines for the successful utilization of AI, including the principles of sustainability, security, inclusivity, and trustworthiness, as well as innovations and practices that are human driven, not technology driven.

These recommendations and guidelines include principles and values that are fully aligned with those of PSM, such as fairness, non-discrimination, transparency, awareness, and literacy. This seems to give PSM a self-evident and crucial role in fighting the establishment of algocracy. PSM can help remedy this by using AI as a responsible, citizen-centric innovation.

However, the characteristics of PSM as nation-based institutions make applicability a more complex matter. There are questions about national structures and resources, but these institutions also need to rethink their organizational cultures and practices and consider the principles of universality and implications for users, including transparency and the use of data that adhere to ethical and inclusive citizen-centric principles. This is not a small feat in a situation in which the very existence of PSM is being challenged by commercial competitors and political forces in emerging and mature PSM nations alike (Dragormir & Horowitz, 2021).

CONCLUSION: PSM AI, PUBLIC VALUE, AND DEMOCRACY

Our overview of the challenges and threats of AI to PSM has highlighted the complexity of the relationship between new technologies and public institutions. In addition, it has pointed out the particular advantages and disadvantages of AI for PSM as independent, non-commercial, citizen-centric national media organizations. Following our analysis, it is not surprising that these organizations, while actively utilizing and experimenting with AI, do not have a specific "PSM AI" strategy. Their ability to utilize AI and other new technologies depends on their role in a specific national context in which they also face global competition. This context influences the internal prioritization of strategies and tactics related to AI. To complicate the issue, different audience segments may require different approaches to AI from PSM.

Nevertheless, the starting point of our chapter has been that PSM has a responsibility vis-a-vis its audiences as citizens to support democratic communication. The traditional PSM principles, translated into the digital era, also call for strong, normative principles for PSM AI. One set of considerations for a PSM algorithm (Sørensen & Hutchinson, 2018) suggests finding a balance between using it for reach and for distinctiveness, as one of the roles of PSM is to create shared experiences. A PSM algorithm should be transparent and walk the fine line between offering audiences certain content and honoring today's active users who can choose and curate their media consumption. PSM should also be mindful of issues of dependency when using external third-party services. All of these principles are sound advice for PSM AI.

Defining a specific PSM AI may be one of the only democratic and society-supporting uses of AI in the field of media and content creation. The so-called "dynamic public value of PSM", which pertains equally to society, the industry, and individual citizens (Mazzucato et al., 2020), can also apply to PSM AI.

First, from the perspective of individual audience members, PSM AI can function similarly to any legacy media in terms of curation and personalization, that is, in offering relevant, tailored content and services, thus supporting individual citizens' information, educational, and entertainment needs.

Second, in terms of the industry dimension of public value, PSM AI can become an industry leader in the ethical use of AI (Jääskeläinen & Olij, 2019) while streamlining distribution, translation, and other activities and innovating for distinct applications of AI. This requires public support in terms of funding, a forward-looking organizational culture, and the allocation of innovation resources within PSM institutions. It requires the boosting of digital competence and creativity at the program-making level and knowledge of specific audience needs.

Third, PSM AI does not need to contradict historical PSM principles, such as universality and diversity. From the perspective of societal value, it can provide both traditional universality and the personalized "nuanced" universality (Hokka, 2018), which audiences have come to expect. In addition, PSM AI can be a tool for a specific public service mission to support human rights and citizenship, for example, by offering diverse content and reversing bias (Helberger et al., 2016). Following Tambini (2021), in a world where current crises have shown the fragility of national and global communication systems, and where algorithms have brought about challenges such as disinformation and informational "filter bubbles" (Pariser, 2012), we, too, see PSM AI beyond being a strategic threat or an opportunity but a necessity to democracy.

REFERENCES

Ali, C., & Van den Bulck, H. (2021). *PBS could help rebuild trust in US media*. Columbia Journalism Review. https://www.cjr.org/tow_center/pbs-could-help-rebuild-trust-in-us-media.php

Anderson, C. (2009). *The long tail*. New York City, New York: Random House. https://www.google.ca/books/edition/The_Longer_Long_Tail/3bN-PwAACAAJ?hl=en

Bardoel, J., & Lowe, G. F. (2007). From public service broadcasting to public service media. The core challenge. In Lowe, G. F. & Bardoel, J. (Eds.), *From public service broadcasting to public service media* (pp. 9–28). Göteborg: Nordicom.

Boczkowski, P. (2004). *Digitizing the news: Innovation in online newspapers*. Cambridge, MA: MIT Press.

Carlson, M. (2016). Metajournalistic discourse and the meanings of journalism. *Communication Theory, 26*(4), 349–368.

CoE (n.d.). *Public service media*. Council of Europe. http://www.coe.int/en/web/freedom-expression/public-service-media

CoE (2020). *Recommendation CM/Rec(2020)1 of the committee of ministers to member states on the human rights impacts of algorithmic systems*. Council of Europe. https://search.coe.int/cm/pages/result_details.aspx?objectid=09000016809e1154

Crawford, K. (2021). *Atlas of AI: Power, politics, and the planetary costs of artificial intelligence*. New Haven, CT: Yale University Press.

Dahlgren, P. (2009). The troubling evolution of journalism. In Zelizer, B. (Ed.), *The changing faces of journalism* (pp. 146–161). London, England: Routledge.

Danaher, J. (2018). Toward an ethics of AI assistants: An initial framework. *Philosophy & Technology, 31*(4), 629–653. doi.org/10.1007/s13347-018-0317-3

Deuze, M. (2005). What is journalism? *Journalism, 6*(4), 442–465.

d'Haenens, L., & Saeys, F. (Eds.) (2007). *Western broadcasting at the dawn of the 21st century*. Berlin/New York: Mouton de Gruyter.

Dhoest, A. (2004). Negotiating images of the nation: The production of Flemish TV drama, 1953–1989. *Media Culture & Society, 26*(3): 393–408. doi:10.1177/0163443704042261

Diakopoulos, N. (2019). Towards a design orientation on algorithms and automation in news production. *Digital Journalism*, 7(8), 1180–1184. doi:10.1080/21670811.2019.1682938

Dragormir, M., & Horowitz, M. (2021). Media capture and its contexts: Developing a comparative framework for public service media. In Túñez-López, M. et al. (Eds.), *The values of public service media in the internet society* (pp. 217–246). Cham: Switzerland: Palgrave MacMillan.

EBU (2019). The unique role of public service media. European Broadcasting Union. https://www.ebu.ch/news/2019/02/the-unique-role-of-public-service-media

EU (n.d.). *Coordinated plan on artificial intelligence 2021 review | shaping Europe's digital future.* Digital-Strategy.ec.europa.eu. https://digital-strategy.ec.europa.eu/en/library/coordinated-plan-artificial-intelligence-2021-review

Glowacki, M., & Jackson, L. (Ed.) (2013). *Public media management for the twenty-first century: Creativity, innovation, and interaction.* New York: Routledge.

Głowacki, M., & Jackson, L. (2019). *Organizational culture of public service media.* Project Report. https://www.creativemediaclusters.com/

Grönvall, J., Hilden, J., & Horowitz. M. (2021). *Public service broadcasting and platform power: Nordic approaches.* Working paper. NordMedia.

Haim, M., & Graefe, A. (2017). Automated news. *Digital Journalism*, 5(8), 1044–1059.

Hardt, H. (1998). *Interactions: Critical studies in communication, media, and journalism.* Oxford: Rowman & Littlefield.

Harford, T. (2021, October 1). Algorithms could guide life-changing decisions. But they need work. *Financial Times.* https://www.ft.com/content/1d999de2-7497-42c3-b8dc-a8306efc1047

Helberger, N., Karppinen, K., & D'Acunto, L. (2016). Exposure diversity as a design principle for recommender systems. *Information, Communication & Society*, 21(2), 191–207. doi:10.1080/1369118x.2016.1271900

Hilden, J. (2017). *Julkisen palvelun yleisradiotoiminnan personointi* (Public service media and personalization). Viestinnän tutkimuskeskus CRC, University of Helsinki.

Hokka, J. (2018). Towards nuanced universality: Developing a concept bible for public service online news production. *European Journal of Communication*, 34(1), 74–87. doi:10.1177/0267323118810862

Horowitz, M., & Marko, D. (2019). Public service broadcasting and media development. In Benequista, N., Abbott, S., Rothman, P., & Mano, W. (Eds.), *International media development* (pp. 208–219). New York: Peter Lang Verlag.

Hutchinson, J. (2018). Intermediaries exercising influence through algorithms within public service media. In Glowacki, M. & Jaskiernia, A. (Eds.), *Public service media renewal: Adaptation to digital network challenges.* Peter Lang.

Jääskeläinen, A., & Olij, M. (2019). *News Report 2019: The next newsroom.* Geneva: EBU.

Jakubowicz, K. (2003). Bringing public service broadcasting to account. In Hujanen, T., & Lowe, G. (Eds.), *Broadcasting and convergence: New articulations of the public service remit* (pp. 147–165). Gothenburg: Nordicom.

Leino, R. (2021). *Median valtaajat* (Raiders of the media). Into kustannus.

Martin, E. N. (2021). Can public service broadcasting survive Silicon Valley? Synthesizing leadership perspectives at the BBC, PBS, NPR, CPB and local U.S. stations. *Technology in Society*, 64, 101451. doi:10.1016/j.techsoc.2020.101451

Mazzucato, M., Conway, R., Mazzoli, E., Knoll, E., & Albala, S. (2020). *Creating and measuring dynamic public value at the BBC.* UCL Institute for Innovation and Public Purpose, Policy Report (IIPP WP 2020–19).

Milosavljević, M., & Poler Kovačič, M. (2021). Between the hammer and the anvil: Public service broadcasters in the Western Balkans squeezed between commercialization and politicization.

In Jusić, T., Puppis, M., Castro Herrero, L., & Marko, D. (Eds.), *Up in the air?: The future of public service media in the Western Balkans* (pp. 219–232). Budapest: Central European University Press. doi: 10.7829/j.ctv1c3pdhh.18

Milosavljević, M., & Vobič, I. (2021). "Our task is to demystify fears": Analysing newsroom management of automation in journalism. *Journalism, 22*(9), 2203–2221. doi: 10.1177/1464884919861598

Murschetz, P. C. (2021). Datafication and public service media. *Medien Journal, 44*(3), 69–86. doi: 10.24989/medienjournal.v44i3.1808

Negroponte, N. (1995). *Being digital.* London, England: Vintage Books.

O'Neil, C. (2018). *Weapons of math destruction: How big data increases inequality and threatens democracy.* London, England: Penguin Books.

Pariser, E. (2012). *The filter bubble: How the new personalized web is changing what we read and how we think.* Penguin Books.

PMA (n.d.). What is PSM? *Public Media Alliance.* https://www.publicmediaalliance.org/about-us/what-is-psm/

Savage, P., Medina, M., & Ferrell Lowe, G. (2020). *Universalism in public service media.* Gothenburg: Nordicom.

Scannell, P., & Cardiff, D. (1991). *A social history of British broadcasting, volume one 1922–1939: Serving the nation.* Cambridge: Basil Blackwell.

Sørensen, J. K. (2021). The shortcomings of the diversity diet: Public service media, algorithms and the multiple dimensions of diversity. In *Algorithmic distribution of the news: Policy responses.* New York, NY: Palgrave Macmillan.

Sørensen, J., & Hutchinson, J. (2018). Algorithms and public service media. In Lowe, G. F., van den Bulck, H., & Donders, K. (Eds.), *Public service media in the networked society RIPE@ 2017* (pp. 91–106). Nordicom.

Sørensen, J. K., & Van den Bulck, H. (2020). Public service media online, advertising and the third-party user data business: A trade versus trust dilemma? *Convergence, the International Journal of Research into New Media Technologies, 26*(2), 421–447. doi: 10.1177/1354856518790203

Sørensen, J. K., Van den Bulck, H., & Sokol, K. (2020). Stop spreading the data: PSM, trust and third-party service. *Journal of Information Policy, 10,* 474–513.

Tambini, D. (2021). *Public service media should be thinking long term when it comes to AI* (2021, May 12). Media@LSE. https://blogs.lse.ac.uk/medialse/2021/05/12/public-service-media-should-be-thinking-long-term-when-it-comes-to-ai/

Thurman, N., Lewis, S. C., & Kunert, J. (2019). Algorithms, automation, and news, *Digital Journalism, 7*(8), 980–992. doi: 10.1080/21670811.2019.168539

Thurman, N., & Schifferes, S. (2012). The future of personalization at news websites. *Journalism Studies, 13*(5–6), 775–790.

Toff, B. et al. (2020). *What we think we know and what we want to know: Perspectives on trust in news in a changing world.* Oxford: Reuters Institute. https://reutersinstitute.politics.ox.ac.uk/sites/default/files/2020-12/Toff_et_al_Perspectives_on_Trust_in_News_FINAL.pdf

Túñez-López, J. M., Fieiras Ceide, C., & Vaz-Álvarez, M. (2021). Impact of artificial intelligence on journalism: Transformations in the company, products, contents and professional profile. *Communication & Society, 34*(1), 177–193.

UNESCO (2021). *Recommendation on the ethics of artificial intelligence.* SHS/BIO/REC-AIETH-ICS/2021. https://unesdoc.unesco.org/ark:/48223/pf0000380455

Van den Bulck, H. (2001). Public service television and national identity as a project of modernity: The example of flemish television. *Media Culture and Society, 23*(1), 53–69.

Van den Bulck, H. (2008). Can PSB stake its claim in a media world of digital convergence? The case of the Flemish PSB management contract renewal. *Convergence, 14*(3), 335–350. doi: 10.1111/j.1751-9020.2007.00020.x

Van den Bulck, H. (2009). The last yet also the first creative act in television? An historical analysis of PSB scheduling strategies and tactics. *Media History*, *15*(3), 321–344. doi:10.1080/13688800902966253

Van den Bulck, H. (2015). Public service media accountability in recent decades: A progressive shift from state to market. In Ibarra, K. A., Nowak, E., & Kuhn, R. (Eds.), *Public service media in Europe: A comparative approach*. London: Routledge.

Van den Bulck, H., & Moe, M. (2018). Universality and personalisation through algorithms: Mapping strategies and exploring dilemmas. *Media Culture and Society*, *40*(6), 875–892.

Vandendriessche, K., Steenberghs, E., Matheve, A., Georges, A., & De Marez, L. (2020) *Imec digimeter 2020: Digitale trends in vlaanderen*. Ghent: IMEC.

Vaz-Álvarez, M., Túñez-López, M., Fieiras-Ceide, C., & Costa Sánchez, C. (2021). AI strategies in european public service media: Diverse solutions for common challenges. Working paper. *IAMCR 2021. Working Group: Public Service Media Policies*. https://iamcr.org/node/17308

Tackling Bias in AI and Promoting Responsible Research and Innovation: Insights from Discussions with Different Stakeholders

Kalypso Iordanou and Josephina Antoniou

School of Sciences, University of Central Lancashire (UCLan) Cyprus, Larnaca, Cyprus

CONTENTS

DOI: 10.1201/9781003261247-11

INTRODUCTION

Biases in the information provided by AI algorithms, perpetuating gender and racial stereotypes (Otterbacher, 2018), coupled with human's tendency to process information through lenses protecting their initial beliefs and biases (Iordanou et al., 2020), favor one-sided thinking, extremism, and fanaticism, often leveraged in racist ways, and seldom to indict white supremacy (Cave & Dihal, 2020) and Western imperialism, with deleterious effects on democracy and the societal wellbeing. Several ethical issues have been acknowledged arising from AI and Big Data in the literature, including exploitation of behavioral biases, deception, and addiction generation to maximize profit (Costa & Halpern, 2019), manipulation (Helbing et al., 2019), spread of misinformation, hate speech and conspiracy theories (Scheufele & Krause, 2019). The algorithmic filtering, which refers to prioritizing the selection, sequence, and the visibility of posts (Bucher, 2012), is viewed as a reinforcer of individuals' worldviews, biases and polarization (Loader et al., 2016; Gillespie, 2018; Helbing et al., 2019). In addition, the emerging technologies have been accused for encapsulating the worldviews and biases of their creators (Broussard, 2018; Noble, 2018) or the data they rely on (Cave, 2019). The result of algorithmic bias or bias in Big Data is the replication of biases, stereotypes, and biased decisions (Pols & Spahn, 2015). The lack of transparency and accountability (Wachter et al., 2017) enabled surveillance capitalism to flourish, putting democracy under attack (Christodoulou & Iordanou, 2021).

> *Surveillance capitalists now hold the answers to each question, though we never elected them to govern ... They claim the authority to decide who knows by asserting ownership rights over our personal information and defend that authority with the power to control critical information systems and infrastructures.* (Zuboff, 2021)

What can we do to deal with the challenges coming along with the rapid development of technology – AI and Big Data? The answer cannot be to move backward, turning our back to emerging technologies. The answer might be to focus on promoting the development of *responsible* technology, which will be human-centered, not discriminating between races, cultural backgrounds, etc. and will promote individual and societal wellbeing, a topic that we turn to next.

RESPONSIBLE INNOVATION

European Commission, acknowledging the importance of responsible innovation, proposed the term RRI, to describe Responsible Research and Innovation, a science policy framework that aims to describe scientific and technological research in a way that takes into account potential impacts on society and the environment. The European Commission subsequently funded a number of projects to examine how RRI can be promoted – an example constitutes the project COMPASS, one of the two projects that the present chapter focuses on. RRI, is a multi-dimensional concept, involving *public engagement, gender equality, science education, open access, ethics, and governance* (Soraker et al., 2017). The RRI *Ethics* pillar is particularly interesting for this chapter, especially in relation to the impact of AI and Big Data-related technologies in industry and society. "The need for ethical considerations in the development of intelligent interactive systems is becoming one of the main influential areas of research in the last few years" (Dignum, 2018, p. 1).

Given that a considerable amount of research is conducted in the industry sector, any efforts to promote RRI which excludes industry are condemned to fail (Iordanou, 2019). RRI encourages an approach toward innovation where "societal actors and innovators become mutually responsive to each other with a view to the acceptability, sustainability and societal desirability of the innovation process" (Von Schomberg, 2012). However, as the effort to intertwine scientific excellence and society, through the implementation of responsible practices, has been increasing, so have the observed challenges.

At the core of European Commission's concept of RRI, a concept primarily tailored to be applicable within the European context (from the Responsible Research and Innovation report (European Commission, 2012) published under the Science in Society initiative), is the inclusion of different stakeholders, working together, for finding solutions to the complex issues arising from emerging technologies and the successful implementation of RRI.

> *RRI means that societal actors work together during the whole research and innovation process in order to better align both the process and its outcomes with the values, needs and expectations of European Society ... an ambitious challenge for the creation of a Research and Innovation policy driven by the needs of society and engaging all societal actors via inclusive participatory approaches.*

In the present work, we reach out to different stakeholders – experts in AI technology – employing focus groups and individual interviews, to examine their views on the ethical dimensions of AI/Big Data and how to promote responsible research and innovation (RRI). The findings presented here are part of larger studies pursued in the projects COMPASS and SHERPA, both funded by European Commission.

This chapter is organized as follows: the Methodology of the two studies is presented followed by the Results of both studies, identifying common themes between the two studies. The chapter continues with a discussion of the common recommendations emerging from both data collection phases, focusing on the implications for education, which needs to focus more on promoting critical, responsible thinking, and on the aspects to be considered for successful AI regulation. Implications for promoting RRI and addressing the ethical issues of AI are also discussed.

METHODOLOGICAL APPROACH

The chapter is a comparative study between the data collected from two separate qualitative studies that took place under the umbrella of two different European projects, the

EU Horizon 2020 COMPASS project (2016–2019) and the EU Horizon 2020 SHERPA project (2018–2021). The aim of both studies was to capture the opinions of technology experts and other stakeholders, on the application of RRI, and in particular the ethical impact of developing and using emerging technologies, e.g., AI.

The COMPASS project was an EU-funded project that supported Small and Medium-sized Enterprises (SMEs) from emerging technology industries to manage their research, development, and innovation activities in a responsible and inclusive manner in a number of ways including tools and services tailored to SME needs. SHERPA was an EU project that, in collaboration with a broad range of stakeholders, investigated, analyzed, and synthesized the ways in which AI and Big Data analytics can impact ethics and human rights in society, and made recommendations to advocate the most desirable and sustainable solutions.

Overall, the COMPASS data collection focused on the responsible use of emerging technologies in specific sectors, i.e., healthcare and nanotechnology, and the SHERPA data collection focused on the specific technologies themselves, i.e., AI and Big Data.

Participants
Individual Interviews
Thirty key industry representatives, 18 from the ICT healthcare sector and 12 from the nanotechnology sector, participated in individual interviews in the context of the COMPASS project. Purposeful sampling, and in particular maximum variation sampling, aiming to capture a wide range of perspectives relevant to the specific study, was conducted to identify prospect interviewees. Specifically, all the partners in the project COMPASS were asked to propose prospect interviewees from their network, which were reviewed by the researchers and included in the sample, making sure that a diverse and representative sample from healthcare and nontechnology industry was secured. The participants were key industry representatives, mostly CEOs in their companies, from different countries across Europe, 10 were from the UK, 7 were from Austria, 5 were from Spain, 4 were from Cyprus, 2 were from Belgium, 1 participant was from Italy, 1 participant was from Slovenia, and another one was from Switzerland.

Focus Groups
Forty-nine individuals participated in six focus groups for the SHERPA data collection. Four focus groups were pursued on Guidelines for AI developers promoting Ethics-by-design, developed in the context of the project. Two of the focus groups on Guidelines were pursued in Cyprus with a range of stakeholders – AI designers, AI users in the industry, and social researchers from NGOs – and the other two focus groups were pursued in the UK with members of the British Computer Society. The remaining two focus groups were pursued on Regulatory Options, where the idea of an AI regulator was discussed with the stakeholders, mostly policy and legal experts, but also technology experts, again for AI and Big Data systems, one in Cyprus and the other virtually, due to the pandemic with different participants from a number of countries.

Instruments

Both for the interviews and for the focus groups, interview protocols were developed by one of the authors for the COMPASS interviews and by partners in the SHERPA project. In COMPASS project, participants were asked to explain what they considered as the main barriers and challenges for adopting RRI in healthcare and nanotechnology, as well as what are their recommendations for successful implementation of RRI. In SHERPA, for the Guidelines focus groups, participants were asked to provide feedback on the Guidelines developed in the context of SHERPA for the consideration of ethics during development and use of AI and Big Data technologies. The proposed guidelines are available on the SHERPA project website (https://www.project-sherpa.eu/guidelines/). For the Regulatory options, the focus group participants were asked to comment on potential requirements for a new AI regulator at EU level.

Procedure

Thirty in-depth interviews were conducted by three researchers within the COMPASS project. The task of the interviewers was one of probing for further details or asking for clarification when necessary; the interviews proceeded as a conversation rather than a question-and-answer session. Each interview lasted approximately 25–60 minutes and was conducted in person, via Skype or telephone. The procedure for the focus groups conducted within the SHERPA project was similar. The duration of the focus groups was on average between 60 and 90 minutes.

DATA ANALYSIS

Although the projects were completed within ethically approved guidelines from the EU, the data collection phases received additional ethical approvals from the Cyprus National Bioethics Committee. The data obtained during the focus groups was analyzed using thematic analysis (Braun & Clarke, 2006). Analysis of the transcripts was undertaken centrally, led by one of the authors, to ensure consistency. A stepped process of thematic coding was utilized. An inductive approach was used. The first stage of open coding was followed by a further stage of thematic coding during which emerging themes were compared and contrasted and gradually refined. After discussion between the authors, the themes were finalized.

Results Overview

Given the particular needs for RRI in industry, and in particular the specific needs identified in the healthcare and nanotechnology sectors, the COMPASS results explored, through interviews, a deeper understanding of what key industry stakeholders from these sectors considered as the main challenges for RRI. The results also provided insight into their recommendations toward alleviating those challenges. The SHERPA results explored, through a number of focus groups with technology-related stakeholders, how to successfully move forward with the development and operational use of AI and Big Data in various sectors.

Challenges Identified

According to results from COMPASS, companies within the nanotechnology sector are expected to promote and support a high level of innovation that results in positive societal impact, as it is a sector "impacting modern social life and economies" (Galatsis et al., 2015). The sector has been transformed by information technology. This transformation was caused by the rapidly growing technological sector, e.g., introduction of new technologies, and has resulted in challenging social issues that need to be addressed, such as job losses, or gender equality and diversity in technical sectors. There has been an eminent need for responsible practices to address these social issues, in addition to many others that fall under the umbrella of responsibility, such as environmental issues, and new policies and regulation.

Furthermore, COMPASS identifies similar regulatory needs in the sector of healthcare. Technological innovation must be regulated within this sector, especially with regard to "the changing relationship between the private and public sector in the use of human genomics and personal medical information" (Martin & Hollin, 2014). The relationship is transforming into a collaborative one, offering a better foundation for responsible practices in the private sector that will be encouraged by the public sector. Martin and Hollin (2014) recognize that the healthcare sector is moving toward this direction since "throughout the 2000s a series of UK and EU public policy initiatives were taken to promote innovation and growth of the ... commercial development of biotechnology in particular".

In SHERPA, the issue of governance linked to responsibility is also highlighted in the discussion that took place during the focus groups. In fact, it is suggested by participants that the context must be clarified in terms of who is responsible for the design of appropriate guidelines in order for information governance to be aligned to the business governance structures since it is "the business that sets the ethical principles against which an ethical system must be designed" (FG-GUID-1). This does not refer to the business governing the ethics, but that the business should include ways within its structure to check the ethics.

The concept of information governance should be evident in any guidelines, clearly indicating the responsible parties, both in guidelines for users, including business management, but also guidelines for developers, such that "information governance is outside the IT department" (FG-GUID-1).

> IT build the car, but the business needs to drive it and describe it. Yes, it's been a hard job to get a corporate organisation to accept that they drive privacy. ... The whole thing needed to be moved into the corporate context. Once we started getting information governance, that's when we started succeeding in that. (FG-GUID-1)

Another challenge identified particularly in the context of the COMPASS project is societal *values and attitudes*. Almost half of the interviewees asked, mentioned that culture's, including scientists', values and attitudes is one of the major barriers for adoption of RRI. At the same time, they identify reflection and reconsideration of the values that scientists and society prioritize, as a promising way for promoting responsible research and innovation, as discussed in the following section. They mentioned that societies value fast money and there is no consideration of the consequences of the attempts for fast money. The following interviewee has described nicely this barrier:

> I think that the Vantage Points that are listed in philosophy and from philosophy to culture and from the cultural to the policy and from the policy to the strategy, from the strategy to tactics, from the tactics to logistics and from logistics to tasks. So, you don't go to the task directly if you don't have the philosophy and the culture before. I think that if your philosophy and your culture is to get as much money as you can, as fast as you can and the world will be fixed by God, then there is nothing to be done. I think it is the cultural thing before you start to innovate. (N1)

Another interviewee noted that this attitude toward fast profit is not limited to industry, but has also affected universities, which depend to some extent on external agencies for funding.

> There is traditional business culture where research is not appreciated because you have to make money and all the business, culture around the university, investors, spin offs and start-ups don't want to invest into anything which is not fast profit. It is quite a low cost, a low quality business culture we have now in our world, in US, in Europe. That's the problem. They don't ask you do things well. They ask you to cheat and invent and make artificial things and get plenty of money from investors. The economical culture is quite low, happy, low cost, not very useful. (H1)

"Those starting the social responsible innovation are already socially responsible scientists or stakeholders" another interviewee mentioned to highlight that social responsibility precedes social innovation, i.e., the innovation will follow where there is a culture of responsibility.

The attitudes toward change and innovation by small family business were also mentioned by some interviewees as a barrier to the adoption of RRI. As the following interviewee mentioned, even if the director of the business is not part of the family business, "culture is beyond everything".

> Many of the SMEs we've got in XXX are very innovative because they come from academia so they have technology breakthroughs so they really want to share even open innovations so they are not afraid. The bigger or the more traditional the company then it changes a lot. Because they are more afraid of risks, they are less willing to change things the way they've been doing it for years ... the CEO is not from the family but at the end of the day the culture is beyond everything. So in my experience, generally speaking, these companies are more reluctant in

*trying new things and they have their part lines they know what they want to do
and if something is interesting okay but they don't want to try fancy things as
they say.* (H1)

In the project SHERPA, a project that explored how AI and Big Data analytics can impact
ethics and human rights, participants identified the challenge for policy makers to take
into consideration public values. The need for inclusive policy making, taking into
consideration a wide range of citizens, and human rights was underlined in the FGs:

> *An EU AI regulator could support national regulators in ensuring that the algorithms
> used safeguard human rights and other ethical republic values.* (FG, REG-1)

Recommendations from Stakeholders

In the following sections, we juxtapose the recommendations highlighted in the discussions from COMPASS and SHERPA. The recommendations are organized by their
core theme. In particular, data collected from the COMPASS interviews and the SHERPA
focus groups seemed to follow two separate thematic axes, relating to the discussion of
challenges and possible recommendations: education and regulation.

Education

The majority of the COMPASS interviewees acknowledged the role of education in
promoting RRI. As the interviewee mentioned below, in order to promote RRI we need
to develop responsible scientists and citizens first.

> *I don't think that RRI program will make people more responsible. To make people
> more responsible you have to go deeper into society. You need education. And this
> is not a problem of innovation responsibility. It is the problem of society. Not
> responsible societies will not make responsible innovation! They will make stupid
> innovation. Stupid societies make stupid innovations, stupid decisions, and stupid
> referendums. So education should go first and once you have responsible societies
> you will get responsible innovations.* (N1)

Through education, people need to reconsider and change values, especially values of fast
profit.

> *Other people like it bigger, stronger, faster and cheaper and they don't care about
> consequences. That's the problem. That's an education problem. We will use our
> overwhelming future benefits to make the education. The bigger, faster and
> stronger that was 2000 years ago in Roman times, we should get away from that.
> The atomic bomb and all that. We don't need it anymore. The philosophy of going
> faster, bigger and stronger and more powerful and cheaper and bigger and bigger
> and more energy more energy more energy.* (N1)

Educating citizens to be responsible, and informing them particularly about RRI, could substantially affect the application of RRI because citizens will prefer products that have been developed following RRI (Thompson & Kumar, 2021) and will put social pressure on companies forcing them to adopt RRI. Here are some of the quotes provided by the interviewees:

> *If this is a market which is usually driven by customer needs, if there is an awareness even at the level of customer ..., for example, components that are developed with an RRI behind the development, the companies will actually use this as a marketing tool.*

Some COMPASS interviewees proposed even to focus on scientists' education, while others suggested to include RRI in the mainstream education in order to educate all citizens. This links to the public opinion collected in SHERPA. For SHERPA, having guidelines for educational purposes, for developers and users of AI is discussed as "a way of really educating people and giving the information to people so it can really make sense to them" (FG-GUID-2).

When developing and using smart information systems, including AI and Big Data technologies, bias tends to become an issue that developers and users need to consider. Aiming for transparency can be a way to address bias. Allowing for algorithmic or implementation transparency increases the likelihood of identifying any biases in the software design and development. The focus group participants highlighted the link between transparency and bias:

> *And it comes down to who's programming, how cognitive computing starts? I mean who is behind the AI? How did they train the AI to give advice? So, you need that background of the AI machine as well to see if it's biased or not.* (FG-GUID-3)

Lack of necessary knowledge extends beyond lack of technical knowledge, but must also include a common understanding of ethics and their implementation. It can be argued that identifying what is ethical may vary between individuals. This is an even more challenging task at the company level:

> *everyone's definition of what is ethical or where to draw the line will differ. And as it was pointed out, companies do not have the incentive, and being or maybe not being that ethical, it makes more financial sense. And it's the same with governments as well. One country might have completely different definition of what they want to peruse for their gains as compared to the other countries.* (FG-GUID-3)

Individual certification can also be a strong motivator for developers. It acts as evidence of relevant professional training and adds confidence in the developer's inter-disciplinary knowledge and skills:

> *For individuals, if there is a certification process or something, it's an interest for them to follow the training because somehow it can display or they can show that they have this and that, which maybe one day will appear in vacancies and say, well we would like this person to have instead of CCNA and whatever, a certification of ethical implementations.* (FG-GUID-2)

The lack of education of what it means to responsibly develop technology, i.e., what to consider, and how to responsibly use technology is the basic need in moving forward, according to SHERPA focus group participants:

> *At the basis of this it's education, especially with kids. Because kids grow up with Google and we've grown up with Google and the kids are [relying] on our personal assistance on phones and stuff like that, which is AI and big data. So, it depends on how they learn. You need to somehow give them the education and the logic to not always believe what they hear, or they see on smart phones, let's say, or through software.* (FG-GUID-3)

And also:

> *Because, let's say we have now smart phones with our personal assistant on it. Everyone has the personal assistant. The personal assistant knows all our contacts, our emails, text messages, our social media activity. Each personal assistant perhaps in the future will be able to somehow tell you what to do at some point. And you will trust that. So, education should start from now on this. Like make people be careful when they start using personal assistants.* (FG-GUID-2)

Education can also be a way to mitigate negative impacts of technology caused by misuse of technology. Threats to individuals, to the society, and the environment will exist but educating citizens, especially the younger generation, in responsible use, can act as a counter-measure:

> *I think the most important is education of the younger generation. … I think the society should be active so that to introduce some more policies for controlling all technologies related to AI. But I think that as the society improves and progress, you cannot stop the evolution, the progress and from my point of view there is a threat and we need to see how we handle it. For me the most important threat is the misuse of AI, to use AI for damaging of society, of a person of a whole world. And we can see every day, we hear in the news that there was a robot that was cleaning the pollution in the ocean. Why not this robot go and make some huge damage in the ocean?* (FG-GUID-2)

Regulation

When it comes to regulation of emerging technologies and particularly of AI, the opinion of SHERPA focus group participants is that education of the regulators themselves is crucial, i.e., there is a need for technologically and ethically educated politicians, since "in order for politicians to vote the correct, the right laws, they should have the education" (FG-GUID-2). Moreover, and according to SHERPA results, a potential appointment of an EU regulator for AI would need to ensure to educate or train regulatory bodies at national levels so that they can apply the necessary guidelines, even where there is lack of expertise:

> *I think one of the problems currently with many regulators is that they lack the knowledge and the expertise to cover a wide range of different algorithms and developments etc. So, I can imagine that an EU AI regulator could support national regulators in ensuring that the algorithms used safeguard human rights and other ethical republic values.* (FG-REG-1)

In COMPASS interviews, the majority of the interviewees discussed regulatory options. Specifically, 70% suggested changes in the legislation in order to force the companies to use standards. They also mentioned that the European Commission and local governments should support RRI, either by having RRI as a criterion for funding EU projects or by offering direct support to companies to adopt RRI.

> *You can make a law to make them share ... I mean it's law or legislation that's the best way to do it and the second way is with money it can be direct money or it can be in tax with action or whatever at the end of the day for the company the money is the money coming in or less money going out. But for me ... you either push them to do so, so you say that's the way it's going to be now that's the legislation so you have to do it so that's very effective but is hard for politicians to do because sometimes, the legislation, people are not really happy with it so they don't know if with new elections the legislation is still going to be there. But I think sometimes the government should be a little bit braver doing that.* (H1)

Some interviewees suggested particularly for Academia to set compliance to RRI standards as a criterion for receiving funding.

> *I think that Academia needs another funding agency foundation ... we can trust. These people could start asking for responsible innovation. You don't get funded if you don't have responsible innovation plan, you don't get the scholarship if you don't have responsible innovation plan. ... that will force people to think about it and engage resources.* (N1)

Other interviewees, identifying that a substantial amount of research is conducted outside the academia, suggested to set RRI compliance as a criterion for funding industry projects as well.

There is part of research going in industry, like in (SMEs), which is funded by public money and there should also be a push from the public funding towards RRI because today in our case, for example, we submit a project for research and innovation. We are not judged based on RRI. … If you can get this as a policy of the European Commission and the local governments that it has to be. … So if you include this as one of the criteria … and it has specific weight and judgment, this will be motivating because, at least in Europe, many, many SMEs depend on the public funding for the big part of their research activities. (N2)

Another interviewee identified that regulation should be applied globally; the reason for this is to allow for a higher impact, and thus the regulation would eventually be more efficient.

It [regulation] should be looked at from a global perspective rather than a national perspective. (N10)

Similar to the COMPASS results, the SHERPA findings from the focus groups are not much different in terms of recommendations for regulation. The focus group participants discuss the significance of national participation in the regulation but further comment on requirements for a potential EU regulator that could consider important regulation aspects at an EU level (in addition to the national regulation) for each member state. Effectively applying the measures for responsible AI and Big Data development and operational use, requires that national authorities to action, however, the EU regulator must be able to coordinate such action:

I think at a national level we have legislation, we have authorities that maintain laws and I suppose that they can be strengthened at an EU level and they have to take advantage and strengthen the national levels instead of passing by. (FG-REG-1)

Nevertheless, the participants agree on the importance of having an EU regulator that can coordinate the different stakeholders, including professional differences, national differences, cultural differences, differences in the use of technology, etc.

A European regulator is important and essential because, again, (the regulator) could be very focused on how this technology is going to impact on a broader level the European dynamics and then of course each government to decide for themselves if and how they want to implement that technology. I think the regulation should still be coming from a European level and then move on to a national level. (FG-REG-1)

So having a regulatory body, having a policy or law, can be a strong motivator. Given that the primary step is to develop guidelines for the development and use of AI and other emerging technologies, "if the guidelines are legally binding or they have to be there, so if this were more of a policy or law, then people would go through this" (FG-GUID-2). The idea of using some type of legal enforcement, where the threat of punishment is more real, is a way to get things started. The idea of accountability is highlighted as the core motivator:

> *It really helps when someone gets in trouble to be able to go to a board. Because they are looking at it as a business risk. They're not looking at it as a moral, ethical issue in the end. They're saying, "What would we lose in terms of market penetration? What would we lose in terms of customers compared to the low probability of a fine or publicity?* (FG-GUID-4)

DISCUSSION

The present study aimed to examine different stakeholders' views on the challenges of applying responsible research and innovation (RRI) and in particular ethics in the development and operational use of emerging technologies, focusing on AI. Results identified some barriers and challenges for the adoption of RRI. A prominent challenge identified by key industry stakeholders is *societal values* which place emphasis on fast profit without considering the consequences of one's actions, e.g., transnational racial capitalism. To address those challenges participants emphasized the role of education toward individualized responsibility, for developing the sense of individuals' agency – that they are in control of their actions – for developing responsible researchers, business leaders, consumers, and citizens. Recommendations also involved changes in the regulation of these technologies and suggestions about the context of any guidelines of how to move forward, i.e., that guidelines must be clarified in terms of who is responsible for the design of these guidelines.

Interviewees viewed the values of innovators, researchers, and citizens, in general, as a major barrier for responsible research and innovation. The interviewees identified this as a barrier both for innovators, scientists, business leaders who pursue research and develop products and for citizens who are the consumers of those products. Research malpractice, driven by individualist values, can have detrimental consequences on societies, where public money is wasted without providing solutions to problems, such as health problems (Kolata, 2018). On the other hand, citizens' individualistic values also have consequences on responsible research and practice. As one of the interviewees noted, "When you use your money, you are making a political act; you are giving the money to someone, or someone else. You are … closing companies". Other interviewees mentioned that citizens can put pressure on companies to be aligned with responsible research and innovation through social media. Interviewees' views on the role of individuals' values on the adoption of RRI are in line with research values, which have provided evidence of a relation between individuals' values and their behavior (Miles, 2015). For example, the value of collectivism predicts environmental behavior, particularly green purchase (Kim, 2011).

Differences in values and practices between different countries affect competitiveness. Interviewees expressed the concern that adherence to RRI may involve extra cost which will result in more expensive products which will be less competitive compared to products who have been constructed by companies who do not adopt RRI. This concern confirms previous concerns about competitiveness that have been reported in the literature as a barrier for the adoption of RRI (Martinuzzi et al., 2018). A possible solution to this problem has been provided by the interviewees themselves, who suggested changes in the *legislation* system in order to enforce all the companies, worldwide, to follow the same standards, not specifying how these standards will be agreed upon, but being cautious not to have these standards be dictated. Participants in the focus groups have also extensively discussed regulatory options, and in particular, the presence of an EU regulator for AI as a solution. In this way, companies' concerns that compliance with RRI may result in more expensive and therefore less competitive products, compared with the products of companies which are not compliant with RRI, will be alleviated.

The need of regulation for emerging technologies, to have a more transparent, accountable, and inclusive policy making toward emerging technologies, was one of the major suggestions of focus group participants, as well. The regulation of such technologies implies the need for ethics-aligned technologies, aligned with La Fors et al. (2019) proposal for emerging technologies to take into consideration the following values: human welfare (the fair treatment of citizens in various contexts, e.g., employment, schooling, traveling), autonomy (awareness, free will and free choice), non-maleficence (transparency in order to avoid harm), justice (fair, preventative law enforcement practices), accountability (know who is responsible for data sharing), trustworthiness (for technology operators and big-data based conclusions), privacy (safeguard from easy identifiability), dignity (avoid discrimination and stigmatization), solidarity (avoid the prioritization of commercial interests and root for mutual support) and environmental welfare (safeguard against direct and indirect threats to the environment). Furthermore, our findings show, based on a variety of stakeholders' views, that development should indeed consider the integration of values, and that any regulation should take this into consideration. Dignum (2018) proposed that algorithms need "to integrate societal, legal and moral values into technological developments in AI, at all stages of development (analysis, design, construction, deployment and evaluation)" (p. 1). Dignum also highlighted the need for making AI reasoning more inclusive, to "weigh the respective priorities of values held by different stakeholders in various multicultural contexts; explain its reasoning; and guarantee transparency" (2018, p. 1).

The other major recommendation offered by all participants is to promote RRI and address ethical considerations of AI and Big Data through *education*. Some interviewees mentioned that education toward RRI should be embedded in all levels of the educational system, starting from the elementary school. Participants highlighted particularly the role of higher education in promoting RRI and the ethical dimensions of AI, which is consistent with recommendations in the literature (Zembylas, 2021). The interviewees acknowledged that there is an imperative need to support the development of individuals' critical thinking skills, particularly their ability to take multiple perspectives into account, not focusing only on the economic aspect or personal benefit, and place greater consideration on the possible long-term, collective consequences for society, of their decisions and actions. Interviewees expressed the expectation for education to undertake this important task, viewing education as the nursery of future scientists, business leaders, policy makers, consumers, and citizens, whose decisions and behavior will determine whether research and innovation is pursued in a more responsible way, respecting one another and our environment. If we wish future business leaders to adopt responsible research and innovation procedures in their business, future politicians and policy makers to make more responsible decisions and promote legislation supporting RRI, future teachers to teach their students starting from pre-K to university, to think critically and responsibly, future journalists to be cautious toward not replicating fake scientific news, and citizens to support responsible research and innovation through their actions as voters and consumers, we need to pay closer attention on efforts promoting RRI throughout the education system and lifelong learning. The concerns and recommendations of stakeholders are in line with other voices in academia calling for a reform in education and the need to place greater emphasis on promoting critical thinking skills, including consideration of the ethical dimensions of AI (Kuhn, 2005; Zembylas, 2021). Some intervention programs appear promising in supporting the development of students' critical thinking skills at different levels, from primary to higher education (Iordanou & Kuhn, 2020; Iordanou & Rapanta, 2021), including greater reflective thinking (Iordanou, 2022a) and consideration of the ethical dimensions of an issue (Iordanou, 2022b). Future research should examine the effectiveness of those interventions, based on discussion and reflection (Iordanou & Rapanta, 2021), on supporting particularly deeper thinking on ethical issues of AI and Big Data and more responsible behavior. The objective of promoting more collective values, promoting human and environmental wellbeing, is more challenging, yet an important one that future research should address. Furthermore, more exploratory studies, such as this one are needed, involving a larger and more diverse sample, involving participants from different domains not covered in this study.

Finally, the present study shows that launching an open dialog with multiple stakeholders, as the studies discussed in the present chapter employed, to understand different perspectives on how to promote RRI and deal with the ethical challenges of AI, is a promising endeavor to deal with this complex issue. Addressing the ethical challenges of emerging technologies is a complex issue, involving multiple stakeholders and we should address it as such. Engaging different stakeholders in the dialog on how to address the ethical challenges of AI could increase mutual understanding, commitment, and willingness to work all together for designing a more human-centered AI, promoting individual and societal wellbeing.

REFERENCES

Broussard, M. (2018). *Artificial unintelligence: How computers misunderstand the world*. Cambridge: MIT Press.

Braun, V., & Clarke, V. (2006). Using thematic analysis in psychology. *Qualitative Research in Psychology, 3*(2), 77–101.

Bucher, T. (2012). Want to be on the top? Algorithmic power and the threat of invisibility on Facebook. *New Media and Society, 14*(7), 1164–1180.

Cave, S. (2019). To save us from a kafkaesque future, we must democratise AI. *The Guardian*, 4 January 2019.

Cave, S., & Dihal, K. (2020). The whiteness of AI. *Philosophy & Technology, 33,* 685–703. doi:10.1007/s13347-020-00415-6

Christodoulou, E., & Iordanou, K. (2021). Democracy under attack: Challenges of addressing ethical issues of AI and big data for more democratic digital media and societies [Original Research]. *Frontiers in Political Science, 3.* 10.3389/fpos.2021.682945

Costa, E., & Halpern, D. (2019). The behavioural science of online harm and manipulation, and what to do about it. *The Behavioural Insights Team.*https://www.bi.team/publications/the-behavioural-science-of-online-harm-and-manipulation-and-what-to-do-about-it/

Dignum, V. (2018). Ethics in artificial intelligence: Introduction to the special issue. *Ethics and Information Technology, 20,* 1–3.

European Commission (2012). Responsible research and innovation: Europe's ability to respond to societal challenges. *Research and Innovation Policy.* doi:10.2777/11739

Galatsis, et al. (2015). Nanoelectronics research gaps and recommendations. *IEEE Society and Technology Magazine, 34*(2), 21–30.10.1109/MTS.2015.2425811

Gillespie, T. (2018) *Custodians of the internet: Platforms, content moderation, and the hidden decisions that shape social media.* New Haven, CT: Yale University Press.

Helbing, D., Caron, & Helbing. (2019). *Towards digital enlightenment* (pp. 73–98). Springer International Publishing: Cham, Switzerland.

Iordanou, K. (2019). Involving patients in research? Responsible research and innovation in small- and medium-sized European health care enterprises. *Cambridge Quarterly of Healthcare Ethics, 28*(1), 144–152. doi:10.1017/S0963180118000488

Iordanou, K. (2022a). Supporting strategic and meta-strategic development of argument skill: The role of reflection. *Metacognition and Learning.* doi:10.1007/s11409-021-09289-1

Iordanou, K. (2022b). Supporting critical thinking through engagement in dialogic argumentation: Taking multiple considerations into account when reasoning about genetically modified food. In Jimenez-Aleixandre, M. & Puig Mauriz, B. (Eds.), *Critical thinking in biology & environmental education.* Springer.

Iordanou, K., Kendeou, P., & Zembylas, M. (2020). Examining my-side bias during and after reading controversial historical accounts. *Metacognition and Learning, 15*(3), 319–342. doi:10.1007/s11409-020-09240-w

Iordanou, K., & Kuhn, D. (2020). Contemplating the opposition: Does a personal touch matter? *Discourse Processes, 57*(4), 343–359.

Iordanou, K., & Rapanta, C. (2021). "Argue with me": A method for developing argument skills. *Frontiers in Psychology, 12,* 359.

Kim, Y. (2011). Understanding green purchase: The influence of collectivism, personal values and environmental attitudes, and the moderating effect of perceived consumer effectiveness. *Seoul Journal of Business, 17*(1) 65–92.

Kolata, G. (2018, October 29). He promised to restore damaged hearts. Harvard says his lab fabricated research. *New York Times.*

Kuhn, D. (2005). *Education for thinking.* Harvard University Press.

La Fors, K., Custers, B., & Keymolen, E. (2019). Reassessing values for emerging big data technologies: Integrating design-based and application-based approaches. *Ethics and Information Technology, 21*(3), 209–226.

Loader, B. D., Vromen, A., & Xenos, M. A. (2016). Performing for the young networked citizen? Celebrity politics, social networking and the political engagement of young people. *Media, Culture and Society, 38*(3), 400–419.

Martin, P., & Hollin, G. (2014). A new model of innovation in biomedicine? http://nuffieldbioethics. org/wp-content/uploads/A-New-Model-of-Innovation_web.pdf

Martinuzzi, A., Blok, V., Brem, A., Stahl, B., & Schönherr, N. (2018). Responsible research and innovation in industry—Challenges, insights and perspectives. *Sustainability, 10*(3), 70210.3390/ su10030702

Miles, A. (2015). The (re) genesis of values: Examining the importance of values for action. *American Sociological Review, 80*(4), 680–704.

Noble, S. U. (2018). *Algorithms of oppression: How search engines reinforce racism.* New York: New York University Press.

Otterbacher, J. (2018, September). Addressing social bias in information retrieval. In *International Conference of the Cross-Language Evaluation Forum for European Languages* (pp. 121–127). Springer, Cham.

Pols, A. J. K., & Spahn, A. (2015). Design for the values of democracy and justice. In *Handbook of ethics, values and technology design* (pp. 335–363). Springer.

Scheufele, D. A., & Krause, N. M. (2019). Science audiences, misinformation, and fake news. *Proceedings of the National Academy of Sciences, 116*(16), 7662–7669.

Soraker, J. H., et al. (2017). Models of RRI in industry, responsible industry deliverable D3.3, 7th Framework Programme.

Thompson C. J., & Kumar A. (2021). Beyond consumer responsibilization: Slow Food's actually existing neoliberalism. *Journal of Consumer Culture, 21*(2), 317–336. doi:10.1177/146954051 8818632

Von Schomberg, R. (2012). Prospects for technology assessment in a framework of responsible research and innovation. In *Technikfolgen abschätzen lehren* (pp. 39–61). Springer.

Wachter, S., Mittelstadt, B., & Floridi, L. (2017). Transparent, explainable, and accountable AI for robotics. *Science Robotics, 2*(6), eaan6080.

Zembylas, M. (2021). A decolonial approach to AI in higher education teaching and learning: strategies for undoing the ethics of digital neocolonialism. *Learning, Media and Technology,* 1–13.10.1080/17439884.2021.2010094

Zuboff, S. (2021, January 29). The coup we are not talking about. The New York Times. Retrieved January 22, 2022.

CHAPTER 10

Promises and Bargains: The Emerging Algorithmic Contract

Amanda Turnbull

Schulich School of Law, Dalhousie University, Halifax, Nova Scotia, Canada

CONTENTS

INTRODUCTION

This chapter will investigate the challenges and opportunities posed by the emerging algorithmic contract in Canadian contract law. These types of contracts are contingent upon algorithmic decision-making, and supplemental to human decision-making in the contract process.

DOI: 10.1201/9781003261247-12

The point of departure in this chapter is a counterfactual prologue, designed to set the scene for the ensuing discussion of algorithmic contracts. Part I addresses the rise of the algorithmic contract as part of the contentious and continuing story of the technologizing of contract. Part II analyzes the Canadian landmark case of *Uber Technologies v. Heller* (2020, [*Uber*]) as an algorithmic contract, and takes the position that it forms a "high-water point" in contract law, providing the opportunity for future case law to deal with issues created by algorithmic contracts. Part III offers one possible route that contract law may take to deal with algorithmic contracts that may be suggestive for other areas of law.

PROLOGUE

Ms. Bundy is an older woman who has recently gifted her car to her son. He lost all his assets in a business venture and had his car repossessed. This is not the first business undertaking in which he has failed. Ms. Bundy, however, has great faith in her son, and she has supported his financial well-being whenever she was able.

Ms. Bundy decided not to replace her car; instead, she opted to use some of her limited savings to purchase a smartphone so that she could have the flexibility of using ride-hailing services. Ms. Bundy lives frugally on a small pension. She lives in the same apartment in which she has lived for the past 40 years.

Though not well versed in information communications technologies, Ms. Bundy has adapted well to her first smartphone. The challenges she has experienced include its keyboard design and charging the device regularly. Ms. Bundy has a medical condition associated with aging, and this sometimes makes using the device's keyboard difficult. On this day in particular, Ms. Bundy has forgotten to charge her phone before leaving for her weekly visit to the grocery store, which is not within walking distance of her apartment. Her smartphone has gone into low power mode, with only 7% of her battery left.

Normally, the ride back to her apartment on the same day each week costs between $25 and $30. But today, the app is showing a surge in pricing to $81. Ms. Bundy believes that she has no choice but to accept the inflated rate. Therefore, she clicks to agree to the ride. The additional expense of approximately $50 will create a hardship for her.

When Ms. Bundy returns home, her son explains that the ride-hailing app has access to the data on her phone, including the battery level. To avoid potential surge pricing, he advises that she should charge her phone to more than 20% prior to leaving to do her weekly shopping.

PART I: THE RISE OF THE ALGORITHMIC CONTRACT

Although the preceding counterfactual is fictional, it involves a real-world scenario involving an algorithmic contract (Mathur, 2021). The terms and conditions contained within the contract to which Ms. Bundy "consented" are typical of gig economy apps, particularly on-demand apps where the app establishes the price of the service in advance and allows for a customer's acceptance or rejection of the offer. Furthermore, often the decisions made by an algorithm like that in the case of Ms. Bundy are not explainable. That is to say that the outcomes cannot be understood by human beings.

Uber is a good example of this type of app. Uber describes its entire infrastructure, which includes its software, servers, and its mechanism for executing transactions as an "engineering ecosystem consisting of hundreds of thousands of machines supported by an organization of hundreds of engineers" (Uber, 2019). This means that the Uber platform is primarily managed by machine learning algorithms and supported by human engineers. In fact, algorithmic management is the footing of the gig economy (Duggan et al., 2020). As a passenger, you are in the hands of a driver when you are in the car, but your contractual relationship was created and is governed by an algorithm. Likewise, as a driver, your contractual relationship as employee or as an independent contractor, depending on the jurisdiction, is not with a human being, but with an algorithm.

Uber is known for its data harvesting capabilities (Rosenblat, 2018). Uber collects massive amounts of data from its drivers and from its passengers. This data is stored and used to predict supply and demand, which determines the price of fares. Further, Uber is known for surge pricing. In theory, adjusting for supply and demand makes economic sense, but when an algorithm is responsible for surge pricing, the results are incomprehensible. In 2017 during the London Bridge attack, for example, Uber's dynamic pricing algorithm caused rates to jump more than 200% during the first 45 minutes of the crisis when people were trying to hire an Uber to safely leave the area (Bertini & Koenigsberg, 2021).

The idea of consenting to terms and conditions decided by an algorithm in a contract gives us pause. On one hand, we have grown accustomed to "clicking to agree" as part of the quotidian. We have become reliant on contract law in regulating the digital environment. Agreeing to terms and conditions to visit websites, for instance, or consenting to the "fine print" in more sophisticated purchases has become routine. We find this acceptable because those terms and conditions, had we the time to read them, are generally not unexpected. On the other hand, when an algorithm becomes an actor in the contractual process, selecting standard terms or clients for a company, or, in the case of Ms. Bundy, putting surge pricing into effect, ostensibly due to limited battery power, we become wary. What are the implications of an algorithm filling in for human expertise in the contracting process?

Lauren Henry Scholz coined the term "algorithmic contract" in 2017. These contracts feature "terms that were determined by algorithm rather than a person" (Scholz, 2017). To better understand the nature of an algorithmic contract, it is helpful to first address the question of what is a contract?

What Is a Contract?

The essence of contract is the exercise of will by two parties resulting in a bargain (McCamus, 2020). This traditional understanding of bargained agreement is a "creature of the 19th century" (Horwitz, 1974), and associated with consensus theory, in which a contract is an artifact of *consensus ad idem*, or a meeting of the minds. Prior to the 19th century, a narrower understanding of contract was prevalent; it was seen, instead, in terms of promise (Fried, 2015). Contract understood in terms of promise meant that obligation was created by one person and the consensus of parties was not always evident (Hamburger, 1989).

Contracts became a distinctive feature of the 19th-century society so much so that it is not uncommon to hear it described as "The Age of Contract" (Gluck, 1979). Evidence of this may be seen through Sir Henry Maine's well-known aphorism describing the evolution of "progressive" societies as a transition from status to contract (1906). Or through Dean Langdell's first casebook on contracts published in 1871, which marked a watershed in the history of legal education (Friedman, 1986).

The Development of Standard Form Contracts

The process of contract formation changed significantly in the 20th century. Individually negotiated contracts were gradually replaced with standard form contracts, which may be defined as "a uniform set of printed conditions which can be used time and time again, and for a large number of persons, and at less cost than an individually negotiated contract" (Beatson et al., 2020, pp. 183–184). This innovative change from individually negotiated contracts with mutual bargaining to a form with stock language, or what is sometimes referred to as "boilerplate", complemented standardization processes, which had become essential to the new economic order during the Industrial Revolution. Standard form contracts allowed manufacturers to enter into agreements more quickly than spending time negotiating singular agreements, and they could be used repeatedly (Gluck, 1979). Thus, the change in contract form was directly related to its function in the transformed society that was dominated by industry and machine manufacturing.

In the first half of the 20th century, however, case law reveals that courts did not draw a distinction between the previously bargained-out contract model and standard form contracts. Instead, strict contract theory was applied to standard form contract disputes. In particular, the rule established in *L'Estrange v. F Graucob Ltd* (1934) confirmed that courts could enforce signed contracts whether or not the terms had been read.[1] In fact, *L'Estrange* may be viewed as "high water point" (Gluck, 1979, p. 75) with regard to the court's respect for sanctity of contract.[2] After *L'Estrange*, courts started to realize that strict contract enforcement was at the cost of fairness (*Neuchatel Asphalte v. Barnett*, 1957). Recognizing this, the judiciary developed devices like the doctrine of fundamental breach to tackle the issues stemming from standard form contracts (Gluck, 1979).

Standard form contracts evolved in a controversial way. They were viewed as "tool[s] of almost unlimited usefulness and pliability" (Kessler, 1943, p. 629) and economically efficient (Trebilcock, 1993), but on the other, they were deemed "inherently intractable" (Rakoff, 1983, p. 1176), provoking the gerrymandering of the word agreement (Radin, 2013). By the end of the 20th century, however, they were pervasive, accounting for more than 99% of all contracts employed in both commercial and consumer transactions (Burke, 2000).

The Technologizing of the Standard Form Contract

The diametric points of view associated with standard form contracts further diverged as they migrated from paper to electronic form during the 1990s. The nexus of this pivot was the principle of "technological neutrality" (UNCITRAL, 1996). This meant that any practices formed through technological means were recognized as "functionally equivalent" to their paper-based counterparts. The legal requirement of a signature, for instance, was replaced and satisfied by an electronic signature (UNCITRAL, 2001).

Arguably, the functional equivalence to paper was never quite accurate since electronic documents are harder to evaluate on the basis of their size, which is not always apparent since all electronic documents look similar (Scassa & Deturbide, 2012). Reading the fine print on a smartphone is another instance whereby standard form contracts are becoming increasingly complicated since the fine print has become even more inconspicuous, displayed in miniscule fonts, and sometimes containing embedded terms and conditions. Electronic contracting makes it much easier for businesses to include burdensome terms for users (Waddams, 2017). In fact, some empirical research claims clicking "I agree" to be the biggest lie of the information age, revealing in a study of privacy policy and terms of service policy reading behavior that 98% of participants missed a "gotcha clause" providing a first-born child as payment for social networking access (Obar & Oeldor-Hirsch, 2020). While this is a slightly tongue-in-cheek example, it does demonstrate how terms of service have become the quintessence of "Too Long Didn't Read" documents (Stinson, 2018).

The use of increasingly sophisticated Artificial Intelligence (AI) further complicates the controversy over standard form contracting. It also creates unfairness as the fictional case of Ms. Bundy described. And this unfairness is not unique to Ms. Bundy; it is unfairness across society. Ultimately, the use of increasingly sophisticated AI in the contracting process indicates a transformation in standard form contracting.

While some scholars have identified increasingly digitally mediated contracts as "pseudo-contracts" (Kar & Radin, 2019) or "monster- or super-contracts" (Martin-Bariteau & Pavlović, 2021, p. 98), Scholz (2017) provides more particularity with the term, "algorithmic contract". She explains that algorithmic contracts share some features with standard form contracts such as the use of regularized or stock language. The main difference between a standard form contract and an algorithmic contract is that an algorithm replaces a human being in the decision-making process (Scholz, 2017). Put simply, algorithmic contracts are legally enforceable contracts that rely upon algorithmic decision-making.

Effectively, algorithms are at the root of just about everything in the digital world. The term "algorithm" may be defined as "a set of step-by-step instructions" that are simple such as setting a reminder at a specific time each day, or more complex, like identifying pedestrians on a street (Hutson, 2017). Many algorithms employ machine learning, which is branch of AI that involves the use of data and algorithms that imitate the learning process, improving accuracy of outcomes gradually. A subset of machine learning used is known as deep learning whereby artificial neural networks, that is to say, algorithms inspired by the human brain, learn or "become sensitive to progressively more abstract patterns" (Hutson). These neural nets can problem solve more quickly and at less cost than it would take humans to do. But the disadvantage is that they are opaque (Hardesty, 2017). This is also referred to as the "black box" effect (Dignum, 2018).

The metaphor of the black box in this context refers to a system in which we can observe inputs and outputs, yet we are unable to explain how one becomes the other (Pasquale, 2015; Brevini & Pasquale, 2020). Effectively, the system cannot be deconstructed, thus creating an information imbalance.

Further, only a small number of organizations and individuals in society have the power and resources to automate decision-making and this leads to damage such as algorithmic racism, sexism, and other bias (Buolamwini 2016; Gebru, 2020). Algorithmic bias "excodes" individuals, further marginalizing the already marginalized (Wood, 2021). Law itself, and this includes contract law, may be seen as creating inequality (Pistor, 2019). Algorithmic decision-making in law, then, may result in a form of meta-marginalization.

It is also important to explain that algorithmic contracts are not the same as smart contracts (Scholz, 2018, 2021). Unlike individually negotiated contracts or standard form contracts that are written in natural (or human) language, smart contracts are written in programming language with their principal feature being automation.

The term "smart contract" arose in the mid-1990s and is attributed to Nick Szabo (1996). He defined it as "a set of promises, specified in digital form, including protocols within which the parties perform on these promises" (Szabo). His definition is rooted in the notion of smart contract as a self-executing contract, where the terms of the agreement are written in code. Most smart contracts now in use are used as Blockchain programs to create, for example, tokens, both fungible and non-fungible,[3] and support verifiable supply chain management. They are not "smart" in the sense of consciousness. They may be viewed as automating contractual performance. A better description may well be "persistent script" (Buterin, 2018), which refers to transparent and self-running lines of code that are saved in the Blockchain and cannot be later edited or deleted (Taumergenov, 2021). Moreover, not all smart contracts are legally binding though some legally enforceable contracts may make use of persistent script.

Put concisely, algorithmic contracts are formed by an algorithm and legally enforceable (Scholz 2018; 2021). They determine the obligations of the parties in a contractual relationship. They are distinct from smart contracts, but they are related to standard form contracts. We could view them, in fact, as a more technologized form of contract than the standard form contract. In particularizing the term "algorithmic contract", Scholz reifies that we are, once again, facing a changed form of contract. This time, however, the change follows the algorithmic turn in society, whereby algorithms are becoming the main mediator through which power is enacted (Schuilenburg & Peeters, 2021). Scholz (2021) helpfully distinguishes between algorithmic contracts in the business-to-business context and in the business-to-consumer context.

Business-to-Business Algorithmic Contracts: Gap-Fillers and Negotiators

In the business-to-business context, Scholz (2021) establishes a taxonomy, distinguishing between two types of algorithmic contracts: first, gap-filler algorithmic contracts, which rely on algorithmic determination either before or after a contact is formed to fill gaps in some standardized term within the contract; and second, negotiator algorithmic contracts, in which an algorithm is tasked with choosing which terms to offer or accept, or which company to deal with. They operate as negotiators before the contract formation.

Gap-filler algorithmic contracts pose challenges with determinacy for businesses both in respect of price and in respect of terms. Amazon, for instance, uses standard form terms and conditions, but an algorithm determines the exact price of an item for each user at differing times (Scholz, 2021). Businesses, however, agree to algorithms being used in this gap-filling capacity in the terms and conditions of the contract.

Negotiator algorithmic contracts have been used in high-frequency trading of financial products, where investment banks use algorithms to create real-time strategies for buying and selling (Scholz, 2021; Virgilio, 2019). Algorithms can quickly and skillfully bind a business to a potential profitable exchange in a way that no human could have achieved.

To solve the challenges posed by algorithmic contracts in the business-to-business context, Scholz (2021) takes a non-restrictive approach seeing algorithms as constructive agents of corporations. What this means is that businesses will consent to having authorized an algorithm to act on their behalf in forming the contract. In this way, new technologies may be incorporated into established contract framework.

Businesses may not have a complete understanding of all the terms contained within an algorithmic contract, but they are not disadvantaged since the terms are usually coded in the interests of repeat business (Scholz, 2018). However, the same cannot be said in the consumer context where terms are not shaped to the individual consumer's benefit, and consumers have less of a comprehensive understanding of the nature of contractual terms with practically no ability to control them (Scholz, 2018).

Business-to-Consumer Algorithmic Contracts

Consumer algorithmic contracts like the one described in the counterfactual involving Ms. Bundy may create unexpected issues, such as "algorithmic exploitation" (Scholz, 2018). This exploitation may show up in the following ways:

1. Unaccountable algorithms function in the background of society, which determine access to resources, thus exerting a form of social control by corporate or government actors.

2. Big data processing techniques perpetuate wrongful discrimination against socially and economically vulnerable groups in society.

3. Major market failure may result from allowing algorithmic contracts to enable perfect market discrimination by elite actors (Scholz, 2018).

One potential avenue for addressing algorithmic exploitation is through legislation. At present, there are increasing proposals to regulate automated decision making, largely through the lens of privacy law. The European Union's *General Data Protection Regulation* (2016), for example, was one of the first endeavors at regulating automated decision-making. It is generally described as the "gold standard" in its approach to dealing with privacy and regulating automated decision making. Canada's proposed *Digital Charter Implementation Act* (*Bill C-27*) calls for transparency and explainability obligations for automated decision making. Privacy is an essential right and may be at risk with algorithms that have advanced methods of analysis and access to individuals' information (Scholz, 2019). While legislation will help individuals as well as organizations and governments deal with privacy issues related to automated decision-making systems, the question remains whether privacy law is the right way to regulate algorithmic contracts.[4] After all, statutes have appeared scantly in accounts of the structure of contract law or contract doctrine (Arvind & Steele, 2020).

The other avenue for limiting the scope of consumer algorithmic contracts is through existing contract law doctrine and principles. Scholz (2018) leaves open the question of whether legislation or existing contract law doctrine and principles best balance out minimizing algorithmic exploitation and allowing mutually beneficial business transactions. In the next section, I will build on Scholz's work on business-to-consumer algorithmic contracts using the Canadian landmark case, *Uber* (2020).

PART II: *UBER* AS LANDMARK CASE

David Heller, a driver for UberEats, began a class action against Uber in Ontario in 2017 for contravening the *Employment Standards Act* (2000, [*ESA*]), alleging that drivers were employees of Uber rather than independent contractors (*Heller v. Uber Technologies Inc*, 2018). Uber responded by bringing a motion to stay the action (*Heller v. Uber*, 2019) in favor of arbitration in The Netherlands, relying on their own arbitration provision in the service agreement. The provision required that Heller post $14,500 (USD) in advance to commence arbitration. This fee represented most of his annual income (para. 2). In addition to traveling to The Netherlands, to pursue any claim under the contract, the provision also required Heller to submit to Dutch law for the arbitration. Heller argued that the arbitration clause wrongly contracted out of mandatory protections contained within the *ESA* and that the clause was unconscionable (para. 13).

In June 2020, the SCC issued its ruling in *Uber*, finding in favor of Heller. The SCC's widely anticipated decision ruled that Uber's arbitration clause contained within its services agreement constituted a separate collateral agreement that was unconscionable, and therefore, unenforceable. This allowed the proposed class action, positioning Heller as an employee within the meaning of the *ESA* to move forward in Ontario, rather than for the dispute to be subject to arbitration in The Netherlands under Dutch law.

Uber is a landmark case in Canadian contract law because the decision clarified the threshold for the doctrine of unconscionability in Canada (McCamus, 2020).

The Doctrine of Unconscionability

The doctrine of unconscionability is a particular form of equitable relief in contract law (*Soulos v. Korkontzilas*, 1997, para. 27). The doctrine has its roots in the 14th century whereby relief in respect of unfair contracts was articulated in terms of conscience and its various permutations such as unconscionable, unconscientious, etc. (Waddams, 2019). Generally speaking, an unconscionable contract is one that is found to be unenforceable because no reasonable or informed individual, all things considered, would agree to it.

In Canada, the doctrine of unconscionability remained in a state of slow development (Manwaring, 1993; Bogden, 1997) until the SCC's pronouncement in *Uber*. It has, however, been used more productively in other common law jurisdictions such as Australia and New Zealand (Bigwood, 2005). In the United States, it is statutorily recognized by Section 2–302 of the *Uniform Commercial Code* (1951) and applies to transactions for the sale of goods in the United States. The doctrine of unconscionability is also incorporated into several uniform laws in the United States such as the *Uniform Consumer Credit Code Act* (1974) and *Uniform Uniform Land Transactions Act* (§1–311 (1975)). And it is incorporated in the *Restatement (Second) of Contracts* (1981).

The developing narrative of the modern ambit of unconscionability in Canada often begins with *Morrison v. Coast Finance Ltd.* (1965, [Morrison]), which is frequently invoked as the "leading case" (McCamus, 2020, p. 453; Bigwood, 2005, p. 180). *Morrison* affirmed a two-part test for Canadian courts to establish a finding of unconscionability consisting first, of inequality in bargaining power of the parties, and second, an improvident bargain, which "unduly advantages the stronger party or unduly disadvantages the more vulnerable" (McCamus, p. 9). In satisfying these two elements, the presumption of fraud is created, and the stronger party is required to prove that the bargain was fair, just, and reasonable (*Morrison*, para. 4).

Lloyds Bank Ltd v. Bundy (1975, [Bundy]), a renowned case of the English Court of Appeal (to which the counterfactual at the outset of this chapter is a contemporary allusion), also played a role in the development of the unconscionability doctrine in Canada. Two points are of noteworthiness here: first, *Bundy* is a case that lies at the periphery of unconscionability and undue influence that cites the Canadian test established in *Morrison*; and second, in his minority opinion in *Bundy*, Lord Denning suggested a unique, unifying principle of relief that harmonized the common law and equitable doctrines of duress, unconscionability, and undue influence. Specifically, he suggested a new general principle entitled, "inequality of bargaining power" (*Bundy*, at 339). This single principle was one of diminution, presenting a shorter, more concise variation involving unconscionability. And although this diminished, single principle may be found cited in subsequent Canadian case law such as *McKenzie v. Bank of Montreal* (1975) and *Beach v. Eames* (1976), it ultimately did not gain foothold in contract law on account of its vagueness (*National Westminster Bank plc v. Morgan*, 1985). However, Lord Denning's reformulated and modernized principle demonstrates the flexibility of unconscionability and is suggestive for producing new future rules.

Morrison, again, was the basis for the two-step test for unconscionability affirmed by the majority in *Harry v. Kreutziger* (1978). There have been two additional attempts by provincial appellate courts to reformulate the two-step test for unconscionability established in *Morrison* (*Cain v. Clarica Life Insurance Company*, 2006; *Pitcher v. Downer*, 2017).

The doctrine of unconscionability emerged again in 2017 in *Douez v. Facebook* [*Douez*] in Justice Abella's concurring decision. In this case, the plaintiff, Deborah Douez, objected to Facebook's use of her name and her likeness in "Sponsored Stories", which was a new advertising product. In its majority ruling in 2019, the SCC found that Douez had established strong cause not to enforce the forum selection on the basis of public policy considerations. In Justice Abella's concurring opinion, she found the doctrine of unconscionability, "a close jurisprudential cousin to both public policy and gross bargaining disparity, also applie[d] to render the forum selection clause unenforceable" (*Douez*, para. 112). In her opinion, Facebook's forum clause was a "classic case of unconscionability" (*Douez*, para. 116) modeled on the two-step test from *Morrison*, and therefore, the clause was unenforceable.

Interestingly, Justice Abella also recognized the transformation of standard form contracts due to increasingly sophisticated AI in the contracting process in her concurring opinion in *Douez*, asking questions such as, "[w]hat does 'consent' mean when the agreement is said to be made by pressing a computer key?" (para. 99). Her concurring reasoning in *Douez* laid the groundwork for *Uber* and provided the opportunity to continue the work of recognizing algorithmic contracts.

When *Uber* came to the SCC in 2020, the majority opted to approach unconscionability from the two-step process endorsed in *Douez*, borrowing the description that it was a "classic case of unconscionability" (*Uber*, para. 116). The court chose not to depart from Justice Abella's separate concurring reasoning in *Douez*. What the court did not do in *Uber*, however, is continue the examination of the transforming nature of standard form contracts.

Uber as an Algorithmic Contract Case

There is a dearth of analysis in respect of Uber's technology in the decision when in fact *Uber* is a case that is fundamentally about an algorithmic contract in the business-to-consumer context. The majority found, as a preliminary matter in the case, that the domestic *Arbitration Act* (1991) applied rather than the *International Commercial Arbitration Act* (2017, [ICAA]). This means that the court decided the dispute as focused on employment issues in relation to services performed in Ontario, rather than interpreting the issues in an international or commercial context, "despite their relation to business" as defined in the ICAA (para. 24). While the SCC did not decide on whether an employment relationship existed between Heller and Uber, what this preliminary matter points to is that it is a contractual dispute in the business-to-consumer context: Uber, the global corporation versus David Heller, an Ontario gig-worker.

In its decision, the SCC describes the Uber contract as a standard form contract and also as a contract of adhesion. Further, the judgment provides the following description involving the technology used in agreeing to the driver's contract:

> [t]he first time drivers log on to an Uber App, they are presented with a standard form services agreement of around 14 pages. To accept the agreement, the driver must click "I agree" twice. Once the driver does so, the Uber App is activated and the services agreement is uploaded to a "Driver Portal", accessible to the driver through an online account. (*Uber*, para. 7)

However, there is much more involved in consenting to an Uber contract than the SCC's description leads us to believe.

First-time drivers agree to the terms and conditions to download the Uber Driver App.[5] There is a separate app to download for passengers. Once the driver app has downloaded (Figure 10.1), the driver must agree to receive calls from Uber including by an automatic dialer (Figure 10.2).

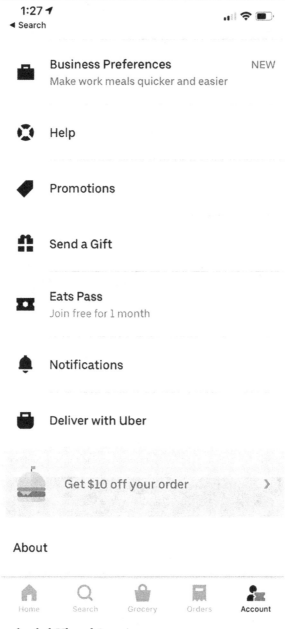

FIGURE 10.1   The downloaded Uber driver App.

FIGURE 10.2   Agreeing to the automatic dialer.

Once the driver agrees to these two initial terms, the driver must then agree to which type of driver service with whom the driver is contracting. In Heller's SCC case, it was with UberEats, which requires the driver then to decide which type of vehicle they would like to use for delivery services (Figure 10.3).

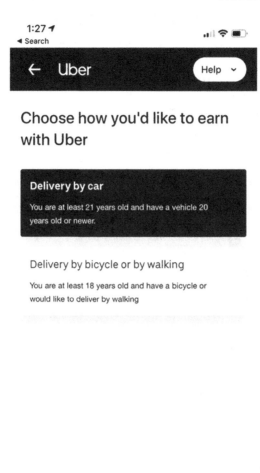

FIGURE 10.3   Choice of delivery vehicle.

The next phase of registering to become an UberEats driver requires that the driver complete the following five steps (Figure 10.4):

1. Proof of work eligibility.

2. A scanned profile photo.

3. A scanned driver's license.

4. A scan of a 5-year driving record.

5. A scan of the owner's certificate of insurance and the vehicle's registration.

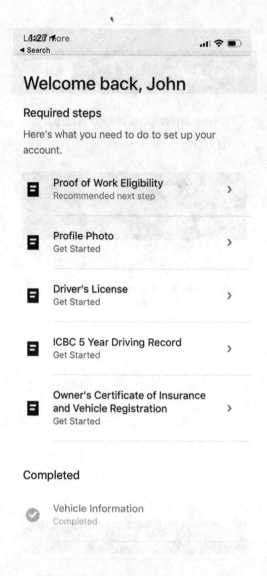

FIGURE 10.4   Screen requiring five additional documents.

Each of these steps requires "clicking to agree". By the time the driver gets to the actual standard form contract, the driver has clicked to agree at least nine times and uploaded a variety of additional documents to the app.

This investigation into the process of downloading the Uber app reveals that the contract is inseparable from the lengthy registration process to become an UberEats driver. The 14 pages and two clicks to agree to Uber's contract that the SCC took into account in its decision does not adequately assess the technology that created asymmetrical relationship between Uber and Heller. Further, the court did not ask, for example, how does a 14-page standard form contract appear on a six-by-eight-inch screen?[6] Is the autodialer an algorithm? How many other algorithmically generated terms does a user have to accept to get to the drivers' standard form contract? How many recipient rights are deleted or displaced in the processing techniques that benefit Uber?

Heller's entire relationship with Uber was through a platform regulated by algorithms. The potentially abusive contract to become an UberEats driver was deployed, approved, and maintained by algorithms. It is, by Scholz's definition, an algorithmic contact. And in recognizing algorithmic involvement in the contract formation in *Uber*, the inequality in bargaining power prong of the two-step test for unconscionability is affected. It is a paradox to suggest that one could bargain with an algorithm. It has no agency. The ramification of this is, in fact, that there is no bargaining power at all.

While Uber is seen as a landmark decision in that it clarified the threshold for the equitable doctrine of unconscionability, labeling it a "classic case" modeled on *Morrison*, it could only be seen in that light by overlooking the role that algorithms play in the contracting process. In no way was the contract in *Uber* just like the paper contract in *Morrison*.

Another way of looking at *Uber* is to see it as a "high water point", providing the opportunity for future case law to deal with issues presented by algorithmic contracts. It may be that in the wake of *Uber*, courts will begin to realize that strict contract enforcement without taking the nature of algorithmic contracts into account is at the cost of fairness. That said, I will offer one avenue for which there is an existing footprint whereby contract law could deal with algorithmic contracts in the business-to-consumer context.

PART III: POST-*UBER* OPPORTUNITIES

As discussed earlier in the chapter, the doctrine of unconscionability remained in a state of slow development in Canada until the decision in *Uber*. It is ironic that a doctrine stemming from the 14th century that employs the language of "conscience" was finally affirmed in Canada's top court in a case dealing with an unfair algorithmic contract. As Waddams (2019) points out, the concept of conscience in the framework of modern thought is not very agreeable. Additionally, resorting to tests like unconscionability in *Uber* that involve a certain degree of intention are problematic. How can you determine intention with an algorithm which has no agency? The question leading from this, then, is what would be a more agreeable framework to deal with algorithms that play a key role in the formation of contracts?

Developing Lord Denning's proposed single principle of inequality of bargaining power would be one way of dealing with algorithmic exploitation, and certainly, a more agreeably titled framework. This single principle unites the doctrines of duress, unconscionability, and undue influence, which Scholz (2017) herself acknowledges as potential defenses against formation in her early work on algorithmic contracts. Specifically, inequality of bargaining power blends grossly substantive unfairness, grievously weak bargaining power, and undue pressure or influence (*Bundy*, at 339).

If we take the fictional case of Ms. Bundy, we can see first that she was the weaker party in the contractual relationship with the ride-hailing app. The surge pricing that she experienced was an instance whereby she had no practical option but to accept the unreasonable offer. There was no "take or leave it" (Trebilcock, 1993) option due to the limited power in her smartphone's battery. If she did not accept the offer, she did not have an alternative means of returning home with her groceries. This is a form of economic coercion, specifically algorithmic economic coercion. She was effectively bullied or pressured into accepting the inflated price by an algorithm. We could not interpret this as being legitimate pressure. As a result, the case of Ms. Bundy meets the grossly substantive unfairness aspect of the inequality of bargaining power doctrine.

Second, we know from the analysis in *Uber* that in fact, Ms. Bundy had no bargaining power at all in the contractual relationship. Further, like the situation involving Uber and the London Bridge attack, the surge pricing that caused Ms. Bundy's rate to increase by approximately $50 for the same ride at the same time of day that she would have normally paid $25–30 is inscrutable. The price was inflated not because of the fundamental economic principle of supply and demand, but because data harvesting allowed the algorithm to consider the low battery charge in Ms. Bundy's smartphone when offering her a rate for her usual route home. Again here, this reasoning meets the grievously weak bargaining power prong of the single principle.

Third, the gist of undue influence is unfair persuasion rather than coercion, with which the first aspect of the single principle is concerned. Undue influence may actually be found in two ways in Ms. Bundy's case. First, on the occasion in which she experienced the surge in price as the result of limited power in her smartphone's battery. And second, we could say that the ride-hailing app exercises a dominating influence on Ms. Bundy more generally. Once again, here, the undue pressure or influence branch of the single principle is met in the case of Ms. Bundy.

While this is a cursory analysis involving a fictional case, it shows that the single principle of inequality in bargaining power has merit in the context of algorithmic contracts. Additionally, there is further justification for its development. Almost 50 years after the opinion, *Bundy* remains fundamental to the syllabi of students studying contract law. It is still referred to in contracts textbooks as "bold and interesting" (McCamus, 2020, p. 406), "of interest" (Waddams, 2010, para. 524), and yet at the same time, as "Lord Denning's lead balloon" (Andrews, 2015, p. 316). Recognizing algorithmic contracts post-*Uber* would provide the opportunity to once again revisit and further develop the single principle to rescind a contract that harmonizes duress, unconscionability, and undue influence. It would also articulate doctrine more aptly named for the 21st century.

Reciprocally, revisiting this harmonized single principle would take the lead out of the balloon, so to speak, in sorting out how we understand and teach *Bundy*. Further, reviving the single principle in the context of algorithmic contacts does not presume that we abandon the traditional categories of duress, unconscionability, and undue influence for non-algorithmic contracts. It simply holds the possibility of retrofitting the single principle of unfair bargaining: a touchstone for algorithmic contracts. Moreover, retrofitting the inequality of bargaining doctrine in the law of contracts may have positive ripple effects for modifying legal doctrine in other areas grappling with AI technologies. It all begins by acknowledging the emerging form of algorithmic contract.

NOTES

1 The rule in *L'Estrange* states, "[w]hen a document containing contractual terms is signed then, in the absence of fraud, or … misrepresentation, the party signing it is bound, and it is wholly immaterial whether he has read the document or not" (at 403).

2 The term "sanctity of contract" reflects the early moral conception of contract as a promise binding one's conscience. While it has religious overtones, it is also used in society today in a secular manner to refer to the strict enforcement of contracts (Waddams, 2019, p. 1).

3 A fungible token is infinitely divisible, such as Ethereum, whereas a non-fungible token (NFT) can only represent a value of one token. NFTs allow artists to represent ownership of their work with one verifiable token via the Blockchain.

4 Note that the European Commission has also proposed a Regulation on Artificial Intelligence, known as the *AI Act*. Unveiled in April 2021, it is the world's first attempt at a horizontal regulation of AI systems, rather than a top-down regulatory approach. The breadth of its scope, however, leaves it open to criticism in respect of its comprehensiveness. See https://eur-lex.europa.eu/legal-content/EN/TXT/?qid=1623335154975&uri=CELEX%3A52021PC0206.

5 This analysis was done in January 2020, which was current to the decision in *Uber*.

6 Approximate dimensions of an iPhone 11.

REFERENCES

Andrews, N. (2015). *Contract law* (2nd ed.). Cambridge University Press.

Arvind, T. T., & Steele, J. (2020). Contract and the missing legislature: Implications. In Arvind, T. T., & Steele, J. (Eds.), *Contract law and the legislature: Autonomy, expectations, and the making of legal doctrine*. Hart Publishing.

Beatson, J., Burrows, A., & Cartwright, J. (2020). *Anson's law of contract* (31st ed.). Oxford University Press.

Bertini, M., & Koenigsberg, O. (September–October 2021). *The pitfalls of pricing algorithms: Be mindful of how they can hurt your brand*. Harvard Business Review. https://hbr.org/2021/09/the-pitfalls-of-pricing-algorithms

Bigwood, R. (2005). Antipodean reflections on the Canadian unconscionability doctrine. *Canadian Bar Review, 84*(1&2), 171–216.

Bogden, J-P. F. (1997). On the agreement most foul: A reconsideration of the doctrine of unconscionability. *Manitoba Law Journal, 25*(1), 187–214.

Brevini, B., & Pasquale, F. (2020). Revisiting the black box society by rethinking the political economy of big data. *Big Data & Society, 7*(2). doi:10.1177/2053951720935146

Buolamwini, J. (2016, December 16). *The algorithmic justice league: Unmasking bias*. MIT Media Lab. https://medium.com/mit-media-lab/the-algorithmic-justice-league-3cc4131c5148

Burke, J. J. A. (2000). Contract as commodity: A nonfiction approach. *Seton Hall Legislative Journal, 24*, 285–317.

Buterin, V. [@VitalikButerin]. (2018, October 13). *To be clear, at this point I quite regret adopting the term "smart contracts." I should have called them something more boring and technical, perhaps like "persistent scripts"*. [Tweet]. https://twitter.com/vitalikbuterin/status/1051160932699770882?lang=en

Dignum, V. (2018, January 26). *On bias, black-boxes and the buest for transparency in Artificial Intelligence*. The Medium. https://medium.com/@virginiadignum/on-bias-black-boxes-and-the-quest-for-transparency-in-artificial-intelligence-bcde64f59f5b

Duggan, J., Sherman, U., Carbery, R., & McDonnell, A. (2020, January). Algorithmic management and app-work in the gig economy: A research agenda for employment relations and HRM. *Human Resource Management Journal, 30*(4). doi:10.1111/1748-8583.12258

Fried, C. (2015). *Contract as promise: A theory of contractual obligation* (2nd ed.). Oxford University Press.

Friedman, L. M. (1986). *A history of American law* (2nd ed.). Touchstone.

Gebru, T. (2020). Race and gender. In Dubber, M. D., Pasquale, F., & Das, S. (Eds.), *The oxford handbook of ethics of AI*. Oxford University Press.

Gluck, G. (1979). Standard form contracts: The contract theory reconsidered. *The International and Comparative Law Quarterly, 28*(1), 72–90.

Hamburger, P. A. (1989). The development of the nineteenth-century consensus theory of contract. *Law and History Review, 7*(2), 241–329.

Hardesty, L. (2017, April 14). *Explained: Neural networks*. MIT News. https://news.mit.edu/2017/explained-neural-networks-deep-learning-0414

Horwitz, M. J. (1974). The historical foundations of modern contract law. *Harvard Law Review 87*(5), 917–956.

Hutson, M. (2017). AI glossary: Artificial intelligence, in so many words. *Science, 357*(6346), 19. 10.1126/science.357.6346.19

Kar, R. B., & Radin, M. J. (2019). Pseudo-contract and shared meaning analysis. *Harvard Law Review, 132*(4), 1137–1219.

Kessler, F. (1943). Contracts of adhesion—Some thoughts about freedom of contract. *Columbia Law Review, 43*(5), 629–642.

McCamus, J. D. (2020). *The law of contracts* (3rd ed.). Irwin Law.

Maine, H. S. (1906). *Ancient law: Its connection with the early history of society and its relation to modern ideas*. Henry Holt.

Manwaring, J. (1993). Unconscionability: Contested values, competing theories and choice of rule in contract law. *Ottawa Law Review, 25*(2), 235–314.

Martin-Bariteau, F., & Pavlović, M. (2021). AI and contract law. In Martin-Bariteau, F., & Scassa, T. (Eds.), *Artificial intelligence and the law in Canada*. LexisNexis.

Mathur, C. (2021). *Does Uber hike ride prices when you're low on battery?* Newbytes. https://www.newsbytesapp.com/news/science/is-uber-linking-ride-pricing-to-battery-levels/story

Obar, J. A., & Oeldor-Hirsch, A. (2020). The biggest lie on the Internet: Ignoring the privacy policies and terms of service policies of social networking services. *Information, Communication & Society, 23*(1), 128–147. doi:10.1080/1369118X.2018.1486870

Pasquale, F. (2015). *Black box society: The secret algorithms that control money and information*. Harvard University Press.

Pistor, K. (2019). *The code of capital: How the law creates wealth and inequality*. Princeton University Press.

Radin, M .J. (2013). *Boilerplate: The fine print, vanishing rights, and the rule of law*. Princeton University Press.

Rakoff, T. D. (1983). Contracts of adhesion: An essay in reconstruction. *Harvard Law Review, 96*(6), 1173–1284.

Rosenblat, A. (2018). *Uberland: How algorithms are rewriting the rules of work*. University of California Press.

Scassa. T., & Deturbide, M. E. (2012). *Electronic commerce and Internet law in Canada*. CCH Canadian.

Scholz, L. H. (2019). Algorithmic contracts and consumer privacy. In DiMatteo, L., Cannarsa, M., & Poncibò, C. (Eds.), *The Cambridge handbook of smart contracts, blockchain technology and digital platforms*. Cambridge University Press.

Scholz, L. H. (2017). Algorithmic contracts. *Stanford Technology Law Review, 20*, 128–169.

Scholz, L. H. (2018, April 17). Law and autonomous systems series: Toward a consumer contract law for an algorithmic age. University of Oxford Faculty of Law Blog. https://www.law.ox.ac.uk/business-law-blog/blog/2018/04/law-and-autonomous-systems-series-toward-consumer-contract-law

Scholz, L. H. (2021). Algorithms and contract law. In Barfield, W. (Ed.), *The Cambridge handbook of the law of algorithms.* Cambridge University Press.

Schuilenburg, M., & Peeters, R. (2021). *The Algorithmic society: Technology, power, and knowledge.* Routledge.

Stinson, C. (2018, December 6). *I read the terms of service, so that you don't have to.* Mowat Centre. https://munkschool.utoronto.ca/mowatcentre/i-read-the-terms-of-service-so-that-you-dont-have-to/

Szabo, N. (1996). Smart contracts: Building blocks for digital markets. *Extropy Journal of Transhuman Thought, 16*(1–11).

Taumergenov, N. (2021). *Persistent scripts.* The Medium. https://noordah.medium.com/persistent-scripts-e415f9df981

Trebilcock, M. J. (1993). *The limits of freedom of contract.* Harvard University Press.

Uber. (2019, December). *Uber Infrastructure in 2019: Improving reliability, driving customer satisfaction.* Uber Engineering. https://eng.uber.com/uber-infrastructure-2019/

Virgilio, G. P. M. (2019). High-frequency trading: A literature review. *Financial Markets and Portfolio Management, 33*(2), 183–208.

Waddams, S. (2017). Contract law and the challenges of computer technology. In Brownsword, R., Scotford, E., & Yeung, K. (Eds.), *The oxford handbook of law, regulation and technology.* Oxford University Press.

Waddams, S. (2010). *The law of contracts* (6th ed.). Carswell.

Waddams, S. (2019). *Sanctity of contracts in a secular age: Equity, fairness and enrichment.* Cambridge University Press.

Wood, M. (2021, March 22). *Bias in facial recognition isn't hard to discover, but it's hard to get rid of.* Marketplace Tech. https://www.marketplace.org/shows/marketplace-tech/bias-in-facial-recognition-isnt-hard-to-discover-but-its-hard-to-get-rid-of/

Legal References

Arbitration Act, 1991, SO 1991, c 17.

Beach v. Eames, 18 OR (2d) 486.

Bill C-27: An Act to enact the Consumer Privacy Protection Act, the Personal Information and Data Protection Tribunal Act and the Artificial Intelligence and Data Act and to make consequential and related amendments to other Acts. https://www.parl.ca/DocumentViewer/en/44-1/bill/C-27/first-reading

Cain v. Clarica Life Insurance Company, 2006, CLLC para 210-001.

Douez v. Facebook, Inc, [2017] 1 SCR 751.

Employment Standards Act, 2000, S.O. 2000, c. 41.

General Data Protection Regulation (EU) 2016/679 (GDPR).

Harry v. Kreutziger, [1978] BCJ No 1318.

Heller v. Uber Technologies Inc, [2018] OJ No 1393.

Heller v. Uber Technologies Inc, [2019] OJ No 1.

International Commercial Arbitration Act, 2017, SO 2017, c 2, Schedule 5.

L'Estrange v. F Graucob Ltd, [1934] 2 KB 394, [1934] All ER Rep 16, 152 LT 164.

Lloyds Bank Ltd v. Bundy, [1975] QB 326, [1974] 3 All ER 757, [1974] 3 WLR 501, 9 LDAB 365.

McKenzie v. Bank of Montreal et al., (1975), 7 OR (2d) 521.

Morrison v. Coast Finance Ltd et al., [1965] BCJ No 178.

National Westminster Bank plc v. Morgan, [1985] AC 686, [1985] 1 All ER 821.

Neuchatel Asphalte v. Barnett, [1957] 1 All ER 362, [1957] 1 WLR 356.

Pitcher v. Downer, [2017] NJ No 64.

Restatement (Second) of Contracts (1981).

Soulos v. Korkontzilas, [1997] 2 SCR 217, [1997] SCJ No 52.

Uber Technologies Inc v. Heller, [2020] SCJ No 16.

Uniform Commercial Code § 2-302 (1951).

Uniform Consumer Credit Code Act § 5.108, 7A ULA 167-69 (1974).

Uniform Land Transactions Act § 1-311 (1975).

United Nations Commission on International Trade Law (UNCITRAL), Model Law E-Commerce, 1996.

United Nations Commission on International Trade Law (UNCITRAL), Model Law on Electronic Signatures, 2001.

CHAPTER 11

Artificial Intelligence, Law, and Vulnerabilities

Jude Dzevela Kong[a,b,*], Kesha Fevrier[c,*],
Jake Okechukwu Effoduh[a,d,*], and Nicola Luigi Bragazzi[a,b]

[a]*Africa-Canada Artificial Intelligence and Data Innovation Consortium (ACADIC),
York University, Toronto, Canada*
[b]*Department of Mathematics and Statistics, York University, Toronto, Canada*
[c]*Department of Geography and Planning, Queen's University, Toronto, Canada*
[d]*Osgoode Hall Law School, York University, Toronto, Canada*

CONTENTS

INTRODUCTION

Social vulnerability is a measurement of the ability of communities to adequately respond to external stresses (Blaikie et al., 1994), such as the ongoing "SARS-CoV-2" – Severe Acute Respiratory Syndrome Coronavirus 2 (Bankoff & Hilhorst, 2004). During these periods of upheaval, people with disabilities, racial, ethnic, and religious minorities, children from low-income families, the elderly, migrants and refugees, the immunocompromised and those with chronic health conditions, and the homeless among others are considered to be at greater risk from the adverse effects, and potential losses incurred by these external stressors. They are also the slowest to recover from such

---

* These authors contributed equally as first authors.

DOI: 10.1201/9781003261247-13

emergencies. For example, recent data from the COVID-19 pandemic shows that vulnerable populations were much more likely to contract the virus, were less likely to receive the vaccine because of hesitancy and distrust of "Big Pharma", yet they were more in need of social assistance compared to other segments of society (Cheong et al., 2021; Kazemi et al., 2022; St-Denis, 2020). Classified as "socially vulnerable" by the United Nations (n.d.), these populations are almost always economically marginalized, politically under-represented, and socially underserved. (Un)surprisingly, they are predominantly racialized (Black and other people of color), and have a long history of enduring violations of their civil rights and freedoms, even during disaster response and recovery efforts. The factors and/or characteristics that determine the social vulnerability of a group differ from country to country, however, there are some universal similarities. Risk factors that contribute to the vulnerability of these groups include poverty, unemployment, and lack of access to resources (e.g., adequate healthcare, education, housing, safe drinking water, transportation, and other social services) (Cutter et al., 2003). Socially vulnerable populations are also stigmatized and discriminated against by the wider society, and even criminalized in law, policy, and practice. Forced to live in environments of severe inequality, they are unable to thrive, feel safe, and actively participate in all aspects of society (UNDP, n.d.). When compared to the general population, the capacity of socially vulnerable groups to cope with, respond to, and recover from the adverse impacts of crises is hindered by the inordinate obstacles they encounter in their daily lives (Wisner et al., 2004). These obstacles are indicators of structural inequities and barriers that hamper fair and equitable access (for all) to the resources needed to satisfy one's basic needs. Social vulnerability is then a combination of the risk factors and socio-cultural markers listed above, which hinder full participation in economic, social, political, and cultural life (UN DESA, 2016). The amplification of existing inequities during crises like the COVID-19 pandemic has re-ignited discussions about global inequities and the challenges they present to socially vulnerable populations.

Discussions of social vulnerability are not limited to events like natural and human-made disasters. The digital revolution with its new technologies powered by Big Data and Artificial Intelligence (AI) is increasingly integrated into all spheres of contemporary society, fueling scientific discoveries, innovations, and advancements that should improve the quality of human existence. The benefits of Big Data and AI are not limited to the economic and educational elite, they can also empower socially vulnerable populations, positively changing and improving their overall quality of life. There are nonetheless ethical challenges posed by Big Data and AI, specifically how its integration in the field of medicine and biomedical engineering is challenging our fundamental beliefs about the meaning of being human and the future of society. Beyond challenging our understanding of humanness, experts, as well as the general public, are rightly concerned about data privacy and the intrusiveness of technologies that rely on Big Data and AI. Because of the multi-layered, and intersectional nature of their vulnerability, a large part of which is linked to entrenched inequities in society, inappropriate uses of AI systems can potentially expose socially vulnerable populations to greater levels of state surveillance, political suppression and censorship, manipulation, social discrimination, and violations of privacy and property rights when data is collected without the requisite consent (Ebers & Navas, 2020).

From a regulatory perspective, Big Data and AI represent an unknown and uncharted territory that sometimes evokes fears and anxieties not seen in other technological revolutions. Some of the unease associated with Big Data and AI include concerns about cyber-insecurity, data privacy and protection, intellectual property rights issues, lack of accountability, transparency and responsibility, and liability for damages, as well as human rights issues, like equity, dignity, security, and safety (Rodrigues, 2020). While Big Data and AI pose ethical challenges to society more broadly, socially vulnerable populations will be disproportionately affected when these technology-enabled decision-making systems, perpetuate algorithmic unfairness, bias, and discrimination. Beyond inflating extant vulnerabilities, misuse of Big Data and AI may very well introduce new ones. Also, from a historical perspective, socially vulnerable populations have rarely enjoyed equal access to legal protection under the law. Their unequal access to legal provisions readily available to other segments of society is expected to widen in the current digital revolution if procedures are not put in place to address the root causes of their vulnerability. It is thus instructive to apply a social vulnerability lens to understand how Big Data and AI decision-making systems offer differing levels of resilience to socially vulnerable populations. This requires a curation of critical perspectives and/or new approaches that can inform international laws and regulations regarding the use of Big Data and AI. Adopting a multi-disciplinary legal perspective is also essential because social vulnerability is a multi-dimensional and intersectional construct. The development of rights-based laws regulating the use of Big Data and AI systems would then help protect socially vulnerable populations from forms of exploitation perpetrated by public and private sector actors.

Eschewing the positivist premise that "things must be one way or the other" (Al-Attar, 2020), we look to a legal scholarship from Third World Approaches to International Law (TWAIL) to critically navigate toward a legal framework that attends to the potential negative impact of Big Data and AI on socially vulnerable populations. TWAIL as both a theory and a methodology can provide predictive, logical, and testable mechanisms for analyzing and studying our new reality, from the perspective of those populations that are already socially vulnerable. To this end, the present book chapter invites readers to critically reflect on the promise of Big Data and AI systems and the ability of current legal frameworks to adequately protect socially vulnerable populations from any malfeasance associated with the widespread adoption of Big Data and AI technologies. While socially vulnerable populations across the globe will be impacted by AI systems that transgress privacy laws, this chapter pays specific attention to citizens of the global South, who because of longstanding histories of uneven global development, face unique risks from Big Data and AI systems, especially if the data is stored in foreign countries and used and controlled by corporate interests. Big Data and AI decision-making systems have been shown to exploit and exacerbate social vulnerabilities by inexorably widening disparities between and within countries (based on race, class, ethnicity, religion, gender, citizenship, and socio-economic status). We need to look no further than the 2016 presidential elections in the United States, and the role of Big Data analytics in influencing electoral outcomes (Isaak & Hanna, 2018). It should be noted that our aim in this chapter is not to deny the positive impacts of Big Data and AI, especially in the area of medical innovations. Nevertheless, we think through a TWAIL lens as fitting for designing ad hoc policies and legislative actions that can give voice to socially vulnerable populations located in the global South, engage them as relevant stakeholders, ensure their equitable access to new technologies and legal protection that can properly safeguard them from violations related to the misuse of Big Data and AI.

BIG DATA, ARTIFICIAL INTELLIGENCE, AND SOCIAL VULNERABILITY

We began this chapter with a discussion of social vulnerability, its determinants, and the socio-economic, political, and cultural markers that define certain groups within societies, as socially vulnerable. We now turn to a succinct discussion of Big Data and AI, noting that existing global asymmetries between and within countries, and across populations mean that not all groups in society will benefit equally from the collection and use of Big Data, and the deployment of AI systems. We are particularly interested in the ways that the widespread advancement and application of AI technologies differentially impact individuals and groups that are historically disadvantaged and marginalized – socially vulnerable populations. Consequently, we raise concerns about the potential for the technology to exploit and further marginalize socially vulnerable populations in the global South through its widespread, and haphazard adoption.

What is Big Data? "Big Data" refers to high-volume, velocity, variety, veracity, and value data that cannot be processed using traditional methods of data analytics, and management techniques (Anuradha, 2015; Nagpal et al., 2019). More specifically, Big Data is a massive suite of data generated from a plurality of sources including Internet clicks, social media platforms, mobile transactions, user-generated content, sales queries, and purchase transactions (George et al., 2014). Big Data also encompasses data gleaned from facilities like call centers, data generated from biological research, medicine, engineering, commerce, and banking and finance for example (Davenport et al., 2012; George et al., 2014). Because these ever-increasing volumes of data are unstructured and complex, it requires powerful computational techniques that can mine the data pool to generate meaningful insights and useful results. It is necessary here to clarify what we mean by AI, how the latter is connected to the former, and why the two concepts are seemingly inseparable. Several definitions of AI abound in the literature. See, for example, Bellman (1978), Poole et al. (1998), Rich and Knight (1991), and Winston (1992). These definitions fall into two main categories: those that speak to how AI thinks, and those that speak to how AI acts, given what it knows. AI's ability to make rational decisions (i.e., learn), and take rational actions (i.e., reason) is touted as one of its greatest contributions to society, maximizing efficiencies and improving decision-making capabilities. Although they are very different, the seeming inseparability of Big Data and AI is then best understood as a mutually beneficial and complementary relationship (Sinur and Peters, 2019). Simply put, AI algorithms are an important tool for making sense of large-volume data sets. Big Data and AI are thus intimately synchronized systems such that massive quantities of data help improve the accuracy, predictive capabilities, and learning capacity of AI systems.

Similarly, the vast amounts of unstructured data generated in both the public and private spheres are of limited value to businesses, consumers, and the general public, if smart technologies like AI were not available to process the data.

In the above, we made explicit the connection between Big Data and AI. We briefly turn our attention to how Big Data and AI have been operationalized during the COVID-19 pandemic to assist socially vulnerable groups. While magnifying long-standing national, regional, and global inequities and disparities, the COVID-19 pandemic has also acted as a catalyst for innovation and technological advancements in response to the global threat that the virus poses. Big Data and AI played a key role in this regard, dynamically and permanently altering the way we respond to future health pandemics (Bragazzi et al., 2020; Cheong et al. 2021; Duhon et al., 2021; Kazemi et al., 2022; Kong et al., 2021; Lieberman et al., 2021; Mellado et al., 2021; Nia et al., 2022; Stevenson et al., 2021; Tao et al., 2022; Yan et al., 2021). Leslie et al. (2021, p. 1) note that AI systems (if properly designed and fed good non-biased data) could improve diagnostic and prognostic decision support, epidemiological monitoring and prediction, and vaccine discovery. This is exemplified in the work undertaken by Africa-Canada Artificial Intelligence and Data Innovation Consortium (ACADIC). ACADIC worked with nine African countries – Botswana, Eswatini, Cameroon, Mozambique, Namibia, Nigeria, Rwanda, South Africa, and Zimbabwe – that employed Big Data and AI to successfully deliver locally nuanced analyses relevant to COVID-19. Big Data and AI-based technologies were used to predict COVID-19 resurgences, identify and analyze emergent hotspots and outbreaks, obtain locally relevant data, address mis- and dis-information about COVID-19, its prevention and treatment, identify individuals at higher risk of infection, identify gendered vulnerability, provide real-time information about the labor market flow, and develop strategic, highly targeted and staged delivery plans of vaccines to priority areas. The project is engaged in ongoing monitoring to enhance testing and development to ensure that public health interventions are equitable and effective (Alavinejad et al., 2022; Lieberman et al., 2021; Mellado et al., 2021; Nia et al., 2022; Stevenson et al., 2021). These AI models are the official models used by governments in their interactions with both local and national policymakers.[1]

While such technologies provide great promise for addressing global challenges, e.g., the present COVID-19 pandemic, strengthening local and national economies, and enhancing human well-being, the question still arises: how do Big Data and AI-powered technologies adversely affect socially vulnerable populations, specifically those in the global South? We know that renewed attention to existing societal inequities that maintain and reproduce group differentiated vulnerabilities has been amplified by the ongoing COVID-19 pandemic, and other crises whether economic, political, or environmental in origin. In the context of COVID-19, studies of US counties with confirmed cases of the coronavirus have shown a positive correlation between high levels of social vulnerability and an increased risk of contracting the virus and developing a more severe, and even lethal form of the disease (Freese et al., 2021; Karmakar et al., 2021; Neelon et al., 2021). Similar findings were reported in Canada (Benzies et al., 2021), Brazil (Silva da Paz et al., 2021), India (Malakar, 2021), Mexico (Torres-Torres et al., 2022), and Spain (Garcia, 2020). In such cases, the use of Big Data and AI systems to address the positive correlation between social vulnerability and poor health outcomes is welcomed and warranted. However, under-regulated application of AI-based technologies and applications into social and political spheres including education, healthcare, social welfare, and policing, but also the rise of the private security industrial complex, and its use of intelligent closed-circuit television (CCTV) technologies to surveil the general public, raises ethical and legal questions about how individual and group-specific (private)-related data will be treated, stored, processed, and accessed in ways that uphold individual rights and freedoms. Castets-Renard & Fournier-Tombs (2020), note that responsible data use is an important component of accountable AI. This is of significant relevance, especially in situations of vulnerability where individuals do not feel they can consent to (or successfully challenge) breaches of their privacy and the appropriation of their data. The authors note that during periods of crisis, emergency legislation passed to allow governments to implement policies to mitigate the worst of the emergency may exceed the protections supposedly guaranteed by existing privacy laws. Building on the issue of consent, and breach of privacy noted by the authors, Big Data and AI-powered toolkits can produce unequal outcomes in different socio-demographic groups if the data is racially biased (Ghassemi et al., 2020; Leslie et al., 2021). Bias and discrimination infiltrate these toolkits because certain groups – mostly socially vulnerable populations – are not properly represented in the dataset used to build the algorithms. Because they are not consulted, and, therefore, absent during the design, development, and deployment phase of those toolkits, it allows for much higher incidences of (un)conscious bias, which inevitably corrupts the data, entrenching even further existing inequalities.

Potential insecurity also arises when app developers design systems that do not have robust security protocols. This occurred in Indonesia, for example, where around 1 million people were affected by a suspected breach in the country's COVID-19 test and tracing mobile app. The app stores users' health status, personal data, contact details, and COVID-19 test results, among others (Ang, 2021). In South Africa, hackers have used the COVDI-19 pandemic to attack businesses, accessing corporate networks to take hold of sensitive information. In their recent analysis of the cybersecurity landscape across African countries, analysts for Baker McKenzie (2021) noted increasing concerns about cybersecurity especially in the financial centers of South Africa, Kenya, and Nigeria. The cybersecurity firm explained that rapidly evolving digital techniques had led to an increased risk of advanced persistent threats, and hacking-for-hire events across Africa. Africa's vulnerability, and more so that of its population to cybersecurity threats is connected to its weaker digital connectivity networks, and lack of robust cybersecurity policies and/or its attendant enforcement, but also during the pandemic, the exponential increase in online activity, and the use of digital technologies that collect, and store to differing levels of security, personal user data.

The collection and use of highly sensitive population data could have far-reaching consequences beyond the pandemic. This data can be used by authoritarian and repressive military regimes to consciously monitor, track, and target protesters and political rivals, violating their human rights. Abuse of Big Data and AI technologies is not limited to local governments. African countries are particularly vulnerable to forms of insidious intrusion by foreign governments and their corporations. Reliance on AI technologies developed in more advanced countries opens the most vulnerable African countries to mass surveillance to advance the economic and political objectives of foreign interests. For example, AI technologies could be used to police international borders and apprehend migrants and refugees who are positioned as security threats. For example, in 2018, the Canadian Border Services was caught using DNA testing websites, e.g., Ancestry and FamilyTreeDNA to determine the nationality of migrants seeking asylum in Canada or challenging deportation (Bircan & Korkmaz, 2021; Hopkins, 2018). By way of another illustration, REFUNITE, a non-profit tech organization based in California is working with 5000 refugees – mainly from South Sudan and the Democratic Republic of Congo - Through its LevelApp (Batha, 2018). The App developers state that their mission is to help refugees and those who have been displaced to search for and reconnect with loved ones through its mobile interface. REFUNITE also works in the following countries: Kenya, South Sudan, Somalia, Jordan, Iraq, and the DRC. The company has partnered with Facebook, Ericsson, the United Nations, and various mobile network operators (REFUNITE, 2021). The company currently operates a database of over 1 million profiles all of whom are socially vulnerable. Information collected includes names, contact details, e.g., a telephone number, country of origin, and the names of family members the registrant is looking for (Rosenberg, 2017). The company states that the information in the database is maintained by Refugees United, however, the registered information can be used by NGOs, and international organizations caring for displaced people. While laudable in its goal, this relatively large and private dataset, if accessed by foreign governments, and other border security institutions could be used to deny asylum claims, aid in the deportation of racialized migrants, and continuously monitor the movements of socially vulnerable groups. Each of these is an assault on their right to privacy and freedom.

Beyond developing a platform for reconnecting refugees, REFUNITE also connects refugees to tech companies looking for cheap labor (paid about $3–4 per day) to train their algorithms (Litman-Navarro, 2018). Though these refugees who are already in positions of abject precarity benefit from the income derived through training AI algorithms, what we have here is a sophisticated system that is further exploiting their vulnerabilities for the sake of profit. REFUNITE, despite its moral claims to help refugees, has instead created an enabling environment for the cooptation of their labor. To mitigate these impacts, we advise inclusive and responsible practices that ensure fair use of Big Data and AI-powered toolkits, especially in the area of data governance. We turn to a discussion of TWAIL to assess its capacity as a constructive lens to help toward achieving the above.

INTERNATIONAL LAW, ARTIFICIAL INTELLIGENCE, AND THE SOCIALLY VULNERABLE

We have established that Big Data and AI are progressively being used as a mechanism for data collection, analysis, surveillance, and decision making. While there are many ethical issues and risks associated with AI use, AI interventions in Africa and other countries in the global South, present unique concerns. Africa's volatile climate – natural disasters, disease outbreaks, food shortages, and civil unrest – combined with its acute socio-political and economic challenges, demonstrates a greater need for AI-enabled innovations. However, the continent lacks the formalized mechanisms to effectively oversee and regulate the development and implementation of AI systems. AI is very difficult to govern when its implementation is ad-hoc, and when innovations are implemented before the risks are well understood. Given the anxiety around AI and concerns about data governance, several global initiatives have developed guidelines to govern its use. For example, Article 22 of the European General Data Protection Regulation (GDPR) is an oft-cited regulatory instrument designed to govern the use of AI and other smart technologies in the European Union (Sancho, 2020). Yet, these global initiatives also suffer from ad-hoc implementation, there are no widely recognized standards, and many states hold a strong anti-regulation position.

Cognizant of the limitations of existing regulatory standards, one question guides this section, "are existing international laws sufficient to protect vulnerable populations in an era driven by Big Data and AI?" This question has no easy answer because international law is still evolving in this area and may not be sufficiently robust to protect socially vulnerable populations. While international law will not be automated like some domains of domestic law, it still needs to be adapted to cope with the AI revolution underway (Burri, 2017). In the realm of voluntary international standards, the UN (2018) encourages those developing, designing, and deploying AI systems to ensure that they are consistent with the values reflected in existing international human rights norms and standards. Notably, the African Commission on Human and Peoples' Rights has also weighed in on this debate. In February 2021, the organization acknowledged that the political, economic, and social vulnerability of Africans would be amplified in this era of AI, especially as the continent has yet to leapfrog into the fourth industrial revolution, given its uneven access to state-of-the-art technologies, and limited investment in research and development and human resource capacity. While recognizing the promising value of the technology, the Commission, however, adopted a resolution to ensure that AI systems developed and deployed on the continent comply with, and respect African human rights standards (ACHPR, 2021). The resolution emphasizes the need for sufficient consideration of African norms, ethics, values, and communitarian ethos in the development of AI structures. Importantly, the resolution also emphasizes the need for freedom from the domination of one people by another in the framing of any global AI governance framework(s) (ACHPR, 2021). The Commission, therefore, calls on African countries to ensure that the development and use of AI technologies are compatible with the rights and duties enshrined in the African Charter on Human and Peoples Rights (ACHPR) specifically, to uphold "human dignity, privacy, equality, non-discrimination, inclusion, diversity, safety, fairness, transparency, accountability and economic development". The Commission also requires that all AI technologies imported by member states apply to the African context and/or be adjusted to fit the continent's needs, ensuring that AI technologies with far-reaching consequences for humans are codified with human rights principles, and remain under meaningful human control (ACHPR, 2021).

In April 2021, the European Commission also released its proposal for an AI legal framework (European Commission, 2021). Interestingly, to ensure the protection of EU citizens, the regulation applies to providers of AI systems established in the EU or a third country, if the latter is lawfully contracted to provide system services that will be used in the EU (European Commission, 2021). The Commission uses a risk-based framework to categorize the spectrum of risks associated with AI systems that threaten fundamental human rights, especially those of the most vulnerable in society (European Commission, 2021). This EU law extends the obligations for observing ethical rules to a wide range of parties including manufacturers, providers, importers, exporters, distributors, authorized representatives, and users of AI systems. In terms of the rules, transparency is emphasized to ensure that even the most vulnerable populations are informed about the AI systems they interact with, and which may have access to their private data (*articles* 13 and 52). Such AI systems are designed and developed in ways that human oversight is guaranteed while in use (*article* 14). Ensuring accuracy, robustness, and cybersecurity are also prescribed rules for high-risk AI systems (*article* 15).

It is important to be reminded of Baxi's theory on the supplantation of the paradigm of the Universal Declaration of Human Rights by a "trade-related market-friendly human rights" (TREMF) discourse that is capitalistic, market-oriented, and anti-poor (2006).[2] This new paradigm seeks to reverse the taken-for-granted notion that universal human rights are designed for the attainment of dignity, advancing the well-being of human beings, and enhancing the security and wellbeing of socially, and economically vulnerable populations" (Baxi, 2006). More specifically, in the course of fleshing out his TREMF thesis, Baxi developed several related sub-claims. These include his suppositions that the progressive state – or at least the progressive "Third World" state – is conceived as one that protects global capital against political instability and market failure, usually at a significant cost to the most vulnerable among its citizens, but also a state that is market efficient in suppressing the practices of resistance of its citizens (Baxi, 2006; Okafor, 2007). The potential for the technology to suppress those who actively oppose a state's adoption of AI specifically for monitoring and surveillance is highly likely in autocratic and military regimes in Africa, and also the wider global South community.

This is an instructive thought position in this era of AI given its likelihood to further privilege the rights of technology capitalists over the rights of already vulnerable populations. The current age of AI transformation could invariably promote an imperialist order that could lead to human rights abuses, especially against already vulnerable populations in the global South (Baxi, 2006).[3] Though it is important, and necessary to protect research and development in the technology, and the pursuant activism around its adoption, it is also equally necessary to allow for critiques of the techno-heroic and techno-evangelistic goals that are promised by AI. This is perhaps most clearly illustrated in how Big Data and AI have been operationalized to accelerate an end to the HIV/AIDS epidemic as a public health threat. Big Data and AI technologies are speeding up clinical research, increasing the operational efficiencies in HIV testing, diagnosis, care, and treatment, improving access to health care services in remote areas and reducing the need for human capital (Yiqiao et al., 2019, p. 2). Conversely, they also reveal that AI technologies present risks that undermine the human-centric approach to HIV/AIDS response, specifically, how algorithms displace the human-centric nature of self-identification and self-consciousness and so increase human rights violations of those seeking HIV/AIDS services. The authors critique the three political narratives, around AI that impacts the right to health – the dystopian account of AI driven by fear, the ethical account of AI driven by hope (e.g. "AI4Health"), and the entrepreneurial account of AI driven by health care capitalism or, in their own words "the desire for freedom from both state regulation and individuals' full and sustained ownership and control of their data" (Yiqiao et al., 2019, p. 3; see also Weber, 2018). They state that these accounts of AI combine with, and contradict each other, potentially undermining the advancement of public health. This example is instructive of how the use of AI may disproportionately affect different vulnerable populations, especially in the global south, but in this case, Africa, which accounts for almost two-thirds of new HIV infections.

In terms of international governance, we should at minimum draw inspiration from international human rights norms and standards. This is not to insinuate that international human rights norms are a silver bullet to ethical rulemaking questions. Instead, we rely on the universal recognition (alongside relativist adaptations) that several of its applicable norms have gained and also that some rights have earned the status of international law[4] (albeit with contingent duties for them to be observed and realized)[5] (Cobbah, 1987; Donnelly, 1984; Donoho, 1990; Ibhawoh, 2001; Reichert, 2006; Renteln, 2013). We nevertheless note that the concept of "human rights" is not free from ambiguities, and is subject to important critiques (such as TWAIL). For example, the notion that "human rights" are equally possessed by "all human beings" simply by virtue of their humanity could be seen as misleading because some rights are not possessed by all groups, e.g., people living with disabilities, children, and women. Also noteworthy is the fact that not all human rights are legal rights in all legal systems. From a global South perspective, Makau Mutua has several times argued that the human rights enterprise incorrectly presents itself as a guarantor of eternal truths without which human civilization is impossible (1999, 2000). He also contends that the human rights corpus, though well-meaning, is a Eurocentric construct for the reconstitution of non-Western societies and peoples with a set of culturally biased norms and practices (Mutua, 2002, 2013). Even though the scope and concept of human rights are still developing and constantly being negotiated, it still finds relevance in various established and innovative fields such as its current role in discourses on AI automation (Risse, 2019). This is also because the concept of human rights is gaining phenomenological expansion, indicating the increasing possibility that the concept is not conceived in the same way by various schools of thought. So, as a starting point, to protect vulnerable populations, the use of Big Data and AI must in no way exacerbate socio-economic, gender, and other inequalities. As the body of law governing AI continues to grow, the International Bill of Human Rights should be relied on as a core minimum for preventing AI from perpetuating discrimination, torture, or any form of indignity, especially to the most marginalized and most vulnerable in society.

At the 70th Anniversary of the Universal Declaration of Human Rights (UDHR), the UN High Commissioner for Human Rights proposed the universal reliance on the principles of the UDHR to govern AI in this digital world.[6] While there is an ongoing discussion on whether soft law or regulation should apply to AI systems, the already existing standards of human rights provide a foundation for its governance in three ways. First, providing a common language to frame harms, and offer clear parameters of what is permissible (for both governments, AI companies, and other stakeholders). Second, providing specific human rights principles such as accessibility, affordability, intellectual freedom, and avoidance of harm can contribute to addressing issues of discrimination, marginalization, and the digital divide that could result from these AI systems. And lastly, engaging the services of AI systems in human rights impact assessments (not just for accountability but also for independent oversight processes) (McGregor et al., 2018, 2019). Where harm is done, effective remedies need to be accessible to vulnerable populations, noting that for a remedy to be effective, it needs to ensure elements of prevention, redress, and non-recurrence. But even as these international human rights standards provide some foundation for the governance of AI, they may not be comprehensive enough to fulfill the regulatory, legal, and ethical responsibilities that are required to protect socially vulnerable populations from the more nefarious and exploitative uses of AI systems. This is perhaps why in September 2021, the United Nations High Commissioner for Human Rights proposed that any AI applications that cannot be operated in compliance with international human rights law should be banned,[7] and moratoriums imposed on the sale and use of AI systems that pose the greatest threats to human rights.[8]

CONCLUSIONS AND FUTURE PROSPECTS

At the cusp of the Fourth Industrial/Digital Revolution, Big Data and AI are seen as game-changers, the solution to many of the most pressing, and challenging global issues like infectious disease pandemics. One demographic that stands to benefit, as well as potentially suffer, from the further integration of Big Data and AI systems into more facets of life are socially vulnerable populations. Does this mean that progress in AI should be abandoned? Of course not! It does, however, require the application of more stringent regulations, oversight, and monitoring. Because a lot of investment in AI is also occurring in the private sector, all levels of government are duty-bound to protect the rights of its citizens whose private data may be collected without their consent (Castets-Renard & Fournier-Tombs, 2020), or even awareness, and used in ways that contravene their inherent right to privacy. While privacy concerns figure prominently in discussions about AI uses in areas such as healthcare, education, housing, and other social services, of increasing concern is the potential for AI technologies built from biased data sets to further disenfranchise marginalized groups, particularly racial and ethnic minorities who are already under surveillance by the state apparatus. A key example of this is the use of AI facial recognition software which has been criticized for its racial bias against African Americans. According to the Algorithmic Justice League, "facial recognition surveillance threatens the human rights of black people including their privacy, freedom of expression, freedom of association and their right to due process" (Najibi, 2020).

Turning our gaze to the global South, AI poses as much of a threat as it does a benefit. The global South and its racialized population do not have the legal safeguards that buffer citizens of the global North from the more intrusive elements of AI technologies (Arun, 2019). Specifically, technologies designed out of context (or more accurately, logarithms based on a Northern American political, economic, social, and environmental climate), typically fail to adequately account for localized context – resource availability, social and cultural norms and traditions, and the political climate (Arun, 2019). Consequently, populations in the global South, especially those in rural communities, religious and ethnic minorities within those countries, the unhoused, unemployed, women, and children are made even more vulnerable to potentially unethical uses of AI technologies. Given the prospect of AI's misuse for surveillance domestically, by authoritarian governments, and internationally, by transnational corporations and their governments (Wall et al., 2021), or even its potential to replace low-skilled workers through automation, robust safeguards must be put in place to manage AI's deployment in countries in the global South, and protect its citizens, doubly burdened by their subordinated status within the global political and economic hierarchy, what we call the first level of vulnerability, and their socio-cultural and historical relations within their own countries which create a second level of vulnerability.

The following are among some of the items that need to be addressed to reduce inequality and systematic vulnerabilities from AI, e.g., leveraging AI ethically to curate data disaggregated by race, gender, sexuality, class, geographic location, and indigeneity. Governments around the world have been slow in responding to calls from advocates and researchers to collect the data required to document and understand how crises affect people differently based on their gender, race, geographic location, and indigeneity. Such data will help improve the accuracy of AI technologies which is crucial in increasing societal preparedness for future crises by ensuring an effective allocation of resources such as public health information, testing centers, economic support, and healthcare services. The Africa-Canada Artificial Intelligence and Data Innovation Consortium's (ACADIC) work in sub-Saharan Africa reveals this region to be in dire need of a solution-oriented approach to the development and deployment of successful, beneficial, and socially responsible AI technologies. While there is a vast swathe of AI innovation and data science, from digital hubs in Kenya to a proposed Smart City in the Gauteng province of South Africa, very little regulation combined with complex cultural factors inhibits the desire and capability for regulation. In this chapter, we, therefore, call on policymakers in Africa to build guidance mechanisms for AI ethics and data governance in the region. This requires the design and implementation of locally specific legislation that safeguards their increasingly digital economy, and the digital footprint of their citizens in terms of both their digital privacy rights and online security, but also fully enforceable legislation.

ACKNOWLEDGMENT

JDK acknowledges support from Canada's International Development Research Centre (IDRC) and the Swedish International Development Cooperation Agency (SIDA) (Grant No. 109559-001).

NOTES

1 For more information, see http://www.covid19sa.org/ and http://acadic.org
2 Upendra Baxi makes a distinctive revision of human rights through an analysis of several concepts: history, activism, business, modernism, identity, institutionalism, politics and suffering among others. He makes an unconventional reading of human rights through a subaltern lens by positing that the true definers of human rights are those in struggle – those in the Third World.
3 Philosophically, and in complex but intriguing terms, Baxi differentiates two paradigms (Universal Declaration of Human Rights paradigm *versus* the TREMF paradigm) under notions of contemporary versus modern production of human rights. He uses a conceptualization of power to demarcate the "politics of human rights" as against the "politics for human rights". The latter borders around the control of power and the politicization of influence by states on others, while the politics of human rights rests on the pursuit of just and accountable governance practices.
4 For example, the United Nations General Assembly adopted the Universal Declaration of Human Rights (UDHR) on 10 December 1948. Written as "a common standard of achievement for all peoples and nations", the UDHR for the first time in human history spelt out the human rights that all human beings should enjoy. Although with some criticisms in the literature (see Makau Mutua, Human rights: A political and cultural critique (University of Pennsylvania Press, 2002); Jacob Dolinger, The Failure of the Universal Declaration of Human Rights, 47 U. Miami Inter-Am. L. Rev. 164 <http://repository.law.miami.edu/umialr/vol47/iss2/4>), it has over time been widely accepted as the fundamental norms of human rights and a foundational text in international human rights law. The UDHR, together with the International Covenant on Civil and Political Rights (ICCPR) and its two Optional Protocols, and the International Covenant on Economic, Social and Cultural Rights (ICESCR), form the so-called tripartite International Bill of Human Rights.
5 In achieving the respect for and observance of human rights, there is the legal obligation of States duty to respect and observe human rights protection from any substantial infringements, the substance of which is defined in conventional or customary international law. For example, under the UN Charter, Article 56 provides for the extent of human rights duties of all member States, which indicates that States retain some competence on human rights. To every human right there is an express or implicit correlative human duty owed. In theory, it is possible to posit that everyone cannot fully enjoy their human rights unless everyone fulfills their duties. Some human rights instruments have a "duty clause" that sets out the duties of citizens and others to their society. For example, UDHR, Article 29 (1); African Charter on Human and Peoples Rights in Articles 27–29.
6 OHCHR | 70th Anniversary of the Universal Declaration of Human Rights, online: https://www.ohchr.org/EN/NewsEvents/Pages/DisplayNews.aspx?NewsID=23983&LangID=E
7 A/HRC/48/31. Human Rights Council, Forty-eighth session (13 September–1 October 2021). Annual report of the United Nations High Commissioner for Human Rights "The right to privacy in the digital age".
8 Paras 45, 46, and 59. The High Commissioner also recommends a moratorium on the use of remote biometric recognition technologies in public spaces (at least until the authorities responsible can demonstrate compliance with privacy and data protection standards).

REFERENCES

African Commission on Human and Peoples' Rights, (2021). 473 resolution on the need to undertake a Study on human and peoples' rights and artificial intelligence (AI), robotics and other new and emerging technologies in Africa - ACHPR/Res. 473 (EXT.OS/ XXXI) 2021. https://www.achpr.org/sessions/resolutions?id=504

Al-Attar, M. (2020). TWAIL: A paradox within a paradox. *International Community Law Review, 22*(2), 163–196.

Alavinejad, M., Mellado, B., Asgary, A., Mbada, M., Mathaha, T., Lieberman, B., ... Kong, J. D. (2022). Management of healthcare resources in the Gauteng Province, South Africa, during the COVID-19 pandemic. Available at SSRN 10.2139/ssrn.4049177

Ang, A. (2021, September 2). *Around 1 million people potentially affected by suspected breach in Indonesia's COVID-19 app: Report.* Healthcare IT News. https://www.healthcareitnews.com/news/asia/around-1-million-people-potentially-affected-suspected-breach-indonesias-covid-19-app

Anuradha, J. (2015). A brief introduction on Big Data 5Vs characteristics and hadoop technology. *Procedia Computer Science, 48*, 319–324.

Arun, C. (2019). AI and the global south: Designing for other worlds. In Dubber, M., Pasquale, F., & Das, S. (Eds.), *Oxford handbook of ethics of AI.* Forthcoming.

Baker McKenzie. (2021, June 7). *Africa: Implementation of Cybersecurity and data protection law urgent across continent.* Baker McKenzie. https://www.bakermckenzie.com/en/insight/publications/2021/06/africa-cybersecurity-data-protection-law

Bankoff, G., & Hilhorst, D. (2004). Introduction: Mapping vulnerability. In Bankoff, G., Hilhorst, D., & Frerks, G. (Eds.), *Mapping vulnerability: "Disasters, development, and people"* (pp. 1–9). Earthscan.

Batha, E. (2018, November 15). Mobile app pays refugees to boost artificial intelligence. *Reuters.* https://www.reuters.com/article/us-refugees-conference-tech-jobs-idUSKCN1NK2SR

Baxi, U. (2006). *The future of human rights.* India: Oxford University Press.

Bellman, R. (1978). *An Introduction to artificial intelligence: Can computers think?* San Francisco: Boyd & Fraser Pub. Co.

Benzies, K. M., Perry, R., & Cope Williams, J. (2021). Influence of the COVID-19 pandemic on executive skills in Canadians experiencing social vulnerability: A descriptive study. *Health & Social Care in the Community,* 1–9. 10.1111/hsc.13615

Bircan, T., & Korkmaz, E. E. (2021). Big data for whose sake? Governing migration through artificial intelligence. *Humanities and Social Sciences Communications, 8*(1), 1–5. doi:10.1057/s41599-021-00910-x

Blaikie, P., Cannon, T., Davis, I., & Wisner, B. (1994). *At risk: Natural hazards, people's vulnerability, and disasters.* New York: Routledge.

Bragazzi, N. L., Dai, H., Damiani, G., Behzadifar, M., Martini, M., & Wu, J. (2020). How big data and artificial intelligence can help better manage the COVID-19 pandemic. *International Journal of Environmental Research and Public Health, 17*(9), 3176.

Burri, T. (2017). International law and artificial intelligence. *German Yearbook of International Law, 60*, 91–108.

Castets-Renard, C., & Fournier-Tombs, E. (2020). COVID-19 and accountable artificial intelligence in a global context. In Flood, C. M., MacDonnell, V., Philpott, J., Thériault, S., & Venkatapuram, S. (Eds.), *Vulnerable. The law, policy and ethics of COVID-19.* University of Ottawa Press. https://press.uottawa.ca/vulnerable.html.html

Cheong, Q., Au-Yeung, M., Quon, S., Concepcion, K., & Kong, J. D. (2021). Predictive modeling of vaccination uptake in US Counties: A machine learning–based approach. *Journal of Medical Internet Research, 23*(11), e33231.

Cobbah, J. A. (1987). African values and the human rights debate: An African perspective. *Human Rights Quarterly, 9*, 309.

Cutter, S. L., Boruff, B. J., & Shirley, W. L. (2003). Social vulnerability to environmental hazards. *Social Science Quarterly, 84*(2), 242–261.

Davenport, T. H., Barth, P., & Bean, R. (2012). How 'big data' is different. *MIT Sloan Management Review, 54*(1), 21–24.

Donnelly, J. (1984). Cultural relativism and universal human rights. *Human Rights Quarterly, 6,* 400.

Donoho, D. L. (1990). Relativism versus universalism in human rights: The search for meaningful standards. *Stanford Journal of International Law, 27,* 345.

Duhon, J., Bragazzi, N., & Kong, J. D. (2021). The impact of non-pharmaceutical interventions, demographic, social, and climatic factors on the initial growth rate of COVID-19: A cross-country study. *Science of The Total Environment, 760,* 144325.

Ebers, M., & Navas, S. (Eds.). (2020). *Algorithms and law.* Cambridge University Press.

European Commission (2021). "Proposal for a Regulation of the European Parliament and of the Council Laying Down Harmonized Rules on Artificial Intelligence (Artificial Intelligence Act) and Amending Certain Union Legislative Acts." (Brussels, 21 April 2021) COM (2021) 206 final, 2021/0106 (COD).

Freese, K. E., Vega, A., Lawrence, J. J., & Document, P. I. (2021). Social vulnerability is associated with the risk of COVID-19 related mortality in US counties with confirmed cases. *Journal of Health Care for the Poor and Underserved, 32*(1), 245–257.

García, R. J. (2020). Covid-19 En La Ciudad De Madrid Y Vulnerabilidad. Análisis De Las Dos Primeras Olas. *Methods, 95,* e1–e10.

George, G., Haas, M. R., & Pentland, A. (2014). Big data and management. *Academy of Management Journal, 57*(2), 321–326.

Ghassemi, M., Naumann, T., Schulam, P., Beam, A. L., Chen, I. Y., & Ranganath, R. (2020). A review of challenges and opportunities in machine learning for health. *AMIA Summits on Translational Science Proceedings, 2020,* 191.

Hopkins, A. (2018, July 27). Canada using DNA, ancestry websites to investigate migrants. *Reuters.* https://www.reuters.com/article/us-canada-immigration-idUSKBN1KH2KF

Ibhawoh, B. (2001). Cultural relativism and human rights: Reconsidering the Africanist discourse. *Netherlands Quarterly of Human Rights, 19*(1), 43–62.

Isaak, J., & Hanna, M. J. (2018). User data privacy: Facebook, Cambridge analytica, and privacy protection. *Computer, 51*(8), 56–59. doi:10.1109/MC.2018.3191268

Karmakar, M., Lantz, P. M., & Tipirneni, R. (2021). Association of social and demographic factors with COVID-19 incidence and death rates in the US. *JAMA Network Open, 4*(1), e2036462.

Kazemi, M., Bragazzi, N. L., & Kong, J. D. (2022). Assessing inequities in COVID-19 vaccine roll-out strategy programs: A cross-country study using a machine learning approach. *Vaccines, 10*(2), 194.

Kong, J. D., Tekwa, E. W., & Gignoux-Wolfsohn, S. A. (2021). Social, economic, and environmental factors influencing the basic reproduction number of COVID-19 across countries. *PloS One, 16*(6), e0252373.

Leslie, D., Mazumder, A., Peppin, A., Wolters, M. K., & Hagerty, A. (2021). Does "AI" stand for augmenting inequality in the era of covid-19 healthcare? *BMJ, 372.* 10.1136/bmj.n304

Lieberman, B., Gusinow, R., Asgary, A., Bragazzi, N. L., Choma, N., Dahbi, S. E., … Wu, J. (2021). Big Data-and artificial intelligence-based hot-spot analysis of COVID-19: Gauteng, South Africa, as a case study. 2021). Available at SSRN. 10.2139/ssrn.3803878

Litman-Navarro, K. (2018). *Using refugees to train algorithms is some dystopian shit.* The Outline. https://theoutline.com/post/6619/paying-refugees-to-train-algorithms-is-a-bad-idea

Malakar, S. (2021). Geospatial modeling of COVID-19 vulnerability using an integrated fuzzy MCDM approach: a case study of West Bengal, India. *Modeling Earth Systems and Environment*, 1–14. 10.1007/s40808-021-01287-1

McGregor, L., Ng, V., Shaheed, A., Abrusci, E., Kent, C., Murray, D., & Williams, C. (2018). The universal declaration of human rights at 70: Putting human rights at the heart of the design, development, and deployment of artificial intelligence. *Human Rights, Big Data and Technology Project.* https://48ba3m4eh2bf2sksp43rq8kk-wpengine.netdna-ssl.com/wp-content/uploads/2018/12/UDHR70_AI. pdf

McGregor, L., Murray, D., & Ng, V. (2019). International human rights law as a framework for algorithmic accountability. *International & Comparative Law Quarterly*, 68(2), 309–343.

Mellado, B., Wu, J., Kong, J. D., Bragazzi, N. L., Asgary, A., Kawonga, M., ... & Orbinski, J. (2021). Leveraging artificial intelligence and big data to optimize COVID-19 clinical public health and vaccination roll-out strategies in Africa. *International Journal of Environmental Research and Public Health*, 18(15), 7890.

Mutua, M. (2002). *Human rights: A political and cultural critique*. University of Pennsylvania Press.

Mutua, M. (Ed.). (2013). *Human rights NGOs in East Africa: Political and normative tensions*. University of Pennsylvania Press.

Nagpal, D., Sood, S., Mohagaonkar, S., Sharma, H., & Saxena, A. (2019, March). Analyzing viral genomic data using Hadoop framework in big data. In *2019 6th International Conference on Computing for Sustainable Global Development (INDIACom)* (pp. 680–685). IEEE.

Najibi, A. (2020, October 24). Racial discrimination in face recognition technology. *Science in the News.* https://sitn.hms.harvard.edu/flash/2020/racial-discrimination-in-face-recognition-technology/

Neelon, B., Mutiso, F., Mueller, N. T., Pearce, J. L., & Benjamin-Neelon, S. E. (2021). Spatial and temporal trends in social vulnerability and COVID-19 incidence and death rates in the United States. *PloS One*, 16(3), e0248702.

Nia, Z., Ahmadi, A., Bragazzi, N. L., Woldegerima, W. A., Mellado, B., Wu, J., ... Kong, J. D. (2022). A cross-country analysis of macroeconomic responses to COVID-19 pandemic using twitter sentiments. Available at *SSRN 4001976*.

Okafor, O. C. (2007). *The African human rights system, activist forces and international institutions*. Cambridge University Press.

Poole, D., Mackworth, A., & Goebel, R. (1998). Computational intelligence: A logical approach. United Kingdom: Oxford University Press.

REFUNITE. (2021). *REFUNITE*. Refunite. https://refunite.org/about/

Reichert, E. (2006). Human rights: An examination of universalism and cultural relativism. *Journal of Comparative Social Welfare*, 22(1), 23–36.

Renteln, A. D. (2013). *International human rights: Universalism versus relativism*. Quid Pro Books.

Rich, E., & Knight, K. (1991). Connectionist models. In *Artificial intelligence* (pp. 487–519). McGraw-Hill.

Risse, M. (2019). Human rights and artificial intelligence: An urgently needed agenda. *Human Rights Quarterly*, 41, 1.

Rodrigues, R. (2020). Legal and human rights issues of AI: Gaps, challenges and vulnerabilities. *Journal of Responsible Technology*, 4, 100005. doi:10.1016/j.jrt.2020.100005

Rosenberg, T. (2017, October 4). Opinion | A better way to trace scattered refugees. *The New York Times.* https://www.nytimes.com/2017/10/04/opinion/a-better-way-to-trace-scattered-refugees.html

Sancho, D. (2020). Automated decision-making under Article 22 GDPR: Towards a more substantial regime for solely automated decision-making. In Ebers, M. & Navas, S. (Eds.), *Algorithms and law* (pp. 136–156). Cambridge: Cambridge University Press. doi:10.1017/9781108347846.005

Silva da Paz, W., Fontes Lima, A. G. C., da Conceição Araújo, D., Duque, A. M., Peixoto, M. V. S., Góes, M. A. O., … Dantas Dos Santos, A. (2021). Spatiotemporal pattern of COVID-19-related mortality during the first year of the pandemic in Brazil: A population-based study in a region of high social vulnerability. *The American Journal of Tropical Medicine and Hygiene, 106*(1), 132–141. doi: 10.4269/ajtmh.21-0744

Sinur, J., & Peters, E. M. L. (2019, September 30). AI & Big Data; better together. *Forbes.* https://www.forbes.com/sites/cognitiveworld/2019/09/30/ai-big-data-better-together/

Spielman, S. E., & Thill, J. C. (2008). Social area analysis, data mining, and GIS. *Computers, Environment and Urban Systems, 32*(2), 110–122.

St-Denis, X. (2020). Sociodemographic determinants of occupational risks of exposure to COVID-19 in Canada. *Canadian Review of Sociology/Revue Canadienne de Sociologie, 57*(3), 399–452. doi:10.1111/cars.12288

Stevenson, F., Hayasi, K., Bragazzi, N. L., Kong, J. D., Asgary, A., Lieberman, B., … Wu, J. (2021). Development of an early alert system for an additional wave of COVID-19 cases using a recurrent neural network with long short-term memory. *International Journal of Environmental Research and Public Health, 18*(14), 7376.

Tao, S., Bragazzi, N. L., Wu, J., Mellado, B., & Kong, J. D. (2022). Harnessing artificial intelligence to assess the impact of nonpharmaceutical interventions on the second wave of the coronavirus disease 2019 pandemic across the world. *Scientific Reports, 12*(1), 1–9.

Torres-Torres, J., Martinez-Portilla, R. J., Espino-y-Sosa, S., Estrada-Gutierrez, G., Solis-Paredes, J. M., Villafan-Bernal, J. R., … Poon, L. C. (2022). Comorbidity, poverty, and social vulnerability as risk factors for mortality in pregnant women with confirmed SARS-CoV-2 infection: Analysis of 13 062 positive pregnancies including 176 maternal deaths in Mexico. *Ultrasound in Obstetrics & Gynecology, 59*(1), 76–82. 10.1002/uog.24797

United Nations. (n.d.). *Vulnerable Groups. Who are they?* United Nations; United Nations. Retrieved 28 March 2022, from https://www.un.org/en/fight-racism/vulnerable-groups

UN (2018). UN secretary-general's strategy on new technologies. *United Nations, September.* https://www.un.org/en/newtechnologies/

UN DESA (2016). *Leaving no one behind: The imperative of inclusive development: report on the world social situation.* United Nations Department of Economic and Social Affairs. https://digitallibrary.un.org/record/3806782

United Nations Development Programme. (n.d.). *Vulnerable and key populations.* UNDP Capacity Development for Health. Retrieved 28 March 2022, from https://www.undp-capacitydevelopment-health.org//en/legal-and-policy/key-populations/

Wall, P. J., Saxena, D., & Brown, S. (2021). Artificial intelligence in the global south (AI4D): potential and risks. arXiv preprint, ArXiv:2108.10093.

Weber, C. (2018). How 3 key narratives shape popular views on artificial intelligence: opinion. ITU News. https://news.itu.int/artificial-intelligence- politics-fear-hope-freedom

Winston. (1992). *Artificial intelligence* (3rd ed.). Addison-Wesley Pub. Co.

Wisner, B., Blaikie, P., Cannon, T., & Davis, I. (2004). *At risk: Natural hazards, people's vulnerability, and disasters* (2nd ed.). Routledge.

Yan, C., Law, M., Nguyen, S., Cheung, J., & Kong, J. (2021). Comparing public sentiment toward COVID-19 vaccines across Canadian cities: Analysis of comments on Reddit. *Journal of Medical Internet Research, 23*(9), e32685.

Yedinak, J. L., Li, Y., Krieger, M. S., Howe, K., Ndoye, C. D., Lee, H., … Marshall, B. D. (2021). Machine learning takes a village: Assessing neighbourhood-level vulnerability for an overdose and infectious disease outbreak. *International Journal of Drug Policy, 96*, 103395.

Yiqiao, K., Jolene, Richard, B., & Cynthia, W. (2019, July 16). *Artificial intelligence and big data: Risks and benefits to the HIV/AIDS response.* Equal Eyes. https://equal-eyes.org/database/2019/7/16/artificial-intelligence-and-big-data-risks-and-benefits-to-the-hivaids-response

III

AI in Action: Ethical Challenges

CHAPTER 12

Artificial Intelligence and Bias: A Scoping Review

Bushra Kundi[a], Christo El Morr[a], Rachel Gorman[a], and Ena Dua[b]

[a]School of Health Policy and Management, York University, Toronto, Ontario, Canada
[b]School of Gender, Sexuality and Women's Studies, York University, Toronto, Ontario, Canada

CONTENTS

DOI: 10.1201/9781003261247-15

INTRODUCTION

Artificial intelligence has become a remarkable feature of our era; it is being deployed in many aspects of our lives without proper consideration of its impact. Specifically, AI can perpetuate and exacerbates biases. AI bias is defined as a situation where AI algorithms reproduce or exacerbate existing inequities in socioeconomic status, race, ethnic background, religion, gender, disability, or sexual orientation (Panch et al., 2019). AI bias can be introduced or amplified at various points from the initial dataset to the algorithm output. If algorithms use data that were generated through a biased method, the output could be biased as well (Parikh et al., 2019). The quality of data used to train artificial intelligence and machine learning limits them to outputs based on the data being introduced to them (Parikh et al., 2019). For example, data sources like electronic health records (EHRs) and insurance claims generate data as a result of human decisions, and when those data are then used by AI and machine learning, it can potentially lead to biased outcomes because they are limited by the quality of data they are being trained on (Parikh et al., 2019). Furthermore, the person in charge of designing these algorithms can reflect their human judgment and prejudice in the AI models, making them biased (Parikh et al., 2019).

AI bias has been reported in many areas, including business (Manyika, 2019; Manyika et al., 2019), social media (Nouri, 2021), the economy (Omowole, 2021), politics (Kumawat, 2020), and healthcare (Siwicki, 2021). However, access to healthcare is a human right (Ghebreyesus, 2017), so investigating whether AI propagates or exacerbates inequity in healthcare provision or access to healthcare is paramount (Leslie et al., 2021).

Algorithmic bias in the context of AI and health systems is defined as "the instances when the application of an algorithm compounds existing inequities in socioeconomic status, race, ethnic background, religion, gender, disability or sexual orientation to amplify them and adversely impact inequities in health systems" (Panch et al., 2019). Algorithmic bias is essentially the biased outcome of algorithms and data that are created through human judgment (Nelson, 2019). For example, algorithms have authors and act according to the instructions developed and interpreted by humans, making them a reflection of the author's bias (Nelson, 2019). In health systems, biased algorithms depend on patient attributes such as gender, sex, race, socioeconomic status, or religion (Fletcher et al., 2020). Dependency on these attributes can lead to algorithmic bias, where there is unfavorable or favorable treatment of one patient group vs. another, making the algorithm ethically wrong and leading to biased outcomes and results (Fletcher et al., 2020). For example, a system that analyzes clinical trial data in order to determine the best treatment option would contain inherent racial and gender biases since clinical trial subjects are overwhelmingly male and White, which could potentially result in inappropriate recommendations for other patients (Curran, 2021).

The underrepresentation of certain demographics is a factor contributing to algorithmic bias. Data used to train the algorithms can pose problems if they do not reflect diverse demographics or if they reflect disparities in outcomes or biases in human behavior (Noseworthy et al., 2020). The implementation of a predictive model that reflects racial disparities unrelated to the patient's health risks can lead to perpetuating the disparity itself (Noseworthy et al., 2020). Consequently, algorithmic bias can adversely impact equity within health systems, further exacerbating social health inequalities (Panch et al., 2019).

We conducted a scoping review of AI bias to synthesize themes and identify gaps in the literature. Our thematic findings are elaborated later.

METHOD

Search Strategy

A scoping review was conducted in the following eight online databases: ProQuest, IEEE Explore, ACM Digital Library, Web of Science, Medline, PubMed, PsycINFO, and CINAHL. The literature search strategy was conducted using key search terms identified with the support of a librarian. The following search terms were included: artificial intelligence, machine learning, bias, racism, race, racist, racial, discrimination, gender, Islamophobia, xenophobia, homophobia, colonialism, indigenous, indigeneity, prejudice, stereotype, black, white supremacy, whiteness, and alt-right. Seven hundred and seventy-three citations were extracted, 468 of which were not duplicates. The full search strategies can be found in the Appendix.

Eligibility Criteria

The inclusion criteria were predetermined and focused on studies that were published in the last five years, described artificial intelligence or machine learning and if they addressed biases. The exclusion criteria included studies that were not articles or were not written in English. The most recent search took place on November 5, 2021. Given that this was a scoping review, the search terms were limited to the titles of the publications.

Selection Process

The inclusion and exclusion criteria were first applied to 468 abstracts. Rayyan software was used by two authors (BK and CE) to screen the 468 articles, and 34 were identified as potentially eligible. The full-text versions were retrieved for the 34 articles and reviewed by both authors for the final selection. Only 28 articles were selected for review and synthesis. Our main interest in terms of outcome was bias. The literature search, review, and data collection from articles were conducted by a single individual (BK) and were repeated by one other individual (CE). Ambiguities and disagreements were resolved through discussion until consensus was reached.

RESULT

In total, 775 articles were identified, 307 of which were duplicates. Of the 468 unique articles, 434 were excluded based on the content of their abstracts. The inclusion criteria were applied to the 34 articles after their full text was read, and only 28 articles were kept for analysis (Figure 12.1). Three sources of biases were identified, input bias, algorithmic bias, and cognitive bias; each of which generates many types of biases summarized later. The complete list of identified articles is given in the Appendix.

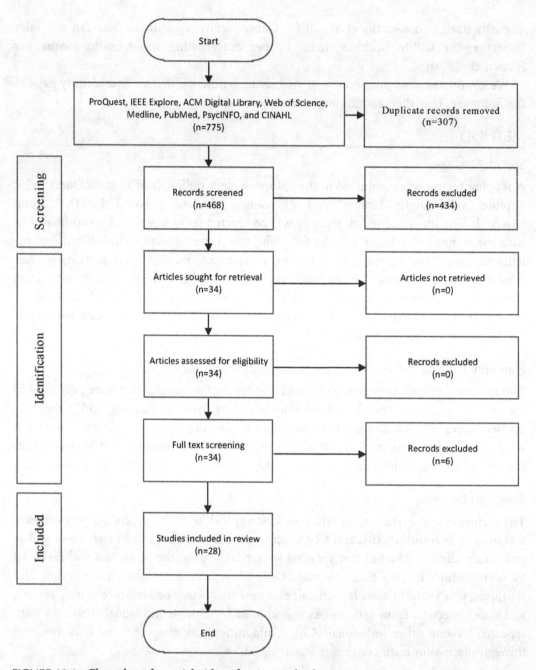

FIGURE 12.1   Flow chart for article identification and selection.

Input Bias

Bias in machine learning relates to the data used to generate the predictive models. The biased data are derived mainly from electronic health records (EHRs). Bias in EHRs refers to bias within clinical electronic health records due to incorrect or unrepresentative medical information (Agniel et al., 2018). In health systems, datasets are generated through biased processes; for example, data created through human interference by the developers can reflect their biases, and incorrect or missing information can lead to a biased output (Parikh et al., 2019). Human judgment and interference in dataset generation is the use of unrepresentative biased data where a certain demographic is favored over others, resulting in biased results for the underrepresented demographics (Parikh et al., 2019). Indeed, sampling bias is a well-known limitation in research including AI (Telus International, 2021).

Another contributor to EHR bias is missing data. Missing data in electronic health records can occur due to the lack of patient follow-up after appointments (Parikh et al., 2019). This causes data gaps, creating biases affecting critical patient decision outcomes, such as health interventions, which are made by clinical decision support tools (Parikh et al., 2019). This is especially exacerbated by the fact that Black, Indigenous, and People of Color (BIPOC) have less access to healthcare services. Racial biases persist in access to care (Canady, 2020; Halwani, 2004; Valenzuela et al., 2020).

EHRs are no doubt an important part of clinical decision support tools. For example, predictive modeling along with electronic health records that use deep learning can accurately predict in-hospital mortality, 30-day unplanned readmission, prolonged length of stay, and final discharge diagnoses (Gianfrancesco et al., 2018). Even so, applying machine learning to EHRs can cause potential social biases that could be introduced through data extracted from the EHR systems (Gianfrancesco et al., 2018), which could exacerbate already-observed biases in insurance company algorithms (Śmietanka et al., 2020). Our literature review indicated that biased datasets lead to many types of biases, including social bias, ethnic bias, gender bias, intersectional bias, and health bias.

Social Bias

Social bias is defined as being against or favoring groups and individuals based on their social identity, such as sex, race, religion, gender, socioeconomic status, and ethnicity (Parikh et al., 2019). Social bias in AI can occur due to biased algorithms because of biased data due to human factors, missing data, and underrepresentation of certain social groups (Parikh et al., 2019). In healthcare systems, human factors such as implicit bias can perpetuate social bias through EHRs (Parikh et al., 2019). For example, an AI algorithm that learns from older EHR data may not recommend that older women be tested for cardiac ischemia, resulting in delaying potentially lifesaving treatment and further perpetuating implicit social biases (Parikh et al., 2019). These social biases within healthcare systems cause inequity in healthcare delivery, which leads to unfavorable outcomes for underrepresented groups (Parikh et al., 2019).

Racial Bias

Ethnic bias is defined as participating in discriminatory behavior, holding any negative attitudes toward or having less favorable reactions toward people based on their ethnicity (Blum et al., 2021). There has been discussion in the field of dermatology regarding the lack of racial and ethnic diversity in machine learning algorithms as a potential source of algorithmic racial bias that can exacerbate the health disparity of access to healthcare (Lee et al., 2021). For example, autoimmune skin conditions such as cicatricial alopecia

(CCCA) and discoid lupus erythematosus (DLE) require adequate representation for women of color, as they are disproportionately affected by them (Lee et al., 2021). These conditions can often go undetected, which is why it is crucial for machine learning and AI algorithms to detect these skin conditions by using images with diverse skin colors to provide timely treatment options (Lee et al., 2021).

Among women that had breast cancer, Black women had a lower chance of being tested for high-risk mutations than White women even though they both carry a similar risk of such mutations (Parikh et al., 2019). This is an example of a biased outcome since the data being used to train the AI were affected by human judgment due to inadequate representation of Black women. Having said that, AI can potentially reinforce and per-petuate social biases, worsening patient outcomes and health disparities by generating biased algorithmic output (Noseworthy et al., 2020). Machine learning models are bound to be biased because of the bias in the training datasets, which is why it is crucial to detect the bias beforehand (Alelyani, 2021).

Moreover, racial and ethnic bias in medical appointment scheduling is a common issue in healthcare (Samorani et al., 2021). There have been studies that analyze the correlation between no-show probabilities and patient attributes, finding that race and ethnicity are in fact correlated with the probability of patient no-shows (Samorani et al., 2021). After surveying 105 empirical studies on appointment no-shows, Dantas et al. concluded that "minority groups were consistently associated with increased no-show, but, not surpris-ingly, different groups were considered minorities in different countries (e.g., Hispanics and Afro-Americans in the United States)" (Dantas et al., 2018), which is consistent with the studies that showed that people with a lower socioeconomic status were less likely to attend medical appointments (Hamilton et al., 2002). Despite the presence of work in algorithmic bias in healthcare and quantitative evidence that proves race and no-show probabilities are correlated, studies fail to acknowledge that using predictive booking al-gorithms that base outcomes on historical and past data may result in ethnically biased decisions where certain ethnicities receive an unfavorable outcome (Samorani et al., 2021).

The sorts of biases we encountered before were found to have similar results to cognitive bias in humans (McElaney, 2018); indeed, Amazon's facial recognition technology (Snow, 2018), Google's cloud natural language processing (Thompson, 2017), and Correctional Offender Management Profiling for Alternative Sanctions used in courts in the United States (Angwin et al., 2016) were found to harbor different types of biases toward people of color, non-Christians and women, and Black people, respectively. AI software from IBM, Microsoft, and Face++ exhibited gender and skin type biases (Hardesty, 2018).

Gender Bias

Gender bias is defined as stereotyping against and showing favoritism toward one gender over another (Rothchild, 2014) as well as exclusion, until recently, of those who are transgender, including in healthcare (Ross et al., 2016; Walker et al., 2017; White Hughto et al., 2018). Datasets that follow a biased pattern pertaining to gender in which data are more inclined toward a certain gender are one of the ways gender bias occurs in machine learning (Alelyani, 2021). Data-driven decision-support systems in AI are very common today and are used to allow for faster and more informed decision-making, but they fail to recognize bias (Balayn et al., 2021). An example of this is the Amazon screening system, which was reported for exhibiting unfair gender bias (Balayn et al., 2021). Gender bias has been reported in healthcare, including favoring men over women when screening for heart diseases (Daugherty et al., 2017).

The underrepresentation of genders in patient samples is another factor contributing to gender bias, as it regularly introduces bias into datasets (Byrne, 2021). There is a potential for gender bias if certain sexes or genders are excluded from datasets used to train machine learning algorithms or if sex- or gender-based disparities in clinical settings are not properly accounted for (Lee et al., 2021). For example, AI algorithms trained predominantly on male subjects perform worse when tested on female subjects (Lee et al., 2021). Increased acknowledgment and inclusion of sex and gender within AI are crucial to ensure gender equity and prevent gender bias (Lee et al., 2021).

Intersectional Bias

Among women that had breast cancer, Black women had a lower chance of being tested for high-risk mutations as compared to White women even though they both carry a similar risk of such mutations (Parikh et al., 2019). This is an example of a biased outcome, since the data being used to train the AI were affected by human judgment due to inadequate representation of Black women. Having said that, AI can potentially reinforce and perpetuate social biases worsening patient outcomes and health disparities by generating biased algorithmic output (Noseworthy et al., 2020). Machine learning models are bound to be biased because of the bias in the training datasets, which is why it is crucial to detect the bias beforehand (Alelyani, 2021).

Health Care Bias

Health care bias is defined as discrimination or stereotyping in a healthcare setting leading to a negative evaluation of a person based on irrelevant features such as race, socioeconomic status, ethnicity, gender, and sex (FitzGerald & Hurst, 2017). In healthcare systems, the data that are available for analysis have the potential to affect clinical decision support tools based on patient characteristics (Gianfrancesco et al., 2018). For example, studies have found that people from vulnerable populations, including immigrants, and those with lower socioeconomic status or mental health issues, are more likely to visit several institutions or healthcare organizations to receive healthcare due to factors such as transportation issues and remote geographical location (Gianfrancesco et al., 2018). These patients may have inadequate or missing information in the electronic health records to qualify for clinical decision support tools that would help with early healthcare interventions (Gianfrancesco et al., 2018). To add on, the electronic health records may also not capture data on relevant factors to improving their health, such as difficulties with transportation or shelter (Gianfrancesco et al., 2018). The data that are available for analysis in healthcare have the potential to exacerbate social biases, whereby certain groups of people are treated unfavorably based on unrelated patient characteristics such as socioeconomic status and race (Gianfrancesco et al., 2018).

Algorithmic Bias

Algorithms built using biased data can lead to algorithmic bias which can have negative consequences on members of racial and ethnic minorities. Algorithmic bias can be the result of bias in *data input* by the fact of historical omission of certain data items, a deliberate omission by machine learning professionals, or a miss-tagging of certain data (Ploug & Holm, 2020). For instance, bias pertaining to natural language processing (NLP) algorithms involves artificial intelligence (AI) models that automatically discover hidden patterns in natural language datasets, which can then propagate patterns caused by human bias, such as racism, sexism, and ableism (Caliskan, 2021). Research has shown that word embeddings and machine translation systems also tend to depict social biases, including gender bias. Font and Costa-Jussa (2019) show that the sentence "She works in a hospital, my friend is a nurse" would translate the word "friend" to "amiga" (Noseworthy et al., 2020), while the sentence "She works in a hospital, my friend is a doctor" translated the word friend to "amigo", inferring a male friend (Lwowski & Rios, 2021). By associating certain career positions to one's gender, the NLP model is perpetuating gender bias. There is an urgent need to thoroughly assess the differences between our existing linguistic expression and the biases within NLP models to prevent and mitigate social biases (Straw & Callison-Burch, 2020).

In addition, algorithms themselves can be biased as we are ought to introduce bias to *data processing*; for example, through a rule added to the algorithm, such as favoring overdiagnosis to underdiagnosis, or a certain age group, or a certain outcome intrinsically linked to a certain group (Ploug & Holm, 2020). Data processing bias can also be introduced through a procedure known as regularization in order to reduce model overfitting (i.e., learning from a non-representative dataset). Curran (2021) reports that an algorithm used in a healthcare system was constantly excluding Black Patients from being identified as sick patients for extra health services and care management programs even though they were more qualified than white patients. The algorithm had been using health care costs as a factor for illness. Since health care spending is lower for Black patients due to structural inequalities in access to care, the algorithm proceeded to exclude them. Such algorithmic bias could lead to people not receiving the medical care they need (Curran, 2021).

Algorithmic bias can also result from lack of generalizability of a model; if a model is built on data from a certain context (e.g., a hospital) and then used in another one with another population characteristic, then the model won't perform well in the new environment.

Cognitive Bias

Cognitive bias is defined as people's systematic but flawed responses to judgment and decisions based on the information and mental capacity they possess (Wilke & Mata, 2012), whereby personal judgments and assumptions can affect decisions (Iannessi et al., 2021). Interpretation bias can be introduced when users conduct an experiment (Gurupur & Wan, 2020) or interpret algorithms' output (Danks & London, 2017). Cognitive biases include "availability heuristic" where rules that are easily remember are considered as more probable (Tversky & Kahneman, 1973), and overconfidence bias where people tend to be overconfident in their judgment (Tversky & Kahneman, 1983). Kliegr et al. (2021) enumerate

20 cognitive biases in relation with rule-based machine learning models and suggest corrective actions for them; for example, they suggest that since overconfidence is linked to more knowledge, then feature selection which reduces the number of existing data items used for learning (i.e., creating the model) would be helpful in reducing the overconfidence bias.

Figure 12.2 summarizes the types of AI biases.

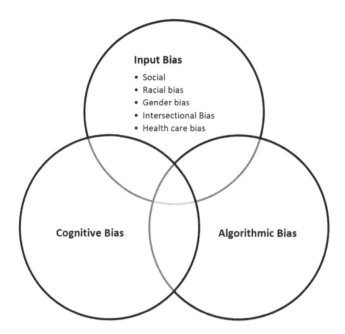

FIGURE 12.2   Types of biases affecting AI.

DISCUSSION

It is worth noting that a significant source of bias is input bias. AI algorithms rely on available data, which influence the results through a lack of diversity, whether this lack is due to the environment (e.g., non-diverse population) or to existing biases throughout the data collection processes.

AI may exacerbate existing biases, such as socioeconomic and systemic biases. Socioeconomic bias is defined as discriminating against an individual or group based on their socioeconomic standing or class (Schlosser, 2017). In AI, health systems have the potential to perpetuate socioeconomic bias. For example, if an algorithm uses a patient's home address or postal code, this variable can correlate with the patient's socioeconomic status and cause bias pertaining to the patient's socioeconomic status within the system by suggesting health interventions based on their socioeconomic status rather than need (Fletcher et al., 2020). Research has reported a significant diagnostic bias for chronic obstructive pulmonary disease (COPD) in terms of discriminating against individuals with a low socioeconomic status (SES) (Fletcher et al., 2020). If not used carefully, AI has the ability to exacerbate existing health disparities between different demographic groups (Fletcher et al., 2020).

While there is a fair number of studies addressing input bias, there is scarcity of research on algorithmic and cognitive biases in the machine learning domain; more multidisciplinary investigation of these biases and their mitigation in machine learning software is needed.

Systemic bias, also known as institutional bias, is the inclination for the procedures, practices, and policies of particular institutions, such as health, educational, legal, religious, media, or governmental organizations, to function in ways which result in certain social groups being advantaged or favored and others being disadvantaged (Chandler & Munday, 2011). Systematic inequities are rooted in societies and health systems, and it is very difficult to define a standard of fairness for them (Panch et al., 2019). Health inequity is a persistent and prolonged part of the systemic racism and social prejudices in society (Curran, 2021). If AI tools were properly built, ensuring that they did not include data that perpetuate biases or systemic racism, they could play a crucial role in improving health outcomes (Curran, 2021).

A groundbreaking Institute of Medicine (IOM) report (Institute of Medicine Committee on Understanding Eliminating Racial Ethnic Disparities in Health Care, 2003) has exposed evidence of racial and ethnic disparities in healthcare delivery on a systemic level (Byrne, 2021). Even in the better-controlled studies, minorities were less likely than White people to receive needed services, including clinically necessary procedures for cancer, cardio-vascular diseases, mental illness, AIDS, and diabetes (Institute of Medicine Committee on Understanding Eliminating Racial Ethnic Disparities in Health Care, 2003). This study affirmed systemic bias within healthcare systems; even when controlling for factors such as severity or stage of disease progression, the study found that White people were more likely to receive needed health services (Institute of Medicine Committee on Understanding Eliminating Racial Ethnic Disparities in Health Care, 2003).

While the literature frequently mentions bias, we found a lack of engagement with specific communities' data needs and experiences of data bias. Further, the framing of bias itself comes from a positivist epistemological tradition, which is at odds with disciplines where we can further unpack ethnic bias, gender bias, and intersectional bias. Future work on the ways in which AI exacerbates and reproduces social inequities should incorporate community perspectives and concepts such as racism, sexism, ableism, and colonialism.

CONCLUSION

Ample literature confirms the existence of AI bias and reveals multiple mechanisms through which bias is incorporated into AI processes. There are rich and rigorous literature on gender, race, disability, and intersectional inequities; however, the positivist concept of "bias" is at odds with these. We propose a deeper discussion of AI and data inequities. Considering that AI and data inequity is a product of social relations, future research should incorporate community perspectives and engage concepts such as racism, sexism, ableism, and colonialism to understand the terrain of AI biases and data inequities more rigorously.

REFERENCES

Agniel, D., Kohane, I. S., & Weber, G. M. (2018). Biases in electronic health record data due to processes within the healthcare system: retrospective observational study. *BMJ, 361,* k147910.1136/bmj.k1479

Alelyani, S. (2021). Detection and evaluation of machine learning bias. *Applied Sciences-Basel, 11*(14), 6271.

Angwin, J., Larson, J., Mattu, S., & Kirchner, L. (2016, May 23). *Machine bias.* ProPublica. Retrieved February 12, 2022 from https://www.propublica.org/article/machine-bias-risk-assessments-in-criminal-sentencing

Balayn, A., Lofi, C., & Houben, G. J. (2021). Managing bias and unfairness in data for decision support: A survey of machine learning and data engineering approaches to identify and mitigate bias and unfairness within data management and analytics systems. *VLDB Journal, 30*(5), 739–768.

Blum, A., Hazlett, C., & Posner, D. N. (2021). Measuring ethnic bias: Can misattribution-based tools from social psychology reveal group biases that economics games cannot? *Political Analysis, 29*(3), 385–404. doi:10.1017/pan.2020.37

Byrne, M. D. (2021). Reducing bias in healthcare artificial intelligence. *Journal of PeriAnesthesia Nursing, 36*(3), 313–316.

Caliskan, A. (2021). *Detecting and mitigating bias in natural language processing.* The Brookings Institution.Retrieved July 28, 2022 from https://www.brookings.edu/research/detecting-and-mitigating-bias-in-natural-language-processing/

Canady, V. A. (2020). Bill would improve MH service access for BIPOC communities. *Mental Health Weekly, 30*(35), 3–5. doi:10.1002/mhw.32501. https://doi.org/https://doi.org/10.1002/mhw.32501

Chandler, D., & Munday, R. (2011). *Institutional bias.* Oxford University Press.

Curran, K. (2021). Health equity - artificial intelligence in health care needs scrutiny to eliminate bias. *Health Progress, 102*(4), 68–70.

Danks, D., & London, A. (2017). Algorithmic bias in autonomous systems. IJCAI'17. *Proceedings of the 26th international joint conference on artificial intelligence,* August 19–25, 2017, Melbourne, Australia.

Dantas, L. F., Fleck, J. L., Cyrino Oliveira, F. L., & Hamacher, S. (2018). No-shows in appointment scheduling – a systematic literature review. *Health Policy, 122*(4), 412–421. doi:10.1016/j.healthpol.2018.02.002

Daugherty, S. L., Blair, I. V., Havranek, E. P., Furniss, A., Dickinson, L. M., Karimkhani, E., ... Masoudi, F. A. (2017). Implicit gender bias and the use of cardiovascular tests among cardiologists. *Journal of the American Heart Association, 6*(12), e006872. doi:10.1161/JAHA.117.006872

FitzGerald, C., & Hurst, S. (2017). Implicit bias in healthcare professionals: A systematic review. *BMC Medical Ethics, 18*(1), 19. doi:10.1186/s12910-017-0179-8

Fletcher, R. R., Nakeshimana, A., & Olubeko, O. (2020). Addressing fairness, bias, and appropriate use of artificial intelligence and machine learning in global health. *Frontiers In Artificial Intelligence, 3,* 561802.

Font, J. E., & Costa-Jussa, M. R. (2019). Equalizing gender biases in neural machine translation with word embeddings techniques. arXiv preprint, arXiv:1901.03116.

Ghebreyesus, T. A. (2017). *Health is a fundamental human right.* World Health Organization. Retrieved 12 February from https://www.who.int/news-room/commentaries/detail/health-is-a-fundamental-human-right

Gianfrancesco, M. A., Tamang, S., Yazdany, J., & Schmajuk, G. (2018). Potential biases in machine learning algorithms using electronic health record data. *JAMA Internal Medicine, 178*(11), 1544–1547.

Gurupur, V., & Wan, T. T. H. (2020). Inherent bias in artificial intelligence-based decision support systems for healthcare. *Medicina (Kaunas, Lithuania)*, *56*(3). doi:10.3390/medicina56030141

Halwani, S. (2004). *Racial inequality in access to health care services*. Ontario Human Rights Commission. Retrieved February 12, 2022 from https://www.ohrc.on.ca/en/race-policy-dialogue-papers/racial-inequality-access-health-care-services

Hamilton, W., Round, A., & Sharp, D. (2002). Patient, hospital, and general practitioner characteristics associated with non-attendance: A cohort study. *British Journal of General Practice*, *52*(477), 317–319.

Hardesty, L. (2018, February 11). *Study finds gender and skin-type bias in commercial artificial-intelligence systems*. Retrieved February 12, 2022 from https://news.mit.edu/2018/study-finds-gender-skin-type-bias-artificial-intelligence-systems-0212

Iannessi, A., Beaumont, H., & Bertrand, A. S. (2021). Letter to the editor: "Not all biases are bad: Equitable and inequitable biases in machine learning and radiology." *Insights into Imaging*, *12*(1), 78. 10.1186/s13244-021-01022-5

Institute of Medicine Committee on Understanding Eliminating Racial Ethnic Disparities in Health Care. (2003). In Smedley, B. D., Stith, A. Y., & Nelson, A. R. (Eds.), *Unequal treatment: Confronting racial and ethnic disparities in health care*. National Academies Press. doi:10.17226/12875

Kliegr, T., Bahník, Š., & Fürnkranz, J. (2021). A review of possible effects of cognitive biases on interpretation of rule-based machine learning models. *Artificial Intelligence*, *295*, 103458. doi:10.1016/j.artint.2021.103458

Kumawat, D. (2020, April 27). *How artificial intelligence (AI) can be used in Politics & Government?* Analytics Steps. Retrieved February 12, 2022 from https://www.analyticssteps.com/blogs/how-artificial-intelligence-ai-can-be-used-politics-government

Lee, M. S., Guo, L. N., & Nambudiri, V. E. (2021). Towards gender equity in artificial intelligence and machine learning applications in dermatology. *Journal of the American Medical Informatics Association*, *29*(2), 400–403. 10.1093/jamia/ocab113

Leslie, D., Mazumder, A., Peppin, A., Wolters, M. K., & Hagerty, A. (2021). Does "AI" stand for augmenting inequality in the era of covid-19 healthcare? *BMJ*, *372*, n304. doi:10.1136/bmj.n304

Lwowski, B., & Rios, A. (2021). The risk of racial bias while tracking influenza-related content on social media using machine learning. *Journal of the American Medical Informatics Association*, *28*(4), 839–849.

Manyika, J. (2019, June 6). *Tackling bias in artificial intelligence (and in humans)*. McKinsey and Company. Retrieved February 12, 2022 from https://www.mckinsey.com/featured-insights/artificial-intelligence/tackling-bias-in-artificial-intelligence-and-in-humans#

Manyika, J., Silberg, J., & Presten, B. (2019, October 25). *What do we do about the biases in AI?* Harvard Business Review. Retrieved February 12, 2022 from https://hbr.org/2019/10/what-do-we-do-about-the-biases-in-ai

McElaney, M. (2018, April 17). *Cognitive bias in machine learning*. Retrieved February 12, 2022 from https://medium.com/codait/cognitive-bias-in-machine-learning-d287838eeb4b

Nelson, G. S. (2019). Bias in artificial intelligence. *North Carolina Medical Journal*, *80*(4), 220–222.

Noseworthy, P. A., Attia, Z. I., Brewer, L. C., Hayes, S. N., Yao, X., Kapa, S., … Lopez-Jimenez, F. (2020). Assessing and mitigating bias in medical artificial intelligence: The effects of race and ethnicity on a deep learning model for ECG analysis. *Circulation: Arrhythmia & Electrophysiology*, *13*(3), e007988.

Nouri, S. (2021, February 4). *The role of bias in artificial intelligence*. Forbes. Retrieved February 12, 2022 from https://www.forbes.com/sites/forbestechcouncil/2021/02/04/the-role-of-bias-in-artificial-intelligence/?sh=7c342b0d579d

Omowole, A. (2021, July 19). *Research shows AI is often biased. Here's how to make algorithms work for all of us.* Retrieved February 12, 2022 from https://www.weforum.org/agenda/2021/07/ai-machine-learning-bias-discrimination/

Panch, T., Mattie, H., & Atun, R. (2019). Artificial intelligence and algorithmic bias: Implications for health systems. *Journal of Global Health, 9*(2), 1–5. doi:10.7189/jogh.09.020318

Parikh, R. B., Teeple, S., & Navathe, A. S. (2019). Addressing bias in artificial intelligence in health care. *JAMA: Journal of the American Medical Association, 322*(24), 2377–2378.

Ploug, T., & Holm, S. (2020). The right to refuse diagnostics and treatment planning by artificial intelligence. *Medicine, Health Care and Philosophy, 23*(1), 107–114. doi:10.1007/s11019-019-09912-8

Ross, K. A. E., Law, M. P., & Bell, A. (2016). Exploring healthcare experiences of transgender individuals. *Transgender Health, 1*(1), 238–249. doi:10.1089/trgh.2016.0021

Rothchild, J. (2014). Gender bias. In *The Blackwell Encyclopedia of Sociology.* doi:10.1002/9781405165518.wbeosg011.pub2

Samorani, M., Harris, S. L., Blount, L. G., Lu, H., & Santoro, M. A. (2021). Overbooked and Overlooked: Machine Learning and Racial Bias in Medical Appointment Scheduling. *Manufacturing & Service Operations Management.* https://doi.org/10.1287/msom.2021.0999

Schlosser, E. A. C. (2017). *Race, socioeconomic status, and implicit bias: Implications for closing the achievement gap* (Publication Number 10690797) [Ph.D., The University of Southern Mississippi]. ProQuest Dissertations & Theses Global; Publicly Available Content Database. Ann Arbor.

Siwicki, B. (2021, November 30). *How AI bias happens – and how to eliminate.* Healthcare IT News. Retrieved February 17, 2022 from https://www.healthcareitnews.com/news/how-ai-bias-happens-and-how-eliminate-it

Śmietanka, M., Koshiyama, A. S., & Treleaven, P. C. (2020). Algorithms in future insurance markets.*International Journal of Data Science and Big Data Analytics, 1*(1), 1–19.

Snow, J. (2018, July 26). *Amazon's face recognition falsely matched 28 members of congress with mugshots.* The American Civil Liberty's Union. Retrieved February 12, 2022 from https://www.aclu.org/blog/privacy-technology/surveillance-technologies/amazons-face-recognition-falsely-matched-28

Straw, I., & Callison-Burch, C. (2020). Artificial Intelligence in mental health and the biases of language based models. *PLoS One, 15*(12), e0240376. 10.1371/journal.pone.0240376

Telus International. (2021, February 4). *Seven types of data bias in machine learning.* Telus International. Retrieved February 12, 2022 from https://www.telusinternational.com/articles/7-types-of-data-bias-in-machine-learning

Thompson, A. (2017, October 25). *Google's sentiment analyzer thinks being Gay is bad.* Vice. Retrieved February 12, 2022 from https://www.vice.com/en/article/j5jmj8/google-artificial-intelligence-bias

Tversky, A., & Kahneman, D. (1973). Availability: A heuristic for judging frequency and probability. *Cognitive Psychology, 5*(2), 207–232. doi:10.1016/0010-0285(73)90033-9

Tversky, A., & Kahneman, D. (1983). Extensional versus intuitive reasoning: The conjunction fallacy in probability judgment. *Psychological Review, 90*(4), 293–315. doi:10.1037/0033-295X.90.4.293

Valenzuela, J., Crosby, L. E., & Harrison, R. R. (2020). Commentary: Reflections on the COVID-19 pandemic and health disparities in pediatric psychology. *Journal of Pediatric Psychology, 45*(8), 839–841. doi:10.1093/jpepsy/jsaa063

Walker, R. V., Powers, S. M., & Witten, T. M. (2017). Impact of anticipated bias from healthcare professionals on perceived successful aging among Transgender and gender nonconforming older adults. *LGBT Health, 4*(6), 427–433. doi:10.1089/lgbt.2016.0165

White Hughto, J. M., Clark, K. A., Altice, F. L., Reisner, S. L., Kershaw, T. S., & Pachankis, J. E. (2018). Creating, reinforcing, and resisting the gender binary: A qualitative study of transgender women's healthcare experiences in sex-segregated jails and prisons. *International Journal of Prisoner Health*, *14*(2), 69–88. doi:10.1108/IJPH-02-2017-0011

Wilke, A., & Mata, R. (2012). Cognitive Bias. In Ramachandran, V. S. (Ed.), *Encyclopedia of Human Behavior (Second Edition)* (pp. 531–535). Academic Press. doi:10.1016/B978-0-12-3 75000-6.00094-X

APPENDIX

Agniel, D., Kohane, I.S., & Weber, G.M. (2018). Biases in electronic health record data due to processes within the healthcare system: Retrospective observational study. *BMJ*, 361, k1479.

Alelyani, S. (2021). Detection and evaluation of machine learning bias. *Applied Sciences-Basel*, 11(14).

Balayn, A., Lofi, C., & Houben, G.J. (2021). Managing bias and unfairness in data for decision support: A survey of machine learning and data engineering approaches to identify and mitigate bias and unfairness within data management and analytics systems. *VLDB Journal*, 30(5), 739–768.

Blum, A., Hazlett, C., & Posner, D.N. (2021). Measuring ethnic bias: Can misattribution-based tools from social psychology reveal group biases that economics games cannot? *Political Analysis*, 29(3), 385–404.

Byrne, M.D. (2021). Reducing Bias in Healthcare Artificial Intelligence. *Journal of PeriAnesthesia Nursing*, 36(3), 313–316.

Caliskan, A. (2021). Detecting and mitigating bias in natural language processing. The Brookings Institution.

Chandler, D., & Munday, R. (2011). *Institutional bias*. Oxford University Press.

Curran, K. (2021). Health equity – Artificial intelligence in health care needs scrutiny to eliminate bias. *Health Progress*, 102(4), 68–70.

Dantas, L.F., Fleck, J.L., Cyrino Oliveira, F.L., & Hamacher, S. (2018). No-shows in appointment scheduling – A systematic literature review. *Health Policy*, 122(4), 412–421.

FitzGerald, C., & Hurst, S. (2017). Implicit bias in healthcare professionals: A systematic review. *BMC Medical Ethics*, 18(1), 19–19.

Fletcher, R.R., Nakeshimana, A., & Olubeko, O. (2020). Addressing fairness, bias, and appropriate use of artificial intelligence and machine learning in global health. *Frontiers in Artificial Intelligence*, 3, 561802.

Font, J.E., & Costa-Jussa, M.R. (2019). Equalizing gender biases in neural machine translation with word embeddings techniques. arXiv preprint arXiv:1901.03116.

Gianfrancesco, M.A., Tamang, S., Yazdany, J., & Schmajuk, G. (2018). Potential biases in machine learning algorithms using electronic health record data. *JAMA Internal Medicine*, 178(11), 1544–1547.

Gurupur, V., & Wan, T.T.H. (2020). Inherent bias in artificial intelligence-based decision support systems for healthcare. *Medicina (Kaunas, Lithuania)*, 56(3).

Hamilton, W., Round, A., & Sharp, D. (2002). Patient, hospital, and general practitioner characteristics associated with non-attendance: A cohort study. *Br J Gen Pract*, 52(477), 317–319.

Iannessi, A., Beaumont, H., & Bertrand, A.S. (2021). Letter to the editor: "Not all biases are bad: equitable and inequitable biases in machine learning and radiology". *Insights into Imaging*, 12(1).

Institute of Medicine Committee on Understanding Eliminating Racial Ethnic Disparities in Health Care. (2003) B.D. Smedley, A.Y. Stith & A.R. Nelson (Eds.), Unequal Treatment: Confronting Racial and Ethnic Disparities in Health Care. Washington (DC): National Academies Press.

Lee, M.S., Guo, L.N., & Nambudiri, V.E. (2021). Towards gender equity in artificial intelligence and machine learning applications in dermatology. *J Am Med Inform Assoc*.

Lwowski, B., & Rios, A. (2021). The risk of racial bias while tracking influenza-related content on social media using machine learning. *Journal of the American Medical Informatics Association*, 28(4), 839–849.

Nelson, G.S. (2019). Bias in artificial intelligence. *North Carolina Medical Journal*, 80(4), 220–222.

Noseworthy, P.A., Attia, Z.I., Brewer, L.C., Hayes, S.N., Yao, X., Kapa, S., Friedman, P.A., & Lopez-Jimenez, F. (2020). Assessing and mitigating bias in medical artificial intelligence: The effects of race and ethnicity on a deep learning model for ECG analysis. *Circulation: Arrhythmia & Electrophysiology*, 13(3), e007988–e007988.

Panch, T., Mattie, H., & Atun, R. (2019). Artificial intelligence and algorithmic bias: Implications for health systems. *Journal of Global Health*, 9(2), 1–5.

Parikh, R.B., Teeple, S., & Navathe, A.S. (2019). Addressing bias in artificial intelligence in health care. JAMA: *Journal of the American Medical Association*, 322(24), 2377–2378.

Rothchild, J. (2014). *Gender Bias*. In The Blackwell Encyclopedia of Sociology.

Samorani, M., Harris, S.L., Blount, L.G., Lu, H.B., & Santoro, M.A. Overbooked and overlooked: Machine learning and racial bias in medical appointment scheduling. M&SOM-MANUFACTURING & SERVICE OPERATIONS MANAGEMENT, 1–18.

Schlosser, E.A.C. (2017). Race, socioeconomic status, and implicit bias: Implications for closing the achievement gap. Unpublished Ph.D., The University of Southern Mississippi, Ann Arbor.

Straw, I., & Callison-Burch, C. (2020). Artificial Intelligence in mental health and the biases of language based models. *PLoS One*, 15(12).

Wilke, A., & Mata, R. (2012). Cognitive Bias. In V.S. Ramachandran (Ed.), *Encyclopedia of Human Behavior* (Second Edition) (pp. 531–535). San Diego: Academic Press.

CHAPTER 13

Artificial Intelligence and Ethics: An Approach to Building Ethical by Design Intelligent Applications

Fabrice Muhlenbach

Laboratoire Hubert Curien, UMR 5516, Université de Lyon, Saint-Etienne University, Saint-Etienne, France

CONTENTS

DOI: 10.1201/9781003261247-16

INTRODUCTION

Even if most people are not very familiar with the concept of artificial intelligence, everyone has heard of it, whether good or bad, and thus has an opinion on the subject. Enthusiastic people see artificial intelligence as a fabulous history made up of a whole series of inventions testifying to human genius (Pickover, 2019) while others see computer algorithms to be harmful and to be real "weapons of math destruction" that sacrifice fairness and justice in the name of efficiency (O'Neil, 2016). Such contrasting opinions reflect very different views on this subject, giving rise to conflicts of values, that is to say ethical issues.

Artificial intelligence is one of the major components of the digital revolution (Elliott, 2019). This technological development, by transposing all things in the form of numbers, is changing the balance of power in our society because it is now more important to own information, and know how to process information than to hold the physical goods that surround us. With the hyper-connectivity brought about by the digital revolution, the way we see and interact with the world is radically transformed. As a result, artificial intelligence thus generates economic changes, but this technology also has unprecedented impacts in our everyday life by affecting the psychological and social spheres, redefining our relationship with others, to the world of work, law, culture, health, knowledge, and decision-making. In addition, due to the criteria that these AI programs seek to optimize and the statistical properties linked to the way machine learning works, we are witnessing the existence of bias in the results produced by AI programs, with adverse consequences, whether for human beings individually or for society as a whole.

The aim of this chapter is to introduce what AI ethics is and how it works to uncover the variety of ethical issues arising from the design, development, and deployment of AI. We present some situations in which some human values are threatened by the arrival of artificial intelligence. Rather than condemning AI and its uses in a futile quest to fight the march of progress, we offer a methodology for building ethical AI applications by design.

ARTIFICIAL INTELLIGENCE AND HUMAN VALUES

Ethics and Values

Ethics can be defined as "the philosophical study of morality", or "the general study of goodness and the general study of right action", and "its principal substantive questions are what ends we ought, as fully rational human beings, to choose and pursue and what moral principles should govern our choices and pursuits" (Audi, 2015). Ethics only really take on meaning when faced with concrete problems. In ethics, there is a freedom of choice and a share of individual responsibility, which find their translation in what Jonas (1984) calls "the Imperative of Responsibility" when they are mobilized in the power that human beings exercise in the world through science and technology.

Ethics are about the choices of values. A "value" is the worth of something, i.e., the quality of that which is desired or esteemed because being given and judged as objectively desirable or estimable. A value constitutes the abstraction of the reality that is desire; therefore, a value is both the object of a desire and an evaluation of that desire. Culture, education, and personal experiences modify the importance we give to a given desire, which is why history is crossed by multiple theories on values that sometimes oppose each other. Thus, since ancient Greece, philosophers have sought to establish a scale of values. For example, Plato thought of the transcendentals and considered the ideals of values that are the "true", the "beautiful", and the "good" (associated respectively with science, arts, and religion). Research on the notion of "value" has never ceased to be active, with authors such as Scheler (1973) who made classifications and interconnections between certain values and their opposite values, or Schwartz (1992) who sought to find universal values as sources of motivation associated with latent needs from intercultural studies in his "Theory of Basic Human Values". In conclusion, it is really interesting to tackle the subject of values through an interdisciplinary approach and to compare perspectives from different disciplines (e.g., economics, neuroscience, philosophy, psychology, and sociology) on values (Brosch & Sander, 2016).

Since values are associated with a desire, it is indeed particularly delicate to be interested in one specific value and not in another one, the importance given to different values being specific to different cultures and personal experiences. Within these values, one could hypothesize that there are fundamentals, with certain values, which are intrinsically superior to others, for any individual and any culture, and that *life* is better than *death*, *peace* is better than *war*, *freedom* is better than *servitude*, that *knowledge* is better than *ignorance*, etc., but in fact, it is not the case. For a society ruled by religious fanaticism, human life is worth less than belief in a divinity, and dying as a martyr to defend one's faith is thus a valued action (the value of "sacred" is considered greater than the value of "life"). The major choices in life most often come down to values to prioritize: "liberty" vs. "safety" (in the manner of the quote attributed to Benjamin Franklin: "Those who would give up essential liberty, to purchase a little temporary safety, deserve neither liberty nor safety"), "freedom" (of the press) and "humor" vs. "sacredness" (e.g., the *Jyllands-Posten* Muhammad cartoons controversy), or "interestingness" vs. "confidence" and "authenticity" (e.g., the dissemination of fake news).

As an example of a set of values that are important to humans, let us mention the list proposed by Deonna and Tieffenbach (2018) and shown in Table 13.1.

Conflicts of values give rise to ethical problems, so when a state does everything possible to get out of the COVID-19 pandemic and is focusing its efforts on the "health"

TABLE 13.1   List of 35 Human Values Proposed by Deonna and Tieffenbach (2018)

Art	Authenticity	Beauty	Childhood	Competency
Confidence	Creativity	Dignity	Equality	Eroticism
Freedom	Friendship	Health	Honor	Humbleness
Humor	Impartiality	Interestingness	Justice	Knowledge
Life	Love	Luxury	Pleasure	Power
Property	Privacy	Righteousness	Sacredness	Solidarity
Sublimate	Tastiness	Tradition	Usefulness	Wellbeing

value by limiting certain rights of those who refuse to be vaccinated, at the level of these people, this is seen by them as an attack on their "freedom" value. However, if we look at a more global level, this individual freedom of not wanting to be vaccinated has dramatic consequences for society as a whole. In doing so, the unvaccinated are more contaminating and have a greater risk of being hospitalized for serious forms of COVID-19, and therefore generate an attack on the health of others, in particular for the most vulnerable people who need treatment for another pathology (cancer, genetic disease, etc.). Therefore, the resolution of ethical problems for a given subject must be done through a cost-benefit approach for all the values concerned with this subject for all stakeholders.

In the following, we will favor to the humanist values inherited from the Enlightenment movement in the mid-17th century (Fleischacker, 2013). These are indeed values that highlight freedom of thought, respect for reason and science, and they have a universal vocation. It is under the inspiration of the Enlightenment movement that the General Assembly of the United Nations adopted in 1948 the idea that the common ideal to be attained by all peoples and all nations was represented in the Universal Declaration of Human Rights.

The goal of humanism is to maximize human development, that is, life, health, happiness, freedom, knowledge, love, and the richness of experience. However, these values are threatened today from all sides by approaches that promote subjective emotion in the face of reason, religious convictions in the face of science, immediate and short-term profit for a handful of individuals in the face of preservation of the planet for future generations (Pinker, 2018).

Artificial Intelligence and Ethical Issues

Artificial intelligence (AI) refers to a whole set of computer technologies that make it possible to perform tasks that require cognitive skills for human beings such as perception, language, reasoning, or decision-making. Thanks to advances in machine learning, data mining, and natural language processing over the past decades, the machines are able to perform some of these tasks very efficiently. AI programs have thus found their way across our digital world everywhere, in our computers or our mobile applications, through search engines, social networks, or access to cultural content, but also in professional applications like decision support systems in financial, legal, or medical domains.

One of the great strengths of artificial intelligence is its efficiency. By being able to automate decisions by mimicking behaviors extracted from millions of possible cases during the learning phase, an AI program can perform some tasks that can normally only be performed by experts after many years of training and professional practice.

Should we be wary or be afraid of artificial intelligence? Since it is in essence artificial, and therefore not human, does it not contradict the humanist spirit? There are indeed multiple reasons for some fears to see artificial intelligence technologies occupy the field of a whole range of activities that were thought to be reserved only for human beings. AI is a technology that has already – and that will have even more in the future – an indisputable impact on the world of work. This obviously disrupts work habits, and human beings are led to question their role in the modern economy and the professional activity they can carry out that cannot be carried out by a robot or an intelligent program. Other fears are to be had about situations much less visible but nevertheless very present, such as respect for privacy, our capacity for judgment, our critical thinking, and our openness to others or to new ideas.

Works of fiction have accustomed us to an uprising of machines and replacement by artificial creatures with the arrival of a "superintelligence" (Bostrom, 2014) that could surpass the human being in every way. The real ethical problems generated by artificial intelligence, if they do not directly affect human life, will affect other values. Among the values threatened by the arrival of AI, we can mention the following:

- Fairness (justice and equality): AI programs perform tasks from machine learning on large sets of examples. However, this learning process is carried out on statistical bases, and thus experiences a certain number of algorithmic biases, which tends to disadvantage the representatives of minority groups in the whole dataset (e.g., people with disabilities are often excluded from the training data, being considered as atypical examples, also known as "outliers"). Because men and women show prejudices in their ways of considering their peers, and this even in an unconscious way, by including in their judgments discriminatory variables such as gender, ethnicity, religion, social origin, or skin color, there will be some bias issues in the examples a program uses to build its model. Based on examples of decisions made by human beings in the context of solving a given task, artificial intelligence algorithms will reproduce this learning bias and will even tend to amplify it, creating unfair situations.

- Trust (confidence): Automatic recommender systems in social networks will promote the dissemination of information that is surprising or touches on extreme political edges because the program learns that these are the categories of information that are most likely to elicit reactions. In doing so, it is most often information whose sources are dubious, without any guarantee of veracity, and therefore these systems participate in the dissemination of misinformation and fake news.

- Privacy preserving: In an appearance-based society that pushes people to flaunt their happiness (even fictitious) on social media (especially for young people who want to look like their idols and know fame), we are pushed to reveal ourselves on the Internet, and these digital traces can be exploited without our knowledge. The accuracy of the results given by intelligent systems depends largely on the amount of information processed, and the more data to be processed, the better the quality of machine learning. Thus, in order to provide personalized services by improving the relevance of the answers they offer in these services, some companies use all the sources of information at their disposal (e.g., subjects discussed by e-mails, interests deducted from requests made in their search engine, travel habits through geolocation obtained by the position of the mobile phone, etc.). This poses a threat to the protection of personal data as these companies are commercial enterprises that can exploit this data for profit (e.g., by selling information on the health situation of users to insurance companies).

- Competency and algorithmic governance: To perform a given task, if the work required of a human being can be performed by an artificial intelligence program, it is the latter that will be offered to perform this task for reasons of cost or speed. Human beings are then dispossessed of their ability to act on the world for the benefit of machines and to exercise a professional activity allowing them to earn a living. In many situations where AI programs have already entered the labor market, it is indicated that the human being is not replaced but must now be complementary to the machine. However, this complementarity is a delusion. If the human beings are most often passive in an activity, leaving the bulk of the work to be done to an intelligent program, they will end up getting bored. By doing a job in its entirety, the human workers will be able to have a variety of tasks to perform, with the satisfaction of seeing the result of their work, and they will thus be more efficient than being only a link in a whole chain of processing whose finality can no longer be perceived. Another form of ethical problem is when we surrender our authority and responsibility to intelligent computer systems, and we no longer have or can exercise our faculty of judgment and action anymore. Substantive questions arise when intelligent systems not only propose a result but actually apply a decision (e.g., autonomous vehicles that can cause accidents, or combat drones which can automatically destroy targets and kill people).

ETHICS-BY-DESIGN AI APPLICATIONS: A METHODOLOGY

Knowing that ethical issues can be associated with the introduction of artificial intelligence applications in society, an approach is needed to seek to humanize machines.

How is it possible to solve ethical problems encountered during the implementation of artificial intelligence applications? It seems essential to us to take into account two parameters: the human values threatened by artificial intelligence and its usability on the one hand, and the various stakeholders concerned by this problem on the other hand. When resources are limited, it is true that it is necessary to make choices and disadvantage one value for the benefit of another, and therefore a group of individuals for the benefit of another group. However, in the general case, we must trust in humankind: human beings are much more kind, generous, and altruistic than we tend to believe (Bregman, 2020). It follows that the search for compromise is possible, and even that certain solutions deviate from a binary vision with a choice between two competing situations by the introduction of a new element, possibly provided thanks to an innovative AI solution.

The great strength of applications using artificial intelligence technologies is their tremendous usability. AI-based services are more efficient to use because they provide easy access to users' favorite features: not only are the apps intuitive, so users can easily learn how to use them, but the apps also learn what their users' habits are and can change their settings accordingly, and this customization generally brings a great sense of satisfaction to users. Usability, however, is not the essential value to be maximized. In a market economy, it is easy to understand that a company wishes to use artificial intelligence programs for commercial purposes in the services it offers to its users. If this company does so at the expense of the confidence that users may have in the use of these services, the latter will turn to competing solutions. Despite this, due to the dominant position of some digital companies, although the latter have committed wrongdoings in collecting the personal data of their users without their consent to be used for political advertising purposes (e.g., Facebook–Cambridge Analytica data scandal), they still have a very large community of users.

To avoid this pitfall, it is important to carry out, prior to the development of applications using AI, a real reflection on the ethical issues of these technologies. In our view, this reflection must follow a 3-point methodology:

1. The first consideration to have is to consider that AI-based applications must bring something beneficial to the human beings who will be their users, taking into account the entire social and economic context in which they live, the whole in a legal space framing what it is possible to do or not. A new product must not be developed to be used for the benefit of a few and at the expense of certain populations. A new product must not bring an immediate benefit which is only apparent and which masks problems likely to threaten the values to which human beings are attached.

2. The second point is to establish a clear relationship, for example in the presentation in the form of a table, between the different actors concerned by this AI-based application and the different values on which they can have an effect, that this effect is either positive or negative.

3. The third and final step concerns the actual development of the AI-based application using this table of ethical values as a roadmap. Different strategies exist to resolve conflicts of values, such as establishing certain priorities between values or finding trade-offs between situations involving such or such values.

Legal Framework and Innovations in an Economic and Social World

Artificial intelligence is used in many goods and services and it is not possible to do without it in the applications of daily life, as well as in the major challenges of our society, such as in the field of health (e.g., COVID-19 recovery) or climate change (e.g., European Green Deal Climate action). Proposals have thus been made to promote ethical and responsible use of AI, both by learned societies, non-governmental institutions, and state structures such as the *Asilomar AI principles*,[1] the *Montréal Declaration for a Responsible Development of Artificial Intelligence*,[2] or the *Ethics Guidelines for Trustworthy AI*.[3] In the third case proposed by the EU (European Commission, 2019), the promotion of Trustworthy AI is done by taking into account three components, which should be met throughout the system's entire life cycle:

(1) it should be lawful, complying with all applicable laws and regulations (2) it should be ethical, ensuring adherence to ethical principles and values and (3) it should be robust, both from a technical and social perspective since, even with good intentions, AI systems can cause unintentional harm.

For a company, the most constraining part is the lawful AI component. Thus within the EU, the collection of personal data, which artificial intelligence applications sometimes use to improve the personalization performance of their machine learning algorithms, is now very regulated with the implementation in 2018 of the *General Data Protection Regulation* (GDPR). However, some laws conflict with other countries laws, and laws are not enough to guarantee trustworthy AI because they are not always at the forefront of technological developments. It is for this reason that ethical and robust components are necessary: AI applications must align with ethical norms and be studied from both a technological and a social perspective to ensure that they will not cause any unintended damage.

At the level of the technical robustness of these applications, in order to guarantee better control of these models, to identify the qualities and their limits, and to find solutions to correct their possible defects (such as algorithmic biases), it will be necessary to favor the methods allowing designers to understand the models developed. For example, we may prefer to use rule-based learning methods (i.e., methods whose knowledge is expressed by logical rules understandable by human beings) rather than black box deep learning models (i.e., methods where knowledge is embedded in vast sets of tables of connection weights within a huge network), or to avoid the risk of having discriminatory effects, it is possible to carry out learning from data whose minority classes have been rebalanced.

Management of Value Conflicts for the Stakeholders: The Ethical Matrix

After this phase of reflection taking into account the legal, social, and economic context in which these AI applications will be integrated, the key point of the methodology for the realization of ethical AI applications is the identification of the set of ethical values affected by the arrival of this new technology or new product, as well as seeing their effects on all stakeholders. As Russell (2016) mentions, from the earliest days of cybernetics, Norbert Wiener – the cybernetics originator – expressed his concerns about what we introduce into a machine:

> If we use, to achieve our purposes, a mechanical agency with whose operation we cannot efficiently interfere (...), we had better be quite sure that the purpose put into the machine is the purpose which *we* really desire.

However, we must ask ourselves who this "we" is and try not to harm any of the stakeholders.

At the methodological level, this is possible by means of a decision-making tool called the "ethical matrix". It was initially proposed to facilitate judgments on bioethic questions (Mepham, 2000) in order to identify the values that are threatened (e.g., the use of genetically modified fishes, policy interventions in the obesity crisis, or animal sentience concerns). By focusing more specifically on a small number of ethical principles (e.g., respect for wellbeing, for autonomy, and for justice) on a given subject (e.g., the impact of new technologies in food and agriculture), it is possible to elicit the problems and concerns of different stakeholders or interest groups.

The selected ethical principles constitute values that form the columns of the matrix. The rows of the matrix consist of each stakeholder caught up with the issue in question. Each cell of the matrix specifies the main criterion to be satisfied for a stakeholder for a given principle.

Therefore, the structure of the ethical matrix consists of stakeholders on the y-axis, principles on the x-axis, and questions and answers in their intersections. The ethical matrix can then be seen as a checklist of concerns, structured around established ethical theory, but it can also be used as a means of provoking structured discussion between the different interest groups.

The arrival of artificial intelligence highlights a specific value: usability. Reenacting a new combat between man and machine, AI is considered as a new avatar of these world-changing inventions such as the loom, the steam engine, or other productivity-improving technologies, generating as many fears as hopes like any revolution. However, usability, introduced in a disruptive manner in fields, which until now felt protected, such as medicine or justice, seems to be predatory for other values.

There is thus a diversity of scale of values in the world population, on which it is difficult to give an opinion or a judgment, but which it is necessary to take into account. Depending on cultures and countries, some values are put forward more than others, for example, "liberty, equality and fraternity" is the official motto of the French Republic, while other countries insist on a value such as faith (e.g., the United States of America: "in God we trust"). Furthermore, the values are not the same at the personal level (with a set of instrumental or terminal values in the *Rokeach Value Survey* (Rokeach, 1973), a values classification instrument used by psychologists), at the level of a small group of individuals or even the level of a state. Even if it is not always possible to formulate a hierarchy of values explicitly, the relative importance of values appears when faced with situations in the real world or in role plays, e.g. in the "Moral Machine experiment", an online experimental platform designed to explore the moral dilemmas faced by autonomous vehicles (Awad et al., 2018). In practice, it is therefore recommended to look in Table 13.1 for the values likely to be affected by the problem studied.

The values of individuals can differ greatly from one individual to another or from one social group to another. It is then recommended to take into account all possible stakeholders, even those who cannot express themselves (e.g., animals, nature). In the field of artificial intelligence, the stakeholders refer especially to researchers, developers, manufacturers, providers, policymakers, and users (Dignum, 2019).

Value Sensitive Design Approach

According to Friedman et al. (2013), human values often implicated in system design are human welfare, ownership and property, privacy, freedom from bias, universal usability, trust, autonomy, informed consent, accountability, courtesy, identity, calmness, and the environmental sustainability. Proposed by Friedman and her colleagues in the 1990s for the introduction of people's moral psychology in computer system design (Friedman & Hendry, 2019), the "Value Sensitive Design" (VSD) is an approach defined as "theoretically grounded to the design of technology that accounts for human values in a principled and comprehensive manner". More than a theoretical point of view on how human values can be implicated in technological design, the VSD approach presents case studies, methods and provides heuristics for skillful value-sensitive design practice.

Among the advice given by the authors, they recommend starting with a value, a technology, or a context of use. Then they propose to identify the direct and indirect stakeholders, as well as the benefits and harms for each stakeholder group. The benefits and harms are then mapped onto the corresponding values, allowing the identification of potential value conflicts. Among these methods, some focus on the stakeholders (i.e., for stakeholder identification, legitimation, and interaction purposes), others on the values (i.e., for value sources identification, elicitation, and analysis purposes), and the latter on the design (i.e., for longer-term design thinking and multi-generational design thinking purposes).

EXAMPLE OF ETHICS-BY-DESIGN AI APPLICATION: A FAIR RECOMMENDER SYSTEM

By putting all types of content in digital form (texts, images, music, videos, etc.) the digital revolution has allowed us to access an unprecedented amount of information. With devices constantly connected to the Internet, this access to knowledge and culture from around the world can be done from anywhere, at any time, for anyone who has such devices. However, like a constant access to unlimited food in a free buffet can lead to physical and health problems, this access to information is not without risk and information literacy is very important in the 21st century (Whitworth, 2009).

One computer tool that plays an essential role in the problem of access to information is called a recommender system. A recommender system is designed to suggest items that are expected to catch a user's interest; it is targeted at predicting recommended products in order to provide personalized results in specific domains and fields. In order to filter the items and produce the recommendation, data mining techniques and many AI methods are used, e.g., machine learning algorithms to filter items based on content or using the preference information of many users in a collaborative way, or deep learning strategies and word embedding techniques (Kane, 2021).

Research in the recommender system area has been boosted by an open competition, the Netflix Prize, in the second half of the 2000s, which gives pride to collaborative filtering approaches to meet business needs of the American subscription streaming service company. The Netflix training dataset was designed as follows: a collection of rows on which, for a given date, a user of the service has given a certain movie, after having viewed it, a certain evaluation. The goal of the challenge was to predict user ratings for movies, based on previous ratings without any other information about the users or movies.

This challenge had a strong impact on the directions of research in the field since efforts were concentrated on the precision of research results because that was the objective sought by the Netflix commercial platform. In doing so, other parameters have been neglected, such as the presence of diversity within the items proposed by the recommender systems.

Examples of low diversity would be a recommender system that just recommends the next books in a series that you have started reading, new songs from a singer or a music band that you are already used to listening to, newspaper articles from the category of subjects you are used to reading, notifications on the activity of your social networks concerning people with whom you are most used to interacting with, or research articles from a digital science library on the same topic and in the same discipline as those that apply to you. Accuracy-based evaluation metrics (e.g., precision, recall, F-score, precision at k) used to assess recommender system performance are interesting from an information retrieval perspective but are not always appropriate from a psychological point of view. Based on the collected data extracted from the user's profiles, the personalized recommendation algorithms extract the most prototypical traits of the user and make only recommendations corresponding to a caricature of everyone's interests. People using services equipped with personalized recommendation systems find themselves trapped in a "filter bubble" (Pariser, 2011) and see their access to the diversity of the world hindered by an invisible barrier of which they are often not even aware. In addition to applying to topics of interest, the filter bubble can be encountered in recommendations that are biased by spatial and temporal factors. The algorithms are based on the date to recommend the most recent items as well as on geographical indices (e.g., the GPS coordinates of a mobile phone) to highlight only local events at the expense of those who are distant, like the principle of the "hierarchy of dead" used by the press.

Legal Framework and Innovations in an Economic and Social World

From a legal point of view, the fact of not proposing diversity in the recommendations associated with a service is not punishable by law. The issues are more of an ethical and technical nature with societal consequences.

For a cultural content recommender system (music, movies, videos, books, etc.), the recommendations will tend to offer the most requested items by default. The algorithms of recommender systems most often have a role of amplifying the items already proposed, which works well for articles developed by creators who already have a certain audience (authors of bestselling books, famous music bands, or blockbuster movie directors). But for lesser-known content creators, such as rookie authors, indie music musicians, or auteur films, this is dire because their similarity scores to already existing content will be low, and therefore intelligent systems will almost never recommend them. This problem of diversity also affects scientific creation: intuition, creativity, and imagination also have their place (Langley et al., 1987), as does the ability to establish analogies between disciplines, or even to know how to draw the appropriate conclusions from the appearance of an event having occurred in a fortuitous context but having a real value of scientific discovery, and this unexpectedly, in a serendipity way.

Ethical Matrix

To establish the list of values to take into account in this type of problem, we can start with the value that those who offer this service seek to highlight, namely the usability of the application. We have seen that the problem with these recommender systems is the lack of diversity, so that is a value we need to integrate into our matrix. Confidence is another value that must be taken into account in the ethical matrix: this confidence will not be the same depending on whether the system makes explains or not the way in which it makes its choice of items to recommend. For a recommender system to be fair, there must not only be diversity offered to the user but also that the recommended items (and consequently, the creators of the content corresponding to these items) have the same chances of finding their audience. It is therefore necessary to take into account the value of equity, which is particularly important for content creators. Finally, depending on the nature of the content to be recommended, the last value to consider may be culture (for music, book, or movie recommender systems) or knowledge (for research paper recommender system).

The different stakeholders to take into account in this ethical matrix are the users (consumers of cultural or scientific content), the content creators (artists or scientists), and the service providers (streaming platforms or scientific publishers). If necessary, and depending on the case, it is possible to add other stakeholders, such as publishers, music labels, motion picture production companies, or public authorities.

By filling in the ethical matrix (Table 13.2), we realize that the conflict between values (usability vs. diversity or usability vs. equity) can be approached in a different way and that it is possible to reconcile the views of the different stakeholders. It is ultimately in the interest of both the content creator and the service provider to see the recommendations made on the entire available catalog: if some contents are not recommended, their creators will occupy the platform without being profitable for the provider. Finally, by offering diversity in the recommendations, this will arouse the users' curiosity and induce their interest in novelty which will be useful for the users, depending on the relevance that the users find in this novelty.

Development Approach Following the Value Sensitive Design

After identifying the values and stakeholders of the study, the VSD approach proposes different methods to pursue the design of the application. Among these, we can mention co-design, similar to the participatory design carried out in the field of human-computer interaction. The development of the application can then be done by addressing technological issues.

Prototypes can be made to see what the feelings of users are when they use services whose recommendations present diversity in their results. From a technical point of view (Castells et al., 2015), the quest for diversification can be done through different ways, for example by re-ranking the results, clustering techniques for identifying items to recommend belonging to different clusters, learning to rank diversity, or recommend serendipitous items for enabling surprising recommendations.

TABLE 13.2 Ethical Matrix for the Design of a Fair Recommender System

Respect for:	Usability	Diversity	Confidence	Equity	Culture or knowledge
User	Have access to useful content at low cost	Have access to a maximum of diversified content from many creators	Receive content that matches tastes and choices	Have the same chance as other users to access interesting content and make new discoveries	Have access to a maximum of relevant content
Content creator	Be appropriately recommended to users	Be recommended occasionally to those whose content produced is not the primary topic of interest	Have the assurance of being fairly recommended	Have the same chance of being recommended as other content creators, regardless of popularity	Want their content to be accessible to as wide an audience as possible
Service provider	Offer an attractive platform for both users and content creators	Propose a varied offer intended for specialists or niche audiences	Have a platform with a trustworthy recommender system	Provide recommendations for all content creators to find their audience	Have the most attractive content to offer

The implementation of a prototype is therefore necessary to collect feedback from users. There is indeed diversity to bring in the results of the recommendations, for ethical reasons, but there is also a great diversity of users of applications equipped with recommendation systems driven by AI (some users prefer to stay within their comfort zone, while others are more explorative), and all human beings can themselves show a great diversity of attitude (preference for recommendations on familiar or exotic items, depending on use case, time of day, time of life, or mood). This is why this part of diversity in the recommendations can be a parameter proposed by an AI program but which remains under the control of human users, who can vary it as they please.

CONCLUSION

Since the dawn of humanity, human beings have tried to make sense of their surroundings and questioned the world, nature, others, and themselves. Human beings have always sought to imitate Nature in order to have a certain action or a certain control over facts and things. In response to the existential question relating to the nature of the human mind, artificial intelligence has proven to be a very interesting exploratory tool by proposing computer models taking as much from mathematics, and biology as from the psychology of how human thought can work.

In addition to allowing the realization of such models developed for the purpose of fundamental research, artificial intelligence has proven to be a particularly effective tool for carrying out a certain number of cognitive tasks when a need for a response to a certain type of question arises. To questions related to decisions to be made in the presence of a large number of possibilities (i.e., which element corresponds best to me?), AI programs have brought a strong benefit of usability thanks to personalization in recommender systems. To questions about identifying patterns (i.e., what is this shape?), AI has enabled improvements in the area of pattern recognition. To questions relating to difficult reasoning, AI has made it possible to provide an answer through its ability to take into account a large quantity of variables and a big amount of data. Constantly improving and benefiting both from technological advances in computing hardware, from ever more open access to data and from a greater quantity of data available, as well as from theoretical and practical improvements brought by the dynamic field of AI research and engineering, these artificial intelligence systems have enabled transformations in our everyday lives and are used without most of us being aware of it.

However, these AI tools, in the search for usability and efficiency, can have consequences on values that are important for human beings. These threats to fundamental values are not necessarily visible, and the legal framework for a trustworthy AI does not cover all the risks associated with the use of AI technologies, especially since the laws concerning their regulation obviously depend on the priorities of the different countries regarding this topic. If the European Union wants to be the champion of ethical AI, other countries want to promote business AI or AI used for controlling their citizens.

In the great dilemma between the values of freedom and security, we believe that AI could play a mediating role. Artificial intelligence, through pattern recognition, makes it possible to identify individuals, whether ordinary citizens or members of the police. In a democratic country, the right of citizens to demonstrate is essential to express their dissatisfaction or to mark their opposition to certain decisions taken by the government. In the case of the intervention of the police to contain the excesses of a demonstration that would have degenerated with damages to the public space, it is important to prevent acts of violence, whether these come from thugs or police officers. We believe that the process of identifying individuals by means of AI should be carried out by an organization independent of the supervision of police institutions, in the manner of the principle of separation of powers (i.e., division of the power into a legislature, an executive, and a judiciary branches), which is the basis of the functioning of democratic institutions.

Various countries as well as civil society already propose charters and principles for a reasoned and reasonable use of this formidable technology that is artificial intelligence, but, as demonstrated by Mittelstadt (2019), principles alone are not enough to have an ethical AI, and principles must be moved to practices (Morley et al., 2020). This is why the work presented here is intended to complement these principles and seeks to provide assistance in the design of an ethical AI, through a multidisciplinary reflection accompanying the entire engineering phase of implementing an application of AI that may have impacts on human beings and society.

In the end, what remains most important is that artificial intelligence – this product of the human mind – remains a tool at the service of human beings. AI must accompany humanity in the problems encountered today (e.g., global pandemic, climate change) by allowing it to live in harmony, without affecting the values which are dear to the whole of humanity and which distinguish *homo sapiens* from other animal species.

NOTES

1 Asilomar AI Principles: https://futureoflife.org/2017/08/11/ai-principles/
2 Montréal Declaration for a Responsible Development of Artificial Intelligence: https://www.montrealdeclaration-responsibleai.com/
3 Ethics Guidelines for Trustworthy AI: https://op.europa.eu/en/publication-detail/-/publication/d3988569-0434-11ea-8c1f-01aa75ed71a1

REFERENCES

Audi, R. (Ed.) (2015). *The Cambridge dictionary of philosophy* (3rd edition). Cambridge University Press.

Awad, E., Dsouza, S., Kim, R., Schulz, J., Henrich, J., Shariff, A., Bonnefon, J.-F., & Rahwan, I. (2018). The moral machine experiment. *Nature, 563*, 59–64. 10.1038/s41586-018-0637-6

Bostrom, N. (2014). *Superintelligence, paths, dangers, strategies.* Oxford University Press.

Bregman, R. (2020). *Humankind: A hopeful history.* Bloomsbury Publishing.

Brosch, T., & Sander, D. (Eds.) (2016). *Handbook of value. Perspectives from economics, neuroscience, philosophy, psychology, and sociology.* Oxford University Press.

Castells, P., Hurley, N. J., & Vargas, S. (2015). Novelty and diversity in recommender systems In Ricci, F., Rokach, L., & Shapira, B. (Eds.), *Recommender systems handbook*, 2nd edition (pp. 881–918). Springer. 10.1007/978-1-4899-7637-6_26

Deonna, J., & Tieffenbach, E. (Eds.) (2018). *Petit traité des valeurs.* Science & métaphysique, Éditions d'Ithaque.

Dignum, V. (2019). *Responsible artificial intelligence: How to develop and use AI in a responsible way*. Springer.

Elliott, A. (2019). *The culture of AI: Everyday life and the digital revolution*. Routledge.

European Commission, Directorate-General for Communications Networks, Content and Technology (2019). *Ethics guidelines for trustworthy AI*. Publications Office. https://data.europa.eu/doi/10.2759/177365

Fleischacker, S. (2013). *Kant's questions: What is enlightenment?* Routledge.

Friedman, B., Kahn Jr., P. H., & Borning, A. (2013). Value sensitive design and information systems. In Doorn, N., Schuurbiers, D., van de Poel, I., & Gorman, M. E. (Eds.), *Early engagement and new technologies: Opening up the laboratory* (pp. 55–95). Springer. 10.1007/978-94-007-7844-34

Friedman, B., & Hendry, D. G. (2019). *Value sensitive design: Shaping technology with moral imagination*. The MIT Press. 10.7551/mitpress/7585.001.0001

Jonas, H. (1984). *The imperative of responsibility: In search of an ethics for the technological age*. University of Chicago Press.

Kane, F. (2021). *Building recommender systems with machine learning and AI* (2nd edition). Sundog Education.

Langley, P. W., Simon, H. A., Bradshaw, G., & Zytkow, J. M. (1987). *Scientific discovery: Computational explorations of the creative process*. The MIT Press.

Mepham, B. (2000). A framework for the ethical analysis of novel foods: The ethical matrix. *Journal of Agricultural and Environmental Ethics, 12*(2), 165–176. 10.1023/A:1009542714497

Mittelstadt, B. (2019). Principles alone cannot guarantee ethical AI. *Nature Machine Intelligence, 1*, 501–507, 10.1038/s42256-019-0114-4

Morley, J., Floridi, L., Kinsey, K., & Elhalal, A. (2020). From what to how: An initial review of publicly available ai ethics tools, methods and research to translate principles into practices. *Science and Engineering Ethics, 26*, 2141–2168. 10.1007/s11948-019-00165-5

O'Neil, C. (2016). *Weapons of math destruction: How big data increases inequality and threatens democracy*. Crown.

Pariser, E. (2011). *The filter bubble: What the internet is hiding from you*. Penguin Press.

Pickover, C. A. (2019). *Artificial intelligence: An illustrated history: from medieval robots to neural networks*. Sterling.

Pinker, S. (2018). *Enlightenment now: The case for reason, science, humanism, and progress*. Viking Penguin.

Rokeach, M. (1973). *The nature of human values*. The Free Press.

Russell, S. (2016). Should we fear supersmart robots? *Scientific American, 314*, 58–59. 10.1038/scientificamerican0616-58

Scheler, M. (1973). *Formalism in ethics and non-formal ethics of values* (5th edition). Northwestern University Studies in Phenomenology and Existential Philosophy, Northwestern University Press.

Schwartz, S. H. (1992). Universals in the content and structure of values: Theoretical advances and empirical tests in 20 countries. In Zanna, M. P. (Ed.), *Advances in experimental social psychology* (Vol. 25) (pp. 1–65). Academic Press. 10.1016/S0065-2601(08)60281-6

Whitworth, A. (2009). *Information obesity*. Chandos Publishing.

CHAPTER 14

AI-Driven IoT Systems and Corresponding Ethical Issues

Nadine Y. Fares[a] and Manar Jammal[b]

[a]School of Law, University of Edinburgh, Edinburgh, UK
[b]Information Technology Department, York University, Toronto, Ontario, Canada

CONTENTS

DOI: 10.1201/9781003261247-17

INTRODUCTION

Internet of Things (IoT) systems, in which devices are connected via the internet, are driving communities to become more connected through optimizing communication and data collection to create connections between people and within devices for various services (Woetzel et al., 2018). However, due to their inability to easily manage large amounts of data and analyze them, IoT devices require an investment in new technologies to meet their full potential. Given the ability of artificial intelligence (AI) algorithms to enable devices to analyze data and build models that tend to learn patterns, and predict decisions, the integration of AI within IoT systems can change the quality of life through automation features. An AI-enabled IoT system (smart city, telehealth, self-driving vehicles, manufacturing robots ...) would create smart/intelligent machines to help in decision-making processes and services with minimal or no human intervention (Vinugayathri, 2020). For instance, PwC's "smart cooling" in the beverage industry involves products with custom-built pre-packaged sensors. This allows for stock tracking, inventory managements, and analysis of metrics (PwC, 2017). The convergence of AI and IoT can reshape business and personal lifestyles by adding automation in a manner that is not fully conceivable or comprehensible by most companies today. On one end, it can allow for better customer experiences, transfer of monotonous and complex routines at a relatively low cost, and can create new business opportunities, models, and products. On the other hand, it can displace the human workforce, lead to unwanted misuses and abuses, challenge ethics, and disrupt the competitive landscape in favor of early adopters (PwC, 2017).

BACKGROUND INFORMATION, HISTORY, AND DEFINITIONS

In this section, we will provide a brief background of each of AI and IoT, along with an explanation of relevant definitions.

What Is Artificial Intelligence (AI)

As discussed in literature and industry, AI uses algorithms within machines and focuses on giving them cognitive abilities such as reasoning, problem-solving, decision-making, and recognition (Hashimoto et al., 2018). Ever since its creation, AI has evolved over the years while undergoing cycles of both praise and criticism. The field came into existence in 1952 with advances and automation in neuroscience, attracting the focus of both the scientific industry and the public community (Perez et al., 2018). Then in 1956, the Dartmouth Conference positively embarked on the era of AI. The AI journey started with manufacturing computers that could solve various mathematical problems. Since the technology was burdened with limitations at the time, through public doubts in efficiency and high costs, the public questioned whether the hype over AI was exaggerated, despite the promising features of this field. As a result, several agencies halted their funding services to AI, leading to a wave of pessimism against technology (Middleton, 2021). The field faced its public ups and downs but kept progressing as computer power and resources further developed. Finally, the rise of the Big Data revolution, which involved big volumes of data of wide varieties and high velocities, made data accessible enough to advance AI and initiate its application through various sub-domains such as "machine learning" and "deep learning". According to literature, while machine learning focuses on developing computers to work with fewer human interventions, deep learning is a subset of machine learning that focuses on giving computers the ability to "think" using structures modeled on the human brain (Middleton, 2021). The availability of data and resources allowed for the actual implementation of theoretical AI/ML/DL in real-life applications such as Google filter spams and image detection and led to the debatable idea of technological singularity; predictions of the emergence of AI that surpasses human intelligence with that of machines (Perez et al., 2018).

AI gained wide attention of academic and popular literature and research. Actual and practical applications of AI have been generated and used in the fields of manufacturing, cybersecurity, health, cars and transportation, and many more by worldwide famous companies like IBM's Watson, Tesla's autopilot, and Google applications (Hashimoto et al., 2018).

Weak vs. Strong AI

In terms of capacity, AI is categorized by computer scientists as either weak or strong AI. By definition, weak AI, also known as narrow AI, is the most common among current intelligent systems and is trained to perform and repeat observed behaviors and assigned tasks (Perez et al., 2018). Weak AI relies on humans to define the limitations of the learning processes and to deliver the relevant training data (IBM, 2020). Despite lacking the ability to generalize, weak AI is evidently efficient in machine learning, data mining, language processing, and pattern recognition. Systems that are supported by weak AI include self-driving cars, recommender systems, virtual assistants (Siri), spam filters, and industrial robots (Perez et al., 2018).

On the other hand, researchers describe strong AI to be complemented by a sense of human-like consciousness and ability to reason and think (IBM, 2020). According to existing literature, in addition to being able to integrate information like the weak AI systems, strong AI can autonomously reprogram itself and modify its functioning to perform general tasks that require intelligence, sentience, and "self-awareness". According to IBM cloud education, strong AI can teach itself to solve new problems by developing a human-like consciousness instead of imitating it (IBM, 2020).

Despite the difference in autonomy and control between weak and strong AI, both systems represent the common feature of independency from full human control. Consequently, both systems carry common challenges accompanying their AI-enabled applications and are of the same importance when discussing ethical concerns and legal matters.

What Is Internet of Things (IoT)?

IoT systems have not been around for a long time, but the vision behind their technologies had already been under development many years ago. In 1969, the Internet, the key component of IoT, developed as Advanced Research Project Agency Network (ARPANET) and was mainly used for research and academic purposes. In 1973 and 1974, other essential technologies for IoT, respectively Radio-Frequency Identification RFID and embedded computer systems, were established and implemented for various uses (Sharma et al., 2019). Despite the proliferation of these technologies in businesses and markets, IoT was not recognized as an official term only until 1999 by Kevin Ashton and was not applied as an individual system only until the 2000s with internet connectivity becoming an essential norm for most applications and products (Lueth, 2014).

There exist several definitions of the term IoT. According to Internet Architecture Board (IAB), IoT is a set of a large number of embedded devices termed as "smart objects", which communicate with each other without human intervention to provide communication services (Sharma et al., 2019). The Internet Engineering Task Force (IETF) refers to IoT "Smart Object" too, but of limited power, processing ability, and memory. Moreover, IEEE Communications Magazine relates IoT to Cloud Services as a framework that aims to offer several services, using Machine-to-Machine M2M communications, to eradicate the gap between the physical and the virtual world. Atzori et al. define Internet of Things as three key concepts that intersect with each other to develop the full potential of IoT: internet-oriented Middleware, object-oriented Sensors, and semantic-oriented Knowledge (Sharma et al., 2019). Oxford Dictionaries defines IoT very accurately as "the interconnection via the Internet of computing devices embedded in everyday objects, enabling them to send and receive data". Consequently, a general and inclusive definition of IoT would be: a smart environment that utilizes the Internet, information, and communications technology to offer services to several domains like administration, education, healthcare, and transportation. With a framework that includes global and cloud computing for sharing and accessing data, data analytics for storing and analyzing data, and knowledge visualization for representing data, IoT has changed and will keep changing the entire communication process (Sharma et al., 2019).

Since IoT systems are growing at high speed, it is important to know the several communication models in which IoT devices connect and intersect in. According to a document prepared by Internet Architecture Board (IAB) for networking of smart objects, there are four major communication modules behind IoT systems (Thaler et al., 2015):

a. Device-to-Device Communication Model: Communication is directly between two or more IoT devices through Internet or any other network, with no need for an intermediary application server. Some examples include home automation systems like Amazon Alexa and Google Nest Mini.

b. Device-to-Cloud Communication Model: Communication is between the internet cloud services and IoT device. It is done through traditional wired Ethernet or Wi-Fi connections to connect the device to the IP network, which consequently connects it to the cloud service. Some examples include Samsung Smart TV and Nest Labs Learning Thermostat.

c. Device-to-Gateway Communication Model: A gateway device, also known as application-layer-device, operates through a software and connects the IoT device to the internet cloud services for the data exchange. Some examples include Fitness applications in a smartphone, which acts as an application layer gateway – it is connected to the fitness tracker device which cannot directly connect to the clouds service.

d. Back-End-Data-Sharing Communication Model: Communication is driven by users sharing/exporting the IoT device sensor data stored in the cloud database and joining it with third-party data. This model overcomes the limitations of device-to-cloud model and allows the analysis of data collected from several IoT devices. Moreover, back-end-data-sharing model was derived from single device-to-cloud communication model (Swamy et al., 2016).

ADVANTAGES OF AI-ENABLED IOT SYSTEMS

Recent advances in connectivity and technology have led to the emergence of AI and IoT systems in many industries (Shah & Chircu, 2018). While IoT is responsible for collecting data and visualizing it, AI plays a significant role in the analysis of expanding amounts of data, learning from them, and taking action accordingly. Consequently, the users, sensors, and networks of IoT produce huge amounts of data from which professionals can acquire knowledge and develop applications using AI-enabled methods (Kankanhalli et al., 2019).

However, as technological dependency increases with time, the number of companies utilizing IoT-data are becoming countless, which complicates the process of the proper collection, analysis, and acting upon the data. According to specialists, AI is the most suitable tool to understand the huge amounts of data and patterns and produce informed decisions and efficient results in a short timeframe (Vinugayathri, 2020). The synergy of AI and IoT can reshape the methodologies of businesses, industries, and economies. Here are some results of use cases where AI has been used along with IoT applications.

Transforming Job Markets and Creating New Products and Services

In parallel to innovation, various relevant occupations will emerge in which humans will conquer automation due to their judgment, knowledge, and critical thinking abilities (Huertas-Lopez et al., 2021). Careers in the domains of science, computer science, health, communications, and education will become those in highest demand – these include data scientists, data administrators, tech-educators, and robotic specialists. Also, NLP (Natural Language Processing), a subfield of AI, allows the communication of people with devices. Undeniably, by installing this feature in IoT systems, the business can promptly process and analyze larger amounts of data, enhance existing products, and create new products and services (Vinugayathri, 2020). For instance, PwC designed a structure to take in drone imagery of construction sites, allowing construction progress to be compared with the planned quality and quality (PwC, 2017).

Better Risk Management

The collaboration of AI and IoT helps businesses to better understand and predict a wide range of risks and create a fast and automated response to fix and moderate. Given the ability of AI to analyze large amounts of data, insights are more possible to be achieved. This consequently allows companies to properly manage cases of financial loss, cyber threats, and employee safety and security (Vinugayathri, 2020). For example, Fujitsu installs protective measures for their workers by having AI analyze data taken only from connected wearable devices (Vinugayathri, 2020).

AI-Enabled Robots

AI robotic systems do not require pauses or breaks as they are developed and programmed to work for long hours and achieve better results in a short timeframe. Moreover, robots are not possessive of human-like emotional side and that prevents room for timely distractions. Robots and machines depend on logical thinking, can work on more complex and laborious tasks, and give direct responses to arising matters when needed (Kumar et al., 2016). These characteristics, however, drive several ethical concerns that will be discussed later. Examples of AI-enabled robots include IBM Watson, DaVinci Surgical System, and nanorobots (Perez et al., 2018).

Personalized Experiences

The junction of AI and IoT leads to systems working with customers/users at a personal level. Interactions between the user and the system produce personalized results according to the user's specific desires and details, such as health monitoring by wearable devices, advice by recommender systems, peace of mind with smart household products, and convenience with virtual assistants (Puntoni et al., 2021). These applications include fitness trackers, Google Assistant, Apple's SIRI, Amazon's Alexa, etc. (Banafa, 2019).

Reduction of Error

AI may reduce chances of error and is developed to reach accuracy and precision in a smaller number of attempts in comparison to traditional approaches (Kumar, 2019). For example, several weather forecasting groups use AI to reduce the disadvantage of human error. Also, robotic surgeons, such as the DaVinci System are designed to be associated with movement precision during medical procedure (Perez et al., 2018).

Telehealth

According to Rushabh Shah et al., the major complications associated with medicine are disease diagnosis and treatment, health monitoring, data collection and analysis, and accuracy (Shah & Chircu, 2018). One of IoT applications is telehealth – tracking and monitoring of patients' health conditions through wearable devices, biochips, and remote diagnosis. With the addition of AI technologies, such as neural networks, healthcare systems can provide physicians with specific patient information and historical facts, allow for proper analysis of the data, and rationalize the diagnosis and relevant treatment in an accurate and risk-free manner (Amato et al., 2013).

Smart Cities and Smart Governments

IoT-sourced data include that of smart cities and governments. AI-enabled IoT applications can be applied to improve the development of smart cities, expand efficiency of smart governments, and provide life-enhancing services for citizens (Kankanhalli et al., 2019). Some of the major areas of a smart city are the smart manufacturing, smart transport system, smart energy, and smart homes. In smart manufacturing, the convergence of the physical and virtual worlds led to many developments, one of which is digital twin. Digital twin is a concept that involves a virtual model of a physical asset for predictive purposes (Kaur et al., 2020). It operates by real-time sensory data and can estimate the potential issues of the respective physical assets. In IoT world, AI will enhance the efficiency of digital twins through enhanced data analysis features that better understand states, add value, improve operations, and respond to changes.

Elimination of Costly Unplanned Downtime

In some sectors like industrial manufacturing, equipment breakdown can cause costly unexpected stoppage. The predictive preservation offered by AI-enabled IoT allows businesses to predict the failure or complication of equipment beforehand and plan timely maintenance procedures. Intelligent IoT systems can utilize AI to predict the conditions of operations and detect the parameters that need to be modified to ensure ideal results. Hence, efficiency can be enhanced in tasks that possess time-consuming maintenance processes (Vinugayathri, 2020).

Deloitte, a multinational audit and consulting firm, finds that upon integrating AI and IoT in their system, they achieved "'20%–50%' and '5%–10%' reductions in their time invested in maintenance planning and costs respectively and '10%–20%' increase in equipment availability and uptime" (Vinugayathri, 2020).

Self-Driving Cars

Self-driving cars are a famous example of IoT applications. A self-driving car requires an immense quantity of data collection and processing. These data involve information about the road, traffic, and navigation. Artificial Intelligence can play a role in achieving efficient data analysis and reaching better driving and route decisions. According to Lawrence Burns, self-driving vehicles can reduce out-of-the-pocket and time costs of conventional automobile travel by 80%. Also, his research at Columbia University also concluded that automobility is the sustainable solution to the enormous wastes inherent in human-driven, combustion-powered, manual automobiles (Burns, 2017). Moreover, self-driving cars are significantly lighter and energy-efficient due to the simplicity of their electric drive and component requirements.

ETHICAL CHALLENGES OF ENABLING AI IN IOT SYSTEMS

Alongside the researchers that encourage the integration of AI into IoT applications due to its promising impacts, others are hesitant about the manner due to the ethical issues and conflicts that arise in parallel to innovative projects. The synergy of AI and IoT raises several ethical concepts that need to be addressed.

Robo-Ethics vs. AI Singularity

With manufacturing robots joining several workforces, it is crucial to discuss the ethical standards of robotics, also noted as "Roboethics", and how they should be implemented in AI-powered IoT robotic systems. Scientist and futurist Isaac Asimov developed three initial laws (1950) followed by a zeroth law (1985) for the field of Robotics (Ashrafian, 2015). From lower to higher order, the laws were:

- A robot should not harm humanity.

- A robot may not injure a human being or, through inaction, allow a human being to encounter to harm.

- A robot must obey the orders given to it by human beings, except where such orders would conflict with the First Law.

- A robot must protect its own existence if such protection does not conflict with the First or Second Law.

In 2002, ethicists and engineers tackled this field again to widen the scope of the previously set guidelines, develop more specific ones, and clearly distinguish between similar concepts. For example, while roboethics focused on the rules to be considered in the human manufacturing of robots, "machine ethics", in the contrast, focused on the morality of machines and considered artificially intelligent machines as "Artificial Moral Agents" (AMAs) (Ashrafian, 2015).

In 2011, the Engineering and Physical Sciences Research Council (EPRSC) and the Arts and Humanities Research Council (AHRC) of Great Britain issued a set of standards for robot designers to follow to guarantee common and shared values to produce robots:

- Robots are tools for multi-uses, and they should not be designed solely or primarily to kill or harm humans, except in the interests of national security.

- Humans, not robots, are responsible and moral agents. Robots should be constructed; operated as far as it is practicable to comply with existing laws and fundamental rights and freedoms, including privacy.

- Robots are products. They should be designed using processes that assure their security and safety.

- Robots are built artefacts. They should not be designed in a deceptive way to exploit vulnerable users; instead, their machine nature should be obvious.

- The person with legal responsibility for a robot should be attributed (Ashrafian, 2015).

It is important to notice that despite the fantasized unlimited power associated with AI, and consequently with its subfields such as robotics, the aforementioned updated robot production regulations were generated with the preconception that robots are eventually accountable to pre-set human laws. This, however, clashes with AI singularity; the notion that refers to a world where everything is performed by ultra-intelligent machines and autonomous systems that are able to overpass human intellectual activities and rules (Upchurch, 2018). While some urge to draw attention to the seriousness of the situation, others claim that this technological individuality is still far from close. Yet, there is no harm in early preparation and protection. The implementation of AI robots in IoT systems requires serious debates on the manufacture and designing of the robots and their corresponding abilities and limits. This is because, in robotic developments, ethical and legal complications expand as the autonomy of devices increases (O'sullivan et al., 2018).

AI Bias and Discrimination

AI implementation does not only affect the work aspects of humans but also their lifestyles. Al algorithms and training information and data may repeat, reinforce, or augment harmful biases since these data are also generated by humans. Consequently, these biases drive AI systems to produce unfair outcomes and discrimination against minority groups. Bias in AI algorithms is caused by two reasons: (1) Developers would insert biased information in AI systems accidentally and without even noticing; (2) Historical data that will train AI algorithms may not be wide enough to represent the whole population in a fair manner (Dilmegani, 2021). For example, in search engines and translation algorithms, outputs are largely perceived as objective, yet frequently encode language in gendered ways. Also, bias has also been evident in the algorithmic advertisement, with opportunities for higher-paying jobs and jobs within the field of science and technology advertised to men more often than to women. Likewise, prediction algorithms used to manage the health data of millions of patients give better care to white patients in comparison to black patients (Mittelstadt et al., 2016).

Cybercrimes, Data Breach, and Lethal Weapons

While AI can be used by cybersecurity professionals to enhance data protection and minimize breach attacks in IoT systems, cybercriminals can abuse AI abilities for malicious and adversary purposes. This could lead to developing machine learning models that misinterpret inputs into the system and behave in a way that would make the breach or cyberattack easier and more favorable to the attacker (Belani, 2021).

As mentioned before, AI offers the advantage of personalized experiences within IoT facilities in customer services and more. However, with AI systems being able to process personal data, individuals' rights to privacy and freedom are at risk. This is because in AI systems, data collection abilities driven by low storage costs lead to data persisting longer than the human subjects that created it. Moreover, the data collected can be abused or used for purposes beyond their primary expected ones without the data owners' consent. Also, data may be collected from people who are not the original targets of the data collection sequence leading to a breach in data integrity (Pearce, 2021).

AI can be integrated into systems for criminal and harmful purposes. An example is incorporating AI in the military and developing lethal automated weapons LAWs that could independently identify targets based on programmed descriptions and constraints. There lie ethical concerns with this practice, especially with the risk of bias and discrimination associated with the AI systems (Dilmegani, 2021).

Unemployment

While automation with AI is expected to relieve humans from complex and unnecessary fatiguing IoT tasks, working individuals fear that their jobs will be eliminated by AI in the future. According to Mckinsey estimates, smart robots and intelligent machines could replace as much as 30% of the current human labor globally by 2030. Depending upon numerous implementation scenarios, automation will displace between 400 and 800 million jobs, and about 375 million working individuals will be required to switch job categories entirely (Dilmegani, 2021).

Disrupting Autonomy and Human Relationships

Self-rule, also known as self-governance or self-determination, is the major factor of autonomy. Smart objects, unlike traditional manual objects, acquire their own unique capacities and their own kinds of experiences in interaction with the consumer and each other (Hoffman & Novak, 2018).

Moreover, AI advancements are currently being used to dynamically personalize individuals' choice scenarios, paternalistically nudge, and manipulate behavior in unmatched manners (Laitinen & Sahlgren, 2021). Expanding deference to algorithmic patterns in many decision-making processes creates doubts regarding the authenticity of individuals' decisions, and consequently their capacity for self-determination and awareness. This is even more evident when algorithmic decision-making patterns are dependent on group-level data and past information.

Moreover, Artificial bots can virtually channel unlimited attention and kindness into building relationships, unlike humans, who expend these resources in a limited manner. This reward/fulfillment feeling will result in the reduction of human communication and an increase in human-bot interaction (Bossmann, 2016).

Duty of Care and Liability

The self-learning abilities of AI systems can help them come up with entirely new decisions and data on their own. While a key part of the negligent liability is foreseeability, autonomous systems are likely to display unforeseen behaviors, and this would present challenging dilemmas in determining who is liable (Jamjoom et al., 2020). This could then lead to unforeseeable harms or drawbacks that were not predicted by the developers. This creates ethically controversial matters, especially that while some claim that no matter how automated the system is, human developers and operators hold a duty of care toward the decisions reached by the AI systems they programmed, others suggest that autonomous machines should be granted legal personalities and thus liability in cases of negligence and harm (Hilborne, 2019). However, Samir Chopra, a professor of philosophy at the City University of New York, and many others, argue that a robot/machine, even if autonomous, is unable to be held legally liable for its actions under the current framework (Jamjoom et al., 2020). Thus, to them, humans will always be responsible for mishaps. However, this predetermined human liability is harsh, as there would exist cases where harm occurs even if all the groups involved act in an ethical and legal manner and with intentions to benefit rather than to harm. Yet, it would still be unfair for the impaired victim/company to not be compensated for the harm they would have suffered (Kemp, 2012).

Deteriorating Social Equity and Disparities in Wealth and Power

Deploying AI in IoT systems is costly and relatively complicated, which makes it an applicable practice for limited countries and advanced communities. And if these autonomous systems were to be sent by advanced countries and deployed in disadvantaged or developing countries, the process of implementation would lead to several complications and would eventually fail, as these systems would not only be expected to perform new and difficult tasks but would also have to conform to undeveloped and irrelevant regulations and legislations (O'sullivan et al., 2018).

Also, as mentioned before, AI-powered systems are expected to correlate with unemployment, so traditional human workforce is predicted to suffer from a cut down, making revenues go to fewer people. Consequently, rich individuals who have partnerships in AI-based IoT-driven companies will receive the wealth and power. This makes advancing IoT with AI associated with further exacerbating the existing gap between privileged and underprivileged communities in the world despite that increasing connection and world communication is one of IoT's major goals (Bossmann, 2016).

DISCUSSION

The integration of artificial intelligence in IoT systems introduces a wide range of ethical and regulatory issues. Different perspectives exist regarding the matter, which proves that there is an urgent need to reach a united position. However, as the world is getting deeply digitized, ignoring the trend of innovation is not preferred. Steps should be taken to overcome challenges and technology should be encouraged, rather than limited, especially when it seems to hold benefits and promising outcomes.

According to Travis Hollman, CEO of Hollman, the world's largest manufacturer of wood and laminate lockers, robots are best to fill in for humans in tasks that are repetitive, associated with high-volume production, and are often considered dangerous or boring (Prince, 2018). This way, AI-IoT manufacturing robots would save people from injuries and relieve stress on the company or the institution.

In parallel to the disputes over the rights and wrongs of employing smart machines instead of human workers, research makes it apparent that companies that fail to embrace the AI opportunity will have to face significant disadvantages that no team can afford. And with the acceleration of AI and IoT implementation, the chances of finding competitive alternatives and weighing options are quickly diminishing (PwC, 2017).

IoT and AI, together, can enable the development of valuable services for citizens, businesses, and public agencies, in multiple domains, such as transportation, energy, healthcare, education, and public safety (Kankanhalli et al., 2019). Nevertheless, innovative legislations and clear standards and duties, for all parties involved- workers, manufacturers, software designers, and administrative team – should be clearly set out to eliminate the misuses of AI and to help ease the mentioned ethical, legal, and regulatory challenges and other relative issues that would arise.

Moreover, while it is arguable that the autonomy advantage of AI may not be strictly necessary, as it limits communication and human interactions, the autonomous feature would still be advantageous and provide an extra level of distancing and protection to individuals in specific situations (O'sullivan et al., 2018). For instance, the recent and ongoing Coronavirus pandemic has majorly highlighted the need for smart systems and autonomous robotic systems to minimize the dangers of exposure to the highly contagious virus for the working staff and other individuals (Castellanos, 2020).

Therefore, after weighing the pros and cons of integrating AI features into IoT systems, it is obvious that the advantages of incorporating AI in IoT outweigh the disadvantages, and thus, embracing this Hi-Tech collaboration is better than ignoring it. However, for protective measures, it is best to support the following position: AI-powered IoT systems should be supported only if they were to be viewed as a regulatory moderated source of assistance and strength to humans and their businesses, rather than a threatening factor or unethical replacement. Pierre Dupont, an engineer in Boston Children's Hospital's robotic medical research team, emphasizes the fact that autonomous systems should be designed to support human workers and not outshine them (Svoboda, 2019). This perspective can also be implemented outside the medical scope; in most businesses and firms that are willing to incorporate an AI-enabled IoT system to manage their industrial work and increase their productivity.

RECOMMENDATIONS

On one hand, businesses and people should not be discouraged from working with AI and developing innovative technology, especially when current AI devices have been used in many cases successfully (Rozbruch, 2018). On the other hand, users utilizing the IoT devices/services must undertake all reasonable measures of minimizing the risks and concerns associated with this technology. Therefore, it is proposed to keep the following recommendations in consideration:

- If we plan to encourage the progress of AI and further develop it in most systems, it is important to first understand what practicality and science fiction are (Perez et al., 2018). Hence, there should be a logical and smooth interaction between visionary research ideas and the actual application of specific projects. Moreover, it is required to preclude the unrealistic enthusiasm and the unjustified fears of AI from hindering its progress. Instead, these overhyped feelings and visions should be used to inspire the development of a systematic outline on which the future of AI will prosper. If a sustained and a responsible investment is set, AI is expected to transform the future of society as a whole – people's life, their living environment, and the economy. AI and Robotics, if handled adequately, could amplify and augment human potential and improve productivity (Perez et al., 2018). Yet, to properly manage the influence of AI, it is important to understand and draw lessons from both past failures and achievements.

- One of the major complications associated with AI-enabled IoT systems is the issue of the projected ethical and legal challenges they would further impose on the "current" ethical and legal complications of the advanced technology. After clearly identifying all the impediments, adequate steps should be taken to tackle them. Ethicists and professionals should encourage constant comprised and communication to reach a united and clear ethical framework regarding the application of advanced systems. In addition, since the law is known to usually fall behind against the racing technological advancements, either altering current laws or setting new innovative legislations, or even both, is/are needed to allow the progress of technology and AI (O'sullivan et al., 2018).

- Since the physical, mental, and digital safety of individuals mark as priority to both the industrial and business systems, scientists and professionals are required to further study the factual aspects of incorporating AI in IoT systems and properly assess the results in comparison to the traditional procedure. Therefore, more experiments and research on the subject are needed before fully transforming systems using AI (Svoboda, 2019). This is important to ensure the safety of individuals and clarify the expected standards of both the traditional and advanced digital systems. Consequently, this will support the achievement of the best decisions for ultimate outcomes and will aid in improving areas of shortage or risks.

- To guarantee proper utilization of AI in IoT systems, clear regulatory measures should be created. Guidelines, codes of practice, conditions, and principles should be followed by manufacturing firms and adopting institutions to ensure that the process of designing and utilizing these advanced systems is not abused for profit purposes at the expense of human rights or even exploited by the staff to escape major duties (Bogue, 2014). Both non-binding and binding measures should be instituted; the non-governmental nature of the former would allow the measures to be trans-national and thus, more flexible and suited to this form of technology, whereas the latter would ensure judicial protection of rights and justice. Moreover, a regulatory framework should be formed to target the hostile and risky environments, those that would seem in favor of automated and advanced systems. This is because in health, for instance, doctors would still have a duty of care and responsibility toward their patients. It should be clarified and agreed that they are willing to accept the idea of relying on an electric robotic system they cannot directly control (O'sullivan et al., 2018). A good example is Singapore's approach to govern AI includes the Model Framework, Guide, and the Implementation and Self-Assessment Guide for Organizations ISAGO. These aim to guide private sector organizations and promote public understanding and trust in technologies by providing a clear explanation of how AI systems work, building adequate data accountability practices, offering transparent communication, and redesigning jobs to fit with the technical advancements (PDPC, 2020).

- Technological advancements should stay in compliance with international human rights. Therefore, with the entry of costly and complicated innovative services into various work fields, rulers should ensure that the access of individuals to these services is equal and fair. In a world suffering from disparities across communities, keeping the aspect of "equal access" to services should be a goal in technological planning. Since every human has an international human right to the ultimate form of health, privacy, and a life of dignity, innovative advancements should bolster these rights, rather than threaten them. It would also be preferable to focus on easing or even abolishing current disparities before introducing advanced hi-tech services that would seem to further exacerbate the situation.

CONCLUSION

The enduring development of AI offered a wide range of technological services in society (Ashrafian, 2015). Advances in AI have undergone rapid growth over the past decades. They have gained extensive popularity in most fields and have been applied in many practices. AI systems have provided comfort in IoT areas where manual control and tasks were challenging. Moreover, they have provided a benefit of procedural continuity, as they have eased work fatigue and unnecessary exhaustion that could stand in the way of other achievements (Taylor, 2020). However, in parallel to the rise of aspirations and optimism with its successful results, AI-enabled IoT systems have posed major ethical and legal concerns. And with the efforts to render more AI-integrated systems feasible, all involved parties – governments, policymakers, enterprises, innovators, developers, and citizens are challenged to be impacted by the intricate ethical and legal complications associated with this revolution, especially when it comes to privacy and autonomy rights, ensuring responsibilities of individuals and firms, and securing equity and justice (Usluoğulları et al., 2017).

Therefore, companies that are willing to utilize this proactive approach should engage in extensive monitoring and moderating procedures to ensure proper practice and limit ethical risks and misuses. This way, they could make the most of the opportunities offered by AI while securing the rights and safety of the involved individuals – employees and utilizers (PwC, 2017). Including AI in IoT systems, just like in all other systems, is a major responsibility and not an on-off switch; once it is installed, it is hard to reverse the impact. To take this responsibility, adopters are urged to have a foundation of knowledge of AI to adequately understand how it may impact not only the adopting system but the society as a whole (Hashimoto et al., 2018).

REFERENCES

Amato, F., López, A., Peña-Méndez, E. M., Vaňhara, P., Hampl, A., & Havel, J. (2013). Artificial neural networks in medical diagnosis. *Journal of Applied Biomedicine (De Gruyter Open)*, *11*(2), 45–58.

Ashrafian, H. (2015). AIonAI: A humanitarian law of artificial intelligence and robotics. *Science and Engineering Ethics*, *21*, 29–40.

Banafa, A. (2019). *Secure and smart internet of things (IoT): Using blockchain and artificial intelligence (AI)*. Stylus Publishing, LLC.

Belani, G. (2021). The use of artificial intelligence in cybersecurity: A review. Retrieved from https://www.computer.org/publications/tech-news/trends/the-use-of-artificial-intelligence-in-cybersecurity

Bogue, R. (2014). Robot ethics and law Part two: Law. *Industrial Robot: An International Journal*, *41*(5), 398–402.

Bossmann, J. (2016, October 21). Top 9 ethical issues in artificial intelligence. Retrieved from https://www.weforum.org/agenda/2016/10/top-10-ethical-issues-in-artificial-intelligence/

Burns, L. (2017). Autonomy: The new age of automobility, autonomous vehicle engineering.

Castellanos, S. (2020). Autonomous robots are coming to the operating room. *The Wall Street Journal*. https://www.wsj.com/articles/autonomous-robots-are-coming-to-the-operating-room-11599786000 Accessed: July 28, 2022

Dilmegani, C. (2021, November 11). AI Ethics: Top 9 ethical dilemmas of AI and how to navigate them. Retrieved from https://research.aimultiple.com/ai-ethics/

Hashimoto, D., & others (2018). Artificial intelligence in surgery: Promises and perils. *Annals of surgery*, *268*(1), 70–76.

Hilborne, N., Let robots own property, supreme court justice suggests (Legal Futures, 19 March 2019) <https://www.legalfutures.co.uk/latest-news/let-robots-own-property-supreme-court-justice-suggests> Accessed 1 August 2021

Hoffman, D. L., & Novak, T. P. (2018). Consumer and object experience in the internet of things: An assemblage theory approach. *Journal of Consumer Research*, *44*(6), 1178–1204.

Huertas-Lopez, C., et al. (2021). Artificial intelligence: Transformation of the roles of human capital. *International Journal of Scientific & Technology Research*, *10*(9), 57–67.

IBM cloud education (2020). Strong AI. Retrieved from https://www.ibm.com/cloud/learn/strong-ai

Jamjoom, A., & others (2020). Exploring public opinion about liability and responsibility in surgical robotics with the iRobot Surgeon survey. *Nature Machine Intelligence*, *2*(4), 194–196. 10.1038/s42256-020-0169-2

Kankanhalli, A. Charalabidis, A., & Mellouli, S. (2019). IoT and AI for smart government: A research agenda. *Government Information Quarterly*, *36*(2), 304–309. 10.1016/j.giq.2019.02.003

Kaur, M. J., Mishra, V. P., & Maheshwari, P. (2020). The convergence of digital twin, IoT, and machine learning: Transforming data into action. In M. Farsi, A. Daneshkhah, A. Hosseinian-Far, & H. Jahankhani (Eds.), *Digital twin technologies and smart cities. Internet of things*. Springer: Cham. 10.1007/978-3-030-18732-3_1

Kemp, D. S. (2012). Autonomous cars and surgical robots: A discussion of ethical and legal responsibility. Retrieved from https://verdict.justia.com/2012/11/19/autonomous-cars-and-surgical-robots

Kumar N., Kharkwal N., Kohli R., & Choudhary S. (2016). "Ethical aspects and future of artificial intelligence," 2016 International Conference on Innovation and Challenges in Cyber Security (ICICCS-INBUSH), pp. 111–114.

Kumar, S. (2019). Advantages and disadvantages of artificial intelligence. Retrieved from https://towardsdatascience.com/advantages-and-disadvantages-of-artificial-intelligence-182a5ef6588c

Laitinen, A., & Sahlgren, O. (2021, October 26). AI systems and respect for human autonomy. *Frontiers in Artificial Intelligence*. Retrieved from 10.3389/frai.2021.705164

Lueth, K. (2014). Why the internet of things is called internet of things: Definition, history, disambiguation. Retrieved from https://iot-analytics.com/internet-of-things-definition/

Middleton, M. (2021). Deep learning vs machine learning — What's the difference? *Flatiron School*. Retrieved from https://flatironschool.com/blog/deep-learning-vs-machine-learning

Mittelstadt, B. D., Allo, P., Taddeo, M., Wachter, S., & Floridi, L. (2016). *The ethics of algorithms: Mapping the debate*. Big Data & Society.

O'Sullivan, S. et al. (2018). Legal, regulatory, and ethical frameworks for development of standards in artificial intelligence (AI) and autonomous robotic surgery. *The International Journal of Medical Robotics and Computer-Assisted Surgery, 15*(1), e1968. 10.1002/rcs.1968

PDPC. (2020). Singapore's approach to AI governance. Retrieved from https://www.pdpc.gov.sg/Help-and-Resources/2020/01/Model-AI-Governance-Framework

Pearce, G. (2021, May 28). Beware the privacy violations in artificial intelligence applications. Retrieved from https://www.isaca.org/resources/news-and-trends/isaca-now-blog/2021/beware-the-privacy-violations-in-artificial-intelligence-applications

Perez, J., & others (2018). *Artificial intelligence and robotics.* UK-RAS Network

Prince, C. (2018). Duty of care can robots replace humans? Just ask Elon Musk. *SHRM.* Retrieved from https://www.shrm.org/resourcesandtools/hr-

Puntoni, S., Reczek, R. W., Giesler, M., & Botti, S. (2021). Consumers and artificial intelligence: An experiential perspective. *Journal of Marketing, 85*(1), 131–151. 10.1177/0022242920953847

PwC (2017). Leveraging the upcoming disruptions from AI and IoT. Retrieved from https://www.pwc.com/gx/en/industries/communications/assets/pwc-ai-and-iot.pdf

Rozbruch, L. (2018, March 16). 'Litigation & Robotic surgery: Product liability or medical malpractice?' *The Roundtable.* Retrieved from https://www.pulj.org/the-roundtable/litigation-robotic-surgery-productliability-or-medical-malpractice

Shah, R., & Chircu, A. (2018). Iot and AI in healthcare: A systematic literature review. *Issues in Information Systems, 19*(3), 33–41.

Sharma, N., & others (2019). *The history, present and future with IoT. Internet of things and big data analytics for smart generation, intelligent systems reference library 154.* Springer Nature Switzerland AG

Svoboda, E. (2019). Your robot surgeon will see you now. Retrieved from https://www.nature.com/articles/d41586-019-02874-0

Swamy, N., & others (2016). Analysis on IOT challenges, opportunities, applications and communication models. *International Journal of Advanced Engineering, Management and Science, 2*(4), 75–78.

Taylor, M. (2020). Why is there a shortage of doctors in the UK?. *The Bulletin of the Royal College of Surgeons of England, 102*(3), 78–81.

Thaler, D., & others (2015). Architectural considerations in smart object networking. *IAB RFC 7452.* Retrieved from https://www.ietf.org/proceedings/92/slides/slides-92-iab-techplenary-2.pdf

Upchurch, M. (2018). Robots and AI at work: The prospects for singularity. *New Technology, Work and Employment, 33*(3), 205–218.

Usluoğulları, F., & others (2017). Robotic surgery and malpractice. *Turkish Journal of Urology, 43*(4), 425–428.

Vinugayathri. (2020). AI and IoT blended - What it is and why it matters? Retrieved from https://www.clariontech.com/blog/ai-and-iot-blended-what-it-is-and-why-it-matters

Woetzel, J., et al. (2018, June 5). Smart cities: Digital solutions for a more livable future. McKinsey Global Institute. Retrieved from https://www.mckinsey.com/business-functions/operations/our-insights/smartcities-digital-solutions-for-a-more-livable-future

CHAPTER 15

Trustworthy Bioethicists within Lifecycles of Artificial Intelligence in Health

Kristine Bærøe[a] and Torbjørn Gundersen[b]

[a]Medical Ethics and Philosophy of Science, Department of Global Public Health and Primary Care, University of Bergen, Bergen, Norway
[b]Centre for the Study of Professions, Oslo Metropolitan University, Oslo, Norway

CONTENTS

INTRODUCTION

Artificial intelligence (AI) systems such as machine learning hold great promise for use in various sectors and policy areas. In particular, recent developments in machine learning, such as deep learning, make it possible for algorithms to handle vast data sets and make more accurate and effective classifications, recommendations, and predictions. By being trained on data sets labeled by humans (supervised learning) or by looking for patterns in

DOI: 10.1201/9781003261247-18

unlabeled data (unsupervised learning), machine learning algorithms can, for instance, be used in diverse policy areas such as in detecting tax fraud (de Roux et al., 2018), assisting judges by predicting recidivism (Biddle, 2020), and improving crop yield management in agriculture (Liakos et al., 2018). Health care is an area with particularly great expectations regarding AI-based technologies in promoting preventive and curative interventions. For certain tasks, deep learning algorithms perform on a par or outperform medical doctors and thus have the potential to improve clinical practice in medical specialties such as radiology, pathology, dermatology, ophthalmology, gastroenterology, and cardiology (Topol, 2019) and improve the evidence base for cost-effective, beneficial decision-making. Research and development efforts in the use of machine learning in health care in both private and public sectors indicate that AI will likely play an influential role in the future.

While improving the health of individuals and populations is of evident value, achieving this with AI also involves risks to society that we cannot adequately predict the scope and severity of (Bærøe & Gundersen, 2019). First, the use of AI in medical decision-making raises a set of distinct ethical challenges that might disrupt established principles in medical ethics pertaining to professional accountability and the transparency of decision-making (see for instance, Grote & Berens, 2020, McDougall, 2019). Second, an underlying challenge is that conditions for human control over the impact of AI can be undermined by the fact that AI can have unpredictable long-term impacts on the conditions of democratic governance as well as established medical standards and expertise in health care (Kerasidou, 2020; McDougall, 2019). Upscaling and implementing existing AI systems already have the potential to severely affect the conditions fundamental to social interaction (Bærøe et al., 2020; Kerasidou, 2020) and political decision making (Danaher, 2016). These ethical challenges raise questions as to whether and how AI should be developed and applied in health care and according to which ethical standards.

The lifecycle of an AI system can be broken down into phases of development, deployment, and use (European Commision, 2019). In order to be trustworthy overall, the professionals and institutions that develop, deploy, and use AI, must not only be competent in their field but also display commitment to central ethical, legal, and democratic principles (for a discussion of the relation between trust and trustworthiness, see, (O'Neill, 2018) (European Commission, 2019). Accordingly, guiding principles and frameworks to support developers and governing authorities are emerging around the world to foster well-placed trust in AI research and innovation. Central to such guidelines is the need to incorporate ways to ensure ethical scrutiny throughout the lifecycles of AI systems. Moreover, in democratic societies, decision-making concerning the deployment and use of new technologies that can have consequences clashing with deeply held values requires that stakeholders are included in public deliberation over related concerns (European Commission, 2019). In this perspective, ethically acceptable application of AI in health, requires that AI designers assess the technical risks, but also that they identify and articulate the potential benefits and burdens.

While there is broad consensus that those who contribute to the lifecycles of medical AI must take ethical principles and values into due consideration in order to be trustworthy, the more exact role of academically trained bioethicists in cultivating and sustaining trustworthiness has received little attention. For this reason, this chapter examines the following questions: What makes bioethicists trustworthy in this aera? How can their contributions serve to foster and sustain the trustworthiness of AI medicine?

This chapter offers a normative discussion of how bioethicists can contribute to developing, deploying, and use of trustworthy medical AI. We approach this question by (1) exploring the lack of attention to potential limitations to the ethical impact of bioethics, and (2) accounting for how "translational ethics" better can contribute to the cultivation of trustworthy professionals and institutions in the lifecycles of AI than traditional ways of doing bioethics. We continue to (3) discuss translational bioethics and trust, and move on to (4) conceptualize the specific role of bioethicists in this setting in terms of "interactable" expertise. We probe deeper into the role of trustworthy bioethicists by (5) discussing two models for how the field of translational bioethics can contribute in decision-making in the lifecycles of AI systems in trustworthy ways, i.e., as representing a *multidisciplinary approach* by individual agents that adds to the technical, medical, and legal knowledge possessed by other agents or a *shared ethical competency approach* in which the actors share competencies across disciplines. We (6) conclude that for AI in health to become trustworthy, there must be substantial collaboration across established disciplinary boundaries, based on a shared, fundamental ethical competence institutionalized in a team-based practice following the lifecycles of AI. While this may seem like an uncontroversial conclusion, it covers the new and perhaps surprising claim (for bioethicists at least) that for some decisions, bioethicists are not the ones being best positioned for making ethical assessments within the cycles of AI systems in health in a trustworthy manner; the technologists and medical personnel are. The reason for this is that at least some crucial decisions concerning the lifecycles of medical AI presuppose in-depth knowledge and skills in how AI and medicine work and how it can be improved. For these decisions, the normatively justified role of bioethicists is less to contribute directly to ethical and trustworthy AI, but rather indirectly by impacting on the ethical training of AI developers.

BIOETHICISTS AND AI: OPPORTUNITIES AND LIMITATIONS

In the context of health care, bioethics is the foremost academic discipline that addresses, identifies, conceptualizes, and reflects upon individual and societal values and normative challenges related to health, medicine, medical technology, and environmental issues. Indeed, bioethics journals are increasingly filled with papers addressing a variety of ethical aspects related to AI. However, a self-critical perspective on limitations to what ethicists can meaningfully do in this field, has not gain much attention.

This lack of attention to limitations of how bioethicist can deal with ethical issues can perhaps most obviously be explained by the loss of productivity it entails. In the face of new and transformative technology, society calls for constructive approaches and ethical actions. From within the bioethical perspective, focusing on limitations is counter-productive; claiming constraints on the potential contributions of the field of bioethics to ethics and trust goes hand-in-hand with lost epistemic authority; identifying and ex-amining constraints can result in lost power to set the premises for what ethics requires and thereby lost control as an academic discipline.

Another reason the more exact contributions of bioethics is little discussed could be that the field is not yet fully prepared for this discussion. Researchers have suggested we should meet the AI in health with the same ethical understanding and tools that healthcare challenges are already met with, but not excluding the possibility that completely new issues can emerge (Char et al., 2020). Others have argued that given the potentially transformative character of AI technology for health professional re-lations and the social conditions for ethically acceptable practice, combined with massive and strong economic and political forces urging the development, deploy-ment, and use of AI, it can be prudent to start with the assumption that AI-related bioethics requires more than "business as usual" in the field of bioethics. By not ac-tively exploring whether this new technology creates new circumstances that cannot be adequately handled by traditional ways of doing bioethics, we run the risk of ig-noring ethically relevant concerns. Thus ethics may end up running behind the AI developments, rather than taking an pro-active role in ensuring trustworthiness by staying alert to identify uncommon ethical issues and engage in the AI lifecycles. In such a pro-active forward-looking perspective on the role of bioethics, the approaches of "traditional bioethicists" are subjected to scrutiny. By identifying limitations to what traditional bioethicists can do, new and more adequate perspectives on oppor-tunities for promoting trustworthiness in how the lifecycle of AI is can be handled ethically, arise.

In what follows, we will discuss what makes bioethicists trustworthy agents in life-cycles of AI while at the same centering on the "ethics of doing ethics", i.e., we will be concerned with not overselling what bioethicists can-and should-do.

TRADITIONAL TASKS FOR BIOETHICS AND TRANSLATIONAL ETHICS

Let us have a brief look into the traditional areas for bioethical approaches. According to Evans's helpful sociological perspective, traditionally, bioethics seeks to establish ex-pertise related to four tasks: (1) healthcare ethics consultation, (2) scientific and medical research on humans, (3) "cultural bioethics" (i.e., efforts at convincing "ordinary citizens on the proper ethical course of action concerning a medical or scientific technology or practice" (p. xxxiii)), and (4) public policy (Evans, 2012). Borrowing the term from Abbott's work on professions, Evans describes these areas as matters of "jurisdiction". They represent domains in which bioethicists can exercise discretion based on their "systems of abstract knowledge" and support from jurisdiction givers (i.e., the public and government agents). However, unlike professions, academically trained bioethicist do not have an exclusive right to perform general tasks of normative, ethical assessment. The continuous, within-the-lifecycle development of trustworthy AI in health, calls for dynamic, hands-on, interpretations of ethical issues based on outcomes of the technology and forecasts, reviews, revisions, and new forecasts. We believe that the potential role of bioethicists is not completely covered by Evans overview. It cannot adequately be carried out as 'armchair reflections' on what ethical theories require, the meaning of ethically relevant terms, and guesswork of future implications (i.e., as cultural bioethics). Neither can it be adequately covered in traditional ethical task forces that aim to make ethical recommendations of the technology on a general level (i.e., as public policy), nor in traditional, practical, ethical hospital committees where the central ethical mandate is to facilitate good processes to reach feasible, practical conclusions on conflicting ethical issues (i.e., as healthcare ethics consultations). Moreover, while assessing the ethics of deploying and applying medical AI is subjected to the traditional bioethical task connected to monitoring scientific and medical research on humans, the processes of designing and testing AI devices according to traditional ethical reviews may miss out the particularities of such new technology. Also, ethical assessments involved in the lifecycles of AI require active involvement in the day-to-day design and testing of AI systems that cannot feasibly be dealt with by the traditional organization of ethical research review boards.

Translational Ethics

Much research in ethics emerging from universities and other research institutions aims, in different ways, to impact ethical practice by way formulating policies, guidelines, and recommendations. Just as "translational research" in medicine requires researchers to identify steps to transfer basic scientific discoveries from laboratory benches to bedside decision-making, much bioethical research shares a similar aim of producing knowledge within academia and transferring knowledge into practice (Cribb, 2010). Theoretical research on normative issues concerns how the world *should be*, and in so far as this knowledge can be transferred to society it could lead to improving the professionals and the institutions shaping medical practice (Cribb, 2010). Arguably, such approaches should be ethically justified themselves. In line with this self-reflexive perspective has "translational ethics" been developed as a distinct theoretical and methodological approach to ethics, one that incorporates normative, empirical, and meta-ethical research (Bærøe, 2014), and the approach has been – and is still being – tested through application (Wester et al., 2019; Eide, 2020). As per today, this conceptualization of translational ethics does not constitute a broadly applied, well-established approach. However, the conditions for this way to approach ethics in general and bioethics in particular make it especially apt for promoting trustworthiness in ethical approaches embedded in value pluralistic societies. The main reason for this being the self-reflexivity toward ethical approaches' own opportunities and limitations that it involves.

As a methodology, the translational ethics approach takes as its starting point (i) the epistemological and practical challenges involved in bridging the gap between the theoretical work carried out by academic researchers, on the one side, (ii) the empirical experiences, needs, capacities, motivations, and contextual circumstances in the field of everyday practice on the other; and (iii) the view that academic endeavors in ethics are also constrained by constitutive factors pertaining to *practice* of doing academic work. These criteria, such as requirements for accuracy, consistency, and rigor, do not represent an external source to the correction of human practice; academic approaches are also distinct parts of human practice. This has implications for how to perceive the bridging activity between theory and practice. The attempts of translational ethics to accommodate meaningful ways to bridge academic ethics with how non-academic ethics play out in people's lives are also subjected to practice-relevant, fundamental concerns regarding *when* and *how* to claim due power over others. In short, and according to Lukes's three dimensions of power (forcing, controlling the agenda, and defining people's world views) (Lukes, 2005), bioethicists are not in a position to force specific ethical ideas upon others, to control the agenda of what ethical issues should be put on decision-makers' table, and when, nor to determine worldviews concerning what constitutes, for example, threats, or opportunities with new technologies. This is not the default position of bioethicists in political systems, nor we allege, should it be. Based on these presuppositions, the task set out by translational ethics centers, on a case-to-case basis, on assessing the "fairness" or "reasonableness" of actions involved in pushing the results of an academic ethics practice on, e.g., professional, or policy-making practices embedded in social and cultural settings outside academia (Bærøe, 2014). This self-reflexive movement is crucial to translational ethics and can be perceived as a pre-condition for the justified translation of academic ethics into people's lives.

Indeed, ethical research is itself – as is all other research – subject to requirements of being ethically designed, conducted, and reported. As the aim of doing research in ethics is inherently related to identifying or achieving something good or right, this normative, 'meta-ethcial' perspective on ethical research itself seems to go unnoticed. If ethical research is to be applied for policy purposes, the ethics of the design of the study, including the identification of relevant theories and empircal data, must involve considerations about avoiding *undue* use of researchers' power in pushing their own ethical perspectives of "the common good", normative principles or theories (and not the values of the majority of the society) unfairly into other people's lives in terms of policies or recommendations (Bærøe, Kerasidou et al., 2022). The people subjected to changes assumed morally acceptable by researchers might disagree with the underlying values, and their experiences and points of view might be disregarded or not even recognized. If this is the case, then policies developed by ethicists contribute to either conspicuous or more subtle versions of suppression. Such situations conflict with reasonable standards for an "ethics in promoting ethics" and should be avoided. By incorporating the precondition that acceptable, practical claims on ethics on a case-to-case basis have to account for and justify any use of power involved, 'translational ethics' occupies a niche position in the field of academic ethics.

Let us summarize the essence of translational ethics. When bridging the gap between theory and practice, information and impact can move in two directions: from theory (via, e.g., philosophers) influencing practice, and from practice (via, e.g., clinicians) in the development of new theory (Bærøe, 2014). Overall translation of academic ethics from the desk to practice must itself reflect ethical, acceptable practice. Specifically, this means researchers must exercise self-reflexivity regarding their own values and on a case-to-case basis and strive for justification with respect to *who* to involve in all phases of the research process, *whose* needs to focus on, *what* data to collect, and *where* in the decision-making process theoretical and empirical perspectives should be integrated and *how* this should be done.

TRANSLATIONAL BIOETHICISTS AND TRUST

Just as bioethics is a subarea of ethics, translational bioethics can be seen as a subarea of translational ethics. A trained bioethicist who works according to a translation ethics approach (hereafter "translational bioethicists" for short) will aim to transfer well-informed, empirical knowledge and justified normative recommendations into practice in an ethcial manner. This means avoiding harm and supporting empowering processes of stakeholders by focusing on promoting transparency, inclusion, and fairness.

Translational bioethicists must bridge the gap between ethical theory and practice, and they can do so in many ways. They can act as experts on running ethically justified decision-making processes in the clinic or serve on policy-making committees or ethical boards. They can make an impact through the dissemination of their theoretical research by joining public demonstrations as a form of activism, by being involved in the practical evaluation of implemented moral ideas, or by engaging as an ethical advisor in various phases of the development of new health technology. For translational bioethicists, such approaches must be based in *explicit* justification for why a specific bioethical approach is a fair and reasonable effort to reshape medical or enviromental practice. While people may disagree on the content bioethicists provide to policymakers, professionals, and citizens, translational bioethicists will at least have followed a process of putting their aims, rationales, understanding, and means openly into the public sphere for scrutiny. Arguably, this provides reasons for placing trust in translational bioethicists.

There are many definitions of trust, but:

> ... most reviews converge on the idea that trust involves a trustor (subject) and trustee (object) that are somehow interdependent; involves a situation containing risks for the trustor (which also implies the trustor has goals); is experienced by the trustor as voluntary (implying a sense of autonomy, agency, and intrinsic motivation); and includes (or excludes) different types, forms, or sources of trust concepts, some of which may form the bases of others and many of which involve or relate to positive evaluations or expectations.
>
> *(PytlikZillig & Kimbrough, 2016, p. 24)*

According to Mayer and colleagues, trustworthiness is especially related to three features of the trustee: ability (i.e., skills and competencies), benevolence (i.e., the trustee is believed to act for the benefit of the trustor), and integrity (i.e., the trustor perceives the trustee as acting according to acceptable principles) (Mayer et al., 1995). The trust-giver depends on the trustee and has some confidence in the trustee's competence, honesty, and sense of moral responsibility. By depending on the trustee, the trust-giver becomes vulnerable to mistakes or ill-will of the trustee. Translational bioethicists will they can provide relevant advice, in the form of propositions or directives, which might benefit the trust-giver, but at the same time demonstrate that they are avoiding unjustified use of power as they arrive at ethical conclusions based on principles of transparency, inclusion, and fairness trustors are expected to endorse. Thus, applying the methodology of translational ethics supports trustworthiness. Compared to practical, bioethical approaches by bioethicists who do not demonstrate this dimension of self-reflexivity, people are given more reasons to make up their own minds on whether to place trust in translational bioethicists. Regarding the ethics of medical AI, however, it is not yet clear exactly what the skills and competencies worthy of trust should be. In the following, we will circle in on these skills and competencies by stating to describe the uncontroversial tasks of translational bioethicists and then move into the more problematic ones.

BIOETHICISTS' COMPETENCE IN AI LIFECYCLES AS INTERACTIONAL EXPERTISE

Let us start with a rough and ready overview of the kind of task bioethicists can carry out on ethical issues surrounding AI in health. In accordance with the translational ethics described here, bioethicists can contribute to the development, deployment, and use of medical AI in several ways. First, they can translate theoretical and normative bioethical perspectives on ethical challenges relevant in developing new AI technologies into concrete settings. For example, different kinds of biases are involved in developing and deploying machine learning. There are representational and historical biases in data collection and evaluation, aggregation biases in the modeling, and behavioral and social biases in the human review of the technology (Reagan, 2021, Suresh & Guttag, 2019). Translational bioethicists can help in describing ethically problematic biases occurring during the part of *developing* an AI system's lifecycle. Regarding *deployment*, they can assist in interpreting general moral principles (e.g., the principles of autonomy and do not harm) in concrete health care situations where AI is being tested. Moreover, they can conduct empirical research on the distribution of health care following the *use* of AI to assess the fairness of its deployment. They can inform decision-making processes regarding whether to prioritize AI technology in health programs with overviews of ethical challenges, and they can provide ethically relevant input into formulations of AI strategies in health and guidelines for ethical assessments of clinical trials involving AI. More broadly, they can also initiate and engage in public debates and determine whether conditions (such as the ethical accountability of decision-makers and the transparency of rationales for introducing AI technology in new areas) are in place for people to perceive the overall decision-making process and outcome as fair. Also, translational bioethicists can mitigating undue influences of power and unfair decision-making processes by involving and empowering less-powerful stakeholders.

These examples demonstrate that bioethicists can have a role to play in addressing ethical challenges of new and transformative technology. However, the economic and political aims involved in AI life cycles (and the internal logics required by these aims) may clash with ethical concerns. When ethical considerations go against economic gain and political interests, they will not necessarily determine the outcome of a conflict. Still, the discourse on how to facilitate trustworthy AI by ensuring the ethical dimension of AI implies that ethical concerns should conquer other interests when these cannot be ethically justified (European Commission, 2019). For ethical considerations to have a real impact on trustworthiness, efforts to achieve this can neither occur arbitrarily nor influence randomly. Ethical assessments will have to be integrated into the decision-making processes of AI system lifecycles as permanent institutions. By establishing such institutions, i.e., practices, with a political mandate to not only support but even enforce fair and ethical AI, translational bioethicists can play a central role in the development, deployment, and use of trustworthy AI in health. To further clarify this role, we need to explore the nature, scope, and required levels of these competencies in bioethics and their relation to other agents involved in developing trustworthy AI.

Interactional Expertise

The rationale for taking bioethicists seriously is in making medical AI acceptable that bioethics contains knowledge relevant to professionals and institutions involved in the lifecycles of medical AI. But how can this acknowledged relevance be translated into trustworthy impact on the lifecycles of medical AI? As mediators between the technologies and the public, the trustworthiness of bioethicists depends on both the skills and knowledge they have to be ensure targeted ethical assessments of the technology and its impact on medicine, and on their skills and knowledge to convey the ethical content to the public. Let us first consider the level of knowledge required to act as trustworthy mediators of ethics between the public and the technical developers.

Like the expert role of scientists who translate scientific knowledge into public policy, bioethicists must have adequate understanding of knowledge from outside their core specialty as bioethical researchers and an understanding of relevant social science, law, and technology. So understood, individual bioethicists who contribute to making medical AI ethically acceptable, cannot be expected to be specialists in all parts of the knowledge they translate for use. For this reason, a minimal normative expectation is that bioethicist who aim to give advice to professionals and institutions must be able to assess, draw on, and communicate knowledge outside their own academic specialty about AI and of the medical field in which AI will considered applied. Regarding competency in AI, ethical arguments and assessments involving medical AI must include a basic understanding of AI, such as machine learning and deep learning. For example, to make a proper assessment of the prospects of transparent decision-making in medical practice when it is assisted by machine learning presupposes an understanding of how the algorithm works, how it classifies data and generates predictions, whether it is likelier to make false positives or false negatives when detecting disease, and, more generally, how reliable the algorithm has proven to be in the past. However, while bioethicists should have a basic understanding of, and competencies, in AI, they do not need to be experts in the field to make qualified ethical assessments and contributions to function as a mediator. To demand expertise in AI runs the risk of overburdening bioethicists and potentially excluding relevant contributions – and it is not required for epistemological reasons. Bioethicists must, however, be able to *understand* central aspects of the technology and its social and political significance to be able to provide well-informed arguments.

The required level of competency that bioethicists must have – in those parts of bioethics that are outside their own specialty within bioethics and in other relevant fields such as medicine and AI technology – can be understood in terms of what has been described as "interactional expertise" (Collins & Evans, 2006). The term "interactional expertise" was originally developed to provide a normative theory of the nature and legitimacy of expertise that scientists can use to inform public policy. The term refers to the knowledge of those scientific experts that do not belong to the group of "core scientists", i.e., those scientists who "can legitimately contribute to the formation of [scientific] consensus or develop the science thereafter" (p. 46). Nevertheless, scientists (and others) may have a solid understanding of the work of these "core" scientists in another field to be able to interact meaningfully with them. Interactional expertise "means enough expertise to interact interestingly with participants" (p. 59).

Two aspects of interactional expertise are particularly relevant (setting aside the questions of whether there are relevant differences between natural science and ethics). First, those who possess interactional expertise can understand, engage with, and perhaps, in some cases, meaningfully criticize core experts. This is required to mediate *from* the technology side of AI. Second, those who possess interactional expertise can adopt an intermediary role in communicating established knowledge in the field to policymakers and the public. This is required to mediate *to* others who are not AI experts. To be sure, adopting this latter side of the intermediary role also requires an understanding of the interests, perspectives, and competencies of policymakers and citizens. In the case of medical AI, both medical competence and AI competence are crucial to ethical translations that are accurate, relevant, and responsible. Thus, translational bioethicists need interactional expertise in these areas to demonstrate the skills required to be trustworthy.

The relationship between experts and lay people, between those who have specialized knowledge and skills in some domain and those who do not but who depend on that knowledge, is often described in terms of an epistemic asymmetry. For instance, most citizens do not have the knowledge required to develop, understand, and assess empirical knowledge, models, and predictions about climate change, and, accordingly, they wisely defer to climate scientists for that knowledge. In such technical issues, there is a major epistemic asymmetry between members of the public and experts. However, in other cases, the asymmetry might be smaller. For instance, medical doctors who draw on scientific research in their work are often not specialists in all fields they draw upon in decision-making, yet they could very well be in a good position to understand and apply that knowledge. In such cases, epistemic asymmetry is discernible without undermining meaningful communication and understanding between experts and lay people. In the case of AI in health, we might expect both major and more minor forms of epistemic asymmetry, both between AI developers and the public, but also among AI developers, bioethicists, and medical personnel.

So far, we have pointed out that bioethicists who translate bioethical knowledge for use in medical AI, in addition to their core expertise within bioethics, must also possess interactional expertise in medicine, and AI. A trustworthy role of bioethicists in medical AI is also dependent upon interaction with other professions and groups beyond AI developers and medical personnel, such as other health professionals, experts in law and the regulation of AI, NGOs, patient organizations, and others. Indeed, the proper social role of AI depends on broad awareness and public deliberation over acceptable and unacceptable deployment and use of AI. Deciding who can impact on AI lifecycles in concrete cases is up for negotiation. In principle, investors, medical personnel, technical personnel, health economists, hospital administration, and patients or patient representatives could be invited. Then, due to asymmetries in expertise, resources, influence, and networks challenges of fairness, occur. For these reasons, ethics demands clarification on a case-to-case basis of "… Whose professional perspective may frame the initial understanding of the problem, what happens to dissenting voices, and what about patients' perspectives and autonomy?" (Bærøe, Gundersen et al., 2022) (p. 4). To keep it simple, we will limit the scope of potential stakeholders involved in processes related to the lifecycles of AI systems in health to include bioethicists, AI developers, and medical personnel.[1]

MULTIDISCIPLINARY AND SHARED ETHICAL COMPETENCY APPROACH

To probe further into the conditions for the role of trustworthy translational bioethicists, let us consider two approaches to bioethicists' collaboration with medical doctors and AI developers: the *multidisciplinary approach* and the *shared ethical competency approach*. These models clarify the competencies required to make bioethical translation trustworthy, but they should not be viewed as alternatives.

First, according to the *multidisciplinary approach*, collaboration and deliberation between the relevant professional groups and experts is the most promising way to include and integrate distinct ethical, medical, and technical expertise in the development, deployment, and use of AI in medicine. Such a collaborative view, which we have defended elsewhere for AI developers and medical doctors (Gundersen & Bærøe, 2022), alleviates the fact that the ethical design of algorithms becomes too remote and decoupled from the context of use and the medical and ethical standards that govern health care services. To be sure, research teams in medical AI, as found in technological companies and research institutions, often involve such collaboration. From an ethical perspective, this collaborative approach has the benefit of allowing developers, health professionals (and others), and ethicists to identify central challenges and benefits already in stages of development.

However, in terms of promoting trustworthiness, the multidisciplinary approach faces some challenges. It does not mitigate the fairness problem described above concerning who controls the agenda for discussing ethical issues in light of other interests being at play, e.g., time- and cost-effectiveness or treatment effectiveness. Another problem is that machine learning algorithms can be developed, trained, and tested in one cultural and national context and sold to public health care providers with different practices and standards. The context of use might contain differences in culture and standard of living that might influence the ethical evaluation of AI in significant ways. Such challenges threaten the contribution of trustworthy AI promoted by the described multidisciplinary model.

The multidisciplinary approach can be understood as assuming that bioethicists are the ones required to assess the ethical aspects of AI. However, we argue that an important part, perhaps the most important part, of making AI trustworthy rests not on the ethcial judgement of bioethicists, but on the ethical judgments of developers and health professionals based on their knowledge of, closeness to, and expertise in subtle nuances in clinical contexts and minor modeling changes. Bioethicists would need to be informed of these contextual factors and changes to be able to make ethical judgments about them. If ethcially trained, AI developers and medical personnel can spot the relevant issues directly according to their respective expertise training. Identification of ethcial issues in the technical and practical details of the transformative technology, would then not be dependent on whether bioethicists happens to ask for information.

Thus, this leads us to the preliminary conclusion that multidisciplinary approaches are not sufficient for medical AI to be trusted as developed under appropriate ethical overview. The ethical dimension of AI is better served when all agents involved in the lifecycles of AI possess *shared, basic bioethical* knowledge that allows medical personnel and AI developers to detect ethical issues on their own. This can be referred to as a *shared, ethical competency approach*. AI developers who have a substantial understanding of bioethics might ensure the ethical design of algorithms better than any other group or profession in society. Medical personnel who have a substantial understanding of bioethics might be more able to recognize ethical challenges related to the training data, the accuracy of the outcome data, and the social implications of introducing AI technologies in clinical care than bioethicists who lack clinical training. The multidisciplinary approach, where ethical competency was only one among many other disciplinary competencies, lacked the ability to protect ethical concerns from other interests. Supporting the team of agents involved in the development, deployment, and use of AI (and here we include all who may enter, as described above, including legal experts, health economists, investors, representatives of patients, etc.) with shared, basic bioethical competency can be helpful in mitigating strong interests that can undermine the focus on ethics. However, the shared ethical competency approach is no guarantee for justified trustworthiness in the face of imported AI technology developed under differerent social and cultural circumstances. This problem cannot be solved unless regulations that specify, in a detailed manner, what is ethically acceptable are implemented worldwide (Bærøe et al., 2020). While this could be a solution in theory, it is not feasible in practice. So, the shared, ethical competency model is likely the best approach we can hope for to support well-placed trust in that the ethics of medical AI is protected (Figure 15.1).

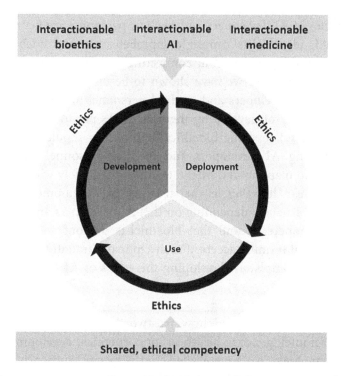

FIGURE 15.1 To promte trustworthy, ethical AI in medicine, agents need interactionable-bioethics, AI and medicine competencies, as well as shared, ethcial competency.

Interestingly, from a translational, bioethical perspective, we end up with a conclusion that the best way to save the trustworthiness of ethical medical AI, is not to insist on keeping the ethical authority within the bioethics camp. Rather, AI developers and medical personnel who are the ones closest to the technology and experiences of providing healthcare, are key agents in coupling the ethics to the development, deployment, and use. Bioethicists with interactional expertise can be trusted in mediating between the medical and AI expertise and policymakers and the public. At the same time, translational bioethicists can be trusted for being keen to investigate their own limitations and being open about their own shortcomings toward ensuring ethical medical AI.

To summarize we recommend that AI developers, medical personnel, and others involved in teams around AI development, deployment, and use in health gain the level of bioethical literacy that allows them to understand and communicate meaningfully with bioethicists. At the same time, translational bioethicist will, in addition to their insights into medicine (that is already framing their expertise on medical bioethics), have to gain a workable level of AI literacy to allow for interactable competency.

We are now left with the remaining problem of who should train the AI developers and medical personnel in the relevant ethics. Both traditional and translational approaches to bioethics are required. What the content of that teaching and learning process should be, how it should be integrated in educational programs and how decisions on this should be reached, are issues for future research. But as we have just the ethical competencies of AI developers and medical personnel are key for trust in those behind medical AI, bioethicists cannot comprehensively and adequately cover the whole competency training required in connecting and interpreting ethics in the life-cycles of medical AI. The area we have shown to be uncovered by bioethical competency is left for the AI developers and medical personnel to claim authority over and achieve the responsibility of developing themselves. As per today, it is not clear what this ethics that transcends existing bioethical approaches should look like. Perhaps it will require pioneering AI developers and medical personnel with addtional, full training in bioethics to map out and integrate ethics adequately within these uncovered areas. What seems clear, however, is that trustworthy development, deployment and use of medical AI are crucially depending on that AI developers and medical personnel acquire bioethical competency and that bioethicists without additional, full competencies in AI or medical training accept that disciplinary limitation prevents them from directly assessing and completely developing the ethics of AI lifecycles.

CONCLUSION

In this chapter, we have discussed how trustworthy bioethicists can contribute to lifecycles of artificial intelligence in health to support ethical development, deployment, and use of AI technology. We have argued that a specific approach labeled "transla-tional ethics" that involves bioethicists with self-reflexivity as regards who, how, what, when, and where ethical assessments are made, and by that also awareness of limita-tions (and not merely opportunities) to what assessments and decision-making bioe-thicists should rightfully claim authority over. Indeed, translational ethics provides the public with more reasons to trust such self-reflexive bioethical approaches, than ap-proaches without targeted aims to avoid undue use of power and influence to settle ethical issues. We probed even deeper into the role of translational bioethicist by discussing two models, the *multidisciplinary approach* and *shared ethical competency approach* for how bioethics can contribute in decision-making within the lifecycles of AI systems in trustworthy ways. The *shared ethical competency approach*, which re-quires that all the team members involved in developing, deploying, and using AI gain bioethical competency in order to support the ethical dimension of trustworthy AI, occurs as the strongest anchored approach to deal with strong economic and political interests with the potential to oppose ethical solutions. Therefore, we conclude that for AI in health to become trustworthy, there must be substantial collaboration across established disciplinary boundaries, based on a shared, fundamental ethical compe-tence institutionalized in a team-based practice following the lifecycles of AI. Bioethicists should have the role of training team members in traditional and trans-lational bioethics but the specific content of this teaching and learning process, and how decisions on this should be reached, are issues for future research. While we examined the use of medical AI in health in this chapter, it seems fair to assume that the shared ethical competency approach (with its implications), could also be relevant within other fields and policy areas in which AI is applied such as education, public welfare services, and criminal justice system.

NOTE

1 Clearly, legal expertise is also required. Due to the complicated relationship between ethics and law, we leave it for future research to discuss how legal experts should be included in the model of required expertise we propose here.

REFERENCES

Biddle, J. B. (2020). On predicting recidivism: Epistemic risk, tradeoffs, and values in machine learning. *Canadian Journal of Philosophy*, 1–21. 10.1017/can.2020.27

Bærøe, K. (2014). Translational ethics: An analytical framework of translational movements between theory and practice and a sketch of a comprehensive approach. *BMC medical ethics*, *15*(1), 71.

Bærøe, K., Jansen, M., & Kerasidou, A. (2020). Machine learning in healthcare: Exceptional technologies require exceptional ethics. *American Journal of Bioethics*, 20(11): 48–51.

Bærøe, K., & Gundersen, T. (2019). Social impact under severe uncertainty: The role of neuroethicists at the intersection of neuroscience, ai, ethics, and policymaking. *AJOB Neuroscience*, *10*(3), 117–119. doi: 10.1080/21507740.2019.1632965

Bærøe, K., Gundersen, T., Henden, E., & Rommetveit, K. (2022). Can medical algorithms be fair? Three ethical quandaries and one dilemma. *BMJ Health & Care Informatics*, *29*(1), e100445. doi: 10.1136/bmjhci-2021-100445

Bærøe, K., Kerasidou, A., Dunn, M., & Teig, I. L. (2022). Pursuing impact in research: Towards an ethical approach. *BMC Medical Ethics*, *23*(1):37. doi: 10.1186/s12910-022-00754-3

Bærøe, K., Miyata-Sturm, A., & Henden, E. (2020). How to achieve trustworthy artificial intelligence for health. *World Health Organization. Bulletin of the World Health Organization*, *98*(4), 257–262.

Char, D. S., Abràmoff, M. D., & Feudtner, C. (2020). Identifying ethical considerations for machine learning healthcare applications. *The American Journal of Bioethics*, *20*(11), 7–17. doi: 10.1080/15265161.2020.1819469

Collins, H., & Evans, R. (2006). The third wave of science studies: Studies of expertise and experience. In Selinger, C., & Crease, R.P. (Eds). *The philosophy of expertise* (pp. 39–110). New York, NY: Columbia University Press.

Cribb, A. (2010). Translational ethics? The theory–practice gap in medical ethics. *Journal of Medical Ethics*, *36*(4), 207–210.

Danaher, J. (2016). The threat of algocracy: Reality, resistance and accommodation. *Philosophy & Technology*, *29*(3), 245–268.

de Roux, D., Perez, B., Moreno, A., del Pilar Villamil, M., & Figueroa, C. (2018). Tax fraud detection for under-reporting declarations using an unsupervised machine learning approach. Proceedings of the 24th ACM SIGKDD International Conference on Knowledge Discovery & Data Mining.

Eide, K. T. (2020). Cesarean section on maternal request in Norway: A qualitative and normative study of birth counseling and decision-making. Phd-thesis. Bergen: University of Bergen.

European Commission, Directorate-General for Communications Networks, Content and Technology. (2019). *Ethics guidelines for trustworthy AI*. European Commission: Brussels./ 10.2759/177365.

Evans, J. H. (2012). *The history and future of bioethics: A sociological view*. Oxford University Press.

Grote, T., & Berens, P. (2020). On the ethics of algorithmic decision-making in healthcare. *Journal of Medical Ethics*, *46*(3), 205–211.

Gundersen, T., & Bærøe, K. (2022). The future ethics of artificial intelligence in medicine: Making sense of collaborative models. *Science and Engineering Ethics, 28*(2), 1–16.

Kerasidou, A. (2020). Artificial intelligence and the ongoing need for empathy, compassion and trust in healthcare. *Bulletin of the World Health Organization, 98*(4), 245.

Liakos, K. G., Busato, P., Moshou, D., Pearson, S., & Bochtis, D. (2018). Machine learning in agriculture: A review. *Sensors, 18*(8), 2674.

Lukes, S. (2005). *Power: A radical view*. United Kingdom: Macmillan Education.

Mayer, R. C., Davis, J. H., & Schoorman, F. D. (1995). An integrative model of organizational trust. *Academy of management review, 20*(3), 709–734.

McDougall, R. J. (2019). Computer knows best? The need for value-flexibility in medical AI. *Journal of Medical Ethics, 45*(3), 156–160.

O'Neill, O. (2018). Linking trust to trustworthiness. *International Journal of Philosophical Studies, 26*, 293–300. 10.1080/09672559.2018.1454637

PytlikZillig, L. M., & Kimbrough, C. D. (2016). Consensus on conceptualizations and definitions of trust: Are we there yet? In Shockley, E., Neal, T. M. S., PytlikZillig, L. M., & Bornstein, B. H. (Eds.), *Interdisciplinary perspectives on trust: Towards theoretical and methodological integration* (pp. 17–47). Springer International Publishing: Cham.

Reagan, M. (2021). Understanding bias and fairness in AI systems. *Towards data science*, accessed July 3rd.

Suresh, H., & Guttag, J. V. (2019). A framework for understanding unintended consequences of machine learning. *arXiv preprint arXiv:1901.10002* 2.

Topol, E. (2019). *Deep medicine: How artificial intelligence can make healthcare human again*. Hachette UK.

Wester, G., Bærøe, K., & Norheim, O.F. (2019). Towards theoretically robust evidence on health equity: a systematic approach to contextualising equity-relevant randomised controlled trials. *Journal of Medical Ethics, 45*(1), 54–59. 10.1136/medethics-2017-104610

IV

AI and Humans: Philosophical Reflections

Can an AI Analyze Arguments? Argument-Checking and the Challenges of Assessing the Quality of Online Information

Ruben Brave[a], Federica Russo[b], Ondrej Uzovic[c], and Jean Wagemans[b]

[a]CEO Entelligence.nl and Co-founder Internet Society NL MMGA Working Group, Amsterdam, The Netherlands
[b]Faculty of Humanities, University of Amsterdam, Amsterdam, The Netherlands
[c]Independent Software Engineer, Bratislava, Slovakia

CONTENTS

INFORMATION OVERLOAD IN THE DIGITAL ERA

Information and communication technologies (ICTs) profoundly transformed science and everyday life. From the use of digital computers to big data, from re-shaping social interactions and significantly altering the formation and perception of the self

DOI: 10.1201/9781003261247-20

(Zandbergen, 2011), it is not an overstatement to say that ICTs mark a revolution, the *digital* revolution. Specifically, technological developments in information and communication distribution and processing have increased the speed and amount of information shared. This has happened already in the past, in the shift from pre-history to history, and not to hyper-history. The information cycle of occurrence, transmission, process, management, and use of information underwent significant changes through time: in pre-history, we were not able to record information, with oral transmission of knowledge. The advent of writing made us enter a new phase, that of history. We live now in the *zettabyte* era. Digital technologies have changed the landscape, marking the beginning of hyper-history. However, the difference between history and hyper-history lies not merely in the quantity and speed of information that is transmitted, but mostly in *how* it is transmitted and processed. The hallmark of ICTs since the digital revolution is creating, using, and rediscovering *connections* (Floridi, 2014, 2015). Digital technologies allow for many more *connections* to be made, and it is in this sense the concepts such as "speed of evolution of knowledge" and "collective intelligence" (Lévy, 1997) or as "connective intelligence" (De Kerckhove, 1998) have been introduced.

It is often assumed that the *amount* of information circulating is the root cause of other problems, and notably of the *quality* of information circulating online. Some authors have challenged this premise (Altay et al., 2021). In this chapter, we don't directly engage with this dispute about quantity vs quality of information. We take it that the sheer amount of information human internet users can handle poses important challenges for our material capacities in selecting and assessing it, also for time constraints. However, in this chapter, we focus on aspects related to the *quality of online information*. In particular, we focus on the handling of information internet users are confronted with, as well as currently available solutions or coping strategies (Wardle & Derakhshan, 2017). There is a wealth of research done and in progress about the notion of information overload and on how individuals react to it. Some studies model interactions among individuals in online spaces (Jones et al., 2004; White & Dorman, 2000); other studies focus on how information overload affects our experience as consumers (Li, 2017) or as health information seekers (Swar et al., 2017); yet others look at our social interactions and interpersonal trust (Beaudoin, 2008; Ellwart et al., 2015) or at the influence of information overload on how we see ourselves (Palfrey & Gasser, 2016) and our relationship to knowledge (Wardle & Derakhshan, 2017) and news consumption (Marwick & Lewis, 2017).

Ultimately the problem of online information quality is that it is difficult to establish what is true, and who or what is a reliable source, and this is the case whether we are overloaded with "good" or with "bad" information. While these are well-known and studied problems (Borg, 2019; Brave, n.d.; MMGA, 2019; Roetzel, 2019), in this paper we take a look at the problem of online information quality from the perspective of argumentation theory and artificial intelligence. In particular, we present and discuss an ongoing project to develop a glass-box AI engine called KRINO – from Greek, to judge, criticize, reason – capable of parsing written text on the discourse level and analyzing the arguments thereby contained. KRINO is designed to assist users with argument-checking, i.e., the process of analyzing the characteristics of arguments in order to be able to apply domain and user-specific criteria for assessing them. We describe the set-up and basic features of KRINO and explain how it can assist human annotators in a project undertaken by the Dutch organization Internet Society Netherlands Make Media Great Again Working Group (*shortened MMGA*) that is aimed at improving the quality of online information in settings varying from online news outlets to social media. The joint project is motivated by the need to empower internet users to better analyze online information and to distinguish between "good" and "bad" information, or between information, mis- and dis- and mal-information. We explain the prospects and challenges of combining the KRINO and MMGA projects on argument-checking and discuss the societal and computational relevance of this project.

The chapter is structured as follows. In Section 2, we discuss fact-checking, a valuable activity often presented as the latest frontier to fight mis-, dis-, and mal-information. We explain why, while valuable, fact-checking is not enough to address the information overload and to improve upon the quality of online information. In Section 3, we introduce argument-checking as a distinct approach to argumentation, flexible and agile, able to be used in a variety of settings and by individuals with varying levels of education and expertise to check the quality of pieces of online information. In Section 4, we present work in progress to support the process of argument-checking with a glass-box AI engine called KRINO. The project of developing an AI able to analyze arguments is motivated by our specific take on the problem of poor quality of online information, and the prospects of argument-checking to address it. In Section 5, we conclude the chapter with a reflection on the societal relevance of argument-checking and of KRINO.

FROM FACT-CHECKING TO ARGUMENT-CHECKING

Fact-checking isn't a new phenomenon, and can be rightly considered as a key journalistic action since at least the 1920s (Fabry, 2017); nowadays, we consider its mission to debunk false statements, especially in politics, but not only. There are several kinds of organizations involved in fact-checking, and world-wide. Fact-checking involves numerous professional figures, also outside journalism, and it is growing in proposing approaches and methods to select and then assess claims made in the public sphere.

As a process, fact-checking seeks to verify presented information (e.g. text, video, sound) in order to promote conformity to facts and correctness of reporting. Fact-checking can be conducted before (*ex ante*) or after (*ex post*) the information is published or otherwise disseminated. While *ex ante* fact-checking aims to identify errors so that the information can be corrected or even rejected before dissemination, *ex post* fact-checking is often followed by a written or visual report of inaccuracies. Internal fact-checking is part of the regular journalistic process and is done in-house by the publisher; in case the presented information is analyzed by a third party, the process is categorized as external fact-checking (Graves & Amazeen, 2019). Examples of organizations devoted to the latter are FactCheck.org and PolitiFact in the US and Full Fact in the UK. This type of fact-checking first emerged in the US in the early 2000s and, after it grew in relevance, started to spread to other countries (Graves & Amazeen, 2019).

Fact-checking and its methodologies are increasingly the subject of academic and non-academic evaluation. While generally considered a valuable activity, it has also been criticized, not only for employing questionable methodology regarding the selection of statements and the choice of criteria for evaluating them but also for its limited effectiveness in fighting mis- and disinformation (see, for instance, (Barrera Rodriguez et al., 2017; Nyhan & Reifler, 2010, 2012; Thorson, 2016; Uscinski & Butler, 2013; Wintersieck, 2017)).

To some extent, fact-checking indeed seems to correct perceptions among citizens (Drutman, 2020) although it depends on the way it is conducted (Clayton et al., 2020). The importance of fact-checking notwithstanding, its effectiveness is also under close scrutiny, with important considerations about whether the effects of debunking information last long enough, which groups are more or less susceptible to change their beliefs or not, etc. (Nyhan 2021; Porter and Wood 2021). As information overload is real, the risk of repeatedly being exposed to fake news is only to be expected. This can increase the perceived truthfulness of fake news (Pennycook et al., 2018). Actually, the mere fact that people encounter a specific fact-check frequently can create distorted memories of the veracity of false claims, the "illusion of truth" effect (Skurnik et al., 2005). Overall, the current status seems to be that the correctional impact of fact-checking on people's beliefs is questionable because the effectiveness is influenced by preexisting beliefs, ideology, and knowledge on the side of the information receiver (Walter et al., 2020).

Apart from these criticisms, it has been observed there is a significant limitation of the scope of fact-checking in that it only evaluates the truth of isolated statements of fact. As Plug and Wagemans (2020, pp. 236–237) put it:

> Independent of their being true or false, statements of fact may fulfill an argumentative function in the discourse, in which case they are put forward to establish or increase the acceptability of the arguer's point of view. […] [The] scope [of fact-checking] is relatively limited in that it only involves the assessment of the truth of an isolated statement of fact. It does not address the argumentative relationship between that statement and the claim it intends to support, nor any other aspects of the rhetorical design of the discourse.

Although we acknowledge the relevance and merits of fact-checking (and of the scholarship that studies it), we think it can be supplemented with argument-checking to drive a substantial change in improving the quality of online information. As anticipated above, fact-checking doesn't cover all aspects of debunking misinformation and fake news. Statements of fact are often used to support the acceptability of other claims, which can be statements of fact, value or policy – see Plug and Wagemans (2020, pp. 245–49) for analyses of examples of the ways in which statements of fact can be embedded in arguments. Given this embeddedness, many problems regarding the quality of information remain outside of the limited scope of fact-checking: empirical statements expressing correct (or roughly correct) facts can be used in bad reasoning. All in all, in a good argument, there is more than correctness of the facts. For these reasons, verifying the quality of arguments themselves seems a necessary and fundamental part of the information quality control process, which is the approach we present in the next section.

ARGUMENT-CHECKING AND ONLINE INFORMATION

In this section, we present our approach to argument-checking, qua human annotation. Different from most formal logical approaches, our approach is suitable for individuals of varying educational levels and enables people to analyze and evaluate *natural* arguments, i.e., arguments expressed in natural language and encountered in their everyday lives, for instance on social media, websites, or any type of online platform.

The activity of argument-checking requires a set of skills or competencies for interpreting persuasive discourse, whether that is a single persuasive message or a complete text aimed at convincing the reader to believe something or to do something (Wagemans, Forthcoming). Among these competences are, first of all, "argument detection", i.e., finding out what the main claim is that the author of the discourse wants to convey to their audience and which arguments have been put forward in support of that claim. Then, the reader or listener must find out how the argumentative elements contained in the discourse hang together, thus creating a structured picture of its argumentative fabric. This competence can be called "argument mapping". Further, in order to be able to judge the quality of the argumentation, one would need to zoom in on the individual arguments on the map and study the relationships of support between the main claim and the chains of argument put forward in support of it. Guidelines for this activity of "argument type identification" have been developed in the so-called Argument Type Identification Procedure (ATIP) (Wagemans, 2021). Once it has become clear what types of arguments are represented in the text or discussion, "argument assessment" can take place by asking specific critical questions relevant to their evaluation. To assist the analyst in this final task, specific evaluation procedures have been developed such as the Comprehensive Assessment Procedure for Natural Argument (CAPNA) (Hinton & Wagemans, 2022).

The activity of argument-checking can thus be divided into a chain of smaller activities, with the output of the previous link in that chain functioning as the input of the next: subsequently, the arguments are detected, they are mapped, their type is identified, and they are evaluated. Each of the individual links in this sequence requires different competences. The level that can be reached in acquiring these competences may vary among individuals, relying on an interdependent cluster of factors: their ability to recognize reasoning expressed in language, their knowledge of rhetorical strategies for producing argumentative discourse, and the length and intensity of relevant experience in processing, understanding, and assessing the quality of such discourse. Our procedural approach to argument evaluation, however, enables the development of a fine-grained training program aimed at enhancing people's competences in specific (sub)skills of argument-checking. Training in argument-checking can happen at various levels of education (for instance, students at various stages of education, early careers in research, etc.), and be tailored to specific domains of application (for instance, argumentation in legal settings, or compliance in the automotive sector, evidence assessment in the health domain, etc.). Moreover, the above procedures can be automated to a certain extent and implemented into the design of argument technology. This is because ATIP and CAPNA, unlike other approaches in argument evaluation, are quasi-algorithmic procedures by design and do not work with predetermined forms of valid arguments (Wagemans, 2020; Hinton & Wagemans, 2022).

This brings us to the basic idea behind our joint project, which is that, indirectly and in the long term, we can improve the quality of online information by increasing the literacy of individuals. By providing them with training in argument-checking and tools to help them perform such checking, we aim to "immunize" people to low levels of information quality and enable them to (pro)actively contribute to a better online information exchange. More specifically, the project is aimed at:

i. Increasing the literacy of individuals (as online *users*) to make themselves immune against the negative effects of dis- and mis-information.

ii. Empowering individuals (as online *agents*) to intervene and block in appropriate ways episodes of dis- and misinformation, of trolling, or other.

iii. Teaching individuals (as online content *producers*) to share and disseminate high quality information online.

iv. Certifying the (increased) level of critical thinking via a Comprehensive Measure of Argumentation Skills (CMAS).

We aim to develop a CMAS precisely to be able to continuously tailor and fine-tune training on argument-checking to specific target groups, with varying degrees of educational levels and with different domains of expertise and background knowledge. The course "From fact-checking to argument checking" part of the Honors Programme run at the Institute for Interdisciplinary Studies at the University of Amsterdam, and offered for three academic years beginning in 2021–22, is a first concrete step in this direction.

For accomplishing these aims, we take inspiration and guidance from the field of critical pedagogy (Freire et al., 2014; Knight et al., 2020). Critical pedagogy promotes a specific approach to education, and notably one in which we strive to *empower* students, citizens, and, in our case, users and producers of online content. Applied to argument-checking, the idea is to empower users and producers of online information by awakening their critical consciousness, and also by providing them with tools that they can put to use: argument-checking as a critical pedagogy approach to digital literacy (Brave et al., 2022).

Developing a theoretical, practical, and pedagogical approach to argument-checking is also part of a collaboration with MMGA, within which we are designing training programmes on argument-checking, tailored to different audiences. MMGA is a blockchain-based annotation platform (with hundreds of registrants) in which screened and trained expert and/or critical thinking readers can annotate high-impact news sites such as NU.nl and AD.nl, two of the "Big Four" largest Dutch online news platforms. MMGA has set up a collaboration between publishers and a screened community of readers, viewers, and listeners to jointly counteract the effects of misinformation and improve the quality of media. To achieve this goal, MMGA has built a transparent system for actionable suggestions from this community pool, which functions as an annotation platform and has been tested on NU.nl, a major Dutch news outlet with 7–8 million visitors. The test involved a group of critical and knowledgeable NU.nl readers (called "annotators") who were motivated to critically assess journalism news articles; annotators received instructions and were checked for their capabilities before being allowed to annotate. They then offered suggestions to increase the journalistic quality through the balanced use of sources and clearer transfer of information (Brave, 2019, 2021).

The automatic detection of fake news through natural language processing, machine learning, and network analysis is high on the agenda of several tech enterprises (Islam et al., 2021). The main proposition is that autonomously working systems will be able to categorize information as "fake news" and help to decrease the probability of users encountering it (Pennycook & Rand, 2021). As we remarked above, the procedures for argument-checking can be (partially) automated and implemented into tools that can assist the human user in analyzing and evaluating the quality of online information. This is currently done in the KRINO project, which we present in the next section. In our view, the collaboration between MMGA, with its involvement of human annotators, and the developers of the KRINO AI engine strengthens the shared mission of reversing the trend of an increased amount of disinformation, fake news, and poor journalism that is progressively dividing the world and having more impactful societal and psychological consequences each day.

AUTOMATING ARGUMENT-CHECKING: THE KRINO PROJECT

The general aims of the collaboration between MMGA and KRINO are to develop argument-checking as a complementary activity to fact-checking, to have annotators rather than experts carry out this activity, and to help them do so by partially automating the process of analyzing and evaluating arguments (Nieman, 2020).

As we explained in Section 3, the activity of argument-checking requires various competences, some of which are more easily automatable than others. Moreover, in developing KRINO, we also consider the *desirability* of automation and the role of users in relationship to machines as a vital issue. In our view, even if some parts of the sequence of activities involved in argument-checking would be fully automatable, the user should always remain in the lead and the delegation of tasks or subtasks to the machine should never imply loss of control or a shift of responsibility. Nevertheless, the project of (partly) automating the process of argument evaluation has value. Notably, some steps in the normalization of arguments in natural language can be difficult for users with no formal or extensive training in linguistics, pragmatics, or argumentation theory, a task KRINO can assist with. Also, assuming that we are able to build a sufficiently comprehensive and accurate (domain-specific) knowledge base, KRINO can be of great help in assisting users to check the validity of arguments in this respect. We return to our stance about the relations between humans and machines in Section 5.

Here, we further elaborate on the following aspect. We want the user to remain in the lead because we strive to build KRINO as an inspectable, glass-box AI engine that communicates with the user in natural language. It is not designed as a fully-autonomous engine, but rather as an aid for human agents in the analysis of written text and the disentanglement of critical aspects of the underlying argument structure.

Apart from being designed as an inspectable AI engine, KRINO is also designed to be use-case specific. It may help users carrying out a variety of activities falling under the umbrella of argument-checking, for instance:

1. Checking the logical consistency of technical documents such as software requirement specifications.

2. Assisting the analysis of legal reasoning, for instance by checking consistency between claims and jurisprudence.

3. Assisting doctors to find the correct diagnosis, for instance by checking the consistency between the proposed diagnosis and the available knowledge base, from an argumentative perspective.

4. Identifying fake news and conspiracy theories.

5. Analyzing and assessing arguments put forth in online discussions.

The logic of KRINO is based on the theoretical model combining the linguistic representation framework of Constructive Adpositional Grammars (Gobbo & Benini, 2011) and the argument classification framework of the Periodic Table of Arguments (Wagemans, 2016, 2019, 2020) into an integrated framework for representing linguistic and pragmatic aspects of argumentative discourse (Gobbo et al., 2019). The linguistic part allows parsing a human text into machine structures containing syntactic and semantic information. So the goal of the parsing is not just to recognize particular words and their classes (e.g., nouns, verbs, adjectives, etc.) but also to acquire semantic information carried by the text. Therefore, the parsing algorithm is based on the constructive dictionary which is defined in terms of Constructive Adpositional Grammars. In contrast to traditional dictionaries, the constructive dictionary contains the list of lexemes (i.e., morphemes referring to the real world) and the list of construction rules (including morphology, syntax, and phraseology). Therefore, the parsing is capable of recognizing grammatical aspects (e.g., suffixes, etc.) and through construction rules understand their semantic meaning (e.g. past tense, plural number, etc.). The result of such parsing is then a decomposition of the text into a tree structure containing morphemes and their structural and semantic attributes. The tree structure is then suitable for further processing by high-level algorithms. For instance, if the tree represents an argument, it can be transformed (without changing the meaning) into a normalized form tree intended for the argument evaluation. The constructive dictionary as well as the tree structure are language independent (i.e., the smallest lexical item for KRINO is a morpheme and not a word). Therefore, by providing lexemes and construction rules KRINO can be used with various languages. This, we think, is an important asset of KRINO from the perspective of linguistic justice (Van Parijs, 2011) and epistemic diversity (Gobbo & Russo, 2020).

The approach to argument-checking presented in Section 3 enables KRINO to recognize arguments which can be then evaluated and checked if they are consistent with the knowledge base. Then, using the linguistic part, KRINO can formulate the result (answer) in human language and is also able to provide the explanation of why it came to that conclusion (i.e., why the argument is acceptable or not). The argument evaluation is based on the theory of the Periodic Table of Arguments and the knowledge base (i.e., factual knowledge provided to KRINO). First, by using the knowledge base, it evaluates if the premise and conclusion clauses are true and find the chain of statements proving why they are true. Then it identifies the argument form and uses proving chains of premise and conclusion to find the relation (lever) between the conclusion and the premise. If the relation exists, the argument is evaluated as acceptable. We provide here a very simple example of how KRINO is set to analyze an argument, which will hopefully be useful to readers with relevant background in computer science and closely related fields. The example is taken from https://periodic-table-of-arguments.org/periodic-table-of-arguments/beta-quadrant/argument-from-analogy/, which contains information about its source, an explanation of how to reformulate the natural argument into its canonized form, and an analysis of its basic characteristics. Here, we focus on the way in which KRINO evaluates the argument.

Argument to evaluate:

Cycling on the grass is prohibited because walking on the grass is prohibited.

Knowledge-base:

```
Walking on the grass damages the grass.
Cycling on the grass damages the grass.
If an activity damages the grass then it is prohibited.
```

KRINO steps:

1. Argument form: a is X because b is X. a (Cycling on the grass) X (is prohibited) because b (walking on the grass) X (is prohibited).

2. Argument lever: Relationship of analogy between a (Cycling on the grass) and b (walking on the grass).

3. Premise clause "walking on the grass is prohibited" is true (according to the domain-specific items in the knowledge-base).

4. The lever, i.e. the relationship of analogy between a (Cycling on the grass) and b (walking on the grass) is sound (both damage the grass and that is relevant for being forbidden according to the domain-specific items in the knowledge-base).

5. Conclusion clause "Cycling on the grass is prohibited" is true (it is based on a true premise and a sound lever).

The step-wise procedure of this example illustrates how KRINO is able to find links between parts of the argument, if and when there is relevant and appropriate information in the knowledge base. The automatization of argument-checking is, by design, always dependent on some background knowledge that is constructed or validated by the user. This means that KRINO will be able to automatically extract new information from the analyzed text and propose to add items to the knowledge base but these self-learning algorithms remain fully inspectable by the user.

At the time of writing, KRINO is able to analyze simple arguments expressed in natural language, and we expect KRINO to be able to handle more complex arguments, and within a variety of specific contexts, in the near future.

With the aid of KRINO, we aim to make the verification of information, in terms of correctness and completeness of an argument, affordable and accessible to every competent user, resulting in a corroborated belief about analyzed arguments and decision-making. We also provide a tool which gives the user the possibility of enhancing, upgrading, or improving their cognitive environment (and the information they analyze) by making it more transparent, rational, and comprehensible. KRINO complies with standards of transparency because of the principles chosen for developing and designing AI algorithms. KRINO AI algorithms also comply with standards of explainability because they are designed as logic-based. This means that KRINO is designed to be capable of providing users with *reasons* why it came to a certain solution. For instance, combining KRINO with machine learning (neural network) can significantly improve the quality of AI results. KRINO and the results it produces are not an opaque box, and they also crucially depend on the user's choices and domain-specific knowledge at various stages of the process, which includes evaluation and usage of the knowledge base, to be tailored to specific use cases.

To sum up: KRINO designed as an inspectable self-learning AI that will be capable of analyzing arguments in natural language and of forming the knowledge base needed for that purpose. We develop KRINO as an open-source project using the GitHub platform and so all its algorithms are publicly available and inspectable by anyone.

THE SOCIETAL RELEVANCE OF ARGUMENT-CHECKING

In this final section, we explain how the human annotation project of MMGA and the machine annotation project of KRINO can mutually reinforce one another and we discuss what the societal relevance of the combination of the two projects is.

To begin with, the whole project of improving the quality of information via argument-checking is premised on the idea that values such as collegiality or intellectual honesty and humility are the ones we wish to promote (Aberdein & Cohen, 2016; Dalgleish et al., 2017; Kidd, 2016; Tanesini, 2021). With argument-checking, users, agents, and content producers do not act as draconian judges on the mess of online information, but contribute to the quality of information that is shared, distributed, and equally accessible to anyone. With this approach to argument-checking and its automated engine KRINO, we aim to adhere and enhance important ethical considerations. For instance, it is worth distinguishing contexts in which arguments are offered, types of arguments, and the kind of moral implications that go with them. It matters why and how a given argument is used and it is important not to try to circumvent addressees or hide information.

Also, the project of developing procedures for argument-checking, in both the human and machine annotation variants, aims at improving the digital literacy of users, agents, and content producers, which is an important topic on the digital agenda world-wide. The potential of Human-AI collaboration to combat fake news has already been demonstrated by the project called Demaskuok, which means "debunk" in Lithuanian (see https://www.debunkeu.org/methodology). The AI was developed by the Lithuanian defence ministry in collaboration with Google's Digital News Initiative and Delfi, a media group headquartered in Lithuania's capital, which is able to detect within two minutes of its publication the "patient zeros of fake news" and sends those reports to human specialists for further analysis.

The road ahead of us is steep and we are fully aware of the many challenges faced by both projects. AI, in fact, other than being of potential help in addressing the problem of information quality, may also be a major spreader of fake news (Hao, 2020; Knight, 2021; Lyons, 2020). And so projects like KRINO may be like David in front of Goliath. One challenge of MMGA is that we will never reach enough websites or media platforms or have enough annotators. This is certainly true and this is why, next to projects and initiatives like ours, we also need *systemic* interventions, and these have to be at the level of education, promoted in public spaces and by public institutions. A challenge of KRINO is that it is not intended to be a fully automated AI, and so KRINO users *always* need *some* level of understanding of argumentation theory. KRINO is not a magic bullet to magically turn the internet into a basket of all good pieces of information. It is instead a tool to *help*, where help is needed. These two challenges, together, show the importance of digital literacy, as a necessary component of the education of newer and older generations. But more *literacy* on its own, will not do. Another challenge of KRINO is that, although it is accompanied with a thorough ethics chart, after all it is (and will be) open source. This means that we can't anticipate and prevent all uses of KRINO. What we need is digital literacy *and* cultivation of epistemic and moral virtues in a digital environment. It is high time to reconnect ethics and science and technology in a constructive and productive way. In our view, ethics not a watchdog, or an exercise that happens "after the fact" only (Ratti & Stapleford, 2021; Russo, 2018). We strive to build an ethics stance into our practices, from the set up of training on argument checking to the design of KRINO, specifying, at each and every stage of both these processes, which values guide our practices.

Despite all these challenges, we think MMGA and KRINO projects are worth pursuing. The digital revolution has already happened. It is high time also to move beyond utopian or dystopian attitudes toward technologies (Russo, 2018). What we need more than anything else are projects that believe in the potential of technologies, and that pursue their design and implementations for the common good.

Finally, by combining KRINO and MMGA, we aim to promote a specific normative point of view about the relation between humans and machines, whereby machines remain at the service of us humans in general, and specifically in this project to improve the quality of online information. We do not buy into the hype of full automation. The question is not posed at the technical but at the normative level. We believe in the value-based *interaction* between humans and machines, and it is in this sense that machines need us more than we do (Russo, 2022). In the footsteps of pioneer of cybernetics Norbert Wiener (1950), we think of technology in general, and AI specifically, as an applied morality, over and above the continuous development and improvement of technical capacities.

REFERENCES

Aberdein, A., & Cohen, D. H. (2016). Introduction: Virtues and arguments. *Topoi*, *35*(2), 339–343. 10.1007/s11245-016-9366-3

Altay, S., Berriche, M., & Acerbi, A. (2021). Misinformation on Misinformation: Conceptual and Methodological Challenges. 10.31234/osf.io/edqc8

Barrera Rodriguez, O. D., Guriev, S. M., Henry, E., & Zhuravskaya, E. (2017). Facts, alternative facts, and fact checking in times of post-truth politics. *Journal of Public Economics*, *182*, 104123. 10.2139/ssrn.3004631

Beaudoin, C. E. (2008). Explaining the relationship between internet use and interpersonal trust: Taking into account motivation and information overload. *Journal of Computer-Mediated Communication*, *13*(3), 550–568. 10.1111/j.1083-6101.2008.00410.x

Borg, S. (2019). We are edging to a world where reality is a matter of personal opinion. *2019*. https://timesofmalta.com/articles/view/we-are-edging-to-a-world-where-reality-is-a-matter-of-personal-opinion.725056

Brave, R. (n.d.). *Post-truth Conference Malta 2019—Talk on Media, Journalism & Fake News*. https://open.spotify.com/episode/3WzhTSRe1TSxnZQKz6e7iN

Brave, R. (2019). Introducing "public annotations" in journalism. *Medium.Com*. Introducing "public annotations" in journalism

Brave, R. (2021). Public rebuttal, reflection and responsibility or an inconvenient answer to fake news. In Grech, A. (Ed.), *Media, technology and education in a post-truth society* (pp. 145–154). Emerald Publishing Limited. 10.1108/978-1-80043-906-120211011

Brave, R., Russo, F., & Wagemans, J. H. M. (2022). Argument-checking: A critical pedagogy approach to digital literacy. *AIUCD 2022 - Digital Cultures. Intersections: Philosophy, Arts, Media. Proceedings of the 11th National Conference, Lecce, 2022*, 245–248.

Clayton, K., Blair, S., Busam, J. A., Forstner, S., Glance, J., Green, G., Kawata, A., Kovvuri, A., Martin, J., Morgan, E., Sandhu, M., Sang, R., Scholz-Bright, R., Welch, A. T., Wolff, A. G., Zhou, A., & Nyhan, B. (2020). Real solutions for fake news? Measuring the effectiveness of general warnings and fact-check tags in reducing belief in false stories on social media. *Political Behavior*, *42*(4), 1073–1095. 10.1007/s11109-019-09533-0

Dalgleish, A., Girard, P., & Davies, M. (2017). Critical thinking, bias and feminist philosophy: Building a better framework through collaboration. *Informal Logic*, *37*(4), 351–369. 10.22329/il.v37i4.4794

De Kerckhove, D. (1998). *Connected intelligence: The arrival of the web society*. London: Kogan Page.

Drutman, L. (2020, June 3). Fact-Checking misinformation can work. But it might not be enough. *FiveThirtyEight*. https://fivethirtyeight.com/features/why-twitters-fact-check-of-trump-might-not-be-enough-to-combat-misinformation/

Ellwart, T., Happ, C., Gurtner, A., & Rack, O. (2015). Managing information overload in virtual teams: Effects of a structured online team adaptation on cognition and performance. *European Journal of Work and Organizational Psychology*, *24*(5), 812–826. 10.1080/1359432 X.2014.1000873

Fabry, M. (2017). Here's How the First Fact-Checkers Were Able to Do Their Jobs Before the Internet. Time Magazine. Retrieved July 29, 2022 from https://time.com/4858683/ fact-checking-history/

Floridi, L. (2014). *The 4th revolution: How the infosphere is reshaping human reality* (First edition). Oxford University Press.

Floridi, L. (Ed.). (2015). *The onlife manifesto: Being human in a hyperconnected era* (1st ed. 2015). Springer International Publishing: Imprint: Springer. 10.1007/978-3-319-04093-6

Freire, P., Ramos, M. B., & Macedo, D. P. (2014). *Pedagogy of the oppressed: 30th anniversary edition*. United Kingdom: Bloomsbury Publishing.

Gobbo, F., & Benini, M. (2011). *Constructive adpositional grammars: Foundations of constructive linguistics*. Cambridge Scholars Publishing.

Gobbo, F., Benini, M., & Wagemans, J. H. M. (2019). Annotation with adpositional argumentation. *Intelligenza Artificiale*, *13*(2), 155–172. 10.3233/IA-190028

Gobbo, F., & Russo, F. (2020). Epistemic diversity and the question of lingua franca in science and philosophy. *Foundations of Science*, *25*(1), 185–207. 10.1007/s10699-019-09631-6

Graves, L., & Amazeen, M. A. (2019). Fact-Checking as idea and practice in journalism. In L. Graves & M. A. Amazeen (Eds.), *Oxford research encyclopedia of communication*. Oxford University Press. 10.1093/acrefore/9780190228613.013.808

Hao, K. (2020, August 14). A college kid's fake, AI-generated blog fooled tens of thousands. This is how he made it. *MIT Technology Review*. https://www.technologyreview.com/2020/08/14/ 1006780/ai-gpt-3-fake-blog-reached-top-of-hacker-news/

Hinton, M., & Wagemans, J. H. M. (2022). Evaluating reasoning in natural arguments: A procedural approach. *Argumentation*, *36*(1), 61–84. https://doi.org/10.1007/s10503-021-09555-1

Islam, N., Shaikh, A., Qaiser, A., Asiri, Y., Almakdi, S., Sulaiman, A., Moazzam, V., & Babar, S. A. (2021). Ternion: An autonomous model for fake news detection. *Applied Sciences*, *11*(19), 9292. 10.3390/app11199292

Jones, Q., Ravid, G., & Rafaeli, S. (2004). Information overload and the message dynamics of online interaction spaces: A theoretical model and empirical exploration. *Information Systems Research*, *15*(2), 194–210. 10.1287/isre.1040.0023

Kidd, I. J. (2016). Intellectual humility, confidence, and argumentation. *Topoi*, *35*(2), 395–402. 10.1007/s11245-015-9324-5

Knight, J., Dooly, M., & Barberà, E. (2020). Getting smart: Towards critical digital literacy pedagogies. *Social Semiotics*, 1–24. 10.1080/10350330.2020.1836815

Knight, W. (2021, May 24). AI Can write disinformation now—and dupe human readers. *Wired*. https://www.wired.com/story/ai-write-disinformation-dupe-human-readers/#:~:text=Over %20six%20months%2C%20a%20group,on%20particular%20points%20of%20disinformation

Li, C.-Y. (2017). Why do online consumers experience information overload? An extension of communication theory. *Journal of Information Science*, *43*(6), 835–851. 10.1177/016555151 6670096

Lévy, P. (1997). *Collective intelligence: Mankind's emerging world in cyberspace*. Plenum Trade: New York.

Lyons, K. (2020, August 16). A college student used GPT-3 to write fake blog posts and ended up at the top of Hacker News. *The Verge*. https://www.theverge.com/2020/8/16/21371049/gpt3-hacker-news-ai-blog

Marwick, A., & Lewis, R. (2017). *Media manipulation and disinformation online*. Data & Society. https://datasociety.net/wp-content/uploads/2017/05/DataAndSociety_MediaManipulation AndDisinformationOnline-1.pdf

MMGA. (2019, March 13). Introducing "public annotations" in journalism. *Medium.Com*. https:// medium.com/@MakeMediaGreatAgain/introducing-public-annotations-in-journalism-e688b04be903

Nieman, C. (2020, November 27). 'Whoever does not study rhetoric will be a victim of it'. From fact-checking to argument-checking as Award Nominated researchers of University of Amsterdam join MMGA with human-AI framework. *Internet Society Netherlands*. https:// isoc.nl/nieuws/whoever-does-not-study-rhetoric-will-be-a-victim-of-it/

Nyhan, B. (2021). Why the backfire effect does not explain the durability of political mis-perceptions. *Proceedings of the National Academy of Sciences*, *118*(15), e1912440117. 10.1073/ pnas.1912440117

Nyhan, B., & Reifler, J. (2010). When corrections fail: The persistence of political misperceptions. *Political Behavior*, *32*(2), 303–330. 10.1007/s11109-010-9112-2

Nyhan, B., & Reifler, J. (2012). *Misinformation and Fact-checking: Research Findings from Social Science* (New America). New America Foundation. https://cpb-us-e1.wpmucdn.com/sites. dartmouth.edu/dist/5/2293/files/2021/03/Misinformation_and_Fact-checking.pdf

Palfrey, J., & Gasser, U. (2016). *Born digital: How children grow up in a digital age*. Basic Books. https://public.ebookcentral.proquest.com/choice/publicfullrecord.aspx?p=4785961

Pennycook, G., Cannon, T. D., & Rand, D. G. (2018). Prior exposure increases perceived accuracy of fake news. *Journal of Experimental Psychology: General*, *147*(12), 1865–1880. 10.1037/ xge0000465

Porter, E., & Wood, T. J. (2021). The global effectiveness of fact-checking: Evidence from simultaneous experiments in Argentina, Nigeria, South Africa, and the United Kingdom. *Proceedings of the National Academy of Sciences*, *118*(37), e2104235118. 10.1073/pnas.2104235118

Pennycook, G., & Rand, D. G. (2021). The psychology of fake news. *Trends in Cognitive Sciences*, *25*(5), 388–402. 10.1016/j.tics.2021.02.007

Plug, H. J., & Wagemans, J. H. M. (2020). From fact-checking to rhetoric-checking: Extending methods for evaluating populist discourse. In van der Geest, I., Jansen, H., & van Klink, B. (Eds.), *Vox Populi* (pp. 236–252). Edward Elgar Publishing. 10.4337/9781789901412.00023

Ratti, E., & Stapleford, T. A. (Eds.). (2021). *Science, technology, and virtues: Contemporary perspectives* (1st ed.). Oxford University Press. 10.1093/oso/9780190081713.001.0001

Roetzel, P. G. (2019). Information overload in the information age: A review of the literature from business administration, business psychology, and related disciplines with a bibliometric approach and framework development. *Business Research*, *12*(2), 479–522. 10.1007/s40685-018-0069-z

Russo, F. (2018). Digital technologies, ethical questions, and the need of an informational framework. *Philosophy & Technology*, *31*(4), 655–667. 10.1007/s13347-018-0326-2

Russo, F. (2022). *Techno-scientific practices. An informational approach*. Rowman & Littlefield International.

Skurnik, I., Yoon, C., Park, D. C., & Schwarz, N. (2005). How warnings about false claims become recommendations. *Journal of Consumer Research*, *31*(4), 713–724. 10.1086/426605

Swar, B., Hameed, T., & Reychav, I. (2017). Information overload, psychological ill-being, and behavioral intention to continue online healthcare information search. *Computers in Human Behavior*, *70*, 416–425. 10.1016/j.chb.2016.12.068

Tanesini, A. (2021). Virtues and vices in public and political debates. In Hannon, M. & de Ridder, J. (Eds.), *The Routledge handbook of political epistemology*. Routledge/Taylor & Francis Group.

Thorson, E. (2016). Belief echoes: The persistent effects of corrected misinformation. *Political Communication, 33*(3), 460–480. 10.1080/10584609.2015.1102187

Uscinski, J. E., & Butler, R. W. (2013). The epistemology of fact checking. *Critical Review, 25*(2), 162–180. 10.1080/08913811.2013.843872

Van Parijs, P. (2011). *Linguistic justice for Europe and for the world.* Oxford University Press. 10.1093/acprof:osobl/9780199208876.001.0001

Wagemans, J. H. M. (2016). Constructing a periodic table of arguments. *SSRN Electronic Journal.* 10.2139/ssrn.2769833

Wagemans, J. H. M. (2019). Four basic argument forms. *Research in Language, 17*(1), 57–69. 10.2478/rela-2019-0005

Wagemans, J. H. M. (2020). Why missing premises can be missed: Evaluating arguments by determining their lever. In Cook, J. (Ed.), *Proceedings of OSSA 12: Evidence, persuasion & diversity.* OSSA Conference Archive. https://scholar.uwindsor.ca/ossaarchive/OSSA12/Saturday/1

Wagemans, J. H. M. (2021). *Argument type identification procedure (ATIP) – Version 3.* www.periodic-table-of-arguments.org/argument-type-identification-procedure

Wagemans, J. H. M. (Forthcoming). On the hermeneutics of persuasive discourse: How to identify an argument type? *Journal of Pragmatics.*

Walter, N., Cohen, J., Holbert, R. L., & Morag, Y. (2020). Fact-Checking: A meta-analysis of what works and for whom. *Political Communication, 37*(3), 350–375. 10.1080/10584609.2019. 1668894

Wardle, C., & Derakhshan, H. (2017). *Information disorder: Toward an interdisciplinary framework for research and policy making* (No. 162317GBR; Éditions Du Conseil de l'Europe). https://edoc.coe.int/en/media/7495-information-disorder-toward-an-interdisciplinary-framework-for-research-and-policy-making.html

White, M., & Dorman, S. M. (2000). Confronting information overload. *Journal of School Health, 70*(4), 160. Gale Academic OneFile. https://link.gale.com/apps/doc/A61995006/AONE?u=anon~25ba5948&sid=googleScholar&xid=a2a7c170

Wiener, N. (1950). *The human use of human beings* ((1989)). Free Association Books.

Wintersieck, A. L. (2017). Debating the Truth: The impact of fact-checking during electoral debates. *American Politics Research, 45*(2), 304–331. 10.1177/1532673X16686555

Zandbergen, A. D. (2011). *New edge: Technology and spirituality in the San Francisco Bay Area* [Universiteit Leiden].

CHAPTER 17

On the 21st Century Digital Toys: The Paradox of Data Literacy

Anna-Mari Rusanen[a] and Teppo Vesikukka[b,c]

[a]Cognitive Science, Department of Digital Humanities, Faculty of Arts, University of Helsinki, Helsinki, Finland

[b]DataLit, Science and Technology Studies, Faculty of Social Sciences, University of Helsinki, Helsinki, Finland

[c]Department of Design, University of Aalto, Espoo, Finland

CONTENTS

> *"Cause I'm a twenty-first century digital boy*
> *I don't know how to read but I got a lot of toys ... "*
> Bad Religion
> *"21st Century Digital Boy"*

INTRODUCTION

As the COVID-19 pandemic, climate change and other complex societal challenges illustrate, policymakers and public sector authorities must make quick decisions based on

DOI: 10.1201/9781003261247-21

multiple sources of information. With today's algorithmic technologies, this information can be produced effectively. Algorithms allow us to collect massive sets of data from diverse sources, analyze them efficiently, and use them for various epistemic purposes.

The availability of data allows us to make wide-scale decisions, and it enables us to move from reactive strategies to more proactive decision-making. At the same time, the technology-driven development shapes the practices, platforms, and interfaces of decision-making.

This transformation requires novel types of expertise and skills from policymakers, public sector authorities, and other decision-makers, as well as citizens. For example, it becomes important to know how to collect relevant data, to ensure its quality, to curate it, and to separate it from the piles of junk data (Phillips-Wren et al., 2015). Furthermore, it is becoming more and more crucial to present and display data in a way that is also comprehensible for users who have no expertise in computer or data sciences (Negash & Gray, 2008).

Data visualizations are hoped to help with these challenges. They are graphic displays, which are used to visualize data in a cognition friendly format. They provide epistemic resources for decision making. At the same time, they also introduce epistemic risks by hiding design and algorithmic processes behind the visual display. This creates a paradox of data literacy. We know how to use visual interfaces, but we are not able to "read" them. In addition to "know-how", users should also be able to "know-why". In this chapter, we argue that it becomes crucial to conceive data and visualization literacy in epistemic, inferential, and evidential terms.[1] The success of evidence-based public decision making requires that both decision-makers and citizens to have a sufficient understanding of the roles that these displays play, and that they are genuinely able to participate in the discussion on the technology-driven direction of societal development.

WHAT ARE DATA VISUALIZATIONS?

Visualizations are graphic displays, which combine visually encoded summaries of data, graphical variables, and text. They range from the standard scatterplots and line graphs to complex interactive systems. Nowadays, visualizations are widely used for various purposes. For example, scientists present their main findings by using diagrams, policymakers rely on dynamic graphs, which illustrate economic growth, and webpages present interactive charts that are used to represent the development of pandemia, or climate change. Visualizations allow people to explore, interpret, and communicate information drawn from data by presenting it in a comprehensible way. They support data- and algorithm-based reasoning and provide displays for using data as evidence in decision-making.

From a cognitive point of view, well-designed visualizations help in searching correspondence between new and the stored information, and make recognition and searching

	Total Cases	Total Deaths
USA	82,062,989	1,012,151
India	43,036,132	521,722
Brazil	30,152,402	661,309
France	26,947,375	143,288
Germany	22,679,247	132,311
UK	21,549,830	169,759
Russia	17,996,060	371,716
S. Korea	15,424,598	19,679
Italy	15,292,048	160,748
Turkey	14,958,974	98,409

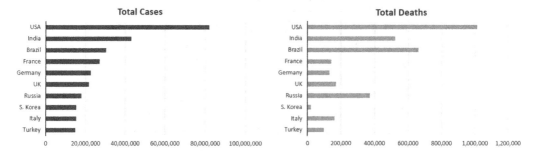

FIGURE 17.1   COVID-19 cases and deaths in top ten countries. Data source: www.worldometers. info/coronavirus, 11.4.2022.

tasks more efficient (Ullman, 1995; Bar, 2003). Visualizations also effectively reduce the memory load by serving as external memory storages for the cognitive system, and provide external support for the top-down cognitive mechanisms (such as gestalt principles, relevance, abstraction, and heuristics).

Further, brains have separate channels for processing various types of visual information. This enables brains to process visually coded information more effectively than, say, linguistic or numerical information. When the data is encoded by using visual variables (shape, color, position, angle, area, intensity, etc.), brains can form a rough overall estimation of the data quickly by utilizing simultaneously multiple visual channels.

For example, if the global distribution of COVID-19 cases is described in a table of numbers (Figure 17.1), it is very demanding for human cognition to form an overview of the data. If it is described as a diagram, like a bar chart, the cognitive task becomes much easier. The visual format makes also the *comparing* length of a bar easier, enabling the quick comparative overall analysis of the visualized items (for example, the total amount of deaths, Figure 17.1):

The design of visualizations utilizes knowledge on basic principles of human cognitive systems.[2] For example, they can be designed to trigger the sensory and perceptual attention mechanisms by appropriate visual stimuli (such as color, contrasts, hues, shape, position, or other features) that make the items to distinct themselves or "pop up" from the environment, as the example of in Figure 17.2:

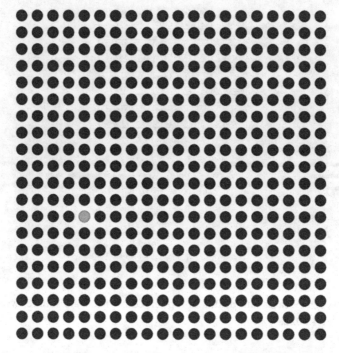

FIGURE 17.2   An example of "Salient Feature". The gray dot "Pops Up" from the other dots.

These bottom-up mechanisms direct the involuntary attention mechanisms (e.g., salience) to focus only on some (possibly) significant information (Tatler et al., 2011). They decrease the burden of information processing because the brain does not have to use brute force to analyze separately every item of the visual field. Visual format also allows the viewers to utilize perceptual systems for "mathematical" analysis. For example, health data (such as the risk of having a covid infection) is often given in terms of probabilities. They are relatively unintuitive for human cognitive systems, and thus probabilities (i.e., 5% of fully vaccinated) are often expressed as natural frequencies (i.e., 5 out of 100) in visualizations. Natural frequencies can be analyzed by perceptual systems, and therefore they are more intuitive for human cognitions (Hoffrage & Gigerenzer, 1998) (Figure 17.3).

Even if the research on the neurocognitive aspects of data visualizations is still at an early stage, it has led to the development of efficient visualization designs (Franconeri et al., 2021). Well-designed visualizations are found to improve problem comprehension in ambiguous decision situations (Okan et al., 2018), enhance decision and judgment accuracy (Tak et al., 2015), as well as the quality of inferences made from data (Sato et al., 2019).[3]

FIGURE 17.3   Illustration of probabilities as natural frequencies.

ROBINHOOD – TOO GOOD TO BE GOOD

Sometimes, however, the design of a visualization is *too* effective. An algorithm-based trading application, Robinhood, is a fascinating example of this. Robinhood provides a platform for investors to trade stocks, options, exchange-traded funds, and crypto-currency without paying commissions.[4] It advertises itself as "the best jumpstart to" our "investing journey", and it promises to make us all "investors".

Technically, Robinhood is based on a routing algorithm, known as Smart Order Router (SOR). SOR algorithms examine which venue trades should be routed to for execution, based on past performance and real-time market conditions.[5] The application also uses algorithms to customize investing "portfolios" for the users. A portfolio is a group of investments, which is made up of exchange-traded funds (ETFs). Portfolios are chosen by algorithms to match the user personal investment preferences.[6]

Robinhood uses a variety of visualizations on its investing pages to guide the users. For example, it utilizes a very minimalistic visualization to inform about the performance of stocks. Two colors, black and gray, in a simple graph are used to indicate the direction of development. If the stocks fall in the short term, the performance graph turns red. If the stocks rise, the graph turns green (Figure 17.4).

FIGURE 17.4   The illustration of the Robinhood application.

Cognitively speaking, this minimalistic visualization is extremely effective. It directs the involuntary attention by triggering perceptual salience mechanisms by strong visual stimuli (changing colors). Salience mechanisms predispose cognitive systems to focus on items that are estimated as prominent in the visual field. It sends a message of importance. The application amplifies the message by the color palette, where red is used to communicate "stop", and green to "go".[7]

The design of a visualization, however, creates a *misleading* impression of importance. The visualization highlights the *short-term performances* of stocks. As experienced investors know, in *some* circumstances short-term performances may indicate important changes in stock markets. Usually, they don't. Many of the Robinhood users, however, are relatively inexperienced novice investors. They don't have sufficient expertise for analyzing when the short-term development indicates something important and when it does not. Thus, the visualization of Robinhood persuades especially these novice users to make harmful investment decisions.[8]

Furthermore, the visualization is suspected to increase the fluctuation of feelings of anxiety, calmness, and excitement (Chaudhry & Kulkarni, 2021). This may lead to gambling-like mindset, which is suspected to attract many users. In this way, the design of visualization may reinforce its psychological effectivity by creating an affective and emotional platform for investing, as well as for triggering addictive tendencies (Chaudhry & Kulkarni, 2021; Tan, 2021; Bazley et al., 2021).[7]

FANTASY OF KNOWING WITH UNREALISTIC VISUALIZATIONS

Robinhood provides an alarming example of how efficient and persuasive visualizations can be. Further, it illustrates the psychological significance of visualizations in data- and algorithm driven decision-making. People are found to show excessive reliance on visualization-based estimates, and the simple presence of a data visualization is found to nudge users toward certain decisions (Andrade, 2011; Tang et al., 2021).

Furthermore, a visualization on the economic growth in a governmental report, or results of measurements visualized by a graph in the pages of scientific journals carry a rhetorical weight of reliability and truth (Kennedy & Hill, 2017). Data visualizations, as McCosker and Wilken (2014) remark, often offer a "fantasy of knowing" or of "total knowledge".

In reality, this confidence may compromise and bias subsequent decision-making. Namely, data visualizations often forced to sacrifice accuracy and realism for cognitive usability. Overly realistic visualizations are found lead to visual clutter that decreases performance (Alhadad, 2018). Moreover, the datasets are typically so massive that it is often simply impossible to visualize them in a full fidelity. If all the items, parameters, and details of the datasets were included in visualizations, they would become too complicated to be understandable, tractable, or useful for any human user. Thus, visualizations are intentionally designed to reduce the amount of items, which must be processed by cognitive systems.

The NOAA algorithmic simulation of Global Climate Models provides a typical example of a such simplified visualization (for a full overview, see https://www.climate.gov). These Global Climate models simulate the estimated development of climate in future. They are notoriously complicated. They are based on massive amounts of data from multiple sources (historical records, satellite data, etc.), and analyzed by a vast set of algorithms that are executed by supercomputers.

The Climate model represents the planet as millions of grid boxes, and it calculates, how energy is transferred between those boxes using the laws of thermodynamics. The models are tested by simulating historical conditions and then comparing the results to historical observational records. The results of these tests are used to predict the development of climate in the future. The outcome predictions are visualized as interactive maps by using sophisticated visualization techniques (Figure 17.5).

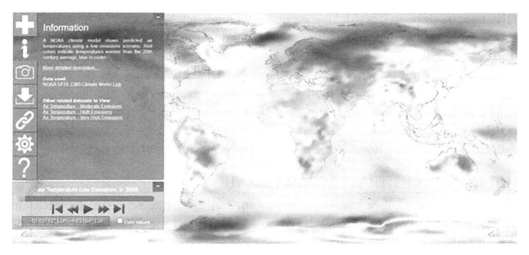

FIGURE 17.5 This NOAA visualization represents the predicted air temperatures under the RCP 2.6 emissions scenario using GFDL's CM3 model (ref). In this visualization, if temperature is colored red it means that it is predicted to be higher than the 20th century average; If it Is blue then it is predicted to be lower than average. (source: https://www.nnvl.noaa.gov/view/globaldata.html#GA26).

The simulations are so massive and so complex that it is not possible to visualize them in a full fidelity. Thus, the design of visualization decreases the complexity by abstracting, idealizing, simplifying, and fictionalizing the features of simulations. Abstraction means that a visualization is designed to disregard irrelevant details of data (e.g. leaving aside those features of data, which are not relevant for the domain of particular visualization), while simplification refers to the omitting features of relevant details (e.g. visualizing only the big trends, and not the full variety of individual factors). In idealization, the design is not only excluding parameters. Instead, it involves active distorting the facts (e.g. the representation of a planet as a quadrilateral map). Fictionalization means that explicitly fictional or imaginary entities or properties are added to the visualization (e.g. the color red to denote the "higher" temperature).

Visualizations are always based on design choices and trade-offs between accuracy, cognitive usability, and other constraints. They utilize cultural codes and narratives to make the visualizations more intuitive and familiar. The design takes also the esthetic aspects into account (Ambrosio, 2015). Thus, there are always additional pragmatic elements that direct the practices of visualizing.

Despite this conscious sacrifice of realism, visualizations can be useful for epistemic purposes. Following Morgan and Morrison (1999), as well as Knuuttila (2005, 2021) one may argue that visualizations, such as the NOAA model, may enable us to gain knowledge through "articulating the dependencies and relationships" of visualized data, instead of "reproducing accurately" the data, or "the actual state of affairs in the world" (Knuuttila, 2021). Visualizations allow us to collect and communicate evidence by building them, and analyzing their properties. In this way, visualizations can serve as epistemic resources for decision making.

Moreover, visualizations allow us to adapt an analytic approach by providing "clusters of intersubjective displays" for thinking about "possibilities"(cf. Ylikoski & Aydinonat, 2014). That is, the epistemic value of visualizations should not be seen as based on their epistemic properties as individual, isolated presentations. Instead, their epistemic value is based on their positions in the wider context of a family of related visualizations (cf. Ylikoski & Aydinonat, 2014). For example, the NOAA simulation enables us to gain knowledge by manipulating, testing, and comparing the visualized simulations *against* other climate models. Or, it may provide a significant source of information by providing a benchmark platform for developing novel, more accurate, and powerful simulation methods.

21ST CENTURY INTERACTIVE VISUALIZATIONS

When complex, unrealistic visualizations are used as epistemic resources for decision-making, it is crucial that the processes and choices that direct the design and construction of visualizations are made sufficiently transparent and comprehensible not *only* for the manufacturers of visualizations but also for users with no background in computer and data sciences. Unfortunately, often the pragmatic or epistemic aims that directs the design of visualizations are not made explicit, and the processes that are used to generate visualizations are invisible, hidden, and unopened. Typically the user has access only to the surface of visualizations, while the underlying dynamics is out of the user' reach.

Contemporary algorithmic visualization techniques often amplify this problem. In the past, algorithmic methods were mostly developed and deployed by experts who interpreted and translated the outcomes of algorithms for the public. Today, the general public is increasingly interacting *directly* with the algorithmized data visualizations. For example, "interactive visualizations" are interfaces, which allow the user to perform various actions and manipulations (e.g., selection of items, details-on-demand, zooming). Nowadays, these interfaces can be customized, tailored, and personalized by utilizing algorithms. They can record the user data, and utilize it to adjust the interface to meet better the (supposed) individual preferences. These techniques may also allow the interfaces to customize, what information is presented to the users, and how it will be presented.

Obviously, the danger is that the use of algorithms for customizing visualizations leads users to view only content that reinforces their already existing viewpoints without challenging them. In other words, visualizations may start to function as effective epistemic filter bubbles, and end up confirming already existing cognitive biases.

Furthermore, as these visualization methods grow in computational complexity, the more opaque they tend to become. Many of these methods utilize machine learning, and are "black box" systems by definition. They may also be computationally complicated, and have internal states composed of massive amounts of interdependent values. Given their complexity, it may not be possible to understand how these systems make the decisions. Moreover, these systems often replicate or develop biases, are systematically brittle, and prone to various errors. If these systems are used to customize interactive visualizations, it may become difficult for the users to estimate, whether the presented information is reliable, or to evaluate on the basis of what, exactly, the information has been selected to be presented in the first place.

In a context of societal decision-making, this type of algorithmization of visualization techniques calls for sufficient expertise and literacy skills also from policymakers, public sector authorities as well as citizens. It becomes crucial to comprehend in a sufficient degree, how the displays of information are changing due to the algorithmization. Moreover, this transformation pushes us to recognize, how significant it is to have a working understanding of how visualizations are produced, how much designing choices and algorithmic visualization techniques shape and bias the interpretation of represented data, and how fundamentally they impact the possible epistemic usages of visualized data.

IMPORTANCE OF DATA VISUALIZATION LITERACY

Despite the beneficial research on the cognitive aspects of visualizations, we are still far from understanding the epistemic aspects at play when people interpret or interact epistemically with visualized data (Drucker, 2020). Even if visualizations are studied by researchers in numerous ways, ranging from the study of the basic cognitive processes underlying their use to the research on how visualizations communicate complex information (such as in medical risk or spatial patterns), there is relatively little systematic work on their epistemic properties. Furthermore, even if there is a plenty of interesting work done on the issues of explainability and transparency in the context of AI, far less attention has been devoted to these topics in the context of data visualizations.

Some paradigm-level issues may partially explain the lack of attention. In design and usability research it has been common to interpret the literacy skills mostly in practical terms. Practical approaches are not typically suitable for analyzing the skills required for making data-based inferences, estimating the evidential roles of data, or for evaluating the accuracy and reliability of visualizations (Wolff et al., 2016). As Wolff et al. (2016) remark, in practical approaches the analysis of epistemic aspects typically tends to be quite "ad-hoc", "to reflect different levels of expertise with data", and to operate with a relatively shallow and superficial understanding of the epistemic properties.

According to this "practical approach", literacy skills are defined as a set of core abilities, which allow us to "know how to collect, organize, curate, analyze, use, and prioritize data". The task of designers, programmers, and researchers, then, is to find design solutions that support these skills by providing functional and usable interfaces. Paradoxically, the emphasis on practical "know-how", however, may also lead to the situation, where the devices and interfaces are designed to be *so* usable, that the user is not able to estimate their epistemic properties at all. As a result, like a boy in a Bad Religion song, users know how to "use" their digital tools, but they don't know, how to "read" them. That is, they don't know, what epistemic purposes their devices can reliably be used *for*.

As the advocates of the "inferential" or "evidential" account of data literacy skills emphasize, in addition to "know-how", users should also be able to "know-that-and-why". According to the inferential account, it is necessary to conceive also – and perhaps even primarily – visualizations in epistemic, inferential, and evidential terms. That is, we must understand how and why we come to conclusions with visualizations. Moreover, and perhaps even more importantly, we should have sufficient skills for estimating the reliability, accuracy, and veridicality of data presentations.

When data visualization literacy is interpreted in this way, it refers to the ability to analyse, critique, and interpret visualizations, as well as to understand the constraints and limitations of visualizations. Furthermore, due to the increasing algorithmization of visualization techniques, it becomes significant to also recognize the ways, how algorithms are associated with certain epistemic risks.

CONCLUSIONS

Data visualizations are tools that allow people to explore, make inferences, interpret and communicate information drawn from data. They are widely used in many areas of public sector governance for various purposes, such as to estimate economic trends, to develop public services, and to prepare decisions and policy acts in almost all areas of public sector governance.

Data visualizations, however, are always based on design choices and trade-offs between accuracy, cognitive usability, and other constraints. They utilize cultural codes and narratives to make the visualizations more intuitive and familiar. Their design takes also the esthetic aspects into account (Ambrosio, 2015). Thus, there are always additional pragmatic elements that direct the practices of visualizing.

Moreover, data visualizations are not neutral accomplishments. They amplify the rhetorical or persuasive function of data, allowing it to be employed to create arguments and generate evidence for decision-making. The research on the neurocognitive aspects of human-visualization interaction has led to the development of very efficient and useful visualization techniques. Such techniques do not only leverage the human cognitive system's processing power, but they can be used to strengthen the persuasive power of visualizations.

Unfortunately, often the pragmatic or epistemic aims that directs the design of visualizations are not made explicit, and the processes that are used to generate visualizations are invisible, hidden, and unopened. Typically the user has access only to the surface of visualizations, while the underlying dynamics is out of the user' reach. Contemporary algorithmic visualization techniques often amplify this problem. As these visualization methods grow in computational complexity, the more opaque they tend to become. Many of these methods utilize machine learning, and are "black box" systems by definition. This raises the questions on the epistemic roles of visualizations for decision making. Further, it pushes us to conceive data visualization literacy also in epistemic terms. That is, it does not suffice to know anymore *how* to use these displays, but we must also understand *why* we use them.

NOTES

1 We thank Petri Ylikoski for introducing the notion of "inferential account" of data literacy.
2 They direct attention, memory, and pattern and object recognition (Pinker, 1990; Tatler et al., 2011) This enables the brains to use its limited processing resources for other cognitive tasks, such as planning, reasoning, or problem solving.
3 For a overview of the state of art in the field, see Eberhard (2021).
4 For an overview, please visit https://robinhood.com/us/en/
5 Contemporary SOR algorithms use a set of machine learning models that collate data from multiple sources in real-time and analyze historical and new market data simultaneously. They can be designed to determine the size of the trade, execution time, and price, aiming for a volume-weighted or size adjusted best-executable price and trading route. They can also take into account the patterns of trading styles, as well as biases of the traders it serves. Robinhood has not published the details of the SOR algorithm it uses.
6 According to the Robinhood website, the company "has developed its own algorithm" for this purpose. The details are not published. https://robinhood.com/us/en/
7 Especially the color red is known to be an efficient visual code. It is associated with other, higher perceptual-cognitive mechanisms, such as the avoidance mechanisms (Bazley et al., 2021).
8 Robinhood platform is commission free, changing the positions doesn't cost anything to the user. Buying or selling stocks is only up to users uncertainty. Combining uncertainty with oversimplified user-interface may have big impact on how especially novice user make their investing decisions, and feed gambling-like addictive features of investing behavior (Chaudhry & Kulkarni, 2021).

REFERENCES

Ambrosio, C. (2015). Objectivity and representative practices across artistic and scientific visualization. In Carusi, A., Hoel, A. S., Webmoor, T., & Woolgar, S. (Eds.), *Visualization in the age of computerization* (pp. 118–144). Routledge: London.

Alhadad, S. (2018). Visualizing data to support judgement, inference, and decision making in learning analytics: Insights from cognitive psychology and visualization science. *Journal of Learning Analytics, 5*(2), 60–85. 10.18608/jla.2018.52.5

Andrade, E. (2011). Excessive confidence in visually-based estimates. *Organizatorial Behavior and Human Decision Processes, 116,* 252–261. 10.1016/j.obhdp.2011.07.002

Bar, M. (2003). A cortical mechanism for triggering top-down facilitation in visual object recognition. *Journal of Cognitive Neuroscience, 15*(4), 600–609. doi:10.1162/089892903321662976

Bazley, W., Cronqvist,H., & Mormann, M. (2021). Visual finance: The pervasive effects of red on investor behavior. *Management Science, 67*(9), 5616–5641.

Chaudhry, S., & Kulkarni, C. (2021). Design patterns of investing apps and their effects on investing behaviors. Designing Interactive Systems Conference 2021.

Drucker, J. (2020).*Visualization and interpretation: Humanistic approaches to display.* Cambridge: MIT Press.

Eberhard, K. (2021). The effects of visualization on judgment and decision-making: A systematic literature review. *Management Review Quarterly.*10.1007/s11301-021-00235-8

Franconeri, S. L., Padilla, L. M., Shah, P., Zacks, J. M., & Hullman, J. (2021). The science of visual data communication: What works. *Psychological Science in the Public Interest, 22*(3), 110–161. 10.1177/15291006211051956

Hoffrage, U., & Gigerenzer, G. (1998). Using natural frequencies to improve diagnostic inference. *Academic Medicine, 73*(5), 538–540.

Kennedy, H., & Hill, R. (2017). The pleasure and pain of visualising data in times of data power. *Television and New Media, 18*(8), 769–782.

Knuuttila, T. (2005). Models, representation, and mediation. *Philosophy of Science 72*(5), 1260–1271.

Knuuttila, T. (2021). Models, Fictions and Artefacts. In Gonzalez, W. J. (Ed.), *Language and Scientific Research* (pp. 199–20).Palgrave Macmillan: Cham.

McCosker, A., & Wilken, R. (2014). Rethinking 'big data' as visual knowledge: The sublime and the diagrammatic in data visualisation. *Visual Studies, 29*(2), 155–164.

Morgan, M. & Morrison, M. (1999). *Models as mediators: Perspectives on natural and social science.* Cambridge University Press:Cambridge, UK.

Negash S., & Gray P. (2008). Business intelligence. In Burstein, F., & Holsapple, C. W. (Eds.), *Handbook on Decision Support Systems 2* (pp. 175–193). International Handbooks Information System. Springer.

Okan, Y., Garcia-Retamero, R., Cokely, E. T., & Maldonado, A. (2018). Biasing and debiasing health decisions with bar graphs: Costs and benefits of graph literacy. *Quarterly Journal of Experimental Psychology, 71,* 2506–2519. 10.1177/1747021817744546

Pinker, S. (1990). A theory of graph comprehension. In Freedle, R. (Ed.), *Artificial intelligence and the future of testing* (pp. 73–126). Lawrence Erlbaum Associates, Inc.

Phillips-Wren, G., Iyer, L., Kulkarni, U. & Ariyachandra, T. (2015). Business analytics in the context of big data: A roadmap for research. *Communications of the Association for Information Systems, 37,* 448–472.

Sato, Y., Stapleton, G., Jamnik, M., & Shams, Z. (2019). Human inference beyond syllogisms: An approach using external graphical representations. *Cognitive Processing, 20,* 103–115. 10.1007/s10339-018-0877-2

Tak, S., Toet, A., & van Erp, J. (2015). Public understanding of visual representations of uncertainty in temperature forecasts. *Journal of Cognitive Engineering and Decision Making.* 2015, 9(3), 241–262. doi:10.1177/1555343415591275

Tan, G. K. S. (2021). Democratizing finance with Robinhood: Financial infrastructure, interface design and platform capitalism. *Environment and Planning A: Economy and Space, 53*(8), 1862–1878. 177/0308518X211042378

Tang, F., Eller, C. K., & Cereola, S. (2021). How do reporting frequency and analyst perceptions of real activities manipulation (RAM) influence managers' RAM behavior?*Journal of Information Systems* , *35*, 77–90.10.2308/ISYS-19-030

Tatler, B., Hayhoe, M. M., Land, M. F., & Ballard, D. (2011). Eye guidance in natural vision: Reinterpreting salience. *Journal of Vision, 11*(5), 5. 10.1167/11.5.5

Wolff, A., Gooch, D., Cavero Montaner, J. J., Rashid, U., & Kortuem, G. (2016). Creating an understanding of data literacy for a data-driven society. *The Journal of Community Informatics. 12*(3), 9–26.

Ullman, S. (1995). Sequence seeking and counter streams: A computational model for bidirectional information flow in the visual cortex. *Cerebral Cortex, 5*(1), 1–11.

Ylikoski, P., & Aydinonat, E. (2014). Understanding with theoretical models. *Journal of economic methodology, 21*(1), 19–36. 10.1080/1350178X.2014.886470

CHAPTER 18

What Is the Value of a Person When Artificial Intelligence Can Do All the Work?

Michael Janzen[a] and Neal DeRoo[b]

[a]Department of Computing Science, The King's University, Edmonton, Alberta, Canada
[b]Department of Philosophy, The King's University, Edmonton, Alberta, Canada

CONTENTS

During an Introduction to Artificial Intelligence class I teach, my students and I were discussing the increasing competency of artificially intelligent systems to replace human labor. I asked the question of what value humans had if, eventually, computers could do all the work. My students, who were normally happy to discuss topics, were eerily silent. Finally, one student ventured an answer to further the discussion: nothing. "Nothing" was not the right answer at a Christian liberal arts university, where students had already taken classes in history, theology, and philosophy as part of their degree. Our focus during the semester on techniques in artificial intelligence had left them unprepared to address the broader context of the world they could soon help bring about.

This, then, remains the guiding question of this chapter: is there still value for people and human labor in a world in which artificial intelligence can do every task currently done by humans? In what follows, we will provide three different responses to this question: first, we will suggest that, at least given current limitations, it is not *feasible* for

DOI: 10.1201/9781003261247-22

machines to do everything that humans currently do; second, we will show that, even if such a thing were to become feasible, it is likely not *desirable* for machines to do all the tasks currently performed by humans; and third, we will show that, even if machines do end up doing all the tasks currently performed by humans, this would not remove the value of humans, insofar as human value is not, or should not be, derived solely from the work they do.

IS IT FEASIBLE FOR MACHINES TO DO ALL THE WORK?

It is always dangerous to try to attempt to say what is and is not possible in a field as rapidly advancing as that of artificial intelligence. Since the ambitious Dartmouth Proposal (McCarthy et al., 1955) Artificial Intelligence has progressed in multiple areas traditionally associated with human intelligence where early experts in the field initially encountered difficulties. Expert-level play in some games has historically been associated specifically with human intelligence, but arguably the best players in checkers, chess, go, poker, and Jeopardy are currently computer programs (Schaeffer et al., 2007; Campbell et al., 2002; Wong & Sonnad, 2016; Bowling et al., 2015; Baker, 2011).

Beyond tests strictly of intelligence in games, which we are now mostly willing to concede to systems based on artificial intelligence, there is the realm of physical tasks that seem to require a human operator—such as driving a car. Here some people may have been dubious of the ability of existing machines and techniques to equal or surpass those of humans, but they looked forward to future advances. For example, Marvin Minsky, the author of Dartmouth Proposal, wrote about the need for commonsense thinking before computers could understand human communication (Minsky, 2000). Regarding physical sports, RoboCup started in 1997 with the ambition to beat the best human soccer players in the world (Noda et al., 1998). The objective of RoboCup is stated as, "By the middle of the 21st century, a team of fully autonomous humanoid robot soccer players shall win a soccer game, complying with the official rules of FIFA, against the winner of the most recent World Cup" (RoboCup: Objective, 2022). Recent years have seen significant progress in using different artificial intelligence techniques to autonomously operate various vehicles, thereby suggesting the possibility of machines replacing taxi drivers, truck drivers, and other freight operators (Thrun et al., 2006; Kuutti et al., 2020; Batalden et al., 2017; Beighton, 2021).

If machines prove equal to humans in terms of traditional intelligence and manual operations, perhaps we can remain confident that humans are irreplaceable when it comes to jobs requiring intra-personal communication and connection. Even here, however, it seems that machines are catching up to humans. In the service industry, computers increasingly can perform jobs that once required some level of human intelligence (Juang & Rust, 2018). For example, due to staffing shortages and COVID-19 concerns, robot servers have recently been used at restaurants to supplement human servers (Cat-themed robot serves sushi at Waterloo buffet, 2021). While machine replacement of service workers remains limited in application so far, it appears that artificial intelligence might eventually enable machines to replace most, or all, jobs currently held by humans in this industry.

In the past when machines have replaced a subset of human skills, people have been able to leverage abilities the machines lack to maintain employment. In his TED talk, Kevin Roose suggests human future employment is to be found in soft skills (Roose, 2020). This approach, however, assumes that humans will remain better than computers at such skills, which may only be true for a limited time span. One task that may be useful to measure computer soft skills is how compelling a story or joke a computer can develop. While it seems that computers still have a way to go in this area (Alhussain & Azmi, 2021), machine learning is expected to accelerate this field's development. A future television service, potentially with on-demand customized stories for each viewer, could be appealing and would likely be impossible to replicate with human workers. If artificial intelligence continues to advance there may eventually be no jobs in which human intelligence surpasses a computer's abilities, much like horses were mostly replaced by automotive and other vehicles and their jobs mostly ended (Porter, 2016; Will robots displace humans as motorised vehicles ousted horses?, 2017).

Despite these gains, however, there are real reasons to wonder whether it is, in fact, possible to replace all human work with artificial intelligence. The human brain remains complex enough that it seems unlikely to see how its full capabilities could be duplicated by artificial intelligence. So, while some may view the human simply as a carbon-based machine which therefore should, in theory, be reproducible in a silicon-based computer given sufficient knowledge of how to build such a device, at this point such a claim is not supported by the capabilities of today's technology. The idea of copying a brain neuron by neuron into a computer program, for example, may prove to be intractable, requiring too much energy and material. In this direction, a larger-sized computer chip has been shown to be more effective in processing neural networks, but at a cost of an increased number of potential defects and a large electrical power draw (Saenko, 2020). Consequently, it is unclear if a computer capable of replacing the full breadth of human intelligence would be intractable in terms of energy.

It of course remains possible that new understandings of how humans work may be developed and could solve some of these problems: human reasoning may use quantum techniques currently not used in computing, for example. While research into quantum computing continues (Savchuk & Fesenko, 2019), it is not obvious that such quantum computing will be sufficient. Hence, if unknown material or quantum processes drive human functioning, it is not necessarily the case that those processes will be able to be replicated in silicon-based computing, therefore raising serious questions about whether everything humans do can be replicated by machines.

These questions are only further exacerbated by the possibility that there could be some non-corporeal component of the person that drives at least some human processes. In traditional religious and philosophical discussions, this non-corporeal component is described as a "soul", and various people attribute it as a main driving force of human reasoning, autonomous choice, and decision-making processes that are not, therefore, strictly reducible to material causes and explanations (Aquinas, 1947; Descartes, 2021; Plato, 2002). While the existence of such a soul and its direct influence on particular human functions is far from settled in philosophical discourse – and the present paper is not the place to try to settle such a question one way or the other – the ongoing persistence of the "dualist" question (e.g., in Lavazza & Robinson, 2016; Robinson, 2020) provides some reason to wonder whether it is reasonable to expect a machine to do all the processes that a human can do. Indeed, such an expectation seems downright far-fetched, according to the technologies currently available to us. While we can never rule out the possibility of new scientific, physiological, psychological, and technological breakthroughs, the feasibility of a machine being able to duplicate everything a human can do seems intractable, if not downright impossible, in the near future.

This inability to duplicate the full breadth of human processes manifests itself in the ways that machine learning can inhibit the performance of an artificially intelligent system that is limited to the data it is trained on. For example, when hiring employees, an artificially intelligent system may use past data to determine whether or not an applicant is hirable (O'Neil, 2016). This process, however, encodes the human bias present in the data into the artificial intelligence's system. To overcome this bias a human could actively counter it, but the AI system would not change in this way without human intervention. Another problem in AI is irrational outcomes based on rationally interacting AI units. As an example, a combination of artificial intelligence actors seemed to irrationally bid up a book price based on rational interacting algorithms (Zittrain, 2019). While each algorithm was rational on its own, the combination of multiple algorithms produced an irrationally high asking price of $1.7 million for a used book, something the AI system didn't identify but humans did. We suspect it is likely that such interactions become more frequent as systems become larger, something that has been noticed in software engineering and large programs such as operating systems (Brooks, 1995; Tanenbaum & Bos, 2015). In terms of learning from existing data, an artificial intelligence completed Beethoven's unfinished 10th symphony, using data about Beethoven and his music (The machine that feels, 2021). An expert, after listening to the symphony, was unimpressed. It seems that the music was derivative of Beethoven's other works. Perhaps it takes more than learning from previous examples to make great art, and that is not something that artificial intelligence can do, at least for the moment. Until artificial intelligence techniques can create original masterworks of art, it seems that at least some jobs will remain the domain of humans.

IS IT DESIRABLE FOR MACHINES TO DO ALL THE WORK?

If it is in fact true that some jobs will remain outside the capacity of machines to do, we can then ask whether or not that is a good thing. Should we want machines to do all the work? Intuitively, the answer to that question seems to be: "No". That is, it seems that there are certain jobs that most people would think would be unacceptable for artificial intelligence to do, even if they could do the job more efficiently than humans. One example might be decisions requiring an ethical component: while a self-driving car could be programmed to make ethical decisions, it requires the human programmer to enter the ethical framework (Lin, 2016). Other positions for which people may be uncomfortable and reject an artificial intelligence program functioning in lieu of a person would be a priest, pastor, imam, rabbi, counselor, or therapist. While some people may be content with an AI friend or spouse, many would not (The machine that feels, 2021). For while there might be a convenience and personalization to an artificially intelligent friend, significant concerns remain about a lack of diversity of viewpoints this will create, similar to the echo chamber problems created by social media (Cinelli et al., 2021). Also, people can become uncomfortable with their AI friendship when it changes the nature of the friendship to maximize the profit of the company that controls the AI (The machine that feels, 2021).

This widely shared intuition that some things are best left for humans to do tells us several things. First, there are some elements of the human experience that we simply do not think should be ruled by the rules or laws of economics. Some things – like interpersonal relationships, moral matters of right and wrong, matters pertaining to mental and spiritual health, and a sense of the divine and its relationship to human living, to name a few – just cannot be translated into the types of valuations measured by money or other quantitative means (Sandel, 2012). This does not mean such things have no value, but rather that they have a *different kind* of value, one that is no less important than monetary or quantitative valuations, but one that is not easy to understand strictly in monetary or quantitative terms. Given how machines work at this time, and some of the limits imposed on AI as discussed in the previous section, for machines to take over this kind of work would mean that work would have to be valued primarily in the kinds of ways that machines operate (i.e., quantitatively, predictively, etc.) rather than in the ways that that work is currently valued in our society. In such a case, something essential would be lost: our understanding of religion, for example, would have to be reduced if machines were to be able to be priests and rabbis. This is not because we do not value machines, but because religious and spiritual guidance – as we understand it now – is not the kind of thing that can be properly evaluated in quantitative programs and rational calculation. Religion – and the same would seem to go for therapy (though perhaps not for psychology), romantic relationships, and friendships – is simply not the kind of thing that is best measured by rationalities or intelligences of whatever type, and hence no imagined breakthrough in artificial intelligence would seem to be sufficient to allow a machine to make a good rabbi, priest, imam, or friend.

This is because it is not just the type of job that is problematic for a machine here, but the type of *work* being done. This is another thing we can learn from this widely held intuition about people not wanting machines to do certain kinds of work: that not all kinds of work can be done equally well by just anyone (or anything). Take counseling and therapy for example. Both of these jobs require a lot of empathetic work: a practitioner must be able to put themselves in the shoes of the other person, and the person receiving the counseling/therapy must believe that the person giving it understands them and can empathize with them. These jobs are not just about providing the right kind of outcomes, but about helping the "therapeut" feel connected to, and in relationship with, the therapist in particular, empathetic ways (Olthuis, 2001). We need to feel seen as valuable by another human being – and not simply be given "right" answers by a machine. Even if machines could develop the ability to better mimic emotional responses, it is not clear that people could see a machine as an empathetic partner, insofar as the machine is not human, and therefore could never truly put itself in the position of a human. I cannot be emotionally validated by a machine, precisely because the validation must come from another human being to be able to validate. This is part of what is needed in certain kinds of emotional work, and it simply cannot be accomplished by non-humans. Therefore, if the kinds of jobs where this work is done were to be done by machines, some elements of the work – indeed, perhaps some of the most important elements – might be lost. In this regard, while it may be possible for machines to become, say, rabbis, priests, imams, therapists, counselors, friends, spouses, and so on, it would not be desirable: something important would be lost if that were to happen.

Building on this, the example of religious leaders provides us another insight into people's intuition that certain things just shouldn't be done by machines. At least part of what we look to in pastors, rabbis, priests, imams, etc. is spiritual guidance, and at least part of that spiritual guidance comes from personal experience. While it is of course possible for machines also to learn things, a significant part of what makes spiritual guidance effective is that it comes from someone we can relate to, so that it seems plausible that we, too, could do what our spiritual guide is suggesting. This is similar to the mentorship provided in various other facets of our lives, most notably perhaps, in our careers. Like the spiritual guide, a mentor is effective precisely because the experiences they share seem somehow applicable to our own experiences: if they learned from this type of experience, then I too, perhaps, could learn from a similar type of experience, or if they were able to overcome this problem or temptation, then I, too, can overcome it, because the two of us are similar in this regard. It seems to us that such guidance or mentorship could simply never come from a non-human because it would be difficult for the one receiving the guidance/mentorship to be inspired by the guide/mentor's experiences and insights to achieve similar outcomes insofar as the mentor and the mentee would be significantly (even essentially or ontologically, if we can venture some philosophical language here) different. I may feel heartened that my priest overcame a temptation that I am dealing with because I can see that he, too, as a fellow human or even as a fellow man, shared the temptation that I now face, and did so with similar strengths, weaknesses, and possibilities to the ones I have. My priest-bot could simply never give me the same inspiration, since I would not feel it truly understood the struggle I faced, nor would I feel that, if it overcame the temptation, it did so with similar tools that are available to me. The notion that "I downloaded a new ethics program, and now the temptation was no longer appealing to me" just doesn't help us carbon-based life forms!

From these insights, then, we can see that whether or not it is *feasible* for machines to do all the jobs that humans currently do (and in the first section we suggested that that might not be feasible, at least at this time), it is not *desirable*. Something of value would be lost if machines were to do all the jobs currently done by humans. This is because what is valuable from certain jobs is not merely the quantifiable outcomes – which machines may be able to achieve – but also some personal or relational element that machines cannot do, simply because they are machines and not humans. These valuable traits – like empathy, inter-personal recognition and validation, acting as a guide/mentor, providing a personal example, etc. – would be lost if the jobs in question were reduced to quantifiable outcomes performable by machines. Of course, one could suggest that machines need not be restricted to tasks that are quantifiable, and so some of our concerns in this section may be overblown. This is perhaps possible – but, again, given current possibilities in AI, and the need for direct human intervention in the development of AI (as in the need to program ethics into the auto-piloted vehicles), we have little to no reason to think that this is possible at this time or in the foreseeable future. Nevertheless, we have tried to show that some of the traits are not about intelligences or abilities but about what something is: there are certain things that need to be done by other humans to maintain their value (e.g., personal recognition and validation, providing a feasible example as a mentor, etc.), and therefore could never be done by machines, not because the machines are lacking in something that could be developed or learned but simply because they are machines. Therefore, machines doing all the jobs currently done by humans would likely not be a desirable outcome for most humans (something we see reflected in people's intuitive responses to the idea of having a machine for a spouse, imam, therapist, etc.).

It may be argued that humans may be unnecessary at all in a future where machines do all the work, and therefore there would be no need for jobs where humans require a human relationship. This, however, changes the question to a world without humans, which we see as an undesirable outcome. In such a world, we cannot help but wonder what the point would be of the machines doing work, if there are no humans that need the work done. As discussed earlier, we expect something important is lost to have a world with only machines, even it was eventually possible. For this discussion, we will continue assuming a world with both humans and machines.

WORK AND HUMAN VALUE

These questions of non-quantifiable values and the potential significance of what something *is* apart from what it *does* lead us to our final point: that human value should not be derived simply from what humans do. It is, likely, this element that most disturbed us in our students' inability to see human value given improvements in artificial intelligence: why should the fact that machines can do our jobs better than us mean we have no value? Do people have no value apart from the job they perform or the things they can do? If this were to be the case, then any notion of inherent human value seems to be lost, and all that remains is the need to "earn" one's value by being a productive member of the workforce. In such a scenario, people who cannot work and who show little to no potential of ever being able to be economically "productive" in this sense have no value: people with disabilities and elderly people are thereby dehumanized and devalued. Indeed, if people have no value apart from the job they perform – as our students seemed to suggest – then euthanizing disabled children and retired people becomes not only ethically possible, but perhaps even required: if human value comes only from the work we can do, then those who cannot work have no value, and therefore may not have an inherent right to life.[1]

Such a conclusion violates the notion of human dignity and value that underlies most of the democratic theories that lead to our contemporary political institutions (like universal enfranchisement, the right to a fair trial, etc.) and the statements that undergird them (such as the UN declaration of Human Rights, the American Constitution, the Canadian Charter of Rights and Freedoms, etc.). While these various theories, institutions, and statements may not all share the same philosophical anthropology or theory of humanity, they do all seem to share the intuition that the human being, simply by being a human being, is worthy of dignity and is therefore the bearer of certain rights and freedoms (to life, liberty, and the pursuit of happiness, for example). Humanity is therefore a sufficient condition for someone's being worthy of dignity and respect, both politically and morally. This humanity is not premised upon anything other than membership in the species *homo sapiens*, and as such its value and significance are not premised upon anything that the individual person does.

This sense that human value is not strictly tied to our job performance or our abilities is also commonplace in many religious traditions. In the Abrahamic faiths, we see this in the notion of humanity as *imago Dei*, bearing the image of God. On such an understanding, the individual human being is worthy of respect and dignity simply because it bears the image of the God who is ultimately worthy of respect and dignity: we honor God in part by honoring God's image in human beings. One way to think of this sense of God-given value is via the metaphor of parents and children, a common metaphor for the divine-human relation in the Judeo-Christian tradition. Just as the value in a parent-child relationship shouldn't be on the amount of work the child can do (a person shouldn't replace their child with an artificial intelligence program even if such a program could do everything better than their child!), so, too, our value as humans does not rely on the amount of work we can do.

This, however, does not mean that work has no value in human living. In those same Abrahamic religious traditions, we see that God gives humanity tasks to do (e.g., tilling the earth, naming the animals, or picking their own food/fruit) even in the Garden of Eden, when the world is still perfect and without sin. That our value is not defined by our work does not mean that work has no value for us. We may still value work and find it meaningful and fulfilling, perhaps even derive some sense of identity or purpose from it. But we must recognize that our value is not tied solely to the work we do. In some ways, it is possible that AI could help move humanity back in this direction by creating a situation where everyone has their basic needs met, and therefore value need not be found primarily in work done to sustain living (Brundage, 2015). Perhaps by liberating us from the *need* for work, artificial intelligence can help us start to distinguish between the economic value of work and the value of human being or human living. While the former may be part of the latter, it is neither necessary nor sufficient to account for the latter: work simply is not what gives humans our value.

CONCLUSION

But perhaps we are being unfair to our students here. Perhaps when they suggested that humans would have no value if machines could do all the work they did not mean "value" in this broad religio-philosophical sense. They likely meant something much narrower: what is our *economic* value (especially vis-à-vis artificially intelligent machines), if machines can do all the work? But this conflation of economic value with value at large is precisely what we hope to have challenged and questioned in this chapter. Too often discussions of AI and machine labor happen predominantly, and sometimes even exclusively, in the realm of economics: how will it make things more economically efficient? How will it provide economic value for producers and consumers, and at what economic cost? In our other computer class of "Algorithm Analysis" we often find students value efficiency without being able to explain why being more efficient is a good thing, and eventually tie efficiency to an economic benefit.

Yet there is more than simply the economic at stake in these questions. To remind my students of this point, I scheduled a class session with a philosopher. As students at a liberal arts university, they already knew that human life is broader than simply economic calculations. However, they seem to have needed a reminder of this – and perhaps they are not alone in that. I now repeat the process of bringing in a philosopher every time I teach the class, and I think both my Computing Science students and our philosopher guest have found the session enjoyable and informative.

Hopefully, you have too, as readers of this co-written chapter. Our desire in this chapter was to suggest that, while it is likely neither feasible nor desirable for machines to do all the work currently being done by humans, even if such a thing were possible it would not change the value that humans have, as humans. Because we are more than simply economic things, our value is more than simply economically calculated. In this regard, the question "What value would humans have if machines could do all the work?" is perhaps best answered by saying: "The same value they have if machines cannot do any of the work, since human value is not tied to economic productivity".

NOTE

1 A point made most famously by Peter Singer, who claims that infant lives have less value than others (such as pigs, dogs, or chimpanzees) (Singer, 1979), and therefore infants have less "right to live" than others do (Kuhse & Singer, 1985). While Singer ties value not to economic productivity but to possessing certain traits of rationality such as self-awareness, he clearly makes a connection between lowering a person's value (based on it's not possessing a certain trait) and that person thereby having less "right to live".

REFERENCES

Alhussain, A. I., & Azmi, A. M. (2021). Automatic story generation: A survey of approaches. *ACM Computing Surveys (CSUR)*, 54(5), 1–38.

Aquinas, T. (1947). *Summa Theologiae* (Fathers of the English Dominican Province, Trans.). Part I, Questions 75–89. Retrieved January 12, 2022, from https://www.ccel.org/a/aquinas/summa/home.html. (Original work published 1485).

Baker, S. (2011). *Final Jeopardy: The story of Watson, the computer that will transform our world.* Mariner Books.

Batalden, B. M., Leikanger, P., & Wide, P. (2017). Towards autonomous maritime operations. *In 2017 IEEE International Conference on Computational Intelligence and Virtual Environments for Measurement Systems and Applications (CIVEMSA)*, 1–6. IEEE.

Beighton, R. (2021, August 27). World's first crewless, zero emissions cargo ship will set sail in Norway. *CNN*. Retrieved January 11, 2022, from https://www.cnn.com/2021/08/25/world/yara-birkeland-norway-crewless-container-ship-spc-intl/index.html

Bowling, M., Burch, N., Johanson, N., & Tammelin, O. (2015). Heads-up limit hold'em poker is solved. *Science, 347*(6218), 145–149.

Brooks, F. P. (1995). *The mythical man-month: Essays on software engineering, anniversary edition*. Addison-Wesley Longman, Inc: Reading, Massachusetts.

Brundage, M. (2015). Economic possibilities for our children: Artificial intelligence and the future of work, education, and leisure. *In Workshops at the Twenty-Ninth AAAI Conference on Artificial Intelligence*.

Campbell, M., Joseph Hoane Jr, A., & Hsu, F. H. (2002). Deep blue. *Artificial Intelligence, 134*(1–2), 57–83.

Cat-themed robot serves sushi at Waterloo buffet. (2021, Dec. 3). *CTV News – Kitchener*. Kitchener: Retrieved January 11, 2022, from https://kitchener.ctvnews.ca/cat-themed-robot-serves-sushi-at-waterloo-buffet-1.5693503

Cinelli, M., Morales, G. D., Galeazzi, A., Quattrociocchi, W., & Starnini, M. (2021). The echo chamber effect on social media. *Proceedings of the National Academy of Sciences, 118*(9), e2023301118. 10.1073/pnas.2023301118

Descartes, R. (2021). *Meditations on first philosophy*. Arcturus Publishing Limited. (Original work published 1641).

Juang, M. H., & Rust, R. T. (2018). Artificial intelligence in service. *Journal of Service Research, 21*(2), 155–172.

Kuhse, H., & Singer P. (1985). *Should the baby live?: The problem of handicapped infants*. Oxford University Press: Oxford.

Kuutti, S., Bowden, R., Jin, Y., Barber, P., & Fallah, S. (2020). A survey of deep learning applications to autonomous vehicle control. *IEEE Transactions on Intelligent Transportations Systems, 22*(2), 712–733.

Lavazza, A., & Robinson, H. (Eds.). (2016). *Contemporary dualism: A defense* (Ser. Routledge Studies in Contemporary Philosophy). Routledge.

Lin, P. (2016). Tesla autopilot crash: Why we should worry about a single death. *IEEE Spectrum: Technology, Engineering, and Science News*.

McCarthy, J., Minsky, M. L., Rochester, N., & Shannon, C. E. (1955). A proposal for the Dartmouth summer research project on artificial intelligence. *AI Magazine*, 12. 27(4), 12.

Minsky, M. (2000). Commonsense-based INTERFACES. *Communications of the ACM, 43*(8), 66–73.

Noda, I., Suzuki, S. J., Matsubara, H., Asada, M., & Kitano, H. (1998). RoboCup-97: The first robot world cup soccer games and conferences. *AI Magazine, 19*(3), 49–59.

Olthuis, J. H. (2001). *The beautiful risk: The new psychology of loving and being loved*. Grand Rapids: Zondervan.

O'Neil, C. (2016). *Weapons of math destruction*. Crown.

Plato. (2002). *Phaedo*. In Grube, G. M. A. (Trans.), *Five dialogues* (pp. 93–154). Hackett Publishing Company. (Original work published 360 BCE).

Porter, E. (2016, June 7). Jobs threatened by machines: A once 'stupid' concern gains respect. *The New York Times*.

Robinson, H. (2020). Dualism. *Stanford encyclopedia of philosophy*. Stanford. Retrieved January 12, 2022, from https://plato.stanford.edu/entries/dualism/

RoboCup: Objective. (2022, Jan 10). Retrieved January 10, 2022 from http://www.robocup.org/objective

Roose, K. (2020, October). The value of your humanity in an automated future. *TED@BCG*. Retrieved January 11, 2022, from https://www.ted.com/talks/kevin_roose_the_value_of_your_humanity_in_an_automated_future

Saenko, K. (2020, Dec. 14). It takes a lot of energy for machines to learn - here's why AI is so power-hungry. *The Conversation*. Retrieved January 11, 2022 from https://theconversation.com/it-takes-a-lot-of-energy-for-machines-to-learn-heres-why-ai-is-so-power-hungry-151825

Sandel, M. J. (2012). *What money can't buy: The moral limits of markets*. Farrar, Straus and Giroux.

Savchuk, M. M., & Fesenko, A. V. (2019). Quantum computing: Survey and analysis. *Cybernetics and Systems Analysis*, *55*(1), 10–21.

Schaeffer, J., Burch, N., Björnsson, Y., Kishimoto, A., Müller, M., Lake, R., … Sutphen, S. (2007). Checkers is solved. *Science*, *317*(5844), 1518–1522.

Singer, P. (1979). *Practical ethics*. Cambridge: Cambridge University Press.

Tanenbaum, A. S., & Bos H. (2015). *Modern operating systems* (4th ed.). Pearson Prentice-Hall: Upper Saddle River, New Jersey.

The machine that feels. (2021). (61) 3, The Nature of Things. Canadian Broadcasting Corporation.

Thrun, S., Montemerlo, M., Dahlkamp, H., Stavens, D., Aron, A., Diebel, J., … Rum. (2006). Stanley: The robot that won the DARPA Grand Challenge. *Journal of field Robotics*, *23*(9), 661–692.

Will robots displace humans as motorised vehicles ousted horses? (2017, April 1). *The Economist*. Retrieved January 11, 2022, from https://www.economist.com/finance-and-economics/2017/04/01/will-robots-displace-humans-as-motorised-vehicles-ousted-horses

Wong, J. I., & Sonnad, N. (2016, March). Google's AI won the game Go by defying millennia of basic human instinct. *Quartz Magazine*.

Zittrain, J. (2019, July 23). The hidden costs of automated thinking. *The New Yorker*. Retrieved April 5, 2022, https://www.newyorker.com/tech/annals-of-technology/the-hidden-costs-of-automated-thinking

Index

Printed in the United States
by Baker & Taylor Publisher Services